SPINOZA AND THE RISE
OF LIBERALISM

Lewis Samuel Feuer, chairman of the Social Science Integrated Course and Professor of Philosophy at the University of California, was formerly on the faculty of the University of Vermont. He studied philosophy at City College and Harvard, where he won the Bowdoin Medal. Dr. Feuer served for several years as the secretary of the Cambridge Union of University Teachers, and in 1955 he was president of the University of Vermont chapter of the American Association of University Professors. He is the author of *Psychoanalysis and Ethics* (published in 1955).

SPINOZA

and the Rise of Liberalism

by Lewis Samuel Feuer

Beacon Press   Beacon Hill   Boston

© 1958 by Lewis Samuel Feuer
Library of Congress catalog card number: 58-6235
Printed in the United States of America

CONTENTS

v

Contents
vii

PREFACE

A thinker can be understood only as we relive his experiences. Spinoza's philosophy was wrought in a time such as ours —one of crisis. The seventeenth century was an age of war, revolution, and social unrest. Cromwell, the Thirty Years' War, the Levellers, the Quakers, the Catholic Inquisition in Spain: these were part of the world in which Spinoza lived. Liberalism was being born in the merchants' republics of his native Netherlands.

Spinoza struggled to understand the crisis of his time. Like political philosophers in the twentieth century, he found that events did violence to his political theories. He was proud of Amsterdam's liberalism, and hopeful that the Dutch Republican experiment would succeed. When political catastrophe came in 1672, Spinoza brooded upon the incapacity of the masses to sustain a liberal government. His social feelings led him to sympathy with the common man; as a social scientist, however, he noted that common men were often irrational and hostile to freedom. He was moved to withdraw to a secluded community of like-minded friends, but he also longed to participate in political action. This young excommunicate gave to the pantheist mysticism of the revolutionary movements its noblest expression; he was also, however, stirred by the marvels which were being opened by the new technology of science, the telescope and microscope. He tried with immense power to identify the God of his mystic vision with a Mathematical God of Science. His system broke apart; scientist and mystic warred within him unreconciled. He worked, a precursor of psychoanalysis, to make men free by helping them to understand their passions; but he also wondered if blessedness came only in unity with God. The path toward freedom seemed often lost in an age of hatred.

I have tried to understand the various components of Spinoza's thought as the outcome of underlying emotional responses to the social conflicts of his time, and to portray his

philosophy as a human document, a landmark in men's efforts
to solve the problem of human freedom. The materials which
I have used have, in large part, been left aside by previous
students of Spinoza, but their use, together with what insight
we can bring of a historical and psychological kind, will enable
us to understand more fully, in my opinion, the enduring
significance of Spinoza's thought.

The research which went into this book was begun many
years ago and continued under circumstances which reflect the
character of our own time. Books would turn up in strange
places, in a troopship library, in the Bibliothèque Bernheim on
the island of New Caledonia, in a ramshackle hut on Iwo Jima.
I am indebted most to the archives of the Widener Library at
Harvard University and to the resourceful librarians of the University
of Vermont. I have also made use of manuscripts and
rare books in the collections at Columbia University and the
Jewish Theological Seminary.

The writing of this book was done while I was teaching
at the University of Vermont. I am grateful to the encouragement
there of William S. Carlson, Carl W. Borgmann, Paul D.
Evans, and the Research Committee. These pages are a tribute
to the liberal spirit which prevailed among Vermonters during
a critical time in American history. I owe much to my teacher,
Professor J. Salwyn Schapiro, who interpreted the history and
philosophy of liberalism with wisdom and learning. My friends,
Professor Horace M. Kallen, Kazuko Tsurumi and Lawrence
Lader, and my wife, Kathryn Beliveau Feuer, were helpful in
various stages of this book's coming into existence. Letitia Kehoe
gave generously of her time in the reading of the proofs.

LEWIS SAMUEL FEUER

Berkeley, California

To the Memory of my Grandmother

Rose Landsman Weidner

and

To Robin

"He that knows himself to be upright does not fear the death of a criminal, and shrinks from no punishment; his mind is not wrung with remorse for any disgraceful deed: he holds that death in a good cause is no punishment, but an honour, and that death for freedom is glory."

B. DE SPINOZA, *Tractatus Theologico-Politicus,*

published in 1670 under a fictitious foreign imprint, and with the author's name suppressed; Chapter XX, "Freedom of Thought and Speech."

CHAPTER 1

The Excommunication of Baruch Spinoza

The Decree of Anathema

A man excommunicate is a man alone. He is severed from his past, his parents, teachers, friends. No community supports him in his weakness; he must draw all sustenance from within himself. He is a stranger in the land.

On July 27, 1656, Baruch Spinoza was excommunicated from the Jewish community of Amsterdam. Rabbi Isaac de Fonseca Aboab read the words of judgment which expelled Spinoza at the age of twenty-four from his fellows:

> The chiefs of the council do you to wit, that having long known the evil opinions and works of Baruch de Spinoza, they have endeavored by divers ways and promises to withdraw him from his evil ways, and they are unable to find a remedy, but on the contrary have had every day more knowledge of the abominable heresies practised and taught by him, and of other enormities committed by him, and have of this many trustworthy witnesses who have deposed and borne witness in the presence of the said Espinoza, and by whom he stood convicted. . . .
>
> With the judgment of the angels and of the saints we excommunicate, cut off, curse and anathematize Baruch de Spinoza, with the consent of the elders and of all this holy congregation, . . . with the anathema wherewith Joshua cursed Jericho, with the curse which Elisha laid upon the children, and with all the curses which are written in the law. Cursed be he by day and cursed be he by night. Cursed be he in sleeping and cursed be he in waking, ... The Lord shall not pardon him, ... The Lord shall destroy his name under the sun, ...
>
> And we warn you, that none may speak with him by word of mouth, nor by writing, nor show any favor to him, nor be under one roof with him, nor come within four cubits of him, nor read any paper composed or written by him.[1]

1

The Jewish Community of Amsterdam

What had provoked the elders of the Amsterdam Jewish community to excommunicate the young Spinoza? Was it an act of narrow-minded orthodoxy? Was it the hatred of liberal philosophy? Or did the theological formulae conceal the fear of new social forces that were in the making, the first glimmerings in modern history of the revolutionary Jewish intellectual? To answer this question, we shall have to reconstruct the tensions of the inner life of the Amsterdam Jews.

The purely external observer might well have regarded the Jewish synagogue as a fortress of rigid, almost Oriental orthodoxy. Its dirges, disorderly wailings, and sexual segregation had a weird exotic quality for the staid Protestant spectator. In 1641, when Spinoza was a boy of nine, the Englishman John Evelyn visited the Amsterdam Synagogue and confided to his diary his amazement with the women, "secluded from the men, . . . shut with lattices, having their heads muffled with linen, after a fantastical and somewhat extraordinary fashion; the men wearing a large calico mantle, . . . while all the time waving their bodies, whilst at their devotions." [2] Ceremonial occasions, however, always find traditional ways in the ascendant. Amsterdam Jewry, though it had outstanding traditionalists, did not live in a cultural ghetto; among its leaders were men attentive to contemporary European culture. Delights of secular knowledge and pagan writers were known to Amsterdam rabbis.

Menasseh ben Israel, for instance, rabbi of the Amsterdam Jews, member of their high court, the Beth Din, principal of their Yeshibah, prided himself on his close personal and intellectual relations with the Gentile world. He had corresponded in warm terms with the renowned jurist Grotius. He was a frequent guest at the home of the Rector of the Remonstrant College. His good friends included the professor of philosophy at the Amsterdam Athenaeum, the Historiographer Royal of France, and the celebrated *femme savante* Anna Maria van Schurman. More significantly still, Menasseh sat for a portrait

by Rembrandt and persuaded the painter in 1655 to illustrate
his book *Piedra Gloriosa*.[3]

Strict orthodoxy among the Amsterdam Jews had evidently
declined, for their prosperous members did not hesitate to have
their portraits done in violation of the Second Commandment
which forbids any pictorial representation. Rembrandt's paint-
ings show that his Jewish subjects, in so far as their dress was
concerned, had adapted themselves to prevalent Dutch ways.[4]
They were burghers or beggars, like their Christian neighbors.
They had begun early to take Dutch women as their wives, and
took them in such numbers that the Burgomaster of Amsterdam
in 1619 had complained "that many Jews fleeing from Portugal
and mostly coming to this country had so conducted themselves
and inter-married with the daughters of this country that it
tended to great obloquy. . . ." It was the Dutch authorities,
not the Jewish community, who forbade intermarriage.[5] The
world of the new Europe had obtruded itself into the book-
shelves of the most confirmed Jewish traditionalist. The library
of Spinoza's judge, Rabbi Isaac de Fonseca Aboab, housed the
works of Montaigne, Hobbes, and Machiavelli; on its shelves,
the priestly church fathers shared a place with the pagans—
Homer, Virgil, Aristophanes, Plutarch, and Cicero.[6] Religious
liberalism had begun to permeate the Amsterdam Jewish community; there were those who doubted the immortality of the
soul, while in Leyden, John Evelyn met a Jew who besides
having a Kentish wife believed that Jesus was a "great prophet,"
and had translated several devotional works into English.

Now the early account of Spinoza's excommunication by
the Lutheran Pastor Colerus ascribed great importance to the
fear aroused in the rabbis by Spinoza's friendship with Gentiles
and his interest in secular learning, "for they did not doubt but
that he would soon leave them, and make himself a Christian."
But the Christian associations of Rabbi Menasseh were as well
known as they were extensive, and they generally elicited the
approval of the Jewish community. Menasseh's friendships with
Gentiles were criticized only when they had overtones of political
liberalism. He was accused "of throwing himself into the Re-

monstrants Party in Holland to gain friends and protectors." [7]
Differences in theological doctrine alone could scarcely have
brought about the severance of Spinoza from his Amsterdam
coreligionists, for the community's leaders undertook to bribe
Spinoza to change his ways. Bribes are not offered to change a
man's opinions; they are meant to change his actions. To his
"evil opinions," Spinoza had added evil "works" and "evil ways";
there were the "enormities which he committed," the heresies
which he "practised." Jewish custom allowed a wide latitude on
questions of theological speculation.[8] Something more than
philosophical daring was involved in the wrath which Spinoza
aroused. To the Amsterdam Jewish community, Spinoza constituted what we call today a "clear and present danger." When
Spinoza rejected the rabbis' offer of a pension of a thousand
florins, he remarked that "if they had offered him ten times as
much, he would not have accepted of it, . . . because he was
not a Hypocrite, and minded nothing but Truth." [9] Colerus
would have it that the bribe's purpose was to secure Spinoza's
appearance "now and then in their Synagogues." If so, this
would have been the only time in history that a Jewish community felt obliged to bribe someone into an intermittent and
perfunctory attendance at their religious services. We must look
more closely into the background of Spinoza's excommunication.
What were the works and ways of Spinoza which called forth the
ostracism of the Jewish community?

Why Spinoza Was Excommunicated

The theory of Spinoza's excommunication which the historic
facts seem most to support may be stated in outline as follows.

The excommunication of Spinoza was the forerunner of
similar episodes which were to take place in the German and
Russian Jewish communities in the next two centuries. With the
secular culture which spread with the Enlightenment and the
Haskalah movement, new winds of unrest blew into the stagnant
air of ghetto containment. Young Jews were rapidly drawn to
extreme liberalism, radicalism, socialism. They became assimila-
tionists; they discarded the doctrine of the chosen people for the

noble ideal of the equality and fraternity of all human beings. Communities were rent by the division between orthodoxy and radicalism; the weapon of excommunication was invoked.[10]

Spinoza is the early prototype of the European Jewish radical. He was a pioneer in forging methods of scientific study in history and politics. He was a cosmopolitan, with scorn for the notion of a privileged people. Above all, Spinoza was attracted to radical political ideas. From his teacher Van dan Ende, he had learned more than Latin. He had evidently imbibed something of the spirit of that revolutionist whose life was to end on the gallows. For Spinoza's political and economic ideas were basically opposed to those held by the leaders of the Jewish community. The Jewish elders were monarchist in their sympathies, loyal to the house of Orange, friendly to the Calvinist party, stockholders in the Dutch East India and West India Companies. Spinoza was an ardent Republican, a follower of John de Witt, a critic of the Calvinist party, its ethics, and its theocratic pretension. Spinoza was associated with the political faction which advocated the dissolution of the great trading companies; he admired the Republican economist who criticized the monopolies. In his youth, furthermore, Spinoza's closest friends were Mennonites, members of a sect around which there still hovered the suggestion of an Anabaptist, communistic heritage. The Amsterdam Jewish leaders could tolerate theological disagreement; they could not tolerate a political and economic radical. They reacted with fear and bewilderment to their first radical intellectual and cast him out from their midst.

The Economic and Political Structure of Amsterdam Jewry

The Amsterdam Jewish community was dominated by a small commercial oligarchy which could impose its will in matters of politics and theology. Economic interest, political ideology, and philosophical conviction were enmeshed in the conflict which led to Spinoza's excommunication.

The Amsterdam Jewish community was not solely a religious group. It was a virtually autonomous socio-economic entity which negotiated with other nations, cities, and Jewish communities.

It had become the strategic center of a network of trading operations which included sister Jewish settlements in the Levant, Barbary, Brazil, and the West Indies. Jewish enterprise was especially vigorous in the silk, sugar, tobacco, diamond, and publishing industries.[11] Amsterdam Jewry was a middle-class community. As Menasseh told the English people in 1656, "mechanicks" are "rarely found among us."[12] Indeed, a resolution of the Amsterdam town authorities in 1632 had excluded the Jews from the craft guilds.[13] The Amsterdam Jews had attained a high measure of affluence. A few months before Spinoza's excommunication, Menasseh described their prosperity in glowing words. His *Humble Addresses,* written to persuade the government of Cromwell to open England's doors to Jewish immigrants, declared that "in this most renowned City of Amsterdam, where there are no lesse than 400 families, . . . how great a Trading and Negotiation they draw to that City, experience doth sufficiently witness. They have no lesse than three hundred houses of their own, enjoy a good part of the West and East-Indian Compagnies. . . ."[14] Indeed, the Portuguese Jews in Amsterdam were extremely well off compared with the population as a whole. Their per capita taxable property in 1647 was evaluated as 1,448 guilders as compared with only 828 for the generality of the citizens.[15]

So thoroughly were the values of the leaders of the Amsterdam Jews pervaded by an economic ethics that the decrees of the stock exchange approached in dignity the decrees of God, while the Dutch East India and West India Companies seemed His appointed instruments. Rabbi Menasseh ben Israel, a prolific theologian as well as Spinoza's teacher in Hebrew, dedicated a Latin treatise, *De Termino Vitae,* to the Dutch West India Company. Menasseh sought the good will of the commercial magnates with books of theology. "I am engaged in trade," he said sadly, "what else is there for me to do?"[16] Again, two years later, in 1641, Menasseh dedicated the second part of his masterpiece, *El Conciliador,* a work on the interpretation of Scripture, not only to the Jews of Pernambuco but also to the General Council of the Dutch East India Company. Menasseh had endeavored in his book "to combine the agreeable of Plato with the profitable of Aristotle."

His theology was moderate and conventional; there was nothing which might disturb the placid reflections of a director of a Dutch India trading company. Man's free will was reconciled with God's foreknowledge, while Biblical passages which implied God's ignorance or sorrow were explained away as having been written with an eye to the limited understanding of the men of the given age.[17]

The mentality of speculative acquisition possessed both Jew and Gentile on the Amsterdam stock exchange. A younger Jewish contemporary of Spinoza, Joseph da Veiga, in a treatise appropriately entitled *Confusion de Confusiones,* gave a hoary scriptural ancestry to the accumulative mania. "Teachers of Holy Writ do affirm that Job might well have been the original shareholder," said Veiga, for he "enjoined his disciples to bear their trials with fortitude." Stocks and shares were affected with divinity; their mysterious mutations were beyond our comprehension. Sad indeed, wrote Veiga, is the lot of the investor. "O travail unceasing! Indescribable agony! Incomparable solicitude! If Investors discourse, it is but of stock; if they go anywhere, they must be guided by shares; . . . do they ever reflect?—only concerning shares; eat?—shares are their roast and savoury; do they think?—yes, of shares, and shares to haunt their dreams. . . ." [18]

The political loyalties of the Amsterdam Jewish leaders corresponded to their economic attachments. Fealty to the house of Orange was their cardinal principle, and it united them, politically as well as economically, with the influential and numerous Calvinist party of the Netherlands. This allegiance dated back to the first arrival of the Jews in 1593. The Jews had been befriended by a succession of Stadtholders. Spinoza was ten years old when the Synagogue was host to a Prince of Orange and a queen of England. Poems of passionate patriotism were recited to celebrate the victory over the hated Spaniards. When William of Orange assumed the throne of England, Joseph da Veiga commemorated the gratitude of the Jews toward the Orange family in his book *Retrato de la Prudencia.*[19]

Wealth in the Jewish community was concentrated, however, in a few hands, and with that wealth went social power. The Jews from Central and Eastern Europe (the so-called Ashkenazim) were twice as numerous in the Amsterdam of 1674 as their Portuguese brethren; yet only twelve of them were as well-to-do as the average Portuguese Jew. Indeed, the average wealth of the Ashkenazic Jews was below that of the Amsterdam citizenry generally. By contrast, the house of the rich David Pinto was so lavishly adorned that the civic authorities intervened, lest its munificence tempt an envious populace to sack the mansion. As in contemporary times, wealth brought a controlling voice in the direction of Jewish educational institutions. It was the brothers Pinto who founded the Talmudical Academy of which Rabbi Isaac Aboab, Spinoza's inquisitor, became head. The brothers Pereira escaped from Spain with their whole large fortune, founded the Yeshibah in Amsterdam, and paid its teachers' salaries. No wonder that the impoverished Rabbi Menasseh, seeking their favor, dedicated to them a legal work which he had compiled. Twenty-five per cent of the shares of the East India Company are said to have been in Jewish hands, but there were many Jews who experienced poverty and felt a deep resentment toward the trading monopolies. Ashkenazic Jews especially lived under disabilities; they were regarded as a lower social caste by their Portuguese and Spanish brethren. In Spinoza's time, they were not allowed to intermarry with Sephardic Jews; permanent places in the Portuguese Synagogue were denied them. Eastern European Jews were often employed as servants or messengers in Portuguese households.[20] Such persons were impotent before the oligarchical structure of the Amsterdam Synagogue.

The constitution of the Amsterdam Synagogue gave a dictatorial power to the *parnassim* (the wardens of the Synagogue). This ruling body was self-perpetuating and unrestrained by any democratic check in the community at large. The seven members of the Council, said Article VI of the constitution, having elected themselves from the previously existent Council of fifteen, "will in the future always elect the new Council." Dissent was repressed in the Amsterdam Synagogue. The constitution gave the power of censorship to the governing board. No book, whether in Hebrew or any other language, could be published without the permission of the *Mahamad* (governing council). Anyone who dared publish so-called libelous writing was to be punished with the *Herem* (excommunication). A similar penalty awaited whoever was guilty of impertinence or disrespect to the presiding authority. The forty-two articles of the constitution of the Amsterdam Synagogue had behind them the weight of the municipal government, which in 1638 had approved their enactment. Separatists and seceders found that they had no avenue of action under the Synagogue's constitution. Article II decreed excommunication for those who, without the prior sanction of two-thirds of the congregation, participated in any other Jewish service within a radius of six miles of the Synagogue.[21] Among Amsterdam Jewry, God could be approached through only one channel of organization.

The Use of Excommunication as a Socio-economic Weapon: the Cases of Menasseh ben Israel and Uriel Acosta

To most of us in the twentieth century, the notion of excommunicating a person seems barbarous. It is all the more important, therefore, to see how the survival of the Jews throughout the Middle Ages was linked to the power of excommunication. The ban and anathema were not unknown to the Jews when they lived in their Palestinian homeland. The need for a procedure of excommunication developed, however, as the Jews became dispersed throughout many lands. As small autonomous enclaves living under foreign rule, the Jewish communities had no customary means for enforcing their ordinances and decisions; they could impose no penalties of imprisonment, death, or exile. And the need for powers of enforcement was overwhelming. Oftentimes, a hostile king or governor would demand from the Jewish community the payment of a huge ransom or financial contribution. The leaders of the Synagogue would then assess the members for their shares in accordance with their respective incomes. But what if some member of the community refused to make his contribution, or what if he refused to divulge the size of his personal fortune? The community's leaders were unable to punish him; they could not invoke the aid of the government of the country in which they lived. They could do only one thing —excommunicate the malefactor and disloyal member. Thus arose the institution of the *Herem Hakahal,* the anathema of the community, which was pronounced not on the authority of one man, but by all the notables of the Synagogue, the *Tove hair,* the worthy men of the town.[22]

The Amsterdam Synagogue, indeed, in Spinoza's time, relied on the power of excommunication to tax its richer members for the help of the poor. In 1670, several prosperous Jews discontinued attendance at the Synagogue in order, it was alleged, to avoid having to make pledges for the poor. The Council of the Synagogue charged that these tax evaders hoped also to evade excommunication by quietly removing themselves from its jurisdiction. The Council therefore asked the town authorities of Amsterdam to grant it the right both to excommunicate and to tax the offenders. The Amsterdam government replied by giving the Synagogue Council these rights for use against such persons "as long as they will belong to Jewish religion." The social structure of the community of Spanish and Portuguese Jews in Amsterdam, its autonomy in all social, administrative, and judicial questions made it imperative that it have the authority to excommunicate.[23]

The power of excommunication enabled the Jews of Europe to make significant social progress. The abolition of polygamy in the eleventh century was enforced in Rabbi Gersom's decree by anathema against its violators. To be excommunicate was to experience a powerful sanction, for the person in that status was deprived virtually of livelihood and legal standing. The excommunicate was neither a regular subject of the host country nor a member of the Jewish group. And in an age when livelihood was linked to social status, the outcast was without economic opportunity. He could neither own land, trade, nor work at a craft, because he was outside any recognized legal class.

Toward the end of the Middle Ages, the power of excommunication began to be abused by the leaders of Synagogues. The reception of Maimonides' philosophy in Western Europe gave rise to an intellectual civil war. Maimonides, in his remarkable philosophic synthesis, had used scientific ideas in an effort to purify Judaism of superstitious elements. The Jews in the towns of southern France, the center of religious liberalism, welcomed his philosophy. For Provence, indeed, was the home of a free and independent middle class which was friendly toward the Albigensian heresy. Maimunist ideas then spread to Spain, where they provided the philosophic groundwork for Jews who were putting orthodox practice aside. The orthodox rabbis finally retaliated against the liberal movement. A fierce war of excommunication and counter-excommunication ensued. Solomon of Montpellier and his pupils pronounced the ban in 1232 against all those who studied Maimonides' philosophic writings. The Maimunist congregations replied by excommunicating the Obscurantists. Then the rabbis of northern France anathematized the leading Maimunist, David Kimchi. The chief congregations of Aragon, however, declared for Maimonides and excommunicated Rabbi Solomon and his associates. The rabbi, having taken leave of his judgment, appealed in 1233 to the Dominican friars of the Inquisition to extirpate Maimunist philosophy. The Inquisition burned Maimonides' works with relish.[24] Soon all the Jews, Maimunists and Obscurantists, were to be driven from these lands to seek homes elsewhere.

The Jews of Western Europe, as the rifts in the medieval system began to appear, forgot the wise injunction of Maimonides to use the power of excommunication sparingly and to emulate those rabbis who had never excommunicated anybody.[25] The leaders of the Amsterdam Synagogue in the seventeenth century had especially forgotten the warning of Maimonides against recourse to anathema.

The oligarchs of the Amsterdam Jewish community did not hesitate to use the weapon of excommunication when they felt their power threatened. Excommunication for them was not primarily a device for the control of theological speculation; it was first and foremost a means by which the unity of the community, as conceived by its affluent leaders, was to be preserved. Excommunication could be used to bend the will of those intractable members who challenged the socio-economic power of the governing group. Spinoza was not the first to be excommunicated by the Amsterdam Synagogue. Others before him had endured its penalty. In one such case, that of Rabbi Menasseh ben Israel, the use of excommunication as a device for socio-economic control stood out in a most naked fashion. Its story is worth recounting for its bearing as precedent for Spinoza's ouster.

In the spring of 1640, Menasseh ben Israel found himself in straitened financial circumstances. When the three Jewish congregations had been united into one Synagogue in 1639, Menasseh lost his post as rabbi. Reduced to an inferior teaching position, he turned to the Brazilian trade which provided the livelihood of many Amsterdam Jews. The trade, however, was controlled by a few Jewish magnates who enjoyed advantageous connections with the colony of Pernambuco and the Dutch West India Company. These oligopolists resented intruders like Menasseh and used their economic power to make things hard for would-be competitors. Then anonymous placards began to appear on the Synagogue gates and on the walls of the Exchange. They denounced certain dignitaries of the Jewish community as unfair monopolists. The governors of the Synagogue retaliated with a Ban, the minor excommunication, against those persons unknown who had thus violated communal discipline. The insurgents, however, were not to be dissuaded from their venture into "trust-busting." Defamatory writings against the dominant magnates began to be circulated clandestinely. An investigation disclosed that Jonas Abrabanel, Menasseh's brother-in-law, had helped compose one of the propagandist leaflets. The Senhores of the Council thereupon pronounced a Ban upon the guilty pamphleteers, but later removed their judgment when the contrite culprits begged forgiveness and paid a fine.

But the dramatic climax was still to come. When Menasseh heard the formal decisions in the Synagogue, he rose from his seat, white with anger. He spoke loudly and at length against the public humiliation of his brother-in-law. He turned to the congregation and appealed for their support against the Council. Two wardens tried to quiet him, but Menasseh, with a prophet's wrath, refused to yield. Then the Council of the Synagogue went into emergency session to decree the Ban of excommunication against Menasseh. A righteous indignation had meanwhile overcome the intended excommunicate. He flung open the door of the Council room, pounded upon the table, and denounced the

Senhores to their face. They told him he was excommunicated. "I under the Ban!" retorted the enflamed Menasseh. "It is I who can proclaim the Ban upon you!" This interchange of excommunicatory utterances over, Menasseh, disgraced, withdrew from the Synagogue. The Ban was revoked after a single day, but Menasseh, besides paying a severe fine, was suspended from rabbinical duties. The bitter memory of the public degradation was not undone. The oligarchs of the Synagogue justified their action "as an example to others, and to further peace and union amongst all in the service of the Most High." [26]

Menasseh, dejected, discouraged, thought of emigrating to Brazil, but finally remained. When the jurist Grotius heard of his friend's difficulties, he wrote: "I had always imagined that the members of the synagogue at Amsterdam were both wealthy and liberal. Now, I realize that I was mistaken. . . ." [27] Like many Gentiles, Grotius had tended to think of the Jewish community as closely knit, homogeneous, and altogether prosperous. But the Jews were riven politically and economically by the same controversies which raged in the surrounding non-Jewish world. Meanwhile, the young boy Spinoza probably witnessed the discomfiture of his teacher, Rabbi Menasseh. The pupil, however, did not learn the lesson of subservience which the Council of the Synagogue hoped to implant.

That same year, in 1640, the young Spinoza no doubt heard and saw much concerning the tragedy of the stormy rebel, Uriel Acosta. The entire Jewish community was involved in a vindictive act, the crushing of a spirit. Uriel Acosta, born to a Marrano family in Portugal, had been enchanted in childhood by the legends and history of his secret people. In manhood, he abandoned his legal career and fled to Amsterdam, where he could assert his identity openly as a Jew. But legend and reality often diverge. Acosta was dismayed by the actualities of Jewish life. He brooded upon the narrow selfishness of the Amsterdam Jews and asked himself whether they were truly the descendants of the people of the book. He came into conflict with the Synagogue's leaders, was excommunicated, recanted, then broke with communal discipline again after a few years, was once more excommunicated, and was finally compelled to submit to a horrifying

public flagellation. Broken in will, he sat down to write his autobiography, then shot himself.

The child Spinoza witnessed the ordeal of the freethinker
Acosta. Children can be made into their elders' images, and the
Amsterdam Jews, wrote Acosta, "set their Children upon me in
the Streets, who insulted me in a Body as I walked along, abusing
and railing at me, crying out, There goes a Heretick, there goes
an Apostate." The adults "spit upon me as they passed by me in
the Streets, and encouraged their Children to do the same." Then
came the spectacle of the last recantation. "I stripped myself
naked down to the Waste," Acosta told; then, his arms bound,
"the Verger came to me, and with a Scourge of leather Thongs
gave me nine and thirty Stripes. . . . During the Time of my
whipping they sang a Psalm. . . . After this . . . I prostrated
myself, the Door-keeper holding up my Head, whilst all both old
and young, passed over me, stepping with one Foot on the Lower
Part of my Legs, and behaving with ridiculous and foolish Ges-
tures, more like Monkeys than human Creatures." The child
Spinoza probably remembered the communal cruelty. In any
case, he mocked his people in later years for their rites of excommunication.

In many ways, Acosta was a philosophic precursor of Spinoza.
Acosta too was drawn to the Greek atomists and materialists. He
had shared the common prejudice against Epicurus, but having
inquired more carefully "concerning him and his Doctrines," he
wrote, "I have found Reason to change mine." Like Spinoza, he
was therefore denounced as an Epicurean. Acosta held, furthermore, that in a nation ruled by right reason, "every one would
contribute his utmost to the relief of his Neighbor under any
Affliction." All that true religion needed, he said, was only "just
and reasonable laws, . . . defending the Cause of the injured
against the violence of the Oppressor." Spinoza was similarly to
define the worship of God as consisting "only in justice and
charity, or love towards one's neighbor," and Piety as "the desire
of doing well which is born in us, because we live according to the
guidance of reason." Like Spinoza, Acosta found no virtue in
religious ritual. He condemned outright "all that fraudulent

Trade, contrived to support the Lazy with the Profits of the Industrious," and declared, "This is the very Cause of our Complaint, . . . that we are misled and deceived in these points by designing Men." Like Spinoza, Acosta sought to base ethical principles on the psychological nature of man. He criticized the Christian injunction to love one's enemies because he held that uneasiness ensues (anxiety, we would say) when we try to conform to commandments contrary to the Law of Nature. Lastly, Acosta had his doubts concerning the immortality of the soul. He regarded rewards and punishments as pertaining to this life only and, like Spinoza, ridiculed a morality which was based on "the Dread of eternal Punishment." [28]

Theological dissent, in and of itself, did not, however, call down upon the dissenter the wrath of the organized community. Acosta was only one among a considerable group in the Jewish community who denied the soul's immortality. These sceptics were called "Sadduceans," after their ancient forebears, and against their trend of thought, the community's exponents of orthodoxy directed an unceasing stream of writings. Menasseh published his *De Resurrectione Mortuorum* in both Spanish and Latin versions, Samuel da Silva wrote a *Tratado da Immortalidade,* and Moses Raphael de Aguilar, principal of the Talmud Torah and friend of the opulent Pereira, contributed a *Tratado de Immortalidade da Alma.*[29] The sceptics, however, were personally unmolested. Something more than theological deviation was required to provoke the penalty of excommunication.

What made the expulsion of Acosta inevitable was his diatribe against the community's Elders. The oligarchs could not overlook bitter words which were aimed against their own socioeconomic status. "The modern Jewish Rabbins," asserted Acosta, "like their Ancestors, are an obstinate and perverse race of men, strenuous advocates for the odious Sect of the Pharisees and their Institutions, not without a view to gain, and, as is justly imputed to them, vainly fond of the uppermost seats in the Synagogue. . . ." Economic self-interest, in Acosta's view, had become the ethics of Amsterdam Jewry; "profits or honour are two prevailing Motives with the People of our Nation," and even Jews cease to be men when they "wallow in the Dirt of Filthy Lucre." Acosta avowed himself a born agitator, with "an Aversion to that haughty and insolent Race of Men, who are apt to despise and trample upon others," and with an ever-present readiness to take "all the Opportunities to defend the Oppressed, and to make their Cause my own." He accepted a mission against those who make "Slaves of Men" and declared his standard as "the natural Rights of Mankind, whom it becomes to live suitably in the Dignity of their Nature. . . ." And finally, Acosta dared to suggest that the Amsterdam town authorities put an end to the autonomous enclave of tyranny which they so tolerantly allowed to flourish in their midst. This was an unpardonable blow at the whole structure of the Jewish community. "I wonder at," wrote Acosta, "how the Pharisees living in a Christian Country, come to enjoy so much Liberty as to judicial power and authority! . . . This is certainly just Matter of Reproach, and what ought not to be tolerated in a free City, which professes to protect Men in the peaceable Enjoyment of their Liberty. . . ." [30]

The values of the market place had interpenetrated those of the Synagogue, and Acosta could not accommodate himself to the mixed constituents of social existence. Prophet in dishonor, he had sustained imprisonment, a fine, and the confiscation of his books. He was ill-prepared to meet the misfortunes which overwhelmed him. Unable to speak Dutch, he was as a merchant dependent on his Jewish connections. He was without the intellectual resources and external friendships which sustained Spinoza in his need. "What can it profit me," wrote Acosta with passionate honesty, "to spend all my Days in the melancholy State, separated from the Society of this People and their Elders, especially as I am a Stranger in this Country, destitute of any Acquaintance with its Inhabitants, or even Knowledge in its Language?" [31] Acosta's suicide was a casualty in the human struggle for free thought.[32] Whatever the flaws in his temperament and character, he had perceived and dared to state the basic issues. Spinoza, cast in a tougher mold, cultivated the heretical seed into a noble system of thought; there was a strength in Spinoza which did not succumb to external forces.

How Spinoza Became a Liberal Republican

The youth of Baruch Spinoza brought him into firsthand contact with the realities of commercial life. Baruch did not pursue the curriculum of studies which led to the rabbinate. He was probably thirteen years old when he joined his father's business. The firm of Michael D'Espinosa was engaged in an extensive import and export trade. It was a successful enterprise. The ledger of the Exchange Bank of Amsterdam shows that in one year Michael D'Espinosa did business with as many as forty-eight concerns. His account during the months from August, 1651 to January, 1652 reached the considerable sum of 61,883 guilders.[33] Baruch himself soon fulfilled responsible functions of business management. He was seventeen years old when his elder brother Isaac died. Bento D'Espinosa, as he was then known, thereupon assumed a more important role in the family business; upon his father's death, he became its manager.

As head of the firm "Bento e Gabriel D'Espiñoza," Spinoza knew the realities of business ethics and capitalist enterprise. Legal documents, only recently discovered, show him pursuing an unfortunate debtor, Manuel Duarte, with all judicial means, and using the threat of a forced sale of goods to produce a settlement. He became aware of the uncertainties and mutabilities of profit-seeking. In 1654, a fleet of Dutch ships was plundered by Barbary corsairs, and merchandise, belonging to "a certain Spinosa," was seized from one of the chartered vessels, *The White Falcon*.[34] The lost goods were probably a consignment from the firm of Bento e Gabriel D'Espiñoza, merchants of Amsterdam.

But Bento was meanwhile beginning to undergo a deep spiritual crisis. From his teens to the age of twenty-four, as he worked upon his father's accounts and supervised the sales and shipments of goods, young Bento, in his mind, was inhabiting a strange world of new ideas and emotions. He made friends outside the commercial circle, and he read books which strengthened his impulse to call into question his mode of daily existence. A life devoted to the pursuit of riches began to seem futile and vacuous, as vain as a life spent in seeking fame or indulging the senses. "I thus perceived," he later wrote, "that I was in a state of great peril, and I compelled myself to seek with all my strength for a remedy, however uncertain it might be; as a sick man struggling with a deadly disease, when he sees that death will surely be upon him unless a remedy is found. . . ." The pursuit of money seemed to him akin to madness. He said in later years: "It has come to pass that its image above every other usually occupies the mind of the multitude, because they can imagine hardly any kind of joy without the accompanying idea of money as its cause." [35] Finally, in March, 1656, Bento D'Espinosa began to retire from business. A legal guardian was appointed to supervise the settlement of his father's affairs and the liquidation of the estate. The interests of a sister, a brother-in-law, and probably a younger brother were involved in this termination. A few months later, Spinoza was excommunicated.

Tradition has it that Spinoza's father had helped make his son into a freethinker. Michael D'Espinosa, a respected man of affairs, had served Amsterdam Jewry in various capacities. He had been a Warden of the Synagogue, a member of the "Santa Companhia de dotar Orphas e Donzellas," a society which provided dowries for orphans, and he had been also administrator of the "Misvah do Emprestino," a bank which provided the poor with interest-free loans. He was evidently, however, both sceptical and anticlerical. According to the oldest biography of Spinoza, he thought that religious people were invariably hypocrites who employed their piety as a cloak for cheating in business, and is said to have influenced his son against superstition.[36] Whatever the truth of this account, it is striking that Michael D'Espinosa's activities were in the direction of social betterment and the assistance of the poor. His conception of religion was evidently a social and practical one.

The influence of Francis van dan Ende upon Spinoza's search for a true way of life was especially enduring; he was, as it were, a second father to Bento. Spinoza sought from Van dan Ende the mastery of the Latin language; it offered him a gateway to the world of European learning and science, to the understanding of the Cartesian philosophy about which he was hearing so much from his Gentile friends. But Van dan Ende helped lead Spinoza as well into the challenging labyrinth of contemporary politics and radical political theory.

Francis van dan Ende was a masterful personality, bold, sardonic, rebellious, a schismatic whose dreams foreshadowed the revolution of the next century. A brilliant student at Louvain, he had joined the Jesuit order, but later left its ranks. He professed himself a pantheist in philosophy, an admirer of the Italian free-thinker Vanini, executed at Toulouse as an atheist in 1619. People called Van dan Ende not only "atheist" but "Lucianist." [37] In the seventeenth century, that appellation signified an attitude of sceptical mockery, of raillery toward conventional beliefs; Lucianism was akin to the later Voltairean impiety and was the charge, for instance, which Voetius, the Dutch theologian, raised against plays which scoffed at Christian dogma. When Spinoza met him, Van dan Ende was running a school in Amsterdam along advanced lines. "That man taught with good Success and a great Reputation; so that the richest Merchants of the City intrusted him with the instruction of their Children, before they found out that he taught Scholars something else beside Latin. For it was discovered at last, that he sowed the first seeds of Atheism in the Minds of those Young Boys." [38] An intimate friendship developed between Spinoza and the unorthodox schoolmaster. Van dan Ende saw Spinoza's loneliness and need and generously "offered to look after him and to put him in his own house," asking only that Spinoza help him in return by sometimes teaching his pupils.[39] Years later Spinoza said that he had wanted Van dan Ende's daughter, Clara, as his wife.

Beneath the Lucianist in Van dan Ende, beneath the satirical laughter, there was the spirit of a radical revolutionist. Visions of a new political world filled the schoolmaster's imagination, and for them he finally gave his life. In 1671, Van dan Ende, living in France, was drawn into a revolutionary project for founding a republic in which all men would be equal. The discontent in Normandy was then severe. The wars of Louis XIV had drained his subjects' resources, and a new sales tax was meeting with bitter resistance. The makers of the proposed revolt, led by the Chevalier de Rohan, planned to convoke the Estates-General after overthrowing Louis XIV. To achieve their aim, they were prepared to accept the intervention of Spanish forces. The whole project came to naught. Its betrayed leaders, Van dan Ende among them, were executed in 1674.

Van dan Ende was the philosophic theoretician of this subversive movement. Among his papers was found a "Plan de gouvernement" in which he had sketched the steps for founding a "popular State in Holland, invincible, always flourishing, always progressing through the unity and efforts of all, to the general liberty and prosperity." He envisaged the morrow of the day of revolution; the citizens would gather in their respective districts to organize a government which would rule in accordance with laws that the people could change. A military council of six hundred men would provide a defensive force for the revolution and supervise the election of a civil assembly; the latter would proceed to the enactment of social reforms. The republican program included the care of widows, orphans, and indigent families, the construction of factories, the promotion of the mechanical arts, and measures against contagious diseases. All children were to be instructed in the fine arts and taught the meaning of liberty. Legislation was planned to assist married couples. The civil assembly was to be the guardian of the people's rights. Everyone over twenty-one years of age and who had served three years in the army would be a citizen. Voting was to be by the secret ballot. Peace would be the objective of the republic's foreign policy. All citizens, whether Catholic or Protestant, were to be equal, provided that they were sincere defenders of liberty and didn't mix religious and political affairs.[40]

The ill-fated revolutionary group in France followed closely Van dan Ende's ideas. In addition, they planned to abolish the hated, onerous taxes such as the "tailles" and the salt impost. They planned to imprison all exploiters, monopolists, and tax collectors of the old régime. The provinces, united with them in an Estates-General, were to build a new order.

Spinoza's liberal ideals were those of his master Van dan Ende. He never, however, as far as we know, subscribed to his teacher's advocacy of armed revolution. The Lucianist raillery of Van dan Ende was, furthermore, uncongenial to Spinoza.[41] The Catholic sceptic might mock at men's foibles, but Spinoza rejected emphatically the outlook of "those who prefer to detest and scoff at human affects and actions than understand them." His scientific "geometrical" analysis of "the vices and follies of men" was therapeutic in intent, not satirical.[42] Among young Mennonite thinkers, Spinoza was beginning to find men with temperaments akin to his own. These men, too, wished to free themselves from the dominion of business enterprise and to live a more philosophical existence. Spinoza, under the aegis of Van dan Ende, was also encountering the fresh, original ideas of the Dutch Liberal Republicans, a group inspired by the talented John de Witt, with a common allegiance to the mathematical method and the scientific study of economic and political questions.

The young Republicans were precursors of Adam Smith, stanch advocates of free trade. They urged the dissolution of the great monopolies, the Dutch East India and West India Companies. In his library, Spinoza possessed the writings of the brothers Pieter and Jean de la Court, the cloth merchants who became the chief publicists of the Republican party. Spinoza estimated Pieter as "that most prudent Dutchman" and admired his economic analysis of the wealth of nations.[43] John de Witt himself had contributed two chapters to Pieter's principal work, *Political Maxims of the State of Holland*.[44]

The wealthy Jewish interests, allied to the dominant trading companies, were, no doubt, disturbed by the barbs of Republican criticism. The East India company, wrote Pieter, "hath impoverished many of our good inhabitants." The company had not been averse to maximizing its monopolistic profit through limiting the supply of foreign imports for, "by causing a scarcity of nutmegs, mace, cloves, cinnamon, etc. [the company] could so raise the price of them. . . ." It had not hesitated to dump cheap Asian goods on the Dutch market, "Japan garments, Indian quilts and carpets. . . ." The trading companies, said Pieter, were once a "necessary evil" because they were needed for carrying on trade in distant lands among armed rival competitors. But Spain was no longer at war with the Dutch, who now had control of the Spice Islands. The practices "of the said companies begin to justle and appugn the general good of this country. . . ." With

the companies dissolved, "an open trade," Pieter declared, could
be instituted for the greater prosperity of the Netherlands.[45]

Such were the new political and economic ideas which young
Spinoza learned in the radical intellectual circle of Amsterdam.
To the elders of Amsterdam Jewry, they seemed a dangerous
wine, confusing to impressionable, immature minds. In Spinoza,
they provoked an intellectual leap from the medieval to the
modern world. He shed the distinctive principles of Judaism
with all the intrepidity of a young explorer who, lured to new,
unknown lands, discards all unnecessary baggage.

Spinoza's Rejection of Jewish Authority

Spinoza had virtually de-communicated himself from Amsterdam Jewry before they excommunicated him. "He resolved," as
Colerus tells us, "to retire somewhere else with the first opportunity. Besides, he was desirous to go on with his Studies and
Physical Meditations in a quiet Retreat. He had no sooner left
the Communion of the Jews, but they prosecuted him Juridically
according to their Ecclesiastical Laws, and Excommunicated
him." [46] When Spinoza heard the news, he commented: "All the
better; they do not force me to do anything that I would not have
done of my own accord if I did not dread scandal. . . ." [47] In
reply to the Elders, Spinoza wrote "an Apology in Spanish for his
leaving the Synagogue." [48] Although it has never been found, its
content is said to have been used in the *Tractatus Theologico-
Politicus.* We can therefore reconstruct the basic propositions of
Spinoza's reply to the Elders. His break with Judaism was of a
most fundamental kind.

In the first place, Spinoza denied the doctrine that the Jews
are a chosen people. As a rationalist cosmopolitan, as a citizen
of the world, he affirmed that "in regard to intellect and true
virtue, every nation is on a par with the rest, and God has not in
these respects chosen one people rather than another." [49] Ethnic
hatreds, he held, were the outcome of unreliable hearsay. Spinoza
was aware that Jewish thinkers maintained that the survival of
Jewry, "without parallel among the peoples," was proof that they
are God's elect. Spinoza answered that the survival of the Jews

could be fully explained on sociological grounds. Gentile hatred and their own wilful separation had kept the Jewish people alive. "That they have been preserved in great measure by Gentile hatred, experience demonstrates." By way of evidence, Spinoza argued that where the Jews had been treated equitably, they had been assimilated into the surrounding population. The Jews, in his opinion, were absorbed into the Catholic population of Spain because they "were admitted to all the native privileges of Spaniards"; they remained unassimilated in Portugal because "they were considered unworthy of any civic honors." [50] Spinoza's approach to the history of the Jewish people was that of an anthropologist with a liberal, universalist ethics.

Indeed, there was an almost Freudian intuition in Spinoza's assertion that "the sign of circumcision is, as I think, so important that I could persuade myself that it alone would preserve the nation for ever." The symbols of separation, says Spinoza, are potent. The Chinese, through a distinctive head-mark, "have thus kept themselves during so many thousand years." Though we may today quarrel with Spinoza's conception of Chinese history, it is astonishing that he made the prediction, confirmed three centuries later, that the Chinese would regain their empire "after the spirit of the Tartar becomes relaxed through the luxury of riches and pride." [51] Spinoza, the sociologist of ethnic relations, had left far behind him the theological dogma of the chosen people.

Moreover, Spinoza held that the "foundations of their religion" had well-nigh "emasculated" the minds of the Jews.[52] The backwardness of the Jewish religion was, in his opinion, an obstacle to the restoration of the Jewish state. He had liberated himself with difficulty from his old teachers, men like Morteira, Menasseh, Aboab; his intellectual development had been arduous: "I have set down nothing here which I have not long reflected upon; . . . though I was imbued from my boyhood up with the ordinary opinions about the Scriptures, I have been unable to withstand the force of what I have said." He regarded his teachers as lost in a Kabbalist morass: "I have read and known certain Kabbalistic triflers, whose insanity provokes my unceasing astonishment." He marveled at the arrogance of such men, their belief "that they alone may be held to possess the secrets of God," and he judged their works as "childish lucubrations." Nor was Spinoza more respectful of efforts such as Menasseh's to conciliate Scripture with science. "The Rabbis," he wrote, "evidently let their fancy run wild. Such commentators as I have read, dream, invent, and as a last resort, play fast and loose with the language." [53]

Lastly, Spinoza denied outright that the Jewish community had the authority to excommunicate anybody. Only the sovereign power has the right to excommunicate a person, and though that right could be granted to a subordinate group, it had not been conferred upon the synagogue by the town of Amsterdam or the Provincial Estates. Spinoza urged that it be retained by the civil government. To separate such rights from the sovereign power, said Spinoza, makes for "division, contentions, and strife." Even in the ancient Hebrew commonwealth, "though the priests were the interpreters of the laws, they had no power to judge the citizens, or to excommunicate anyone: this could only be done by the judges and chiefs chosen from among the people." The evils of a divided sovereignty and clerical excommunication are shown, says Spinoza, in the way the Roman Pope acquired superiority over the German Emperors. The secular authorities must not grant such powers to any clerical elite, for such prerogatives are most powerful in the manipulation of public opinion. They confer "the most complete sway over the popular mind." [54]

Spinoza's Judges: the Commercial Magnates and Rabbis Aboab and Morteira

Spinoza was tried by a court in which the influence of wealthy commercial magnates was paramount. Who were his judges? The Mahamad, the governing council of seven men, was the supreme authority of the Synagogue. It possessed the final power of excommunication. In a case, however, as momentous as that of Bento D'Espinosa, the Mahamad felt it expedient to ask the elders as well as the rabbis to join in its deliberations and decision. Such was the procedure which was followed in the contemporaneous, though much less significant, case of Daniel de Prado.

The decree of Spinoza's excommunication indeed alluded to the fact that he had been examined "in the presence of the elders," who had joined together with "the chiefs of the council" in proclaiming the anathema. The judgment of the Mahamad, with its enlarged tribunal, carried the full weight of the Synagogue. The court which excommunicated Spinoza in the summer of 1656 was in all probability composed of the following sixteen men: Joseph de los Rios, J. Selomo Abrabanel, Ishac Belmonte, Jaacob Barzilay, Abraham Pereira, Abraham Pharar, Abraham Nunes Henriques, Saul Levi Morteira, Isaac Aboab, Benjamin Musaphia, Semuel Salom, Dor. Ephraim Bueno, Imanuel Israel Dias, Izak Bueno, David Osorio, Abraham Telles. These were the names recorded in the community's minutes for similar proceedings with respect to Daniel de Prado which occupied the council at the same time and in the months immediately following its decision of Spinoza's case.

Of Spinoza's probable sixteen judges, five were listed among the chief shareholders of the Dutch West India Company in 1656 and 1658—Abraham Pereira, Izak Bueno, David Osorio, Joseph de los Rios, and Dionnis Jennis. The last name "Dionnis Jennis" was an alias of Rabbi Isaac Aboab, who announced the decree of Spinoza's excommunication. David Osorio was, according to the tax returns of 1631, the richest of the Jews and the leading importer and exporter in the Levantine trade. Another councilor, Ishac Belmonte, was the brother of the third wealthiest member of Amsterdam Jewry (according to the tax accounts of 1674), while he himself became in 1664 agent-general for the Spanish king in the Netherlands. Ishac's affluent brother, Jacob, also served as superintendent of the Hebrew Academy "Etz Chayyim" (The Tree of Life). Councilors Pereira and Osorio were leading personages in the Bank of Amsterdam and Stock Exchange. Another judge, Abraham Nunes Henriques, was evidently an immediate relative of Jacob Nunes Henriques, mortgager of the Swedish crown jewels and, within a generation, the principal Jewish shareholder in the Dutch East India Company. The shareholders of the India companies were the aristocrats of their time. As the famous Dutch commercial leader Usselinx said: "The greatest nobleman is he who invests in the India Companies." If we add to the chief shareholders among Spinoza's judges the probable number of minor shareholders, the preponderance of the commercial aristocracy in the court of excommunication becomes clear.[55]

Three other councilors—Abraham Pharar, Benjamin Musaphia, and Dor. Ephraim Bueno—were prosperous physicians associated with the most religious orthodoxy. Pharar and Musaphia had been born in Portugal and Spain; they were loyal to Judaism with the complete dedication of those who had chosen its creed despite all the insidious power of the Inquisition. Pharar did, indeed, hold that "philosophy takes precedence over the Talmud and the Kabbalah," but he nevertheless regretted his lack of education in Hebrew and faithfully tried to make amends by studying one hour daily with Rabbi Morteira. For those like himself, he made a compilation in Portuguese of the 613 precepts of the Mosaic code, so that, as he wrote, "all of us who come from Portugal and Spain, and for our sins do not understand Hebrew, shall rightly know what they are." The title page of this volume proudly identified its author as "a Jew of the Portuguese Exile." As a French proverb has it, *Ce sont les derniers convertis qui sont les plus farouches.* Pharar, an exiled son returning to orthodoxy, must have looked upon the young radical Spinoza as thoroughly disloyal and insensitive. Benjamin Musaphia, his fellow councilor, had served as physician to the king of Denmark and was also the author of theological works. Benjamin's devotion to the Jewish nation outran his scientific judgment. A few years after Spinoza's excommunication, Benjamin was among those who hailed the pseudo-Messiah, Sabbatai Zvi, as the liberator of Israel. The third of the physicians, Ephraim Bueno, eminent in his profession, was among the very first Jews to be admitted into the Amsterdam surgeon's guild. His father, Joseph Bueno, had been physician to Maurice, Prince of Orange. Ephraim was a powerful pillar of orthodoxy and helped edit in 1661 the code of Jewish law and ritual, the *Shulchan Aruch.* Together with Councilor Pereira, he founded in 1656 (the year of Spinoza's excommunication) the society *Torah Or* for the study of the Law. With still another councilor, Jonas Abrabanel, he published in 1650 a Spanish translation of the Book of Psalms. Abrabanel was now a prosperous merchant; he had in 1642 been chosen to deliver the welcoming address to the Prince of Orange and queen of England when they visited the Amsterdam Synagogue. Abrabanel rejoiced in the victories of the "most exalted" Prince over their common enemy, the Spaniard. Political, economic, and religious orthodoxy all commingled among the elders and Governing Council of the Amsterdam Synagogue in 1656.

The motives of judges, like most human beings, are an amalgam of a striving for justice and the communal welfare together with a concern for their own status and self-interest. The elders of the community were men of influence and distinction. Spinoza might deride them, but they had served the community well.

The elders of Amsterdam Jewry had watched with concern the actions and associations of Baruch Spinoza. They observed his intimacy with the unfrocked Jesuit, Van dan Ende, a man notorious for his political and philosophic freethinking, and linked with the extreme republican wing. They observed the young Spinoza renounce his business career and betake himself to comradeship with Mennonite religious communists and republican antimonopolists. The elders valued their holdings and influence with the trading companies. They were able to use and had used their economic power to help their less fortunate, persecuted brethren abroad. Only recently, in 1654, they had intervened against the Governor of far-away New Amsterdam, Peter Stuyvesant, who had asked the directors of the Dutch West India Company for authority to expel the handful of Jewish immigrants. The Amsterdam Jews, moved by a plea from their colonial coreligionists, had reminded the company that Jews were among its principal stockholders and its most loyal defenders in the days of its adversity. Whereupon the directors of the company in 1655 reluctantly informed their governor in New Amsterdam that they must deny his request to oust Jews "especially because of the considerable loss sustained by this nation, with others, in the taking of Brazil, as also because of the large amount of capital which they still have invested in the shares of this company." [56] In 1653, the elders of the

Amsterdam Synagogue had similarly exerted their influence with the Dutch West India Company to prevent the curtailment of Jewish rights to pursue retail trade and the handicrafts in Brazil. The Jewish people could withstand a hostile environment only through the strategic use of its economic power. The young cosmopolitan Spinoza might enjoy discourse upon the rights of man with Mennonites and Republicans, but he had forgotten what the Dutch Jews in Brazil had undergone a few months before. Were all nations equally just and rational in the eyes of God? Rabbi Aboab, as he sat upon Spinoza's court of judgment, could answer this question another way.

Rabbi Isaac de Fonseca Aboab had from 1642 to 1654 been the spiritual leader of the Jewish colony in Pernambuco, Brazil. Those had been intense, unforgettable, dramatic years. For more than a generation, Amsterdam Jews had worked to help build the distant settlement. Together with the Dutch West India Company, they had financed the campaigns to drive the Portuguese from Brazil. Jewish soldiers and officers aided a Dutch army of liberation. In 1645, the Jewish population of Dutch Brazil almost equaled that of Amsterdam Jewry; its 1,450 persons were more than half the total number of the colony.[57] Then in 1646 began an era of ordeal for the Jewish pioneers. They were assailed by a powerful Portuguese force which, with fanatical religiosity, hoped to exterminate the Jews.

There was an intense nationalist feeling among the Jews who had fought for their lives and liberty against the hated minions of the Inquisition. The young Spinoza chose to ridicule the notion that the Jews were a chosen people. Those, however, who had survived massacre and torture could ask: what did this crackpot youth know of what his people had experienced? Had he seen the madness of the Portuguese and the fortitude of his own blood? Rabbi Isaac Aboab had commemorated in poetry the siege of Pernambuco; his people's hour of trial had been their vindication as God's elect: "Volumes would not suffice to relate our miseries. The enemy spread over field and wood, seeking here for booty and there for life. Many of us died, sword in hand, others from want; they now rest in cold earth. We survivors were exposed to death in every form; those accustomed to luxuries were glad to seize mouldy bread to stay their hunger." The beleaguered Brazilian Jews, dying of starvation, had yet refused to surrender. Aboab went among them, exhorting them never to yield and offering prayers to the God of their fathers. The slain Jewish warriors had sanctified the soil around them. Then on the ninth of Tammuz, their destruction had been averted. As by a miracle, a Dutch fleet appeared on the horizon, putting the enemy to craven-hearted flight. The Jews, delivered like their ancestors at the Red Sea, sang with joy: "Who is like Thee among the gods, O Lord!" [58]

Rabbi Aboab recalled the Portuguese, "an abomination of Amalek." They had persisted in harassing the Brazilian colony until the Jewish population dwindled to less than half its number. Then finally another Portuguese army, abetted by an uprising of Negro slaves, captured Pernambuco in 1654. The Synagogue on the Street of the Jews became a prize of war to the Portuguese commander, while the Jewish cemetery was the booty of a Negro insurrectionist.[59] Rabbi Aboab returned with most of his congregation, in defeat, to Amsterdam. Now, a year later, this scoffer at his people and their ways, Baruch Spinoza, stood before him, arguing logically, making his points. The rabbi listened to the witnesses who testified that they heard Spinoza "scoff at the Jews as superstitious people born and bred in ignorance, who do not know what God is, and who nevertheless have the audacity to speak of themselves as His people, to the disparagement of other nations. . . ." [60] Probably he remembered the guns and swords at Pernambuco; God was known in His people's sorrow and suffering, not in callow syllogisms.[61]

The hope of Isaac Aboab that God's People in his time would triumph was still a living one. Ten years later, in 1666, Amsterdam Jewry went wild with the rumor that a Messiah, Sabbatai Zvi, had made his appearance in Smyrna. Isaac Aboab, Abraham Pereira, and Benjamin Musaphia were swept into the vortex of fantasy. In the Synagogue, there was music and dancing to celebrate the pending redemption of Israel. The printing presses were tireless in producing literature glorifying the self-revealed Messiah. All the rabbis and presidents of schools in Amsterdam joined in sending a collective letter of homage to

Sabbatai Zvi. Deep was the chagrin in Amsterdam when their redemption proved to be a delusion, and their redeemer a pathetic, vain convert to Islam. Such, however, was the fantasy world of longing and unreality in which the minds of Spinoza's judges dwelled. Centuries of persecution and flight through countries and continents had made the Jews neither rationalists nor lovers of humanity. They had turned inward upon themselves, clinging to the dream of a powerful Messiah who with plentiful miracles would turn the tables on their persecutors. Messianic irrationalism fed on the phrases of the Kabbala. The Messianic dream was a mixture of grandiosity, paranoia, the narcissism of the persecuted, an "inadequate idea," as Spinoza would have called it. But Spinoza, a scientific radical, freeing himself from the ties of his boyhood environment, trying to emerge into the world of a new Europe, had no energies to spare for understanding his people with compassion. If he had been less ruthless in destroying the cord of birth which attached him to his people, his philosophy probably never would have been born.

Together with Isaac Aboab on the Beth Din, the judicial tribunal, sat the senior rabbi, Saul Levi Morteira.[62] Since 1619, he had been the spiritual guide of Amsterdam Jewry. Born in Venice, however, Morteira had grown to maturity in an atmosphere heavy with mysticism.[63] At the court of Marie de Médici in Paris, he had become sceptical of Christian charity. When an anti-Jewish edict compelled him to leave France, Morteira settled at Amsterdam, where he transmitted to his students a taste for Kabbalist obscurantism. His favorite pupil, Moses Zacuto, later rabbi at Venice, corresponded with him in 1650 with regard to the ransom of Jews captured by the Tartars of Crimea. Zacuto, who also succumbed to the Sabbatian frenzy, celebrated his master Morteira as the sun of charity, the sun of sacred eloquence, the sun of dialectic and polemic. But this sun had long since set for Spinoza. Zacuto was famous in Amsterdam Jewry for the forty days' fast which he had undertaken so that he might forget Latin; Morteira's favorite pupil had come to believe that language incompatible with Kabbalistic insight.[64] By contrast, Spinoza was working laboriously with Van dan

Ende to acquire this linguistic master key to science. Morteira was the author of a Spanish treatise which remained in manuscript form because it bristled with anti-Christianity. This work, *Providencia de Dios con Israel Verdad y heternidad de la lei de moseh,* contained a chapter which inveighed against secular sciences; the Mosaic Law, Morteira held, was sufficient for Jews, and its precepts were altogether superior to anything the Gospels had to offer.[65] Saul Levi Morteira embodied the ideal of ghetto separatism. Spinoza turned away from its heavy mist and looked for the light of the new science. It was Morteira, the self-righteous guardian of darkness, who provoked Spinoza to his most scornful outburst against Amsterdam Jewry:

> After Morteira had exhausted his rhetoric, without being able to shake the determination of his disciple, then as Chief of the Synagogue he urged him in a most formidable tone to make up his mind for repentance or for punishment, and he vowed he would excommunicate him if he did not immediately show signs of contrition. Undismayed, the disciple answered him: "That he knew the gravity of his threats and that, in return for the trouble which he [Morteira] had taken to teach him the Hebrew language, he was quite willing to show him how to excommunicate." [66]

This was Spinoza at the age of twenty-four addressing Rabbi Saul Levi Morteira. And Morteira, like Aboab, could recall other occasions whose significance seemed to have been lost on Bento D'Espinosa. Only a few years before, on December 15, 1647, the Portuguese had burned at the stake a brave and talented young Jew, also twenty-four years of age, Isaac de Castro Tartos. Isaac, a relative of an Amsterdam family, had been born in Pernambuco. One day he dared to visit Portuguese Brazil. He was recognized by spies, transported to Lisbon, where he refused before the Inquisition to renounce his Jewish faith. He died with such courage amidst the flames that for years afterward people in Lisbon remembered him. His death caused a great sorrow among the Amsterdam Jews. Rabbi Morteira himself delivered the memorial sermon on young Isaac's martyrdom.[67] His words had evidently meant nothing to Bento D'Espinosa.

Bento was the friend of liberals and anti-Calvinists. But Aboab, Morteira, and the Amsterdam Jews shared a common bond with the Dutch Calvinists. Each hated the Spaniards and Portuguese. Each had fought on land and sea against the Catholic powers. Each abhorred the Inquisition. Liberal political philosophy must have seemed as much a treason to Morteira and Aboab as it did to Jews centuries later when they battled for survival in the Warsaw ghetto or in the village settlements of Israel.

Such was the character of the men who judged Spinoza. If to him they seemed the pathetic exponents of superstition and reaction, they were to the community at large the living symbols of its unity. Daniel Levi de Barrios, the so-called Poet Laureate of Amsterdam Jewry, rejoiced in the "Sapientissimo Saul Levi Morteira," who with his pen had fought "contra el Atheismo en defensa de la Religion" and triumphed over impious freethinkers like Spinoza. He sang the community's praise of their Rabbis:

> A los que enseña Ishac Aboab sapiente
> del Talmud gloria, de la Ciencia Oriente
>
> O, que gloria Mortera alcanço
> con la ciencia, y amor que enseño.
>
> [To those whom teaches Ishac Aboab, the sage,
> Glory of the Talmud, Beacon of Knowledge,
>
> O what glory did Morteira attain
> with knowledge, and the love he taught.]⁶⁸

There have been worse judges and more cruel men than those who excommunicated Spinoza. The real tragedy was that the persecuted Jews had imbibed something of the intolerance of their persecutors. One always hopes that the downtrodden will behave like heroes; it comes as a shock how like they are to their oppressors, that men are indeed equal.

The Trial

The seventeenth century was an age of revolutions. The small, scattered Jewish communities of Western Europe were inclined to proceed cautiously and not to commit themselves irrevocably to any side. Their sympathies tended to be conservative. The Amsterdam Jews, for instance, were by and large benevolently disposed toward the English Royalists in their civil war with Cromwell and the Parliamentary Army. Indeed, several wealthy Jews gave financial support to the cause of the Stuarts. There was a brief flurry of friendliness toward Cromwell in 1656 when Menasseh ben Israel undertook his mission to secure the readmission of the Jews to England. But when that mission seemed a failure, Dutch Jews promptly disowned Menasseh and resumed their royalist attachment.[69] A newly established minority community tends to be timid politically. When a sister Jewish community in London succeeded a few years later in coming into existence, its timidity was so great that during the Revolution of 1688 it enacted a solemn decree threatening to excommunicate any member who dared to participate in political activities or who voted in any political contest of the English kingdom.[70]

As an alien minority, dependent for their perhaps temporary residence on the good will of their rulers, the Jewish leaders in early modern times felt most secure with the existent order. When a crisis occurred, they abstained for safety's sake from the national politics of their host country, but clearly preferred a return to the tried familiar order of things. A new species of liberals and radicals was to arise, however, among young Western European Jews, eager to join fully in the life about them. With ardor, they swept minority consciousness aside, rejected a ghetto culture which had become a self-imposed alienation. For their ancient orthodoxy they substituted a new political religion, with its creed of human equality and liberty, and with projects of social reform. Spinoza was the first Jew in modern times to be fully and consciously consecrated in the new faith.

The council of the Amsterdam Jewish Synagogue, the Kahal

Kados Amstelodama, searched for a way to rid itself of the young radical Spinoza. It was difficult to find sufficient grounds for an indictment against Baruch. He was guarded in his words, gentle in his ways. Shortly before Spinoza's case, the council had begun to deal with Daniel de Prado, a physician who had also expressed doubts concerning the doctrine of the chosen people. But Prado's relations with women had transgressed the communal code, and his excommunication, milder in its terms than Spinoza's, had left open the door for his migration to the colonies; Prado himself was anxious to have the excommunication rescinded.[71] But Baruch Spinoza, morally blameless, gave no cause for offense, beyond his association with the circle of radical Dutchmen. The council of the Synagogue searched for actionable evidence; it could not introduce political and economic grounds, for besides being inexpedient, there was no constitutional basis for such a procedure. Unlike the antimonopolists of 1640, Spinoza had neither committed breaches of decorum nor circulated inflammatory leaflets. The council of the Synagogue turned to methods of investigation customary to all agencies for ideological control. The council asked certain young men of Spinoza's acquaintance to ascertain Spinoza's views on theological matters in informal conversation.

The oldest document of Spinoza's life tells the story with simple eloquence. "Among those who were most eager to associate with him were two young men, who, professing to be his most intimate friends adjured him to tell them his real views. They represented to him that whatever his opinions were he had nothing to fear on their part, as their curiosity had no object than to clear up their own doubts." Spinoza, wishing to avoid incidents, advised them that if they were true Israelites, they should turn to Moses and the Prophets for answers to their questions. Spinoza's questioners persisted with specific doctrinal queries until finally Baruch avowed "that since nothing is to be found in the Bible about the non-material or incorporeal, there is nothing objectionable in believing that God is a body." Then Spinoza dared to defend the Sadducean standpoint associated with Acosta and the dissenters among Amsterdam Jewry. "We do not read that the Jews excommunicated the Sadducees," he said. He bluntly affirmed that the Scriptures gave no support to a belief in the soul's immortality. Spinoza, his suspicions belatedly aroused, subsequently avoided the company of the two interrogators. After some hesitation, the two young men decided to proceed against him: ". . . when they saw that there was no hope of being able to bend him, then they vowed to take revenge; and in order to do it more sensibly, they commenced by depreciating him in the mind of the people."

The two informers said that, having frequented Spinoza's company upon Rabbi Morteira's request, they had found Spinoza contemptuous of the Mosaic Law. They declared that Spinoza unchecked would be the Synagogue's destroyer, that Morteira, indeed, had misplaced his confidence in this errant pupil. They alluded to Rabbi Morteira's reluctance to authorize their queries. Whether this was a kind or tactical effort to separate the rabbi from the onus of provocative interrogation, or whether Morteira indeed had been compelled by external pressures to initiate an inquiry for which he had no heart, we do not know. In any case, the two young men now pursued their quarry vehemently: "When they saw the proper time to push it more actively, they made their report to the Judges of the Synagogue, whom they incited in such a manner that they thought of condemning him without hearing him first."

'Spinoza went to his trial with good courage; "on his part, feeling that his conscience had nothing to reproach him, he went cheerfully to the Synagogue." Before his judges, he denied formally the one charge that had thus far been made, "contempt for the Law." Thereupon the two accusers came forward to prefer new charges. They had heard Spinoza, they said, scoff at the Jews as a superstitious people, ignorant of God; they had heard him say that the Law "was instituted by a man who was forsooth better versed than they were in the matter of Politics, but who was hardly more enlightened than they were in Physics or even in Theology; with an ounce of good sense one could discover the imposture, and one must be as stupid as the Hebrews of the time of Moses to believe that gallant man."[72]

The ground of the accusation against Spinoza had thus been moved from the simple issue of overt conformity to the

Law to more profound questions of philosophy; Spinoza's advocacy of scientific method and his disbelief in the dogma of the Chosen People were now the gravamen of the charges. The young radical, future author of the spirited *Tractatus Theologico-Politicus,* could scarcely disclaim that scientific and cosmopolitan outlook which he shared with his Republican friends. The technical indictment of Spinoza could be sustained before the judges; the excommunication followed with all the unctuous logic affected by the intellectual ancillaries of the status quo.

It is noteworthy that Spinoza did not appeal to some older, more respected Jewish community to help him in reversing the decree of the Amsterdam Council. There was ample precedent for such a procedure. David Farrar, for instance, had been charged in 1618 by the Amsterdam Rabbis with being "a despiser of the words of the sages and a denier of the oral law." Farrar, a rationalist, who rejected Kabbala, appealed for support to the honored and long established congregation of Venice. Upon the advice of its Rabbi, Leon de Modena, the Council of the Venetian Sephardic Community declared that Farrar was a loyal Jew, "believing all that is incumbent upon a Jew to believe." [73] In 1656, the excommunicated Prado had likewise appealed to the Hamburg congregation to intercede on his behalf. But Spinoza took no such step. He accepted the verdict of excommunication. Many centuries before, the sage Hillel had said: "Separate thyself not from the congregation, and trust not thyself until the day of thy death." Spinoza spurned the received wisdom; he chose the way of separation.

Henceforth, there was a bitterness in Spinoza toward the people who had cast him out, an anger not unlike that which in later centuries overcame those who broke with the ghetto to become international revolutionists. He rejected the people which had rejected him. "The Hebrew nation," he wrote, "has lost all its grace and beauty (as one would expect after the defeats and persecutions it has gone through) . . ." His sociological parenthesis did not mitigate the adverse judgment. The Jews were to him "Pharisees," a term Spinoza used with its connotation of opprobrium and arrogant mien; they extirpated heresy, defended superstition, and took a perverse pride in their long list of martyrs. He grieved that the compilation of the Scriptures had been in the hands of such an ignorant group as the ancient rabbis.[74]

Spinoza separated himself furthermore from the main stream of Jewish thought. He wrote caustically concerning the most venerated name in Jewish theology. He regarded Maimonides' metaphorical interpretations of the Bible as "harmful, useless, and absurd"; Maimonides' vaunted philosophy, far from being a guide to the perplexed, was to Spinoza's mind a further entrapment for the bewildered, a work which was "the acme of absurdity," "mere nonsense," an attempt "to extort from Scripture confirmations of Aristotelian quibbles." As for Maimonides' belief that blessedness could not be attained without subscribing to the Mosaic revelation, such views, said Spinoza, were "mere figments." He felt that Maimonides' disregard for the common sense of mankind tended to make for "a new form of ecclesiastical authority, and a new sort of priests or pontiffs. . . ."[75] To Spinoza, Maimonides exemplified the sectarian and inverted pride of the Jews. When Spinoza praised a Jewish thinker, it was someone like the near heretic, Ibn Ezra, or the opponent of Aristotle, Chasdai Crescas—someone not in the dominant authoritative tradition.[76]

In our own time, when institutions desire to oust from their midst radicals or subversives, it is a commonplace principle of administration that whenever possible the grounds for such expulsions should be the violation of some statutory rule or precept of the social mores. Administrative wisdom advises against raising the real, underlying political issues. The excommunication of Spinoza seems to have partaken of this character. Spinoza, the first great radical in modern Jewish history, was radical in his politics, economics, and associations.[77] His "guilt by association" with Van dan Ende and other extremists was obvious enough to the pillars of the Amsterdam Synagogue. His theological heresy was the formal instrument invoked to achieve his excommunication. Spinoza went his way to become the founder of the philosophy of liberalism.

CHAPTER 2

Revolutionist in Mystic Withdrawal

The Periods of Spinoza's Thought

Spinoza, the excommunicated Jew, could scarcely hope to take a full part in the political life of his time. In early manhood, he was moved by strong feelings of revolutionary extremism which, though they later receded, never vanished. Their last residual expression was found in a strange painting. To amuse himself, Spinoza had taken to drawing portraits. He left behind him, indeed, "a whole Book of such Draughts, amongst which," wrote Colerus, "there are some Heads of several considerable Persons, who were known to him, or who had occasion to visit him." Most striking of these was a portrait of a fisherman whose face "did perfectly resemble Spinoza," but whose dress and attitude, on the other hand, were "very much like that of Massanello, the famous head of the Rebels of Naples." [1]

A man's deepest feelings are often those unspoken. A hostile society will send words into hiding until they finally issue only as reverberations from the unconscious. In a work of art, however, in painting, poetry, or music, repressed feelings find a direct medium and spring to life, revived by the breath of communication.

In fantasy, Spinoza projected his own face in the costume and personality of a revolutionary leader. Who was Masaniello? He was a young fisherman of Naples, illiterate, ignorant, but full of energy and eloquence, who in 1647 led an insurrection against the hated Spanish ruler. Before he was murdered by the Viceroy's agents, Masaniello won notable victories for the poorest classes, principally the abrogation of onerous taxes and the promise of constitutional reforms. All this took place within six days, which, in their fashion, shook Europe. Masaniello's uprising was followed in Naples by a movement which aimed for both national independence and the abolition of feudalism. The rebels cried: "Down with Spain! Long live the Republic!" Though finally crushed, they amazed Europe with their successes against the trained Spanish forces.[2]

In Masaniello's guise, Spinoza identified himself with the aspirations of democratic revolution, perhaps also, with their ultimate defeat.

The pale pages of academic histories may portray Spinoza's political philosophy as a kind of unified abstract doctrine, the intellectual emanations of a recluse. It was nothing of the sort. Spinoza was a man who shared the political feelings of his time. He lived in an age of revolution and war, the time of Cromwell and De Witt, when democracy and liberalism were struggling to be born. The experience of our own era has shown that the political philosophy of persons associated with radical movements changes with the rise and decline of their hopes. It was so even in Spinoza's time. An ardent Leveller such as John Lilburne ended his days as a mystic Quaker, saying as he became converted in 1655, "I shall never hereafter be an user of a temporal sword more, nor a joiner with those that so do"; apostles of outward revolution became missionaries of the inner light. Radicalism and quietism tended to change into each other, so that even Cromwell, the revolutionary leader, with tears in his eyes, could tell the mystic pacifist, George Fox: "Come again to my house; for if thou and I were but an hour of a day together, we should be nearer to one another." [3] The political evolution of Spinoza likewise seems to have moved through three distinct stages, each of which left its impress on his thought.

Spinoza's early years, spent largely in association with Mennonite thinkers, were touched with the hues of their Utopian communist outlook. As he approached the age of thirty, Spinoza became discontented with the Mennonite ethics of withdrawal; he became critical of its escapism. He began to wish to participate in the political debates of his time and to take his place in the lists of the Republican defenders. Life in the Utopian oasis of a religious community no longer satisfied him. Urged by political associates, Spinoza left his Collegiant friends of Rijnsburg and moved to The Hague. There he put metaphysics aside to write the *Tractatus Theologico-Politicus,* the great philosophic statement of the Republican party. The practical political philosopher emerged, the optimistic advocate of Amsterdam liberalism, the analyst of the problems of the Dutch Republic. Then came the cataclysmic events of 1672, the failure of De Witt's policy for the maintenance of peace, the invasion of the French Army, the English declaration of war, the mob murder of the outstanding Republican leader, the return to power of a Prince of Orange. The Republican optimism of Spinoza vanished in the bloodshed and reaction. Spinoza experienced an emotional and intellectual crisis; the third and last stage of his thinking was marked by melancholy. He was no longer stirred to rapture by Amsterdam liberty. He pondered the problem: Why did John de Witt, Europe's most liberal and scientific statesman, fail in his efforts to establish a durable republic in the Netherlands? Spinoza was now a less confident advocate of democracy. Instead, he was prepared to discuss how any mode of government, whether monarchical, aristocratic, or democratic, could be rendered stable. He was at the end concerned with showing how every governmental form could be made consistent with the life of free men. The political reformer was in abeyance; the free man was ready to accommodate himself to the existing dominion.

Such, then, were the three stages of Spinoza's political development—from youthful Utopian religious communist, to mature Republican partisan, to, lastly, the chastened political scientist. Maximal hopes for changing the world gave way at the end to concern for the minimal safeguards of individual freedom.

The First Stage: Retreat Among the Religious Communists

As a merchant, Spinoza observed the impact of the pursuit of wealth on men's lives. The desire for commercial advantage led the English and Dutch to make war upon each other. During June and July of 1653, Spinoza witnessed the effects of the English naval blockade upon his native city. Amsterdam, the sovereign city of the world's commerce, was depopulated and deserted, with three thousand houses empty. Workmen were unemployed; "the land is choke-full of beggars," said the Admiralty of Amsterdam.[4] Even the dividends of the Dutch East India Company sank that year to a low $12\frac{1}{2}$ per cent from their high of 47 per cent in 1646.[5] During these years prior to his excommunication, Spinoza seems to have reacted strongly against the pattern of competitive capitalism. "He had frequent conversations with some learned Mennonites," and when he left the environs of Amsterdam, his choice of residence was most significant; he went to live in Rijnsburg, the center of a group of Collegiant-Mennonites, most akin to the Quakers.[6] At Rijnsburg, periodic Collegiant meetings took place which were known as "the Assembly of the free minded." Each followed his own opinion, and, as an English contemporary described them, "everyone that will has the liberty of making an Exhortation."[7] In this Collegiant environment, Spinoza pursued his philosophic studies peacefully.

Who were these Collegiant-Mennonites? What was their way of life? The Mennonites were the lineal descendants of the Anabaptists, that group of religious communist revolutionaries whom Preserved Smith has aptly called "the Bolsheviki of the sixteenth century."[8] The Münster communist experiment of 1534, which was suppressed with frightful bloodshed, had something of the aura in the seventeenth century that the Paris Commune would have for socialists in twentieth-century Europe. The Anabaptists flourished especially in the Netherlands among the urban handicraftsmen—tailors, smiths, bakers, shoemakers, carpenters—who were drawn to the social doctrine that "among the Brethren all things should be in common." Despite persecution, they had multiplied in secret. They were called "Anabaptists," that is, "rebaptisers," because they held that the baptism of a helpless, uncomprehending infant could mean nothing; baptism was bestowed only on grown persons who joined their fellowship, as a symbol, one might say, of admission into the revolutionary party. Pantheistic and mystical ideas were widespread among them.[9]

With the passage of years, the ways of the Anabaptists mel-

lowed. The Mennonites developed as a moderate offshoot of
their revolutionary forebears. They still nourished, in Spinoza's
time, vague ideas of communist cooperation among themselves.
Indeed, in 1663, one of their brotherhood, Pieter Plockhoy,
managed to persuade the Amsterdam government to support his
effort to establish a cooperative commonwealth of 41 persons
along the banks of the Delaware River.[10] The Mennonites, however, renounced the use of violence to achieve social change;
their communism was of a voluntary and benevolent kind.[11]
Furthermore, they repudiated the idea of free love which had
been associated with the first Anabaptists. In Spinoza's lifetime,
the Mennonites were estimated to constitute one-tenth of the
Dutch population; they were largely skilled artisans and persons
of the lower middle class.

An ethic of withdrawal from the political world prevailed
among the Mennonites. They were estranged from the actual
order, and if they had surrendered chiliastic dreams, they were
also without ambitions for present power. They were pacifists
who refused to bear arms. But they were a loyal community.
When the States-General appealed to them for help during the
critical days of 1672, the Mennonites, within a few days, provided
money and thousands of shoes, hose, and shirts.[12] Their pacifism
had led them to retire from the large Dutch capitalist ventures.
Early in the seventeenth century there had been Mennonites
and Anabaptists among the stockholders of the Dutch East India
Company. Uncompromisingly, however, they opposed the
Company's war against the Portuguese and resisted the arming
of the company's ships. When capitalist policy triumphed over
pacifist ethics, the Mennonites sold their stock.[13] Their social
philosophy aroused a great debate in the Netherlands. On behalf of the Dutch East India Company, the jurist Grotius wrote
his *Commentary on the Law of Prize,* arguing that the Christian
religion did not forbid war, and that even a private company
could wage a "just war." The whole Mennonite way of life
was despised by Grotius. He thought communism was the road
to ruin. "Common ownership," he wrote, "would bring nothing
but discontent and dissension. . . . For it is reasonable that

what is open to all should go to the man who first takes it to keep for himself." [14]

Among the Mennonites, there were no ordained ministers. They chose their ministers by a vote of the majority, and those selected had no special authority. They believed that the word of God was internal, that its source was neither sermon nor Scripture. The Collegiants were Mennonite adherents who met in so-called *collegia* rather than churches in order to evade the government's religious restrictions.[15] The Rijnsburg Collegiants had been much influenced by Cartesian philosophy, and employed its language in stating their religious standpoint. In their writings, a mysticism very similar to that of the English Quakers was set forth in Cartesian terminology.

Spinoza's Mennonite Friends

To signalize his break with the ethics of competitive capitalism, Spinoza abandoned trade and commerce and undertook to earn his livelihood as a craftsman, as a lens-grinder.[16] The imaginative Colerus saw in this vocational choice a loyalty to the Talmudical precept that every man should be the master of some profession or mechanical art. Actually, as we have seen, there were few "mechanicks" among the Amsterdam Jews; the community's values were commercial, and the artisan held a low place in their social scale. When most under Jewish influences, Spinoza did not seek a craftsman's livelihood. He became an artisan when he left business and the Amsterdam Synagogue.

Spinoza's abandonment of commercial life was a pattern of behavior not uncommon among the Collegiants and Quakers. It was part of their search for a more communal, less self-seeking, less exploitative way of life. Jarig Jelles, the good friend who paid for the publication of Spinoza's first book, *The Principles of Descartes' Philosophy*, gave up active participation in his spice business in 1653 to seek that knowledge which he considered "better than choice gold." Jelles wrote the Preface to Spinoza's *Posthumous Works* in 1677, in which he described

with approval Spinoza's renunciation of business, "freeing himself from all kinds of occupations and the cares of business affairs,
which, to a large extent are an obstacle to the search for truth." [17]

Life for the young philosophers who rejected the commercial ethics was a kind of *Pilgrim's Progress*. They wrote their
intellectual autobiographies, narratives of the pilgrimage of the
spirit from the false values of monetary and sensual enslavement
to liberation in the mystical knowledge of God. Jelles' account
of his religious development, *Confession of the Universal
Christian Faith*, won Spinoza's commendation. The first part of
Spinoza's essay, *On the Improvement of the Understanding*, is
indeed one of the genre of *Pilgrim's Progress* autobiographies.

"After experience had taught me," Spinoza wrote, "that all
the usual surroundings of social life are vain and futile, . . .
I finally resolved to inquire whether there might be some real
good, . . . of which the discovery and attainment would enable
me to enjoy continuous, supreme, and unending happiness."
He wished to cast off enthrallment to Riches, Fame, and the
Pleasures of Sense. "With this end in view I made many efforts
but in vain." "I could not forthwith lay aside all love of riches,
sensual enjoyment, and fame." But the very process of philosophic reflection itself, says Spinoza, helped to turn his thoughts
"from his former objects of desire" so that gradually he came to
see that as means, not as ends, they could help man to achieve
his "highest good"—"the knowledge of the union existing between the mind and the whole of nature." This "highest good"
was linked to the outlook and projects of the social reformer,
for to achieve it, Spinoza wrote, it is necessary "to form a social
order such as is most conducive to the attainment of this
character by the greatest number with the least difficulty and
danger." For "it is part of my happiness to lend a helping hand,
that many others may understand even as I do. . . ." [18]

Spinoza's *Improvement of the Understanding*, although not
published till after his death, was being written during 1662
while he was living at the Collegiant center, Rijnsburg.[19] At
that time, Spinoza's close Collegiant friend was Pieter Balling,
who was also engaged in writing his testimony of spiritual experience, *The Light upon the Candlestick*. Spinoza's friendship

with Balling was warm and intimate. Balling translated Spinoza's book on Descartes into Dutch in 1664. When Balling's child died that year, Spinoza, from his new residence at Voorburg, wrote to comfort the beloved father: "my anxiety daily grows more; and therefore I beseech and adjure you by our friendship not to mind writing to me fully." [20]

Especially striking is the similarity of spirit, quest, and conviction which pervaded the self-analyses that the two friends, Balling and Spinoza, were writing at this time. The Light which, according to Balling, should guide men is much like Spinoza's intellectual love of God. It is the Light "which leads man in Truth, . . . yea, brings him Union with God, wherein all Happiness and Salvation do consist." This "Light is a clear and distinct Knowledge of Truth in the Understanding of every Man, by which he is so convinced of the Being and Quality of things, that he cannot possibly doubt thereof." Like Spinoza, Balling desired a "Principle certain and infallible," and he found "the Knowledge of God must first be, before there can be knowledge of any particular things." [21] Like Spinoza, he used the Cartesian language to convey the mystic union with God. Balling's essay became a Quaker classic.

The Rijnsburg Collegiants were deeply interested in the promotion of the Cartesian mode of philosophizing. It was at Rijnsburg, for a pupil's help, that Spinoza composed a summary of Descartes' philosophy, in the geometrical manner. It became Spinoza's first published book. Balling acted as a courier between Spinoza and Amsterdam friends who were arranging for its publication. [22]

Jan Rieuwertsz, a Collegiant bookseller in Amsterdam, published all of Spinoza's works. He was a publisher after the fashion of Victor Gollancz in England during the nineteen-thirties. His bookshop was a gathering place of radical thinkers. Courage was required on the part of such a publisher in Spinoza's time, for the power of the Calvinist clergy and the Orange party was strong. The identity of Rieuwertsz as the printer was concealed in all of Spinoza's books with the exception of the one on Descartes. Even the author's name was omitted from the title page of the *Tractatus Theologico-Politicus*, which was given the fictitious imprint of a firm in Hamburg. The Mennonite-Collegiants were the friends upon whom Spinoza relied in death as well as in life. When he was dying, he asked his landlord "that immediately after his death, his Desk, which contained his Letters and Papers, shou'd be sent to John Rieuwertzen, a Printer at Amsterdam." [23] Rieuwertsz, safeguarding the desk from Spinoza's relatives, guided through his press the first publication of the *Ethics* in the *Posthumous Works* of 1677. At that time, political reaction in the Netherlands was so pronounced that, as Colerus says, "the Person who published it, did not care to be known."

Two hundred years later, when scholars were seeking literary manuscripts and remains of Spinoza, their greatest find was in the Collegiant orphanage at Amsterdam. Jelles had contributed liberally toward its construction in 1675. Perhaps it was in this building that Spinoza's friends met to discuss the publication of his works.[24]

Together with his Mennonite friends, Spinoza held that the greed for money was the ruin of commonwealths. In 1671, Spinoza wrote to Jelles of his conviction that "among friends, all things are in common." Spinoza was prompted to reiteration of this principle by his reading of a small book, *Homo Politicus*, which like Mandeville's *Fable of the Bees* affirmed money and honors to be man's highest good and justified, in their pursuit, "simulation, promising without giving, lying, perjury." Spinoza contemplated writing a reply to this acquisitive ethics, in which he would show "the restless and wretched plight of those who are greedy for money and covet honors, and lastly show, by clear arguments and many examples, that through the insatiable desire for Honours and Riches commonwealths must perish and have perished." But this work against the economic self-destruction of civilizations was never written. Spinoza did affirm, however, that communal cooperation was the way of wisdom. "How much better and more excellent the thoughts of Thales of Miletus were than those of the above-mentioned writers. Among friends, he said, all things are in common; the wise are the friends of the Gods (and all things belong to the Gods); therefore all things belong to the wise." [25] This expression betokened Spinoza's underlying loyalty to the ethical communism of the Collegiants.

In a world where men are rarely friends and seldom wise, it was not, however, an alternative for practical political action. Nevertheless, some of Spinoza's daring economic proposals in the *Tractatus Politicus* were related to his strain of religious communism.

Spinoza's Meeting With an English Quaker Missionary

In this time of social crisis, there was a great restless movement between England and the Netherlands of Quaker missionaries, Leveller agitators, royalist agents, and Cromwell's envoys.[26] The city of Amsterdam seethed with political intrigue as extreme Levellers plotted with Royalists to overthrow Cromwell. Amsterdam Jewry figured in these plots and counterplots. Richard Overton, the Leveller representative, sought its help, but found at that time "they are in conjunction with Cromwell; some of their Rabbies are learning English on purpose to live in England." Menasseh ben Israel was indeed on his momentous mission to Cromwell to secure the readmission of Jews into Britain. A few years earlier, in 1650, Menasseh had published a little book in Latin, *Spes Israelis* (The Hope of Israel), dedicated to the Supreme Court of Parliament, the English revolutionary government, whose "favor and good-will" he besought for "our nation, now scattered over all the earth." This book Spinoza owned in its Spanish translation. It abounded in the millenarian, Messianic ideas which were current in that revolutionary era. "I prove at large," wrote Menasseh, "that the day of the promised Messiah unto us doth draw near."

There was a community of spirit between the English radicals and the hardier souls of the Amsterdam Synagogue. The English radicals were philo-Semites. Their God was the God of the Revolutionary prophets who called for social justice, the God of Samuel who warned his people against taking unto themselves a king. There was a succession of English radical pamphlets portending a new era for the Jews; one predicted their conversion in 1656, another foresaw their return to Palestine in 1655, others were tracts advocating the readmission of the Jews to England. Margaret Fell, later the wife of the founder of Quakerism, George Fox, addressed two pamphlets to the Amsterdam Jews. The first in 1656 was entitled: *For Manasseth Ben Israel, The Call of the Jewes out of Babylon which is Good Tidings to the Meek, Liberty to the Captives, and for the Opening of the Prison Doores.* The second, *The Loving Salutation,* published in 1658, had a brisk circulation of 170 copies among the Amsterdam Jews.

Millenarian enthusiasm carried leftist radicals such as Everard the Leveller to even further lengths. As a contemporary wrote: "Everard said, He was of the race of Jews; as most men called Saxon and other, properly are. . . . That the time will suddenly be, when all men shall willingly come in and give up their lands and estates, and submit to the Community of Goods." His language was like that of the Fifth Monarchy Men who spoke of the wars of the latter days which would usher in the new age: "Then shall the oppressors cease and no more complaining be heard in the streets. Taxes should be no more . . . then peace and safety, plenty and prosperity, should overflow the land." These radicals far exceeded in their demands anything that Cromwell intended for Britain. Some millenarians went to Amsterdam and were formally received into the Synagogue. No wonder that Cromwell, in denouncing the mystic ultrademocrats in 1654, charged that they aimed to bring in the "Judaical Law," that they did not regard property as one of the badges of the Kingdom of Christ, and that they proposed that Christ's Law "be abrogated, indeed subverted." Subversives were regarded by Cromwell as "Judaisers." Thus, at the beginning of modern history, socialist and communist ideas came somehow to be thought of as Jewish. The orthodox Amsterdam Jews must have been as anxious to rebut the charge as their successors three centuries later.

Spinoza, cast out from the Jewish Synagogue, searched among the radicals for a way of life to which he could make a complete commitment. If the God of the Pharisees had failed him, there was still, he felt, a God among the radical free men to whom he could offer his deepest loyalty. His quest brought him to a meeting with William Ames, an eloquent English Quaker who was trying hard to persuade the Dutch Mennonites to join the

Society of Friends. In principle, the two sects were virtually identical, but the Quakers in Holland had so widespread a reputation for advocating communism with violent means that the Dutch Mennonites were hesitant to unite with them. But William Ames met an excommunicated Jew, who doubtless was Spinoza, with whom he experienced at once a community of conviction. They shared the same ideas on the inner light of reason, and they both rejected the interpretation of Scripture by authority. Spinoza promised he would attend the Quaker meeting, but William Ames was meanwhile arrested by Dutch authorities. A remarkable letter of William Ames to Margaret Fell written on April 17, 1657, less than a year after Spinoza's excommunication, gives us an unforgettable glimpse of the young Spinoza as he searched for the true way of life among the philosophical-political underworld of mystical, radical agitators. The letter, so striking in its significance, has been overlooked by scholars. Ames wrote:

> there is a Jew at Amsterdam that by the Jews is cast out (as he himself and others sayeth) because he oweneth no other teacher but the light and he sent for me and I spoke toe him and he was pretty tender and doth owne all that is spoken; and he sayde tow read of moses and the prophets without was nothing tow him except he Came toe know it within: and soe the name of Christ it is like he doth owne. I gave order that one of the duch Copyes of thy book should be given tow him and he sent me word he would Come toe oure meeting but in the mean time I was imprisoned.[27]

Communist feeling in Dutch Quakerism was at its highest in that year—1657.[28] A contemporary account spoke of one Quaker group in Rotterdam which was persuading "the rich that they should forsake the world and the poor that they should hold all their goods in common . . . they were joined by many of the rabble who had gladly seen that all their goods had become common property. But the Rulers of Rotterdam having regarded the affair as being fraught with great danger of tumult, arrested seven or eight of the leaders." A Dutch newspaper that month bewailed the Quaker meetings "to which the rabble flocked; for the latter took much joy in the Quakers' text that all goods should be owned in common, and, if they had seen an opportunity, would probably have liked to plunder a good burgher's house." [29] William Gerritsz, a Dutch Quaker whom the Collegiants found too stormy to assimilate, held up the example of the early Christians who used their money "which they did not consider their own" for the communal welfare.[30]

The religious communist yearning of the Quakers no doubt was appreciated by Spinoza. But he was probably perturbed by their reputation in the Netherlands as advocates of armed revolt. Indeed, the Quakers were subsequently believed to have participated in the violent uprising of the Fifth Monarchy Men in England in 1660. Passages from William Ames's pamphlet against the Amsterdam magistrates certainly did not lack the phraseology of violence: "the wrath of the Lord is kindled, his sword is driven from its scabbard, it is grasped in his hand; it is ready for the fray: In your blood, oh ye powerful of the earth, it shall be bathed." [31] To dispel this impression of their philosophy, English Quakers published in Amsterdam Dutch pamphlets which disclaimed any sympathy for insurrection or violence.[32] The image of the Quaker as a social revolutionist was, however, too fixed to undo in Holland. Pieter Balling, Spinoza's friend, failed to join the Quakers despite the fact that his book was translated into English by Benjamin Furly, the most eminent Rotterdam Quaker. Serrarius, who was Spinoza's trusted agent in the transmission of correspondence, published a pamphlet against the Quakers denying that they were the restorers of the primitive Christian community.[33] As these revolutionary associations ebbed, however, Dutch Quakerism merged with the Liberal Republican movement. Benjamin Furly in Rotterdam placed in his house "a plaster bust of Jan de Witt on a pedestal," and the heroic English Republican exile, Algernon Sidney, was his friend as well as De Witt's.[34] The Grand Pensionary evidently used his influence to allow the Quakers to meet freely in Rotterdam.

Spinoza always retained something of the pacifist outlook of the Mennonites and Quakers, who in that era of war held that war was unrighteous and the bearing of arms sinful. The dislike of militarism and nationalism found a curious expression in

Spinoza's theory of knowledge, as first formulated in the *Short Treatise*. Patriotism, he held, does not derive from true ideas but from opinion only. It is the kind of love which tends "to our ruin"; its hold on people, he observed, is similar to "the attitude of children to their father; because their father tells them that this or that is good they incline towards it, without knowing anything more about it. We see it also in those who from Love give their lives for the Fatherland. . . ." [35] Militarist patriotism is assigned by Spinoza to the lowest grade of knowledge; it ranks beneath clear ideas and belief in its claims. As Freud would say, its influence on us proceeds from a cultural superego of nationalist tradition, not from rational insight, and such an idea, Spinoza says, is inadequate. There are youths, moreover, Spinoza noted, who, in rebellion against their parents, likewise make the irrational choice of the military life—they "fly to the army, choosing the discomforts of war and the rule of a tyrant . . . , suffering all kinds of burdens to be imposed upon them in order that they may revenge themselves upon their parents." [36] Descartes conceived his philosophy while serving as a volunteer in the armies of Europe. Spinoza's philosophy was born in the circles of radical pacifist protest.

During the second Anglo-Dutch War which broke out in 1665, Spinoza made his most antimilitarist pronouncement. In a letter to the secretary of the Royal Society of England, Henry Oldenburg, Spinoza said he looked forward to the time "when the warriors are sated with blood"; then the scientists of England and Holland might resume their friendly interchanges. The spectacle of the war moved him to bitterness. "If that famous scoffer [Democritus] were alive today," said Spinoza, "he would surely die of laughter." [37] Spinoza found his pantheist faith tried by the actions of men at war. He elaborated a philosophic defense mechanism which would transmute his often low opinion of men into a component of his admiration for God. "These disorders, however, do not move me to laughter nor even to tears, . . . when I consider that men, like the rest, are only a part of nature, and that I do not know how each part of nature is connected with the whole of it. . . . And I find it is from the mere want of this kind of knowledge that certain things in Nature were formerly wont to appear to me vain, disorderly, and absurd, because I perceive them only in part and mutilated, and they do not agree with our philosophic mind. But now I let every man live according to his own ideas. Let those who will, by all means die for their good, so long as I am allowed to live for the truth." God, Nature, in its infinite power, produced even irrational militarists. Who then was the thinker who would dare to find an absurdity in things, to legislate his human-distorted preferences against the infinite power of God? To this device of repression, Spinoza was driven by his loyalty to the pantheist philosophy of seventeenth-century radicalism.

Spinoza's Pantheism and the Radical Thought of the Seventeenth Century

In 1650, Cromwell's Parliament passed an ordinance against certain "blasphemous and execrable opinions." It provided "that any person not distempered in their brains who shall maintain . . . that the true God . . . dwells in the creature . . . or that there is not any real difference between moral good and evil" should suffer six months' imprisonment, and be banished, if he didn't mend his opinions. Thus did Parliament take note of the pantheist mysticism which was spreading among the common people during the social ferment of the Commonwealth.[38] There was a widespread searching and questioning which broke through the confines of established sects. So-called "Ranters" and "Seekers," besides preaching the community of goods, held that God is identical with the universe, and indwelling in every creature and object. "They maintain," wrote an observer, "that God is essentially in every creature," that there is no such thing as what men call sin, that men are "living in God and God in them," and that in prayer, it was God in them that prayed.[39] They even rejected the belief in immortality, so that a contemporary versifier satirized these homespun metaphysicians:

> They prate of God! Believe it, fellow creatures,
> There's no such bug-bear: all was made by Nature
>   . . . and that they grossly lie
> That say there's hope of immortality. . . .[40]

The air was filled with the uncertainties of revolutionary possibilities and intoxicating visions of social reconstruction. And with the political leveling emotion went a new conception of man's relation to the universe. For the first time in Western Europe, pantheist and mystical ideas became diffused among groups of ordinary people. Pantheistic ideas were the common intellectual property of left Republicans in Spinoza's time.[41] Gerrard Winstanley, the colorful apostle of Christian communism who led the English Diggers in 1649 in their ill-fated experiment in collective farming, expounded his pantheism in a series of political and theological tracts.[42] His ideas were known in Holland. Winstanley's theological tracts and his *The True Leveller Standard Advanced* found their way into the library of Benjamin Furly, Rotterdam Quaker. God, said Winstanley, "dwells in every creature according to his orbe within the globe of the creation. . . ." God "knits every creature together into a oneness; making every creature to be an upholder of his fellow; and so every one is an assistant to preserve the whole." The "goer to church," the man who "looks for God without Himself," said Winstanley, will not find him, "but he that looke for a God within himselfe . . . hath community with the spirit that hath made all flesh in every creature within the globe." Winstanley's "community" with all existence is an expression of the same pantheist mysticism which Spinoza saw as the union of the human mind with nature. Like Spinoza too, Winstanley held that scientific knowledge is a knowledge of God: "To know the secrets of Nature is to know the works of God; And to know the works of God within the creation, is to know God himself, for God dwells in every visible work or body." [43] As Spinoza was to say: "The more we understand individual objects, the more we understand God." [44] Both men regarded the Calvinist fear of damnation as a source of mental disorder.

The philosophical questioning of the Levellers took them in a direction shared with Spinoza. Richard Overton, an intellectual spokesman of the movement, was often in Holland conducting dubious intrigues on its behalf. In 1644, he published a pamphlet in Amsterdam against the conventional notion of immortality. Man, he wrote, "is a compound wholly mortal, con-

trary to that common distinction of Soule and Body." [45] Spinoza
too held to a view which was tantamount to a denial of personal
immortality: "The mind can imagine nothing, nor can it recollect
anything that is past, except while the body exists." Like Spinoza,
Overton denied that the "soul" was "any selfe distinct Being"; as
Spinoza would put it, the human mind is not a substance, but a
mode. The Leveller philosopher looked to the ancient materialists for inspiration, not to Plato and Aristotle. The three "most
rationall" philosophers, said Overton, were Democritus, Leucip-
pus, and Epicurus. [46] Spinoza's words were much the same. "The
authority of Plato, Aristotle, and Socrates," he wrote one of his
correspondents, "has not much weight with me." The Calvinist
divines, in Spinoza's words, continued "to rave with the Greeks,"
to teach "the speculations of Platonists and Aristotelians." His
own respect was reserved for the Atomists—"Epicurus, Democritus, Lucretius." [47] During this time, the ancient materialists were
coming into their own. A *History of Philosophy* published in
1656 by Sir Thomas Stanley devoted 112 pages to Epicurus, more
than any other philosopher received, and that same year appeared
John Evelyn's *Essay on Lucretius*. [48]

Pantheist ideas thrived also among the numerous small sects
and conclaves in the Netherlands searching to know God directly,
without the refracting intervention of sacred text or minister's
authority. Besides the Mennonites, there were Borellists, Enthusiasts, Quakers, Tremblers, and Seekers. There were numerous Socinians. A hostile observer in 1673 remarked that they
were mostly uneducated men, merchants and artisans, who had
none the less a remarkable talent for explaining the Scriptures.
These freethinkers, he added, were usually pantheist: "Most of
them believe that there is one Spirit of God, which is in all living
things, which is diffused throughout everything, which is and
which lives in all creatures: That the substance and immortality
of our soul is nothing else than this Spirit of God: That God himself is nothing other than this Spirit: That souls die with the
bodies. That sin is nothing. . . ."

In Spinoza's thought, pantheistic mysticism, the standpoint
of the seventeenth-century philosophic radicals, reached its culmination of rigor and profundity. "I could not separate God

from Nature," wrote Spinoza to Oldenburg in 1662, "as all of whom I have any knowledge have done." He spoke in his *Ethics* of "that eternal and infinite being which we call God or Nature." The explorations of Collegiants, Quakers, and Levellers were added up in his simple proposition: "Whatever is, is in God, and nothing can either be or be conceived without God." [49] Spinoza's contemporaries were aware of this affiliation of his thought. Robert Hooke, the indefatigable English scientist, recorded in his diary for July 24, 1678, that he was engaged in "much discourse about Spinosa quakers," while John Howe, formerly chaplain to Cromwell, attacked Spinoza's pantheism in his *The Living Temple*.[50] When the Reformed Church at The Hague in 1697 denounced Spinoza's ideas as blasphemous, a pamphlet defending its action characterized the typical Spinozist as a communist— "avec ses idées de communisme il tache de détourner les hommes et les jeunes gens de la bonne vie [with his ideas of communism he tries to lure men and young people from the good life]." [51]

The question, of course, arises: Why did the radical democratic thought of the seventeenth century find pantheist metaphysics its natural expression? [52] For it is a fact that after 1649 and 1650, the radical social consciousness of Europe expressed itself largely in pantheist mysticism. One historian has tried to explain this phenomenon with the hypothesis that mystical enthusiasm arose among the discontented classes because they had no avenues for political expression.[53] According to this explanation, pantheistic mysticism is the outcome of repressed political action. There is strong evidence, however, against this fantasy-repression hypothesis. Two centuries later, pantheistic mysticism flourished once more in the transcendentalist philosophy of New England.[54] Emerson, Thoreau, Hawthorne, the cooperators of Brook Farm, were men who opposed slavery; they expressed their views forthrightly, unrepressed. What their philosophy provided them was a doctrine of the inherent worth of all men, including the enslaved Negroes.

The Calvinism of Spinoza's Holland, like the Puritan orthodoxy in Massachusetts, was prepared to grant salvation only to a few, to the fortunate predestined elect of God. According to Spinoza and the transcendentalists, however, all men partook of the immanent divine. To the harsh Calvinist doctrine of the elect, Winstanley the Digger had replied: "Jesus Christ . . . will dwell in the whole creation, that is, in every man and woman without exception," and Lilburne, the Leveller, had similarly said: "The Lord hath promised his enlightening spirit unto all his people that are laborious and studious to know him aright." [55] The Quakers found the Light present even in wild Indians who had not heard of Christianity.[56] Spinoza, like his fellow seekers, drew a liberal consequence of salvation from his pantheist metaphysics: "The highest good of those who follow virtue is common to all, and all may equally enjoy it.[57] The aristocratic sadism in the Calvinist theology was alien to the spirit of radical democrats.[58] For this reason, pantheistic mysticism became the metaphysics of the nascent liberal democracy of the seventeenth century.

In later years, Spinoza still endorsed certain aspects of the Collegiant-Quaker secession from society. He shared, for instance, their aversion toward oaths which are taken in God's name. "Those, whom the law compels to take an oath," he wrote, "will be more cautious of perjury, if they are bidden to swear by the country's safety and liberty . . . than if they are told to swear by God." [59] For man's relationship to God is private, whereas his relations to his fellows are public and verifiable. In his personal habits, Spinoza remained very much the Collegiant. It was said that his clothes "were not better than those of the meanest citizen," and that when an eminent Councillor of State, who was visiting him, reproached Spinoza for what to the Councillor's eyes was shabbiness, "Spinoza answer'd him, that a Man was never better for having a finer Gown. To which he added, It is unreasonable to wrap up things of little or no value in a precious Cover." [60] This story may be apocryphal, but what is noteworthy is that it coincides exactly with the Collegiant philosophy of dress. The Mennonites discarded all personal ornaments; they were precise and simple in their clothing and furniture. Benjamin Furly, the Dutch Quaker, even queried in his pamphlet of 1661, *The World's Honour Detected:* "Is there any Difference to be made in Cloths in the worship of God?" [61] Toward the vanities of authorship, Spinoza likewise retained to the end a

Collegiant-Quaker outlook. The Dutch Quakers published books without using a single capital letter. Their motives were not those of a literary avant-garde; rather, they felt that to begin a man's name with a capital letter "was as bad as to render him hat-honour." [62] Spinoza was not so drastic in his rejection of literary ego-enhancement, but he cited with approval Cicero's saying that "even the philosophers who write books about despising glory place their names on the title-page," and as the editor of his *Posthumous Works*, Jelles, tells us, "shortly before his death he asked explicitly that his name should not figure on his *Ethics*," because "he did not want his teaching to derive its name from it." [63]

But there were deeper aspects of the Collegiant withdrawal with which Spinoza was becoming discontent. He was beginning to long for a return to the world of political strife and contention.

CHAPTER 3

Political Scientist in the Cause of Human Liberation

The Political Philosopher as Political Participant

In Spinoza's character there was a tension between two components. On the one hand, there was the mystic who chose the life of withdrawal at Rijnsburg, the seeker who longed to immerse himself in the intellectual love of God. On the other hand, there was the man who was restless with the retired ways of his Collegiant friends, and who aspired to take his place in the councils of the republic.[1]

The Collegiant-Mennonite mode of life was indeed a secession from the political conflicts of the time. One-tenth of the population disfranchised itself from civic activity. The Mennonites excluded themselves voluntarily from all military and governmental posts and the civil service. Spinoza came to believe at last that the Collegiant-Mennonite secession was indefensible. He wrote in the *Tractatus Theologico-Politicus*: "It is certain that duties towards one's country are the highest man can fulfill; for, if government be taken away, no good thing can last, all falls into disrepute, anger and anarchy reign unchecked amid universal fear." He criticized the Mennonites' refusal to use the courts of law. One's obligation to the state, Spinoza argued, should outweigh the literal Christian ethics of submission: "For instance, it is in the abstract my duty when my neighbor quarrels with me and wishes to take my cloak, to give him my coat also; but if it be thought that such conduct is hurtful to the maintenance of the state, I ought to bring him to trial, even at the risk of his being condemned to death." [2] The ethics of political participation was surmounting, in Spinoza's mind, that of political withdrawal.

The Republic, moreover, had need of the talents of a political philosopher. The Republican party of John de Witt had its interpreter of Dutch history in the person of De Wicquefort, author of the *History of the United Provinces;* its economist was Pieter de la Court, author of *The Political Maxims of the State of Holland,* published in 1662; while its political scientist was Pieter's brother, Jean de la Court, author of the *Political Discourses,* likewise published in 1662. But Jean de la Court died prematurely in 1660, and there was a gap in the ranks of Republican spokesmen.[3] A thinker who could cope with political ideas, who was a master of the analyses of Hobbes and Machiavelli, and whose own liberalism was unquestionable was welcome among the Republicans. Spinoza, for his part, was delighted at the prospect that his ideas might now exert their influence in political circles. He removed in April, 1663, from Rijnsburg to Voorburg, a little town but a half-hour's walk from The Hague, the capital of Holland.

The change of residence marked a major step in Spinoza's intellectual evolution. The mystic was now to be superseded in large part by the political philosopher. A few months after he removed to Voorburg, Spinoza confided to Oldenburg the hope that his little book on Descartes, in process of publication, would confirm his own qualifications in the eyes of the Republican political leaders. "Perhaps, on this occasion," he wrote, "there will be found some who hold the first places in my country, who will desire to see other things which I have written and which I acknowledge as my own; and they will make it their business that I should be able to publish them without any risk of trouble. Should this indeed happen, then I have no doubt that I shall publish some things immediately." Spinoza at this time was no recluse. There was an admixture of pride in his complaint that his time was so little his own: "Since my return to this village, in which I now live, I have scarcely been able to be my own master, because of the friends who deigned to visit me." [4] His intellectual distinction won the attention of eminent men in the government. The political philosopher could regard himself as making a direct contribution to statecraft. As Colerus described Spinoza's life at Voorburg: "He lived there . . . three or four years; during which time, he got a great many Friends, at the Hague, who were all distinguisht by their Quality, or by Civil and Military Employments. They were often in his Company, and took a great delight in hearing him discourse. It was at their request that he settl'd himself at the Hague at last." [5]

During the first years at Voorburg, Spinoza worked hard at his chief book, the *Ethics*. By June, 1665, he was able to show his friends a work which was already advanced to the eighteenth proposition of a Third Part. So immersed was he in its composition that he was reluctant to take time for discussion of points in the Cartesian philosophy. Suddenly, however, he dropped his studies in ethics and metaphysics and turned to the writing of a book which was to become the *Tractatus Theologico-Politicus*. Spinoza announced his decision to write this political book in the same letter of 1665 in which his diatribe against the warriors and human nature was bitterest. Three months before, he had confessed his disquietude concerning the irrationality of the people at large and their incapacity for understanding the decisions of the Republican leaders: "The populace does not cease to apprehend all things evil, nor can any one find a reason why the fleet does not sail. Indeed, the matter does not yet seem to be safe. I fear that our people there [at The Hague] wish to be too wise and far-seeing. . . . I should like to hear what our people there think. . . ." [6] There was a gap which Spinoza saw between the scientific aristocracy of the Republican merchants and the superstitious Calvinist, monarchist masses. Unless the people too could be won to reason, the Republic was in danger of foundering.

The book which Spinoza undertook to write was directed against the political and social doctrines of the Calvinist party. He set forth in 1665 the reasons for his project:

> I am now writing a Treatise about my interpretation of Scripture. This I am driven to do by the following reasons: 1. The Prejudices of the Theologians; for I know that these are among the chief obstacles which prevent men from directing their minds to philosophy; and to remove them from the minds of the more prudent. 2. The opinion which the common people have of me, who do not cease to accuse me falsely of atheism; I am also obliged to avert this accusation as far as it is possible to do so. 3. The freedom of philosophizing, and of saying what

we think; this I desire to vindicate in every way, for here it is
always suppressed through the excessive authority and impudence
of the preachers.[7]

The project grew beyond the initially intended bounds. When
the book was published five years later in 1670, it had come to
embrace a political analysis of the problems of democracy in the
Netherlands cast in the guise of a Scriptural discussion.

The Political Setting

What was the political setting in which Spinoza's thought
was shaped, and in which he was as an individual involved? The
great dominant fact, which posed the primary problem for
Spinoza's political reflections, was the experiment in the republican form of government in the Netherlands. It was an experiment unprecedented in Europe; the old Venetian Republic was
nothing like it in size or scale. The Dutch Republic had not been
conceived with explicit design.[8] It was born in 1579 during the
struggle for independence from Spain, and like the Third French
Republic, it came into existence largely by chance, before the
citizens were clearly aware of what was occurring.

The Dutch Republic had a precarious hold on the loyalty of
its citizens. The masses were still monarchist in their emotion
and tradition, bound by close attachment to the house of Orange,
which had given them their leaders in the struggle for independence. The civilian Republican spokesmen were not figures of
glory; the house of Orange was the repository of the national
military honor. The Republican leaders appealed to the economic self-interest of their countrymen, to the stake which all
citizens had in the peace, prosperity, and trade of the Netherlands; they were rationalists in politics. The house of Orange
appealed to the deepest levels of irrational feeling in the Dutch
people generally. "The Name or Title of Prince," remarked the
visiting French *libertin,* St. Evremond, "is what they submit to
with Pleasure," and at The Hague, only two men, John de Witt
and a friend, dared pronounce the word "Republic." [9]

This republic, without the people's allegiance, dared not be a democracy. The Republican government rested on the support of the merchant class, philosophic liberals and exponents of peace. As Sir William Temple, the distinguished English ambassador said, the republic of Holland was no democracy but "a sort of oligarchy and very different from a popular government." [10]

The two parties in the Netherlands differed profoundly with respect to their conception of the Dutch Union. The monarchist party stood for a centralized, unified Netherlands, while the Republican party was faithful to the principle of provincial sovereignty. This issue was no abstract disputation in constitutional law. Holland, which was the richest, most commercial, and most populous of the seven provinces, had borne the lion's share of the expenses of the war against Spain. It wanted relief from the burden of a standing army. It wanted peace, trade, not the bellicosity of vested military interests. Holland disliked the military bureaucracy which had grown up around the house of Orange. With the advent of peace with Spain in 1648, Holland's demands for economy and the reduction of the army became more strenuous. But its voice was ignored in the States-General of the United Netherlands, where it had only one vote like each of the other six provinces.

The house of Orange was the powerful centralizing force of the Netherlands. The Prince of Orange was usually the executive officer, the Stadtholder of several provinces, and, as such, commanded their respective armies of mercenary troops. In 1650, there ensued one of the recurrent crises in the troubled relations between liberal, commercial Holland and the ambitious house of Orange. The province undertook to reduce its armed forces that year. Outbursts of wrath from the pulpit, press, and the people descended upon the provincial leaders. The lower classes refused to see their idolized prince humiliated by arrogant burghers. The Prince of Orange, for his part, was engaged in private plans for the restoration of the Stuarts on the English throne and an invasion of the Spanish Netherlands. He decided to make a coup d'état, and ordered his soldiers to seize Amsterdam. The besieged city capitulated after a brief resistance. It looked, indeed, as if the Republican party was finally to be eliminated from the Dutch political world. But the smallpox intervened, and William II,

who had become the virtual absolute monarch of the Netherlands, died in his twenty-fourth year.

Chance had brought the Republican party an unforeseen
historic opportunity. The house of Orange was bereft of a chief;
its fortunes were insecure, dependent on an infant born posthumously to William II. The Republican leaders of Holland
seized the initiative and summoned the provinces to a Great
Convocation in 1651. Its outcome was a basic republican revision
of the constitution of the Netherlands. There was no longer to
be an over-all captain-general of the Netherlands Armies. Most
of the provinces abolished the office of the stadtholder entirely.
Provincial sovereignty over armed forces was recognized; officers
and men were to swear obedience to the civilian authorities of
their respective provinces. It was said that Holland resorted to
bribery to win the majority of the three hundred delegates. The
Hollanders could reply that the liberties of every province and
town were now safeguarded against the encroachments of arbitrary monarchical ambition.

The Republican leaders of the Netherlands were unable,
however, to bring peace and tranquillity to their country. They
wanted friendly relations with Oliver Cromwell's government in
England, but the Calvinist clergy had so excited the masses by
denouncing as parricide the execution of Charles I that Cromwell's ambassadors in 1651 were greeted with jeers from The
Hague populace, "Cromwell's bastards, King's murderers." [11]
Cromwell proposed a noble, breath-taking scheme, to coalesce
the two Republics for the defense of their common Protestantism
and Republicanism. The Dutch leaders, however, were mindful
of the people's hostility to the regicide. In the meanwhile, commercial rivalries between the English and Dutch were aggravated
by the English Navigation Act of 1651, and from 1652 to 1654 the
two countries were at war.

Peace came through the efforts of John de Witt, who in 1653
became Grand Pensionary of Holland. When the stadtholderate
was abolished, the functions of a foreign secretary devolved upon
the office of the Grand Pensionary. De Witt came to be the
virtual Prime Minister of the Estate of Holland, with a paramount influence upon the other provinces. De Witt was inclined

to accept Cromwell's proposal for a great European Protestant Alliance. The ardor and faith of the international revolutionist were strong in Cromwell. To win the Dutch to his scheme, he offered to concede to them the whole East Indies trade and to re-call every English ship and resident in the Far East. All to no avail. The States-General were bound by the monarchist emo-tions of the Orangist masses and Calvinist clergy; there was also the consideration of their interest in trade with Catholic coun-tries. Thereupon De Witt embarked upon a secret diplomacy with Cromwell. The war was terminated in return for De Witt's con-sent to an Act of Exclusion which stipulated that no Prince of Orange should ever be appointed stadtholder or captain-general in the Netherlands. To Oliver Cromwell, this was more than a guarantee of the permanence of the republican form of govern-ment in the Netherlands. It was a safeguard that the Dutch land would not be used as a base for rebellions on behalf of the Stuarts, the close relatives of the Orange family.

John de Witt thus achieved peace through a series of strata-gems. The States-General were compelled to accept the Act of Exclusion as a *fait accompli*. Throughout the Netherlands, the ordinary citizens, the laborers, the shopkeepers, the farmers, hated John de Witt because he had done wrong to the little Prince of Orange.[12] The Grand Pensionary of Holland became known as the most eminent Dutchman of his time, an adroit, skillful Re-publican leader. But the republic he led was hardly stable, for its fragile foundation in the reason of a few men was always menaced by the rejection in many men's feelings.

Was the Republic then a form of government ahead of its time for the Netherlands? Could men of reason persuade the ordinary people that a republic would make for their greater happiness? Could men of reason undermine the irrational author-ity which benighted Calvinist divines exercised upon their con-gregations? How could the multitude be taught that freedom was their highest virtue? These questions were in Spinoza's mind as he wrote the *Tractatus Theologico-Politicus*.

The Birth of Liberalism

The political philosophy of Spinoza is the first statement in history of the standpoint of a democratic liberalism. It was written during the high tide of Republican rule. The experiment in scientific republican government had lasted for a decade and a half, and could claim more than a measure of success. So Spinoza wrote with joyous optimism: "Now seeing that we have the rare happiness of living in a republic, where everyone's judgment is free and unshackled, where each may worship God as his conscience dictates, and where freedom is esteemed beyond all things dear and precious, I have believed that I should be undertaking no ungrateful or unprofitable task, in demonstrating that not only can such freedom be granted without prejudice to the public peace, but also, that without such freedom, piety cannot flourish nor the public peace be secure." He wrote with pride of his native city:

> The city of Amsterdam reaps the fruit of this freedom in its own great prosperity and in the admiration of all other people. For in this most flourishing state, and most splendid city, men of every nation and religion live together in the greatest harmony, and ask no questions before trusting their goods to a fellow-citizen, save whether he be rich or poor, and whether he generally acts honestly, or the reverse. His religion and sect is considered of no importance: for it has no effect before the judges in gaining or losing a cause, and there is no sect so despised that its followers, provided they harm no one, pay every man his due, and live uprightly, are deprived of the protection of the magisterial authority.[13]

Amsterdam indeed had become the envied center of all who loved freedom in Europe. A fellow of the Royal Society described the high estate of liberty in Holland at this time:

> Here is the greatest Equality in the World. It is ordinary to hear a mean Fellow in a dispute with a Citizen say, *I am as much as you; if you be richer than I, 'tis well.* . . . Certainly when I do reflect upon the miserable condition of some Christians in

Europe; as of the peasants in Lytuania, and almost all over Poland, where the Lords have the power of hanging them, when they run away from their tyranny; in Bohemia, and some other place of Germany; in Denmarke and Sweden, where the Gentlemen do highly abuse the Commons; I cannot chose but cry out, *O happy Holland, that hast preserved that precious jewel of Liberty; preserve it well, for with its loss, goes that of thy happiness!* [14]

Holland had become the exemplar land to all those who sought a free commerce and a free thought. Thomas Hobbes in surly fashion blamed the English Revolution partially on the Dutch example. He wrote in his *Behemoth:* "the city of London and other great towns of trade, having in admiration the prosperity of the Low Countries after they had revolted from their monarch, the King of Spain, were inclined to think that the like change of government here would to them produce the like prosperity." [15] But when English repression descended upon its advocate Hobbes, he turned to free Amsterdam for the opportunity to plead his case. On October 17, 1666, the House of Commons of a restored monarchy ordered a committee "to receive information touching such books as tend to atheism, . . . and in particular the book of Hobbes called the Leviathan. . . ." Thomas Hobbes, an absolutist too straightforward in his reasoning to be tolerated by a governing absolutism, began to burn his papers. He was never able again to publish his ethical and political writings in England. But in free Amsterdam, Hobbes in 1668 published the works which the English censor had refused to license. No wonder that Hobbes, on reading Spinoza's *Tractatus Theologico-Politicus,* commented to a friend that Spinoza "had out throwne him [Hobbes] a barres length, for he durst not write so boldly." [16]

The commercial prosperity of Amsterdam, Spinoza held, was the outcome of its religious and intellectual freedom. The Liberal Republicans of Holland made this proposition a cardinal tenet of their philosophy. Pieter de la Court made the point again and again in his *Political Maxims of the State of Holland.*

"Freedom or toleration," wrote Pieter, "in and about the service or worship of God, is a powerful means to preserve many inhabitants in Holland, and allure foreigners to dwell among us." Holland had won its commercial supremacy because it cherished freedom more than its rivals; "besides, neither in France nor England was there any liberty of religion, but a monarchical government in both, with high duties on goods imported and exported. . . ." [17] Liberalism in economy was conjoined with liberalism in religion. Trade had always thrived most, Pieter held, under Republican governments, and like a tradesman's Toynbee, he went back into the antiquity of the Phoenician towns to sustain his vision of the high historic destiny of the commercial republic.[18] The backwardness of England relative to Holland, said Pieter, arose from such monarchical policies as its exclusion of foreigners from guilds.

The liberal political philosophy, despite the power of its economic rationality, was confronted, none the less, by the fact that the majority of Dutch people, especially among the lower classes, was often neither liberal nor rational. The majority was Calvinist and fanatical. When the Amsterdam city council enacted a statute of religious toleration in order to attract more foreigners to its domain, fiery Calvinist preachers protested loudly that it would be far better to lose some trade than to permit the poisonous doctrines of heretics to circulate within Amsterdam's walls.[19] The Calvinist divines were troubled by the secular cast of the economic motive. At home, in Holland, they imposed their will on the directors of the Dutch East India Company, which adopted rules requiring its officials to be members of the Reformed Church, and forbidding the public practice of any other religion within its territories. But in the Far East, religious intolerance was curtailed by the company's desire for profit. In Java, Calvinist ministers were horrified by the indifference with which the company allowed Chinese and Mohammedans to go unconcernedly about their ritualistic observances without troubling themselves about original sin. When the Calvinist consistory of Batavia reminded the Governor-General, Maetsuycker (1653-1678), that the Law of Moses forbade the tolerance of non-

Christian religions, he replied in words which are a paraphrase
of Spinoza's doctrine: "The laws of the old Jewish republics have
no force in the territory of the Dutch East India Company!" [20]

The desire for economic well-being can help make people
rational. Here, then, was a strategic flaw in the Calvinist standpoint. Economic motives could clash with Calvinist intolerance,
and as a consequence of this conflict freedom might be extended
to hitherto closed domains. Spinoza therefore explicitly endorsed
the wisdom of the Dutch East India Company in its policy of
religious liberalism in the Far East. The Dutch treaty with the
Japanese, he said, was an instance of sound principle in the international adjustment of religious differences. The Dutch company's outpost in Japan had indeed in 1641 forbidden the observance of Sunday in order to conform to the domestic Japanese law,
and had actually also allowed its vessels to be searched for cruci-
fixes and Bibles. "The Dutch were there to make money, not
Christians." [21] And Spinoza commented with approval on the
rule of economic reason: "those who live in a country where the
Christian religion is forbidden, are bound to abstain from such
rites, and can none the less live in a state of blessedness. We have
an example of this in Japan, where the Christian religion is forbidden, and the Dutch who live there are enjoined by the East
India Company not to practice any outward rites of religion." [22]

Perhaps it was strange that liberalism and tolerance should
look for support in the search for trade. But from Spinoza's time
on, through the eighteenth century, philosophers hoped that the
commercial spirit which animated middle-class republics would
give birth to an era of international peace. A hundred years after
Spinoza, Immanuel Kant, the critical philosopher, was to voice
the same forlorn hope, conceived in the longings which the
French Revolution had awakened: "It is the spirit of commerce
that sooner or later takes hold of every nation, and is incompatible with war." [23]

Together with the Governor-General in the East Indies,
Spinoza affirmed that "the whole Mosaic Law, had reference
merely to the government of the Jews, and merely temporal advantages." Even the Christian rites, he added, are merely external signs, "not as having anything to do with blessedness, or

possessing any sanctity in themselves." Ceremonies were solely ordained, in Spinoza's opinion, for the preservation of specific societies; they have no universal obligation. Christian rulers had done well therefore in not hesitating "to make treaties with Turks and heathen," and in telling their subjects abroad to abide "either in things secular or religious" by the foreign laws. The Calvinist spokesman, Gysbertus Voetius, Professor of Theology and Oriental Studies at the University of Utrecht, complained that the Dutch East India Company had made so small a number of converts in Asia, but to Spinoza, the Asians could find the highest good in their own ways. Professor Voetius harassed free men everywhere; as Spinoza observed, he had "once maligned Descartes," blaming him for the spread of immorality, and had persuaded his University in 1642 to condemn the Cartesian philosophy. Cosmopolitanism was the outlook which Spinoza advocated against the Calvinist ethnocentrism.[24] Ethnic hatreds, he held, arise from the errors of hearsay, the pitfalls of untested words; they have no place in the mind of the free man who knows the universal laws of human nature. "The two archenemies of the human race," Spinoza wrote, "are Hatred and Remorse"; hatred and guilt, we should translate today, are the arch-oppressors of men.[25]

The Calvinist Party in the Netherlands

Despite its name, the *Tractatus Theologico-Politicus* is a book which was designed to terminate the influence of theology on politics. In the seventeenth century, religious passions entangled themselves in the political and economic disputes of men. Social questions could not be dealt with in their own terms realistically; Calvinist ministers were placing the hegemony of their church above the people's material and cultural well-being. To win the citizens' support for the Republican polity of John de Witt, the first step, as Spinoza saw it, was to undermine the primary institution which helps make men irrational. Voltaire, in the France of the eighteenth century, was the harbinger of social revolution when he hurled his challenge to the church, *"Ecrasez l'infâme."* And Spinoza, in the setting of a precarious

Republic, which sustained itself from month to month against Calvinist "prophets" and "agitators" who enflamed the populace, had taken the same stand. The glory and prosperity of Amsterdam were the achievement, he argued, of Republican freedom. He carried the polemical warfare into his opponents' citadel of biblical texts. Scriptural criticism and interpretation provided Spinoza with the grounds for the dismissal of Calvinist claims to hegemony. His analysis of the ancient Hebrew confederation was with pointed parallel reference to the contemporary Dutch Union. He wrote a plea for intellectual liberty which was meant to revive the fire of freedom even in those immured in slavery.

Religious controversies, Spinoza said, must not be allowed to obtrude themselves into political questions. Religious differences, superimposed on political ones, exacerbate men and make them irrational. Spinoza called on the political-religious history of the Netherlands to bear witness to the baneful effects of religious ideology in politics: "when the religious controversy between Remonstrants and Counter-Remonstrants began to be taken up by politicians and the States, it grew into a schism, and abundantly showed that laws dealing with religion and seeking to settle its controversies are much more calculated to irritate than to reform, and that they give rise to extreme license: further, it was seen that schisms do not originate in a love of truth, which is a source of courtesy and gentleness, but rather in an inordinate desire for supremacy." [26]

At its inception, the liberal principle of minority rights was in conflict with the principle of majority rule. For the intense loyalty of the Dutch people to Calvinist religion was unquestionable, and liberal tolerance had always to press its case against a latent intolerance. What explains the attachment of the Dutch multitude to the Calvinist creed? To understand the problem of Spinoza's liberalism, we must turn for a few moments to the story of Calvinism in the Netherlands.

Calvinism was no religious opiate distilled by the upper classes for the befuddlement of the workers. It was a powerful stimulant to action which the workmen largely brewed for themselves. As the distinguished historian Henri Pirenne stated: "It was, however, among the working class that Calvin's teaching spread most rapidly. The chief centres of its growth were to be found just where the great industries were supreme." The ports of Holland became bases of Calvinist faith. "Above all, it triumphed where the worker was reduced to a precarious existence. . . . Discontent, the spirit of revolt, and the hope of bettering his lot, worked without exception in favour of Calvinism." [27] According to Marxians, the revolutionary masses tend to be scientific and irreligious. Actually, the opposite is more often the case. People in revolution are drawn to millenarian, mythological, and visionary modes of thought. Redemptive metaphysics rather than empirical science captures the mentality of the masses in crisis.

The stern Calvinist creed rallied the Dutch people against the Spanish oppressor. When the social revolutionary movement of the Anabaptists declined in the Netherlands, some of its adherents, as we have seen, took the path of secession into communities of gentle religious souls inspired by primitive communal Christianity. The greater number, however, were drawn to Calvinism, which aimed to reform the state through a church which was organized, to use a modern analogy, like the party vanguard of a proletarian dictatorship. Calvinists were the leaders and inspirers of the struggle against Spain which followed the "beggar's revolt" of 1572. The lower classes, driven to despair by new taxes, rose against the Spanish authority. The Calvinist creed endowed fishermen, the poor people, with the conviction that they were the elect, the servants of the Lord, warring against the damned. The Duke of Alva, Captain-General for the Spanish king, cruel in his Catholic zeal, was confronted by a novel weapon of social warfare, the general strike: artisans closed their workshops to protest his decrees. Calvinist crowds drove Catholic magistrates and deputies of the States-General from their seats of office.[28] Calvinist pastors were everywhere the guides and spokesmen for a citizenry in revolt.

The triumph of the Dutch revolt, however, produced an unanticipated consequence; it took away the revolutionary crisis which had brought Calvinists to leadership. A new governing class began to emerge, the regents, the liberal commercial class of the Netherlands. There ensued what has beeen called a "return of the patriciate." Calvinism had been the austere doctrine of national and social upheaval; it gave expression to the resentment of the poor, inspired them with the conviction that they were God's elect, channeled their aggressions against the oppressors, the damned. Calvinist rigor made a virtue of the poverty of the poor, and a sin of the beauties and pleasures which only the rich could afford. Calvinism was a theology of crisis, an ethics of scarcity. But as the crisis dissolved in men's memories, as the Netherlands grew, with unparalleled prosperity, to become the great carrier and trading nation of Europe, the desire arose among comfortable Dutch citizens for a more liberal philosophy, one less harsh and cruel in attitude toward others.

Spinoza was a lineal descendant of this liberal movement in Dutch philosophy. The regents were often men who in their youth had come under the influence of the gay, kindly, tolerant Erasmus. The liberals at the beginning of the seventeenth century were called by the Calvinist clergy "libertines"; they frankly regarded Erasmus as their spiritual ancestor. Erasmus' influence grew even more pronounced later in the century. A French translation of the *Praise of Folly,* published at The Hague in 1642, when Spinoza was ten years old, ran into three editions. Pierre Bayle placed an engraving of Erasmus on the title page of his *Nouvelles de la République des Lettres,* and in 1703 Jean Leclerc, a Socinian who had come to terms with Spinoza's ideas, began to publish the complete edition of Erasmus' works.[29] And it is noteworthy that when Spinoza in his *Short Treatise* wrote a dialogue concerning his pantheist ideas, he gave to the interlocutor the name "Erasmus."[30] It was to the men of the liberal party, the followers of Erasmus, that he most directly addressed his philosophy.[31]

In effect, there was the rise in Holland of a hedonist insurgence against the Calvinist ethics. A movement of thought began against Calvinism which was not unlike the protest of Emerson against New England Puritanism, or Bentham's use of the Principle of Utility against the Principle of Asceticism.[32] A religion was desired which would not take a sadistic delight in the predestined damnation of others; a religion was sought which would, indeed, be less Messianic, and more kindly toward men's pleasures—a religion gentler and more of love.

The liberal patricians were led during the first decades of the seventeenth century by men of great force and character— such men as the courageous John Oldenbarnevelt and the erudite Hugo Grotius. Oldenbarnevelt's philosophy was summed up in the motto, *Nil scire tutissima fides* [the safest faith is to know nothing].[33] The liberals wanted no Calvinist theocracy after the model of Geneva. They proposed that the Reformed Church should reform itself toward tolerance. The liberal religious group became known as the "Remonstrants"; they rejected the doctrine of predestination, according to which God, in his own pleasure, had condemned some to eternal bliss, others to eternal damnation. Christ, they said, had died for all men, not for a group of elect. Remonstrants and Calvinists now engaged in political-religious conflict. Each side pressed the Estates of Holland to convene a national synod to give authoritative direction on religious questions. A war of pamphlets on the question of predestination helped arouse all the emotions which only theological (or ideological) controversy can engender.[34] Politics and religion were henceforth interwoven in an inextricable confusion.

The orthodox Calvinist party could invoke on its behalf the political fears and anxieties of Netherlanders. It portrayed the liberals as imperiling the national security. It reminded townsmen that a Catholic offensive in Europe was always a real threat; there were rumors of the formation of a Catholic League. The Calvinists called for a monolithic unity of Dutch Protestants; mindful that the bulk of the Dutch peasantry still remained Catholic, they stirred fears and suspicions concerning the enemy within who might lend aid and comfort to the enemy without. Prince Maurice of Orange, Captain-General of the army, had until 1616 troubled himself little about theology. He said bluntly: "I know nothing of predestination, whether it is green or whether it is blue." [35] But even Maurice, ignorant of theology's profundities, began to take heed when people warned him that the defeat of the Reformed religion would be followed by a subversive movement for political freedom. Then he too began to assert that Oldenbarnevelt's "libertine" recklessness added to the dangers of European Protestantism, always menaced by a Catholic encirclement.

The Liberals, or Arminians as they were called (after Arminius, the liberal theologian at the University of Leyden), had become, as Sir William Temple observed, "a party in the state rather than a sect in the church."[36] Taken as pure abstractions, there was perhaps, as Grotius said, "no considerable difference between the theologies of Remonstrants and Contra-Remonstrants." [37] Political and economic differences, however, had enveloped themselves in theological garments. The Remonstrants were the liberal merchants, advocates of provincial autonomy, cosmopolitan in their outlook, opposed to monarchist and clerical influences. The Contra-Remonstrants were austere men of orthodoxy, stern spokesmen of the frugal proletariat and lower middle class, suspicious of anything that smacked of internationalist or papist associations, advocates of a strong centralized state under the house of Orange. The Calvinists said: "there may be only one religion in the state; all heretics must be driven out; for better is a desolate city than a trafficking city full of sectarians." [38]

In such ways, as Spinoza said, differences in religious doctrine had become the fulcrum of a struggle of groups for power.[39] Provinces and municipalities were torn by fierce, unyielding dissension. The majority of the governing commercial class, sympathetic to the liberal philosophy, controlled the Estates of Holland, but Amsterdam itself was won by the Contra-Remonstrants. The conflict, more and more, took on a political complexion; it became a struggle between Maurice of Orange and Oldenbarnevelt, between Stadtholder and the Estates of Holland. The prince, together with his Calvinist allies, determined to impose their religious totalitarianism on the country. At the National Synod in 1618, they expelled the Remonstrant delegates, and condemned them as heretics, disturbers, and teachers of falsehood. They arrested the aged statesman Oldenbarnevelt and submitted him to many days of rigorous, protracted interrogation. Their questions ranged over his liberal

theological opinions, his views on foreign policy, and his resistance to the monopolist Dutch East and West India Companies.[40] The courageous old man challenged their jurisdiction,
defended the sovereignty of Holland, and reminded the self-ap-
pointed court that they were emulating the ways of the Spanish
oppressor. He defended the right of individuals to freedom of
opinion on such questions as predestination. The judges
wavered, but then sentenced him to death; they found him
guilty of trying to establish states within states, of trouble-making
in church and political affairs. The old man refused to ask for
pardon or to acknowledge any guilt. He was executed on May
13, 1619. Such was Oldenbarnevelt's reward for his lifetime of
service to the Dutch people.

The Liberal Republicans of Spinoza's time still remembered
the repression that had taken place under Calvinist auspices.
Two hundred Remonstrant preachers at that time were removed
from office. Some recanted; many chose exile. Sheriffs and
secretaries in various towns were driven from the governmental
service. "Lovers and upholders of religion and government"
replaced those deemed disloyal. At Antwerp, some die-hard
Remonstrants published pamphlets denouncing the Calvinist
party as "little monsters of the new Holland inquisition." [41] But
the political power of the Liberal was broken for a generation.

Ideas can bide their time in men's unconscious, and when
censors are weakened, they issue with reborn vigor from their
hiding places. In Spinoza's time, the mantle of Oldenbarnevelt
was transmitted to John de Witt. The inheritor was to suffer
the same reward for his services. Spinoza, as a Liberal Republican philosopher, was to be confronted more poignantly than
ever with the problem—how to found a democracy if a people
is prone to unreason and hatred and capable of destroying its
benefactors. Meanwhile, he wrote the *Tractatus Theologico-
Politicus* with hope, working to persuade those who would listen
that their own self-interest was best served by putting aside religious quarrels, separating religion from politics, and evaluating
all political issues by the criterion of the welfare and prosperity
of the community.

Spinoza and John de Witt: the Geometrical
Method in Politics

It seems to be a universal sociological law that whenever an advanced political idea is superimposed on a backward population, either the perversion of the idea or the destruction of its proponents is likely to occur. The Republicans of Holland were enlightened men, scientific, with liberal conceptions of economics and policy; would their scientific method win the people's loyalty?

The personality of the Republican leader, John de Witt, was truly imposing. He was "the most scientific statesman of his time." [42] He was singularly immune to the prejudices of the day. He was uninfected, for instance, by the violent anti-Catholicism which characterized many of his Calvinist countrymen, so that a foreign ambassador wrote: "he seemed inclined to accord them the most perfect freedom in their religion." [43] But how was scientific method to be applied to the rule of men? De Witt pondered this problem. Immensely talented, devoted to the welfare of Holland, there was nevertheless something about De Witt which irritated people. He reasoned too clearly, saw things too distinctly; he couldn't conceal his superiority over others, perhaps even his pitying contempt for them. And when crisis came, he was to discover that the scientist's character rather than his method was what most concerned the people he governed.

John de Witt had grown to maturity under the influences of the Cartesian scientific movement. At Dordrecht where he went to school, his head master had been Dr. Beekman, a mathematical friend of Descartes.[44] At the University of Leyden, Europe's intellectual center at the mid-century, John studied mathematics intensively. He made original contributions to the science which won the praise of Descartes himself. His *Elementa linearum curvarum,* published at Leyden in 1650, was admired by both Newton and Condorcet.[45] Would the mathematical method light the way to a science of man and politics?

The use of the geometrical method in social science was,

indeed, the contribution of John de Witt. When Spinoza applied the geometrical method to questions of ethics and psychology, when he announced his intention to "consider human actions and appetites just as if I were considering lines, planes, and bodies," when he spoke of mathematics as providing the rule of truth which would liberate "the human race" from "darkness to all eternity," Spinoza was following a path which John de Witt, Republican statesman, had already opened.[46] Among his papers, De Witt left "a scheme in which he represented human societies as great geometrical constructions, where all operated as in nature in conformity with certain and fixed laws, to which the free will of each individual, after more or less variation, always ended by obeying." [47] De Witt envisaged a new science, to which he gave the name "social mathematics"; he conceived of social geometricians calculating the evolution of societies as astronomers predict the advent of eclipses and comets. There was a common philosophical axiom which was shared by both the social mathematics of John de Witt and the political science of Spinoza—the conviction, in Spinoza's words, that nature "is always and everywhere one. Her virtue is the same, and her power of acting; that is to say, her laws and rules, according to which all things are and are changed from form to form, are everywhere and always the same; so that there must also be one and the same method of understanding the nature of all things whatsoever, that is to say, by the universal laws and rules of nature." [48]

De Witt, the pioneer of social mathematics, was also among the founders of statistical science. Even in this field he found that the application of science to social problems awoke the resistances of powerful vested groups. Leibniz tried hard to secure De Witt's statistical writings, but in vain; the States-General of the Netherlands, in subservience to selfish business interests, had suppressed his principal statistical treatise. For John de Witt had calculated a system of life annuities whereby the government might secure money at a low rate of interest. Cheap money, however, was no more welcome to the States-General than were similar Keynesian measures in a later era. Wealthy capitalists wished to continue to receive a high rate of interest from their loans to the government. The States-General acquiesced to the financiers' wishes and kept the knowledge of De Witt's researches from the people.[49] The rate of interest was a relatively minor political question. How immense, then, would be the power of human prejudice, hatred, jealousy, and unreason, how intense the resistances to the scientific statesman, when he would go coldly about his task, impervious and aloof, to solve the great political questions as he would a mathematical equation.

John de Witt did not think that the Dutch needed a "great man." His was the rationalist's fallacy—to misread the power of reason in an irrational world. But intellect alone would not win the hearts of men, no matter how just its aims, no matter how correct its arguments. De Witt was finally destroyed, not for any mistakes or blunders, but rather, as Pieter Geyl has said, "because the mob resented a man who had never courted their favor, who approached political questions with cold intellect, and despised passion, who embodied all the virtues of the unpopular ruling class." [50]

The ruling oligarchy of patricians was indeed unpopular; town governments were closed corporations, vacant offices were filled by co-optation from a small group of ruling families. Could De Witt set out to win the support of the people as a whole? De Witt and his spokesman, Pieter de la Court, wrote that "he who possesses with the affection of his soldiers, that of the lower class, can make himself the undisputed master of the whole State." [51] But in his geometrical equations, De Witt could not find the solution to the problem of winning the people's love. The arts of the demagogue were not his, and he had no conception of how a democratic republic, under the conditions of his time, could be founded. To extend the franchise to "the ignorant and Orange-worshipping populace" would have meant their raising "the dreaded House to power with shouts of loud acclaim." There was no alternative to De Witt's mind but the continued rule of the enlightened middle class. In his hands, and with his own province, Holland, in a dominant position, there would be wise government and administration. The people were not fit to rule.

The republican form of government, as De Witt conceived

it, was a method for bringing the ablest men to power. It was a device for giving rule to the most virtuous, not to the masses, a device for keeping power from the hands of monarchs and hereditary nobilities. In 1654, De Witt wrote a defense of his actions which, translated into Latin, circulated throughout Europe as a kind of manifesto of the Dutch Republicans.[52] Its principles found their way into Spinoza's political philosophy. The Republican faith, wrote De Witt, is "the unanimous opinion of all political writers that the highest dignities stand open to virtue; and that as much should never be deferred to possessions, family connections, qualities of ancestors, or other adjuncts of fortune, as to the piety, capacity, and merits of men themselves." The true descendants of great princes and heroes, he added, "are not those who spring from their loins, . . . but those who are truly the issue of their souls, and who, following in their footsteps show in fact that they inherit in reality the eternal treasure, namely, the virtues of the same great princes and heroes."

Liberties vanish, said De Witt, when monarchs rule men. "Liberty and freedom is more secure in the keeping of many good men," he wrote, "than in the hands of one person called in to take charge of it, but on whom the same good men at all times have kept and still must keep a watchful eye." He recited the roll of the cruel wars in the time of dukes, counts, bishops, and lords. He reminded his readers of the testimony of history concerning the house of Burgundy, the Emperor Charles, the Spanish King Philip. He recalled the more recent intrigues of nobles, "province being set against province, town against town, subject against magistrate; with discord, dissension, disruption, and the beginnings of civil war. And of later noble heads, we have the example still before our eyes." Thus De Witt warned against the house of Orange, with its monarchist ambitions, as a fomenter of civil war.

The interests of monarchs and their peoples, De Witt held, must necessarily diverge. That, in his opinion, was a basic law of political psychology. "Heads of quality have oftentimes their own private interests to forward, differing from the interests of the State, yea, sometimes in direct contradiction to the common weal," and this divergence cannot be remedied "unless they could draw the human nature out of themselves." Men of conscience must therefore inevitably come into conflict with princely heads. The freedom of the Republic, moreover, said De Witt, is endangered when any house or person receives hereditary prerogatives, and freedom likewise becomes precarious if any man is endowed with the privileges of a dictator. Experience teaches, said De Witt, that "all the Republics of the whole world not one excepted, . . . even almost all those which had only entrusted the might of the State to one person for life, and many who had entrusted it to one man for a long period, had been brought under subjection, and reduced to a state of Monarchy."[53] Such were the Republican principles, set forth with much learning and in logical paragraphs in De Witt's *Deduction of the States of Holland.*

Spinoza and the Mass of Mankind

Spinoza could subscribe wholeheartedly to John de Witt's theory of a republic demonstrated in the geometrical manner. He shared too De Witt's low regard for the political capacity and understanding of the masses. If a theory of democracy must be founded on a high evaluation of the common man, then it would be impossible to classify Spinoza among the democrats. He addressed his *Tractatus Theologico-Politicus* to the "Philosophic Reader," even though he disclaimed any originality in its ideas: "I know that its leading propositions are to Philosophers but commonplaces." His book, Spinoza emphasized, was not written for men at large, because they were too prejudice-bound, cowardly, and anxiety-ridden to give his ideas a hearing: "To the rest of mankind I care not to commend my treatise, for I cannot expect that it contains anything to please them: I know how deeply are the prejudices embraced under the name of religion; I am aware that in the mind of the masses superstition is no less deeply rooted than fear; I recognize that their constancy is here obstinacy, and that they are led to praise or blame by impulse rather than reason. Therefore the multitude, and those of like passion with the multitude, I ask not to read my book; nay, I would rather that they should utterly neglect it, than that they should misinterpret it after their wont."

To the theme of the irrationality of the masses, Spinoza returned again and again. "The mass of mankind," he wrote, "remains always at about the same pitch of misery, it never assents long to any remedy, but is always the best pleased by a novelty which has not yet proved illusive." The basic cause for war and revolution, according to Spinoza, is the irrational character of the masses: "This element of inconsistency has been the cause of many terrible wars and revolutions; for as Curtius well says, 'The mob has no ruler more potent than superstition'. . . ." [54] Long before John Stuart Mill had become sensitive to the "tyranny of the majority," and wondered how liberalism could be united with democracy, Spinoza had raised the question of how a free state might be founded on the precarious substructure of fear-driven ordinary men.

The free man, in Spinoza's philosophy, always retained an estrangement from the masses. He felt no identification with their ways and could indulge in no illusions concerning their worth. This estrangement Spinoza stated as a theorem in the *Ethics,* demonstrated in the geometrical manner: "The free man who lives among those who are ignorant strives as much as possible to avoid their favors." A free man should maintain his aloofness from the masses "in order that he may not be hated by the ignorant nor yet yield to their appetites." Since even the free man, of necessity, must dwell in a common society with the multitude, he must cultivate tact so as not to offend people with whom he wishes to have only a tangential association. "For although men are ignorant, they are nevertheless men, who when we are in straits, are able to afford us human assistance —the best assistance which man can receive. It is often necessary therefore to receive a favor from the ignorant, and to thank them for it according to their taste; and besides this, care must be used, even in declining favors, not to seem either to despise the givers or through avarice to dread a return, so that we may not, while striving to escape their hatred, by that very act incur their displeasure." [55]

The social reformer in Spinoza was not, however, prepared

to accede without resistance to the melancholy recognition of men's irrationality. Like every radical thinker, he hoped for acceptance by the very masses who would reject him.[56] As a scientific liberal, Spinoza was led to criticize the one social institution which, in his opinion, operated most to keep men slavish and superstitious—the church.

The Christian religion, wrote Spinoza, should mean "love, joy, peace, temperance, and charity to all men." Instead, it had come to signify "rancorous animosity" and "bitter hatred"; such was "the readiest criterion of their faith." "Popular religion," he added, "may be summed up as respect for ecclesiastics." Churchmen were assiduously laboring to enslave people's minds; under their guidance, "the love of diffusing God's religion degenerated into sordid avarice and ambition. Every church became a theater, where orators, instead of church teachers harangued, caring not to instruct people, but striving to attract admiration, to bring opponents to public scorn, and to preach only novelties and paradoxes, such as would tickle the ears of their congregation. This state of things necessarily stirred up an amount of controversy, envy, and hatred, which no lapse of time could appease. . . . Piety, great God! and religion are become a tissue of ridiculous mysteries. . . ." [57] Whatever his doubts concerning the ultimate success of people's government, Spinoza was prepared to defend the liberal principle that "everyone should be free to choose for himself the foundation of his creed, and that faith should be judged only by its fruits; each would then obey God freely with his own heart, while nothing would be publicly honoured save justice and charity." This principle he would defend even against the multitude itself. To this liberal principle, Spinoza applied all the resources of the political and social science of his time.

Determinism and Social Science: the Guide to Action and the Apotheosis of Acquiescence

The doctrine of determinism was Spinoza's axiom as a social scientist. "Man does not act from freedom of the will," said Spinoza; "but the mind is determined to this or that volition by a cause, which is also determined by another cause, and this again by another, and so on ad infinitum." [58] Belief in this doctrine, Spinoza held, "contributes not a little to the advantage of common society, in so far as it teaches us by what means citizens are to be governed and led; not in order that they may be slaves, but that they may freely do those things which are best." Determinism was thus the philosophic foundation for an applied political science.

Tyrants and despots, Spinoza knew, had also been shrewd practitioners of social science. His purpose, however, was to use causal analysis to help achieve liberal goals. "But if, in despotic statecraft," as Spinoza wrote, "the supreme and essential mystery be to hoodwink the subjects, and to mask the fear, which keeps them down, with the specious garb of religion, so that men fight as bravely for slavery as for safety and count it not shame but highest honour to risk their blood and their lives for the vainglory of a tyrant," there was also another statecraft which could delineate the conditions of "a free state." [59]

Social science then could help one make a society in which men would "freely do those things which are best." Social science, with its determinist postulate, would enlighten the way for effective democratic leadership. At the same time, however, there were circumstances in which the determinist postulate could justify submission to things as they are. Once again, there was a duality in Spinoza between the seceder and the participant. For science might demonstrate that the individual is unable to affect historic process, that he is almost powerless against the rigidities of tradition, prejudice, and hatred. The message of determinism, in that case, said Spinoza, was that it "teaches us how we ought to behave with regard to the things of fortune, or those which are not in our power, that is to say, which do not follow from our own nature; for it teaches us with equal mind to wait for and bear each form of fortune because we know that all things follow from the eternal decree of God, according to that same necessity by which it follows from the essence of a triangle that its three angles are equal to two right angles." Determinist social science would explore the domain of human power, but it would also find the limitless domain of human impotence. At that point, Spinoza tried to surmount political defeat, the rule of tyranny and the destruction of individual freedom, by invoking the belief that man's highest happiness, his blessedness, consists in the knowledge of God. "The highest possible peace of mind," "the intellectual love of God," arises when we perceive the essences of things as logically involved in the attributes of God. This knowledge, said Spinoza, brings repose to the soul. Determinism then provided more than a philosophy of resignation to the cosmic necessities in things. It was made the basis for an automatic human approval of all cosmic legislation.

How much repose to the soul, we may ask again, would this doctrine bring? The intellectual love of God was the last refuge for the defeated political reformer. In our own day, we have seen tired Marxian revolutionaries turn from history to eternity, from social science to theology. In Spinoza's time, incendiary Levellers, like the Anabaptists before them, were finding their spiritual resting place in such quietist sects as the Quakers. In Spinoza's work, at the outset of his formulation of the theory of liberalism, there is a premonition of the limits of social reconstruction, and the frustration which stalks the political radical. The knowledge of things under the aspect of eternity is then supposed to bring blessedness. But what blessedness indeed? This was a knowledge that could bring unending melancholy. Let us suppose, for instance, that the history of the human race, its wars, massacres, hatreds, are seen as manifestations of certain universal laws of psychology and zoology. And let us suppose, further, that we apprehend these laws as expressions of God's attributes, His thought and extension. Is the tale of human misery transfigured because it is given an eternal, necessary status? Spinoza would reply that the varieties of human suffering illustrate the perfection of God as a whole: "Because to Him material was not wanting for the creation of everything, from the highest down to the very lowest grade of perfection; or, to speak more properly, because the laws of His nature were so ample that they sufficed for the production of everything which can be conceived by an infinite intellect. . . ." [60] Someone once said that metaphysics is misery dissolved in words. Spinoza's notion of the perfection of God is masochism translated into metaphysical language. The anguish and the agony of men, according to him, illustrate the variegated combinations and permutations of the laws of psychology. We are supposed by Spinoza to be moved to the love of God by seeing how our pains are an expression of Nature's abundance. We are supposed to love infinite variety for its own sake, even if we are broken upon its wheel. Spinoza speaks of the intellectual love of God; it would be even more consistent with his argument to affirm an intellectual hatred of God. Determinism, says Spinoza, has a moral value; it guides action, comforts us in defeat with the consolation of its inevitability, and teaches "us to hate no one, to despise no one, to mock no one, to be angry with no one, and to envy no one. It teaches every one, moreover, to be content with his own and to be helpful to his neighbor. . . ." But defeat is no less defeat because it is inevitable, or because the domain of effective action is limited. Human impotence is no less real because it is determined, and determinism, from this standpoint, is a doctrine always suffused with sorrow. To this subject we shall return more fully in a later context.

In our time, men have rebelled against the impotence of the individual in a determinist world. Against Spinoza's arguments for the moral value of determinism, they have counterposed a defense of the moral values of indeterminism. Man struggles to be free in a metaphysical sense even while actualities overwhelm him. At its noblest, determinism, when believed sincerely and practiced as a philosophy of life, has enabled persons such as Clarence Darrow and Mark Twain to rise above hatred, and to take men as pitiful existents, pathetically sentient creatures struggling in a night whose darkness will engulf them. Such men, however, have never loved the Eternal Nature of things. Rather, they have hated it, as the author of the folly of all human life. But Spinoza, in his Quaker-Collegiant mysticism, wished to devise a reliable anodyne for the defeat of political and personal hopes which was always on the horizon. He provided a philosophy for applied social science, but he was always in spirit prepared to retreat from The Hague to Rijnsburg, to renounce political participation in favor of withdrawal. The anxiety of defeat, of isolation, of hermitage in a peopled world never left his philosophy.

CHAPTER 4

The Promise and Anguish of Democracy

The Limits of Democracy and the Futility of Revolution

The Liberal Republican philosophy lacked the contagion of enthusiasm, that faith in the multitude, without which it could not hope for popularity in the minds of Dutch citizens. Spinoza and De Witt had the attitudes of an intellectual elite. To be sure, as a pantheist mystic and social reformer, Spinoza rejected the Calvinist concept of election for a minority; as we have seen, he held that "the highest good of those who follow after virtue is common to all, and all may equally enjoy it." The theology of guilt and human weakness was repugnant to Spinoza. The nature of man, he said, could not condemn him to perdition; for the highest good "is deduced from the human essence itself," and is common to all men. He denied the cardinal tenet of the Calvinist ethic: "repentance is not a virtue," wrote Spinoza, "that is to say, it does not spring from reason; on the contrary, the man who repents of what he has done is doubly wretched or impotent." At the same time, however, Spinoza, the political scientist, was compelled to avow that men generally had not the strength of mind to accept his liberal philosophy. The winds of reason were too much for them, for they threatened moralistic structures built on fear. For men at large, then, the shoddy theology of guilt might provide a makeshift substitute for the life of freedom. "Inasmuch as men seldom live as reason dictates, therefore these two affects, humility and repentance, together with hope and fear, are productive of more profit than disadvantage, and, therefore, since men must sin, it is better that they should sin in this way. For if men impotent in mind were all equally proud, were ashamed of nothing, and feared nothing, by what bonds could they be united or constrained? The multitude becomes a thing to be feared if it has nothing to fear." [1]

The psychological core of a political theory consists of its emotional attitudes toward people. The seventeenth century had unleashed new revolutionary movements upon society. The masses, with the approach of the Industrial Revolution, were beginning to assert their will in political action. Spinoza, a democratic liberal, voices the first concern as to the role that the multitude of men will play. When he says that the multitude must have something to fear, he speaks as a disciple of Thomas Hobbes. In the state of Nature, as Hobbes said, "the life of man" is "solitary, poor, nasty, brutish, and short." Civilized societies are but slightly removed from the savage state; the man who takes a journey, observed Hobbes, locks his house and thereby tells mankind what he really thinks of it. Governments, in Hobbes' view, are coercive powers whose purpose is the "introduction of that restraint" upon men which will curb their natural passions. [2] And Spinoza, making the first efforts toward a philosophy of liberalism, finds himself at every turn confronted by a multitude whose minds have been shaped in fear, whose violence was the mirror of the absolutist rule under which it had almost always lived.

The lower classes, the poor workmen of Amsterdam, remained predominantly and fanatically attached to orthodox Calvinism. [3] Economic hardship and unemployment made men miserable and susceptible to harsh theological doctrine. The denizens of the slums lived on doles from the parish, and the Calvinist consistory "which controlled the relief work used the almsgiving as a lever of mob violence." [4] The rich seemed to be growing richer and ever more ostentatious in exhibiting their riches newly acquired from the Dutch East and West India Companies; the poor were growing poorer. There was an ever widening gulf between the classes. In 1660, the almonries of the Reformed Church distributed in Amsterdam alone 238,000 guilders, apart from other charities to the poor which sometimes reached 600,000 guilders, figures, which as the historian Blok remarks, "indicate the great number of the poor." Calvinism, as a religion of rigor and resentment, was used by the workmen and the unemployed to denounce the pleasures which only the rich could afford. Pamphlets contrasted the luxuries of the few with the poverty of the many, for whom the high cost of bread was a primary problem. Measures were demanded to relieve the lot of the poor, and municipal governments considered proposals for reviving old statutes against luxury at weddings and feasts, costly dress and ornament. Profits were being accumulated in ventures which it was regarded as bad form to mention, ventures such as the lucrative slave trade of the West India Company on the Guinea coast.

To the lower classes, the liberal philosophy of the Republican party might well seem like an affectation of the leisure class, which was exempt from the grim day-by-day trials of ordinary men's lives. Calvinism was a religion of envy, but it was their lot and station in life which made the poor envious. Envy, a disastrous feeling, a passion, as Spinoza said, but withal, it held the stirrings of a conception of justice. Meanwhile, the people at society's base remained miserable. In Malthusian fashion, pestilence destroyed them in their slums. In 1656, the year of Spinoza's excommunication, 18,000 persons died of epidemic disease in Amsterdam, more than one-tenth its population of 150,000. Leyden the preceding year lost 13,000 persons, one-fourth of its numbers.[5]

There was no avenue through which the Dutch workmen could directly express their economic protest. They were forbidden by law to organize in combinations. At times, they dared to join in secret societies. As late as 1692, such efforts at clandestine organization were threatened with the penalty of death. Frustrated in their efforts to articulate their discontent, the lower classes found the Calvinist wrath and the monarchist agitation available instruments for venting their feelings of aggression. The movement on behalf of the house of Orange, with its appeal to military glory and national unity, was a seventeenth-century version of later movements for a "man on horseback." The "democratic despotism," which worried De Tocqueville, was first exemplified in the Orangist party; it was the forerunner of the parties of Louis Napoleon, Boulanger, and the modern fascist trends. The rule of Orange was counterposed to the republican oligarchy in much the same way that dictatorial strong men were later contrasted with weak, unglamorous parliamentarians.[6] Communist ideas, as we have seen, arose among religious sects as an alternative outlet of protest. But the way of love meant a withdrawal from existence into unreal Utopia. Calvinist bitterness, with its apocalyptic aspect, offered a readier expression for anger. The Republican liberals, men like De Witt and Spinoza, never solved the problem of achieving in the environment of their social forces a stable equilibrium for democratic liberalism.

When Spinoza wrote the *Tractatus Theologico-Politicus,* his mood, however, was one of rare hopefulness. The peace of Breda with England in 1667 gave promise of a period untroubled by war. De Witt wrote that his faith had been justified that the state "within the time of two years would be in a better condition, in greater reputation, and in higher credit than ever before." [7] Spinoza pondered such modifications of Hobbes' pessimist theory as would provide a basis for Liberal Republicanism. The Republicans sought the maintenance of their political status quo. They were not a party of revolution. Ideas of violent uprising which still persisted were held by the Calvinist-Orange partisans, and Spinoza, seeking to reinforce the stability of the Republican regime, was led to argue against the ideology of revolution. The anomaly of Spinoza's political theory was that he, a democrat, was none the less opposed to revolution. It was precisely the unique conditions of Dutch politics which gave to Spinoza's political philosophy a cast so different from that of John Locke, the philosopher of the Glorious Revolution of 1688.

Demonstration of the Futility of Revolution

The philosophy of revolution in the sixteenth and seventeenth centuries was born among religious thinkers. After St. Bartholomew's Day, Huguenot philosophers ransacked the Bible to find texts which would justify revolution against tyrannical Catholic monarchs.[8] The so-called Monarchomachs were the first thinkers to enunciate the right of revolution. Duplessis-

Mornay, the French Huguenot, and perhaps the most eminent of the Monarchomachs, had a considerable influence on Calvinist-Orange thought.[9] Catholic philosophers, in their turn, were also led to a doctrinal justification of tyrannicide; Jesuit spokesmen, appalled by the prospect of a Henry IV mounting the throne of France, devised theories to justify violent uprising.

Liberal Dutch Republican opinion, however, was alienated from the philosophy of revolution. It had been disillusioned by the course of the English Puritan Revolution and Oliver Cromwell. Spinoza owned a *Historia van Karel de II*, a translation of *The History of his Sacred Majesty Charles II, King of England,* and he was concerned with the implications of the English events for his political theory.[10] During the first stages of the English revolution, the overwhelming majority of the Dutch people, led by Holland and Zealand, had sympathized warmly with the Puritan rebellion.[11] They saw the Puritan movement as a revolt against a king who had been betraying his people to Popery. For eight years, the Orange party sought to embroil the Dutch Republic into efforts and intrigues on behalf of Charles I, but the Dutch people had steadfastly refused such involvement. Public opinion, however, was altered by the execution of the English monarch. To clergy and citizenry alike, to the people of both the Orange and anti-Orange parties, this execution was parricide. A special mission was sent by the States-General to intercede with Parliament to prevent the sentence from being carried out on the king; it failed. "The tragedy on the scaffold at Whitehall produced a profound revolution of feeling in the Seven Provinces. Amazement and horror, then indignation, next widespread compassion; for the heart of the people was touched. The clergy and the body of the people, all except the governing and various other classes of Hollanders and Zealanders, deserted the Parliamentary cause. It was a complete transference of their sympathy to the Stuarts. This was not the generation that had risen against Philip. . . ."[12]

The Republican regents continued to hope that a common religious and political bond would unite their country in peace with the government of Cromwell. Instead, within a few years, two bitter and costly wars were fought, and Cromwell's Pro-

tectorate showed itself extremely aggressive in promoting English
commercial interests against the Dutch. To the mind of John
de Witt, Oliver Cromwell was indeed something of an incompre-
hensible phenomenon. De Witt, it is said, was "as cold and
guarded as a mathematical demonstration"; Cromwell, on the
other hand, was a charismatic mixture of Messianic religious
vocation and political radicalism. De Witt consulted with a
clergyman of Dordrecht concerning Cromwell's "humour on the
subject of religion." Three centuries later, Franklin D.
Roosevelt, trying to understand the primal power of Hitler,
was similarly moved to ask a clergyman questions about
Kierkegaard and the irrational recesses of human nature. Cromwell, in a speech to the Dutch in 1653, declared that his "first
thought" was "the outspreading of the kingdom of Christ." [13]
De Witt and his associates honestly professed themselves as
interested only in the extension of their commerce, and they
recognized that the mission of Christ's kingdom could embrace
in its theological grasp a multitude of secular aims. When the
restoration of Charles II took place, the Republican statesmen
hoped for genuinely improved relations with England.[14]

Spinoza, as a Republican political philosopher, undertook
to explain why Cromwell's revolution was a failure. His explanation led him to a theory of social change not unlike that of
contemporary conservatives. Spinoza opposed all revolutionary
movements which were directed against the traditional forms
of government in the given country. He was against a republican revolution in a monarchical country, and by the same token,
he held that a monarchist revolution in a republican land was
an unjustified usurpation, without prospect of success. In these
terms, Spinoza was able, on the one hand, to criticize the
revolutionary hopes of the house of Orange, and on the other,
he could express the reasoned disillusionment of the Dutch
Republicans with Cromwell's revolution. Modes of government,
Spinoza argued, are rooted in the psychological characteristics
of their respective peoples. The English people, he wrote, are
accustomed to monarchy and cannot adapt to any other political
form. The Dutch people, on the contrary, have always known
republican institutions. It is a general principle of political

sociology, according to Spinoza, that a people cannot change its form of government; revolution, therefore, is impossible. Spinoza consequently advises acquiescence in the established political order. In the Netherlands, this was tantamount to the assertion that any Orangist *coup d'état* would be contrary to the laws of political science. Spinoza's demonstration of the impossibility of revolution in political systems is simple:

> Lastly, we see how disastrous it is for a people unaccustomed to kings, and possessing a complete code of laws to set up a monarchy. Neither can the subjects brook such a sway, nor the royal authority submit to laws and popular rights set up by anyone inferior to itself. Still less can a king be expected to defend such laws, for they were not framed to support his dominion, but the dominion of the people, or some council which formerly ruled. . . . The representative of a new monarchy will employ all his zeal in attempting to frame new laws, so as to wrest the rights of dominion to his own use, and to reduce the people till they find it easier to increase than to curtail the royal prerogative. I must not, however, omit to state that it is no less dangerous to remove a monarch, though he is on all hands admitted to be a tyrant. For his people are accustomed to royal authority and will obey no other, despising and mocking at any less august control.
>
> It is therefore necessary, as the prophets discovered of old, if one king be removed, that he should be replaced by another, who will be a tyrant from necessity rather than choice. . . .
>
> Hence it comes to pass that peoples have often changed their tyrants, but never removed them or changed the monarchical form of government into any other.

Then Spinoza applies his general analysis of the impossibility of revolution to the English Puritan rebellion:

> The English people furnish us with a terrible example of this fact. They sought how to depose their monarch under the forms of law, but when he had been removed, they were utterly unable to change the form of government, and after much bloodshed only brought it about, that a new monarch should be hailed under a different name (as though it had been a mere question of names); this new monarch could only consolidate

his power by completely destroying the royal stock, putting to death the king's friends, real or supposed, and disturbing with war the peace that might encourage discontent, in order that the populace might be engrossed with novelties and divert its mind from brooding over the slaughter of the king. At last, however, the people reflected that it had accomplished nothing for the good of the country beyond violating the rights of the lawful king and changing everything for the worse. It therefore decided to retrace its steps as soon as possible, and never rested till it had seen a complete restoration of the original state of affairs.[15]

The Protectorate, according to Spinoza, was a monarchy in everything but name. The English Puritans had proposed to build a parliamentary republic; the inevitabilities of political evolution, however, generated an absolutist dictatorship, and the subjective intentions of the English revolutionaries counted for nought against the workings of social law. The means that Oliver Cromwell had to use to consolidate his power, according to Spinoza, made it impossible for the parliamentary dreams to be realized. The execution of Charles I, Pride's Purge, the imprisonment of the Levellers—these were all necessary consequences of the violent seizure of power for political reconstruction. The new order turned out to be the old with new faces. *Plus ça change, plus c'est la même chose,* Spinoza could say with the old proverb. What change did ensue was for the worse. Spinoza maintained that the primary cause for the Anglo-Dutch war during Cromwell's time was the Protector's desire to divert the discontent of the English people toward an external object. With psychological insight, Spinoza held that the English people were afflicted with the guilt anxieties of their regicide.[16] And the burden of regicide, like parricide, is presumably lightened when it is turned away from one's self toward another. The nation torn with guilt seeks war or a scapegoat to escape from itself. In this fashion Spinoza expressed the general Dutch Republican disillusionment with Cromwell's revolution.

The republican form of government, however, was, none

the less, according to Spinoza, the normal, stable polity for the Netherlands. An anti-republican revolution, a monarchist movement, was therefore contrary to the spirit of Dutch institutions:

> As for the United States of the Netherlands, they have never, as we know, had a king, but only counts, who never attained the full rights of dominion. The States of the Netherlands evidently acted as principal in the settlement made by them. . . ; they always reserved for themselves the authority to keep the counts up to their duties, and the power to preserve this authority and the liberty of the citizens. They had ample means of vindicating their rights if their rulers should prove tyrannical, and could impose such restraints that nothing could be done without their consent and approval.

Spinoza alluded to the attempt of William II, Prince of Orange, to subvert the republican institutions of Holland in the *coup d'état* of July, 1650: "Thus the rights of sovereign power have always been vested in the States, though the last count endeavored to usurp them. It is therefore little likely that the States should give them up, especially as they have just restored their original dominion, lately almost lost."

The pretensions of the Orange party were to Spinoza's eyes without validity. He professed himself confident that the Republican party would remain in power. He recognized how serious the crisis of 1650-1651 had been, but evidently believed that Republican stability and tradition were powerful enough to survive the hostility of Calvinists and Orangists. Spinoza's confidence was soon to be shattered. But in 1670, he could still appeal to political science to vindicate the Republican status quo: "These examples then, confirm us in our belief, that every dominion should retain its original form, and indeed, cannot change it without danger of the utter ruin of the whole state." [17]

The modern theory of liberal republicanism was thus born as a theory of Dutch exceptionalism. The liberal republic was not advocated by Spinoza as a form of government suitable for other people; it was not an article for ideological export. The liberal republic was the constitutional form which had arisen under the fortunate, unique conditions of the history of the

Dutch provinces. Just as there have been historians who have attributed the origins of American democracy to the unique influence of the American frontier, so Spinoza would join hands with those Dutch historians who have found the genesis of Netherlands liberties in the struggle of a people in a land which was literally a frontier upon the ocean, a land which one fought to safeguard and extend with dikes against the ravages of the sea.

Spinoza, blessed by the happy confluence of Dutch circumstances, was a democratic liberal, but he had no doctrine of revolutionary liberation for those not so fortunate. There was thus something provincial about this first democratic theory. It came wrapped in swaddling clothes redolent of the submissive past. What could foreigners learn from a theory which refused to link democracy with a right to revolution? What could Englishmen and Frenchmen, confronted with the absolutist pretensions of Stuarts and Bourbons, borrow from a doctrine which urged acquiescence even to tyrants? The great influence which Spinoza was to have on European political thought was to be, in considerable measure, despite himself. For Spinoza, like all great political thinkers, like Marx, like Mill, was not one self, but many, and the eighteenth century was to brush aside the disclaimers, disregard the qualifications, and learn from Spinoza the radical, whose utterances on behalf of liberty of thought and speech transcended Dutch provincial boundaries to become part of the deathless struggle of free men everywhere.

Spinoza, with his vision of the unity of nature, tried furthermore to base his opposition to revolution on metaphysical grounds. He turned Hobbes' doctrine of submission to legal authority into a corollary of the philosophy of pantheistic determinism. The laws of secular rulers, Spinoza wrote, are the laws of God (or nature); God does not speak to men directly, as the revolutionary enthusiasts say, but his decrees proceed through the decrees of governments. "We cannot conceive," he wrote, "God as a prince or legislator giving laws to mankind." The divine precepts "do not receive immediately from God the force of a command, but only from those, or through the mediation of those, who possess the right of ruling and legislating. It is only through these latter means that God rules among men, and directs human affairs with justice and equity."

At this point, clearly, Spinoza's pantheism, drawn into the ideological service of a doctrine of acquiescence, betrayed its cosmic neutrality. For on what grounds can one say that God, through His mediators, directs men's affairs "with justice and equity"? Spinoza recognized that "the same lot befalls the just and the unjust, the pure and the impure." He allows that this fact "causes Divine Providence to be doubted by many," a recognition of the growing agnostic, sceptical currents of his time.[18] Spinoza criticized the sceptics for expecting a God who would direct all nature for men's benefit, though he himself, seeking to defend political acquiescence, gave God this ideological function. A consistent pantheism, however, could just as soon find the decrees of God in the actions of revolutionary movements against tyrannous governments. Pantheism, as a metaphysical doctrine, is politically neutral, and Spinoza, in his desire to demonstrate his ideology in a geometrical manner, was substituting his own preference for proof; he illicitly converted the alterable laws of "secular rulers" into a special case of laws of Nature which are God's immutable activities.

The government must always be obeyed, Spinoza insisted, even if it be the government of a tyrant. There has been only one exception to this rule, says Spinoza, that of Christ and the Apostles, and they are not to be emulated—"all are bound to obey a tyrant, unless they have received from God through undoubted revelation a promise of aid against him; so let no one take example from the Apostles unless he too has the power of working miracles . . . we must therefore admit that the authority which Christ gave to His disciples was given to them only, and must not be taken as an example for others." [19] The condition of slavery itself, according to Spinoza, does not justify revolt. The prophet Jeremiah admonished the Hebrew captives to submit to the king of Babylon, " 'and seek the peace of the city.' " "Now, they could not seek the peace of the city as having a share in its government, but only as slaves, being, as they were, captives; by obedience in all things, with a view to avoiding seditions.

. . ." Government is so all-important to man's good, Spinoza held, that no disobedience can be countenanced. The spirit of Hobbes dominates Spinoza's formal theory; it has no room for Thoreauesque sentiments of civil disobedience. "It is certain that duties towards one's country are the highest that man can fulfill; for, if government be taken away, no good thing can last, all falls into dispute, anger and anarchy reign unchecked amid universal fear." [20]

To Spinoza's mind, revolutionary agitation was identified with Calvinist preachers calling for the overthrow of the liberal republic. Revolution meant a theocratic counterrevolution. The notion of a progressive social revolution was something alien to Spinoza's philosophy.[21] To undermine the credentials of Calvinist agitators, Spinoza went far in the Hobbist direction. He denied the doctrine of the separation of church and state, and made the state sovereign in all matters of religion. Liberalism today makes an essential tenet of the separation of church and state. But in Spinoza's day, when social institutions were in violent conflict, the idea of a pluralistic compromise had not been conceived. The state, Spinoza declared, must retain all sovereignty; then it will redefine the true religion to mean simply human behavior in accordance with piety and charity. True religion will signify ethical conduct. And the wise sovereign will follow a policy of toleration toward all specific creeds which are in harmony with ethical religion. But the sovereignty is the state's, and no Calvinist preacher should set himself up against the Republic; Spinoza writes:

> Perhaps I shall be asked, "But if the holders of sovereign power choose to be wicked, who will be the rightful champion of piety? Should the sovereigns still be its interpreters?" I meet them with the counter-question, "But if ecclesiastics (who are also human, and private citizens, and who ought to mind only their own affairs), or if others whom it is proposed to entrust with spiritual authority, choose to be wicked, should they still be considered as piety's rightful interpreters?" It is quite certain that when sovereigns wish to follow their own pleasure, whether they have control over spiritual matters or not, the whole state,

spiritual and secular will go to ruin, and it will go much faster if private citizens seditiously assume the championship of the Divine rights.[22]

The Calvinist agitators of the seventeenth century, in England and Holland, were imbued with Old Testament fervor. They looked upon themselves as the modern successors of the Hebrew prophets, and they proclaimed that "prophets could, in virtue of their mission, choose a new king, and give absolution for regicide. . . ." The Old Testament, in the seventeenth century, had become a revolutionary tract for the times. Hobbes had bewailed the subversive consequence of its translation into English: "After the Bible was translated into English, every man, nay, every boy and wench that could read English, thought they spoke with God Almighty . . . and every man became a judge of religion, and an interpreter of the scripture to himself." [23] Spinoza coldly dismissed the would-be prophet-revolutionaries of modern times with the remark that the age of prophecy is over. "Consequently the rulers of modern times, who have no prophets and would not rightly be bound to receive them (for they are not subject to Jewish law), have absolute possession of the spiritual prerogative. . . ." Any attempt at revolution is treason, says Spinoza, a crime which he defines as any effort "to seize the sovereign power, or to place it in different hands." There are no mitigating circumstances, Spinoza wrote, to this crime. "I recognize no difference whether an attempt should be followed by public loss or public gain." [24]

Spinoza was a thoroughgoing political monist. Sovereignty, from his standpoint, is as indivisible as substance. Whosoever wishes to divide sovereignty, he affirmed, "is desirous of dividing the dominion; from such division contentions and strife will necessarily spring up, as they did of old between the Jewish kings and high priests, and will defy all attempts to allay them. Nay, further, he who strives to deprive the sovereign power of such authority, is aiming (as we have said) at gaining dominion for himself." The evils of divided authority, Spinoza asserted, are evident in political history. The Pope of Rome "gradually acquired complete control" over the German Emperors through an adroit misuse of clerical pretensions. The history of the Catholic encroachment on the secular sovereign, their devices of "multiplying the dogmas of religion" in order to vest authority in a leisured "skilled philosopher and theologian"—all that is a warning to maintain intact the sovereignty of the liberal Dutch republic from Calvinist intrigues.[25]

Did Spinoza grasp the profound character of the revolution which had begun in his time? As a sensitive, rationalist philosopher, he had recoiled from the hatreds and irrationalities which abounded in the lower classes. He placed his faith in the enlightened representatives of the Dutch middle class. Revolution was the political mode of passions, a manifestation of the life of bondage, the slave's futile revolt against the laws of nature. But deeper social changes had taken place as a result of the English revolution than Spinoza recognized. Charles II, it is true, had been restored to the throne of England, but it was a different throne, over a people which had changed itself and, in some measure, its social system. The French ambassador at London, in 1664, four years after the Restoration, wrote with discernment to Louis XIV: "This government has a monarchical appearance because there is a King, but at bottom it is far from being a monarchy." [26] The poor ambassador was bewildered by the tumultuous atmosphere of free discussion in London. Feudal military dues had been abrogated, and considerable lands of the nobility, lost in forced sales, were permanently alienated. The English middle classes had risen to new prestige and influence upon commercial policy. The supremacy of parliament in finance and taxation was acknowledged by the king. Star Chamber was permanently abolished. Cromwell's revolution had not been an interlude without fruit. The reign of law in social phenomena is not equivalent to the immutability of social systems. Spinoza, the disciple of De Witt's social mathematics, had tried to impose too simple an equation upon social realities. The fact of social revolution was recalcitrant to his scheme.[27]

It was mandatory for the Liberal Republicans, as an anti-revolutionary party, to succeed in winning away the allegiance of the poor from the Calvinist-Orange party to themselves. Here and there Spinoza showed himself mindful of the economic roots of the problem. The Calvinist consistories were administering the relief of the poor, and making strategic use of their doles to influence their recipients. Spinoza proposed instead that the state, the sovereign power, have the control, "lastly, of providing for the poor." In the *Ethics,* he wrote that the care of the poor is a problem which surpasses the bounds of private charity. "The care, therefore, of the poor is incumbent on the whole of society and concerns only the general profit." [28] A governmental program of poor relief might have removed the poorest workmen from their subservient relation to the Calvinist leaders. Spinoza had learned from Josephus that religious opinions are often distributed according to class. The Pharisees, he observed, consisted "chiefly of the common people," and in Spinoza's analysis of Jewish history, the Pharisees are the forebears of the Calvinists.[29] But how was the allegiance of the common people to be deflected from the purveyors of superstition? The Liberal Republicans never really approached this question. Indeed, there were problems enough, unending and critical, to absorb the energies of John de Witt—above all, the overriding threat of war, which made domestic questions seem small and secondary.

What Is Democracy?

Spinoza was the first political philosopher of modern times to avow himself a democrat. He was not, however, a democrat because he in any way idealized the people, plebs or proletariat. He had no mystic faith in the common man. Rather, he was an advocate of democracy because he believed it to be the best way to assure the liberties of men. Majority rule, in his opinion, would interfere least with minority rights, with the rights of the individual. This approach to the problem of democracy is indeed a landmark in political thinking.

Hobbes had considered government as the instrumentality of "peace and safety." [30] But what is "peace"? Hobbes tended to identify peace with quiescence, with the fear of the intimidated, with the frustrated submissiveness of the terrified. To Spinoza, however, as to a modern political psychologist, a broken, frustrated people is not a peaceful one; it is at war with itself, with passions and aggressions directed against itself. In the *Ethics*, Spinoza declared: "He who is led by fear, and does what is good in order that he may avoid what is evil, is not led by reason." [31] This proposition is directed as much against the Hobbist as the Calvinist. For it is a free society which Spinoza sought to help achieve, as far as that society is possible. To the Hobbesian apotheosis of fear, Spinoza replied that fear cannot be the basis of a true commonwealth:

> Of a commonwealth, whose subjects are but hindered by terror from taking arms, it should rather be said, that it is free of war, than that it has peace. For peace is not mere absence of war, but is a virtue that springs from force of character. . . . Besides, that commonwealth, whose peace depends on the sluggishness of its subjects, that are led about like sheep, to learn but slavery, may more properly be called a desert than a commonwealth. . . . For a free multitude is guided more by hope than fear, a conquered one, more by fear than hope: inasmuch as the former aims at making use of life, the latter but at escaping death. The former, I say, aims at living for its own ends, the latter is forced to belong to the conqueror; and so we say this is enslaved, but that free.[32]

Security and the preservation of life are not the full aims of government. A despotism can achieve these ends. But, as Spinoza said, the ends of different forms of government are not the same. The purpose of a democracy is to bring into existence a "free multitude," a society of men who are without anxiety and fear, who know their own values and desires, and who are as free from bondage in their emotional lives as they are from slavery in external ways.

"The true aim of government is liberty," says Spinoza. He believes in democracy because he thinks it is an obstacle to interferences with liberty: "In a democracy, irrational commands are still less to be feared: for it is almost impossible that the majority of a people, especially if it be a large one, should agree in an irrational design: and, moreover, the basis and aim of a democracy is to avoid the desires as irrational, and to bring men as far as possible under the control of reason, so that they may live in peace and harmony: if this basis be removed the whole fabric falls to ruin."

In a democracy, Spinoza continues, obedience to law does not make man a slave. "Action in obedience to orders does take away freedom in a certain sense, but it does not, therefore, make man a slave, all depends on the object of the action." In a democracy, especially, "the weal of the whole people, and not that of the ruler, is the supreme law. . . ." The basic conception of Spinoza's ethics, as we shall see, is the *free man.* Democracy, as a mode of government, is the social environment in which free men will most be found. Spinoza's political theory is thus a corollary to the values which are fully set forth in the *Ethics.* "Therefore that state is the freest whose laws are founded on sound reason, so that every member of it may, if he will, be free; that is, live with full consent under the entire guidance of reason." Even at this point where he stated the democratic faith most strongly, the component of emotional withdrawal in Spinoza's character asserted itself. There was a fear in Spinoza lest he commit himself too far to any political program, even the democratic one. In the last analysis, man's blessedness lies in his intellectual love of God, not in his enjoyment of political democracy, and the man who lives under tyranny can also know the mystic unity with God. So Spinoza adds a footnote of caution. "Whatever be the social state a man finds himself in, he may be free";[33] and therefore, he will always "respect the laws of his country, and obey the commands of the sovereign power to which he is subject."

As the philosophy of democracy emerged in Spinoza's thought, it was divided against itself. His political analysis, his impulses of political participation led him to an impassioned advocacy of the free society. His feelings of withdrawal, mistrust of the multitude, his desire not to know the disillusionment which must come with every political movement and faith prompted him to the reminder that a man can be free under any political circumstances. What is the free man's freedom, however, if he be condemned to a slave's life by some despot? Is he then to meditate that his slavery is the outcome of the laws of social development, and that his misery shows the infinite resourcefulness of God? The philosophy of democracy should logically have led to a vindication of revolution, but Spinoza shrank from such a consequence, and fell back upon the distorted "freedom" of self-hatred which can thrive under any social system.

The amazing thing about Spinoza's theory of democracy is that he found himself, despite his mathematical method, quite unable to provide a consistent definition of "democracy." The components in Spinoza's political theory simply would not fit together. As a Republican, as a loyal follower of John de Witt, Spinoza found himself aligned with the polity of the enlightened middle class, sharing their low estimate of the "multitude." But the radical reformer in Spinoza's feelings led him to trespass beyond the confines of the aristocratic middle-class republic. Liberty would best be preserved in a democracy, wrote Spinoza. "I think I have now shown sufficiently clearly the basis of a democracy: I have especially desired to do so, for I believe it to be of all forms of government the most natural, and the most consonant with individual liberty. In it no one transfers his natural right so absolutely that he has no further voice in affairs, he only hands it over to the majority of a society, whereof he is a unit. Thus all men remain, as they were in the state of nature, equals." [34]

To illustrate the advantages of democracy, Spinoza described the liberty and prosperity of Amsterdam, "in order to prove that from such freedom no inconvenience arises." But Amsterdam was certainly no example of a city with democratic government. It was, indeed, an oligarchy.[35]

Amsterdam was an oligarchy, yet it was the home of freedom. Spinoza's question in political theory was the same which De Witt faced in action: Should he advocate an extension of the franchise, an enlargement of the electorate to include the multitude? From this step he desisted. But in that case, how could Spinoza call Amsterdam a "democracy"? Was there, then, another sense in which Amsterdam, despite its lack of majority rule, was still a democracy, a sense of "democracy" more philosophical perhaps than the purely numerical significance? Unwilling to become a revolutionary democrat, as he would have had to if he had espoused the rule of the majority, Spinoza tampered with the meaning of "democracy." He redefined the term so that Amsterdam, an oligarchy, could still be called a "democracy." Thus, at the inception of its theory, democracy was born with those ambiguities which are too well known today. In our time, revolutionary thinkers have declared that the dictatorship of the proletariat, or the dictatorship of a party vanguard, is more really a "democracy" than the formal democracies of majority votes. And Spinoza, in the seventeenth century, trying to defend the Liberal Republican party of John de Witt, the party of scientific statesmanship, unwittingly embarked upon similar devices of ideological rationalization.

Democracy, Spinoza therefore said, is a society "where men with one consent agree to live according to the dictates of reason." The emphasis in this definition is on the ethical purpose of the state, the rational community which it promotes, rather than on the criterion of the majority. Then Spinoza defined "democracy" in a way which made it compatible with oligarchical rule. It is a society, he wrote, in which "if each individual hands over the whole of his power to the body politic, the latter will then possess sovereign natural right over all things; that is, it will have sole and unquestioned dominion, and everyone will be bound to obey, under the pain of the severest punishment. A body politic of this kind is called a Democracy, which may be defined as a society which wields all its power as a whole. The sovereign power is not restrained by any laws, but everyone is bound to obey it in all things. . . ." [36] In this sense of the word, any absolute monarchy, any government which claimed in some primordial sense to rest on powers and rights which were surrendered to it by the citizens, would be classified as a "democracy." A democracy would then be a government in which the citizens have reserved for themselves no rights—a government, in other words, which has the absolute powers of a dictatorship. At such moments in his theory, the Hobbesian absolutist overshadowed the liberal in Spinoza's thought. An oligarchical group could claim to wield the social power as a whole on behalf of the ethical welfare. A benevolent bureaucracy, in this sense, could be called "democratic." John Stuart Mill told his fellow philosophic radicals in the nineteenth century that their task was to achieve a government by the middle class on behalf of the working class.[37] Spinoza had a similar conception of "democracy" in 1670.

The theory of total sovereignty enabled Spinoza to stamp as seditious the activities of Calvinist agitators against the Republic. If a man believes that "a law is repugnant to sound reason," said Spinoza, he should submit "his opinion to the judgment of the authorities (who, alone, have the right of making and repealing laws)." As a "good citizen, [he] meanwhile acts in nowise contrary to that law. . . ; but if he accuses the authorities of injustice, and stirs up the people against them, or if he seditiously strives to abrogate the law without their consent, he is a mere agitator and rebel." This theory of total sovereignty, however, made the foundations of liberalism tenuous. In disabling the Calvinist agitators, Spinoza was at the same time undermining the liberal philosophy. For, unless there are rights of free thought and speech reserved to the individual, what are his safeguards against the omnipotent state? The democracy, wielding its power as a whole, can overwhelm the individual with its tyranny. Democracy can engulf liberalism and sweep freedoms away, as the multitude can rise and destroy the person who has not done obeisance to its idols. Confronted by this incompatibility between total democratic sovereignty and the rights of the individual, Spinoza began to modify his conception of the absolute powers of government. "Yet such unlimited power," he declared, "if it exists at all, must belong to a monarch, and least of all to a democracy, where the whole or a great part of the people wield authority collectively. This is a fact which I think everyone can explain for himself." [38] In a basic sense, common to all the modes of government, there are limits to absolute power, Spinoza argued, limits which arise from the very fact that no government can supervise the private thoughts of men:

> However unlimited, therefore, the power of a sovereign may be, . . . it can never prevent men from forming judgements according to their intellect, or being influenced by any given emotion. It is true that it has the right to treat as enemies all men whose opinions do not, on all subjects, entirely coincide with its own; but we are not discussing its strict rights, but its

proper course of action. I must grant that it has the right to rule in the most violent manner, and to put citizens to death for very trivial causes, but no one supposes it can do this with the approval of sound judgement. Nay, inasmuch as such things cannot be done without extreme peril to itself, we may even deny that it has the absolute power to do them, or consequently, the absolute right; for the rights of the sovereign are limited by his power.

There is a critical ambiguity in this whole passage which nullifies Spinoza's attempt to unify democracy, liberalism, and the sovereignty of the state. The state has the "strict right" to persecute men for their opinions, but Spinoza struggles in the next sentence to deny that the state has this right. These were the birth pangs of liberalism; it had not yet found its vocabulary. The first liberal had to state his case in the language of absolutism, and he fell into contradictions. The idiom was that of Hobbes, the aspiration was toward the rights of men, toward the world of the American and French revolutionists, and it was desperately seeking in the seventeenth century to find its proper garment.

Spinoza tried to solve his contradiction by emphasizing that men cannot alienate their rights of free judgment to the sovereign, that there are inherent limitations to the rights which can be assigned to the sovereign, and that the right of free thought is necessarily reserved to the individual: "Since, therefore, no one can abdicate his freedom of judgement and feeling; since every man is by indefeasible natural right the master of his own thoughts, it follows that men thinking in diverse and contradictory fashions, cannot, without disastrous results, be compelled to speak only according to the dictates of the supreme power." According to this line of reasoning, the state, if it could do so, would automatically possess the right to curb free thought; but since it is unable to control men's thoughts, it does not have the right to do so. Yet if these propositions were true, there would have been no need for Spinoza to have written his great defense of free thought. For the state, to begin with, would (according to his standpoint) have lacked the power to interfere with its citizens' opinions; its power and right would be limited by the fact of the privacy of human thought and feeling. Spinoza's whole treatise, in that case, would have been a colossal redundancy, an emotional advocacy of what already was the case and couldn't possibly have been otherwise. It would have been as relevant to political theory as a treatise urging that we enact the law of gravitation.

Manifesto for Freedom

In actual experience, Spinoza knew the power of the state to mold and control human opinions. He knew how the state could intimidate people, how it could sway passions and reduce the efficacy of reason in the community. While he was writing the *Tractatus Theologico-Politicus,* he saw the resources of repression brought to bear against his friend and disciple, the physician, Adrian Koerbagh. In 1668, Koerbagh published two works which aroused the vindictive hatred of the Calvinist clerics. His *Een Bloemhof van allerley lielykheyd sonder verdriet* (A Flower-garden of all sorts of charms without ill-humor) and *Het Licht schynende in Duystere Plaatsen om te verligten de voornaamstesaaken der Gods geleertheyd* (A Light shining in Dark Places to enlighten the chief points of theology) were remarkable for their criticism of orthodox religion and their outspoken advocacy of a hedonistic ethics.

Koerbagh's *Bloemhof* was a kind of philosophical dictionary, the forerunner of such works by Bayle and Voltaire. Its definitions were conceived in the spirit of Spinoza's philosophy. Miracles, in the customary sense, he wrote, cannot have occurred, for nothing can happen which is contrary to nature. His definition of metaphysics affirmed that there is only one nature, and nothing outside it, so that there can be no science apart from natural knowledge. He identified Jesus as a great and good man whose father was unknown, and he ridiculed those who conceived of paradise as a heavenly pleasure spot, who forgot that the kingdom is within us. His article on the Bible echoed Spinoza's view that its books were probably compiled by Ezra, whose name, however, Koerbagh inaccurately set down as Esdras. His definition of concubine was a provocative application of Spinoza's ethics; sexual promiscuity is not wrong in and of itself, said Koerbagh, but, like polygamy, it is forbidden by law on rational grounds. Like Spinoza, he criticized those who forsake humanity, and go off to live alone in the forests in the company of beasts. Like Spinoza, Koerbagh scorned episcopal corruption and the thirst for power, and in a memorable article on excommunication, he summed up, in effect, Spinoza's experience. In Holland, the man who is cast out from the official church, said Koerbagh, lives fortunately in a country where people have the right to unite in small communities where tolerance and light continue to find a home. Koerbagh's brother, indeed, had been accused of having, like Spinoza, attended Collegiant meetings. Koerbagh's world-view, moreover, was Spinoza's: There is but one substance, he wrote; thought and extension are its pervasive attributes, and whatever exists, exists in that substance. His definition of democracy, more pessimistic than Spinoza's, also made its existence in the Netherlands a fortunate exceptional occurrence rather than an advancing political form: "here and in other places, indeed a shadow of it is still found, but its force has already suffered a bit." But, like a good Republican, Koerbagh still proclaimed his faith that a man is a nobleman, though he be born of the poorest beggar, if he is blessed with wisdom, while a man is ignoble, though he be born of kings, if he lacks understanding.[39]

Koerbagh was arrested and tried by an ecclesiastical commission. During the interrogation, he was closely questioned as to his friendship and relations with Spinoza. Koerbagh steadfastly refused to involve Spinoza in responsibility for his ideas, though he did not deny their friendship. The interrogators were cruel in the manner of men searching to destroy the doubter who has raised questions which cannot be stilled in their own unconscious.[40]

It is especially significant that the magistrates cross-examined the unfortunate Koerbagh concerning the doctrine of the *Schechinah,* with which they tried to link Spinoza's name. The doctrine of the *Schechinah* is the Talmud's closest approximation to a theory of the immanence of God in the world. *Schechinah* literally means "dwelling"; its use connotes the presence of God everywhere. It denotes the underlying subject of all experience so that a man in deep crisis would identify his experience as the *Schechinah*'s. The *Schechinah* was a Talmudic form of pantheism.[41] The interrogation of Koerbagh tried to elicit whether he had been persuaded by Spinoza to import into Dutch thought a doctrine of Jewish pantheism. The inquiry thus took on something of the character of an investigation into un-Dutch activities and modes of thought.

Adrian Koerbagh did not long survive the ordeal of intolerance. He was fined 6,000 florins, sentenced to imprisonment for ten years, with subsequent banishment. Koerbagh had experienced the spectacle of human beings at their ugliest level, he had watched the sanctimonious judges enjoying their sessions of socially approved vindictiveness, and heard a member of the court demanding as a punishment appropriate to the crime of free thought: that Koerbagh's right thumb be cut off, that his tongue be bored through with a red-hot iron, that he be imprisoned for thirty years, and his fortune confiscated. It was enough to destroy any man's will to live. Adrian Koerbagh died in prison the next year.

All this Spinoza knew. He knew that men were intimidated by the destruction of their boldest thinkers. He had no desire for martyrdom and could not understand persons in whom the death-wish was strong.[42] But to the memory and honor of the martyrs of freedom, Spinoza wrote his noblest words: "He that knows himself to be upright does not fear the death of a criminal, and shrinks from no punishment; his mind is not wrung with remorse for any disgraceful deed: he holds that death in a good cause is no punishment, but an honour, and that death for freedom is glory." [43]

Spinoza was thus acutely aware that an inquisition, a police state, a society of informers and hysterics can stamp out men of independent mind. An effective inquisition is not impossible according to the laws of human psychology. According to Spinoza's formal political theory, an inquisitorial state would have all the right to those activities which it could effectively prosecute. And Spinoza thereby found himself caught in the coils of his own formulae of God and nature, of power and right. His liberalism could not articulate itself within the scheme of his pantheistic metaphysics. The social reformer who envisages an alternative political order, the social reformer who wishes to liberate men's energies is challenging one system of recognized rights in behalf of another; his touchstone is the advancement of human happiness, and he does not bow before the powers and rights that exist. The men who overthrew the feudal order, for instance, began with all right and power pitted against them. But Spinoza was trying to be a *scientific* liberal, to ground liberalism in the laws of nature, much as Marx, in a later century, tried to be a scientific socialist, and to make the socialist world a corollary of the inevitable laws of social development.

"For it is certain that nature, taken in the abstract," wrote Spinoza, "has sovereign right to do anything she can; in other words, her right is co-extensive with her power. The power of nature is the power of God, which has sovereign rights over all things; and, inasmuch as the power of nature is simply the aggregate of the powers of all her individual components, it follows that every individual has sovereign right to do all that he can; in other words, the rights of an individual extend to the utmost limits of his power as it has been conditioned."

Once more, there is the note of masochist submission in Spinoza to the powers of nature. Just as the contemporary worshiper of the Marxian dialectic accepts the will of history, genuflects before historical necessity, and tries to identify himself with the total historical process, which he regards as transcending the individual's ethical questioning, so Spinoza bows before the powers and manifestations of nature, and declares them to be "right": "For instance, fishes are naturally conditioned for swimming, and the greater for devouring the less; therefore fishes enjoy the water, and the greater devour the less by sovereign natural right." "By the rights and ordinance of nature, I merely mean those natural laws wherewith we conceive every individual to be conditioned by nature, so as to live and act in a given way." [44]

The masochist acquiescence in the greatness of nature could be united with the mystic's withdrawal from political participation; it could even give a scientific veneer to Spinoza's views by its arbitrary definition of "right" as "power." But Spinoza's own political sense continued to look for an ethical vocabulary in which one could challenge the repressive powers of the established order. He searched for an ethical idiom in which he could set himself against the powers of the European political world as Job once challenged the greatness of God:

> Oh that I knew where I might find him! that I might come even to his seat!
>
> I would order my cause before him, and fill my mouth with arguments.
>
> I would know the words which he would answer me, and understand what he would say unto me.
>
> Will he plead against me with his great power? [45]

And Spinoza likewise, despite his formal political theory, appealed to an ethical right which is not reducible to political power. He became the spokesman for the liberties of men against the tyrannies of governments:

> How much better would it be to restrain popular anger and fury, instead of passing useless laws, which can only be broken by those who love virtue and the liberal arts, thus paring down the state till it is too small to harbour men of talent. What greater misfortune for a state can be conceived than that honourable men should be sent like criminals into exile, because they hold diverse opinions which they cannot disguise? What, I say, can be more hurtful than that men who have committed no crime or wickedness should, simply because they are enlightened, be treated as enemies and put to death, and that the scaffold, the terror of evil-doers, should become the arena where the highest examples of tolerance and virtue are displayed to the people with all the marks of ignoring that authority can devise? . . .
>
> What purpose then is served by the death of such men, what example is proclaimed? The cause for which they die is unknown to the idle and the foolish, hateful to the turbulent, loved by the upright. The only lesson we can draw from such scenes is to flatter the persecutor, or else to imitate the victim.

The state has the power and the "right" to pass laws which interfere with freedom of thought, but Spinoza affirmed his belief that it would be "better" not to enact such statutes: "for laws of this kind prescribing what every man shall believe and forbidding anyone to speak or write to the contrary, have often been passed as sops or concessions to the anger of those who cannot tolerate men of enlightenment, and who, by such harsh and crooked enactments, can easily turn the devotion of the masses into fury and direct it against whom they will."

Radical by temperament, Spinoza desired to extend the domain of the individual's free thought. But his "realistic" tendency to recognize the state's power led him to allow encroachments on free thought which fitted ill with his radical defense. The "best government," Spinoza pleaded, would promote free thought. It would allow freedom of thought and expression for all ideas short of those which are seditious and would judge men primarily by their overt acts, not by their philosophic thoughts:

> If we hold to the principle that a man's loyalty to the state should be judged, like his loyalty to God, from his actions only —namely, from his charity towards his neighbors; we cannot doubt that the best government will allow freedom of philosophical speculation no less than of religious belief. I confess that from such freedom inconveniences may sometimes arise, but what question was ever settled so wisely that no abuses could possibly spring therefrom?

The "best government," according to Spinoza, would abstain from any efforts to regulate the detail of men's lives. He adumbrated an argument which was to grow to full force in Mill's *On Liberty:*

> He who seeks to regulate everything by law, is more likely to arouse vices than to reform them. It is best to grant what cannot be abolished, even though it be in itself harmful. How many evils sprang from luxury, envy, avarice, drunkenness, and the like, yet these are tolerated—vices as they are—because they cannot be prevented by legal enactments. How much more then should free thought be granted, seeing that it is in itself a virtue and that it cannot be crushed! Besides, the evil results

can easily be checked, as I will show, by the secular authorities, not to mention that such freedom is absolutely necessary for progress in science and the liberal arts. . . .[46]

Spinoza urged the state to emulate the model of the "best government." But what if the state declines to follow the way of enlightenment? There are no reserved rights upon which the individual can insist; against the dominion of the state, the individual has no higher recourse. He cannot claim that the terms of the social compact have been violated; he is ineffectual against the state's power. And this is the final weakness in Spinoza's political theory; his doctrine pleads for wisdom but merges into quiescence rather than deed. For without an ultimate right to revolution, wise men are impotent before tyranny. Without a right to revolution, wisdom issues not in action, not in the assertion of man, but in the apology for inaction. Wisdom turns into the self-hatred in which the individual reflects not upon his power, but upon his impotence.

Without a right to revolution, Spinoza's theory sets definite limits to thinking critical of the established order. In American jurisprudence, the doctrine of Justice Holmes concerning freedom of thought has become widely influential. Justice Holmes held that there was only one boundary to critical political thinking—that where words created a "clear and present danger" of violence against the state, the restriction of freedom of expression would be justified. The "danger," however, which justifies repression must, according to Holmes, be real, not academic, a "present danger of immediate evil or an intent to bring it about that warrants Congress in setting a limit to the expression of opinion. . . ." [47] Spinoza, however, imposed much narrower confines upon the political philosopher. In Spinoza's view there are subversive thoughts which should be suppressed, not because of any concrete danger which issues from them, but simply because they are subversive.

"From the fundamental notions of a state," Spinoza writes,

we can no less easily determine what opinions would be seditious. Evidently those which by their very nature nullify the compact by which the right of free action was ceded. For instance, a man who holds that the supreme power has no rights over him, or that promises ought not to be kept, or that everyone should live as he pleases, or other doctrines of this nature in direct opposition to the above-mentioned contract is seditious, not so much from his actual opinions and judgements, as from the deeds which they involve; for he who maintains such theories abrogates the contract which tacitly, or openly, he made with his rulers.[48]

From Spinoza's standpoint, philosophies which are subversive of the bases of the social order are seditious and justly suppressed. Political doctrines such as those of Kropotkin, Nietzsche, and Mandeville would in his eyes be seditious. This is a large limitation on freedom of thought, especially since opponents of freedom are prone to consign unpopular ideas to the subversive group. If one accepts the notion that seditious ideas merit suppression, the core of the argument for freedom is surrendered. Many of Spinoza's contemporaries thought his own ideas were subversive of the social order. But Spinoza concedes to his own critics the principle of the repression of subversive ideas, and then undertakes to argue that he is not subversive. To the charge that he was an atheist, Spinoza replied by pointing to his manner of life: "For Atheists are wont to desire inordinately honours and riches, which I have always despised, as all those who know me are aware." [49] And he was prepared to retract anything in his book which the government deemed seditious. The *Tractatus Theologico-Politicus* is a manifesto of freedom, but it ends with freedom's voice muffled and subdued: "I have written nothing which I do not most willingly submit to the examination and approval of my country's rulers; and that I am willing to retract anything which they shall decide to be repugnant to the laws, or prejudicial to the public good."

Hesitantly and uncertainly, Spinoza groped for the first statement of the philosophy of liberalism. At one point, he seemed to reach for a distinction between thought and action which would have been the equivalent of the Holmesian "clear and present danger" doctrine. Spinoza then wrote: "Thus we see how an individual may declare and teach what he believes, without injury to the authority of his rulers, or the public peace; namely, by leaving in their hands the entire power of legislation as it affects action, and by doing nothing against their laws, though he be compelled often to act in contradiction to what he believes, and openly feels, to be best." [50] But seditious, subversive doctrines were none the less barred by Spinoza on grounds of their incompatibility with the social contract. Two centuries later, John Stuart Mill was prepared, in the strength of his matured liberalism, to admit before the bar of discussion all doctrines, subversive, apologetic, orthodox, heterodox, conventional, and heretical; Mill was confident that free discussion, like the selective environment, would allow only the sturdiest intellectual fruit to survive. But Spinoza, struggling to be a liberal in an atmosphere beclouded with intolerances, trying in a century which had known the fiercest of religious wars to breed the first seeds of liberalism, had produced a variety which was still impure. His liberalism was hybrid, mixed with strains of concession to absolutism, but, none the less, a mutant in a world of intolerance, the intellect's first offspring with variations of freedom. It was a seed which, in the hands of friends, might grow into a magnificent assertion of the powers of the free human mind.[51]

A society which suppresses freedom, said Spinoza, is one which makes for hypocrites, one which suppresses the good faith of men in one another. A society of hypocrites is one in which all men suspect each other, in which all men are spies and spied upon: "But let it be granted that freedom may be crushed, and men be so bound down, that they do not dare to utter a whisper, save at the bidding of their rulers; . . . the necessary consequences would be that men would daily be thinking one thing and saying another, to the corruption of good faith, that mainstay of government, and to the fostering of hateful flattery and perfidy, whence springs stratagems, and the corruption of every good art."

In a more defiant mood, Spinoza refused to grant that freedom of speech could be suppressed:

It is far from possible to impose uniformity of speech, for the more rulers strive to curtail freedom of speech, the more obstinately are they resisted; not indeed by the avaricious, the flatterers, and other numskulls, who think supreme salvation consists in filling their stomachs and gloating over their money-bags, but by those whom good education, sound morality, and virtue have rendered more free. Men, as generally constituted, are most prone to resist the branding as criminal of opinions which they believe to be true, . . . hence they are ready to forswear the laws and conspire against authorities, thinking it not shameful but honorable to stir up seditions and perpetrate any sort of crime with this end in view.

Laws which suppress the free thought of the "generous-minded," Spinoza argues, "cannot be maintained without great peril to the state." [52] Spinoza lived before the modern totalitarian state applied the sciences of man to induce new levels of fear and anxiety. His own political theory, however, would preclude Spinoza from more than a sorrowful sympathy with the conspirators for freedom.

Spinoza's emotions took him toward an aspiration for freedom, toward defiance of tyranny; this was the Spinoza who had withstood the wrath of the Jewish community. But outside the Jewish community, there was an intolerance, too, which threatened the alien radical. Spinoza's strain of defeatism, which counterbalanced the striving toward liberation, forbade him to join with conspirators or revolutionists. He appealed to governments to be rational, but if governments were irrational, Spinoza resignedly advised only submission. The political philosophy of Spinoza was the harbinger of freedom in Europe, not its tocsin.

Despite all caution and conciliation, however, a conspiratorial secrecy hovered about Spinoza's own political writing. For after all his qualifications and professions of loyalty, there remained his simple stark advocacy of freedom of thought. When he heard in 1671 that the *Tractatus Theologico-Politicus* had been translated into Dutch, and that someone proposed to publish it, Spinoza wrote anxiously to his friend Jarig Jelles:

"I therefore beg you most earnestly please to find out about this, so as, if possible, to stop the printing of it. This is not my request only, but also that of many of my good friends who would not like to see the book prohibited, as will without doubt happen, if the book is published in Dutch. I firmly trust that you will do me and our cause this service." [53]

To work for "our cause," Spinoza's book had been published without the author's name and with a false imprint of a publisher's firm. The agencies of repression, however, were exceedingly vigilant. A few months after the publication of Spinoza's work, the Reformed Church Council of Amsterdam pronounced its condemnation of the book, and a series of lesser councils and consistories swiftly followed its example. With reaction soon to take the ascendancy after the murder of John de Witt, the light of liberalism would flicker weakly in the darkness. Spinoza's name was damned together with that of John de Witt by the enemies of freedom. The latter printed in 1672 an alleged catalogue of the books which De Witt possessed; they attributed this pamphlet to the society of *Nil Volentibus Arduum* [They Who Like Nothing Serious], which was led by Spinoza's close personal friend and physician, Dr. Lodewijk Meyer. Among their items was No. 33, *Tractatus Theologico-Politicus,* which they described as follows: "Produced by the renegade Jew Spinoza from Hell in which it is demonstrated in an unheard of, atheist manner that the word of God must be explained and understood by philosophy which is published with the knowledge of Mr. Ian." And still again: "Forged by the renegade Jew together with the devil in Hell and published with the knowledge of Mr. Ian and his accomplices." [54] Spinoza submitted to such calumny in silence; it was the part of the wise man, he believed, under certain circumstances, not to do battle. "The virtue of a free man," he wrote in the *Ethics,* "is seen to be as great in avoiding danger as in overcoming it." "Flight at the proper time, just as well as fighting, is to be reckoned, therefore, as showing strength of mind in a man who is free. . . ." [55] Submission in silence, Spinoza held, was not capitulation. Perhaps so, we may observe, but neither was it the ultimate assertion of human freedom; it led to no action. Spinoza's feelings went out to the fighters; men like Masaniello, the revolutionist, moved his unconscious. "Death for freedom is glory." But his political theory drew him back, a creature of compromises, from conflicts with established authorities. Meanwhile, however, he had carried the signal of freedom far beyond any previous outpost. He had surmounted Europe's heritage of "inadequate ideas" to a point where free action was sure to emerge because thought had dared to assert its right to freedom.

To Preserve the Republic

As a Republican political scientist, Spinoza undertook to analyze the problems which beset the Dutch Republic. This discussion, curiously enough, was the substance of his chapter on the Hebrew theocratic republic. Behind the façade of Biblical scholarship, we find a point-by-point analysis of the great issues which were being debated by the Republican and Calvinist parties. The ancient Hebrew confederation was the convenient analogue around which Spinoza made his incisive reflections on Dutch politics. He frankly indicated the contemporary bearing of the study of Biblical politics: the Hebrew tribes, he observed, "were, in fact, in much the same position (if one excepts the Temple common to all) as the United States of the Netherlands." [56]

Spinoza's problem was one in political sociology; what, he asked, were the causal conditions which made for the stability of the Hebrew commonwealth? From this experience, he believed, much could be learned of value for the Dutch Republican experiment. It was the fashion for all political parties at that time to search for the support of Biblical passages. Spinoza remarked sardonically that there is a proverb in Belgium, *geen ketter sonder letter*, "no heretics without a text." In this sense, Spinoza too was engaged as a Biblical master in vindicating Republican policies with scriptural texts, and putting to flight the Calvinist party with a barrage of sacred missiles. Meanwhile, as a by-product, Spinoza developed a sociology of the Bible, a sociological analysis of ancient Hebrew history. It was the first such sustained inquiry of the social bases of a political form.

Spinoza classified the ancient Hebrew confederation as a theocracy. He defined theocracy in two ways, one secular, the other religious. In the religious sense, a theocracy is a government in which "all the people owed allegiance to God, their supreme Judge, to whom they had promised obedience in all things." In the secular sense, a theocratic government is one in which there is a separation of powers, so that neither monarch, nor aristocracy, nor masses have complete sovereignty. Spinoza thus wrote: ". . . after the death of Moses no one man wielded all the power of a sovereign; as affairs were not all managed by one man, nor by a single council, nor by the popular vote, but partly by one tribe, partly by the rest in equal shares, it is most evident that the government, after the death of Moses, was neither monarchic, nor aristocratic, nor popular, but, as we have said, Theocratic." [57] In this secular sense, the Dutch Republic, like the Hebrew state, was likewise a theocracy, for it too was managed neither by one man, nor by a single council, nor by the popular vote, but partly by one province, partly by the rest in equal shares. Spinoza conceived of the Dutch Republic as a confederation which possessed only a limited, delegated sovereignty; his analysis coincides with that which De Witt had made.[58]

Why did Spinoza use the term "theocracy" in a scientific study? The classical terminology of political science from Aristotle to Hobbes spoke only of monarchies, aristocracies, and democracies. This was regarded as the essential exhaustive classification. Spinoza departed from the classical models, even from his much admired Hobbes, and on this point, chose to adopt the deviant, forgotten classification of Flavius Josephus. It was Josephus who first maintained that theocracy did not fall into the Hellenic classification of governments: "Some legislators have permitted their governments to be under monarchies, others put them under oligarchies, and others under a republican form; but our legislator had no regard to any of these forms: But he ordained our government to be, what, by a strained expression, may be termed a Theocracy, by ascribing the authority and the power to God, and by persuading all the people to have a regard to him as the author of all the good things that were enjoyed either in common by all mankind, or by each one in particular. . . ." [59]

Spinoza's use of "theocracy" was designed for the discomfiture of the Calvinist party. The Calvinists, following their master in Geneva, urged that the law of the Old Testament, the Hebrew theocracy, be re-established in Europe. Spinoza therefore undertook to show what the Hebrew theocracy really was. He borrowed a "slogan-word" from the Calvinist party and filled it with a content which no member of that party could accept. "You desire a theocracy," he in effect, told the Calvinist preachers; "look then and see what the Hebrew theocracy really was, how it subordinated priests like yourselves, and let our Dutch Republic follow the wise example, in these respects, of the ancient Hebrew commonwealth." In this sense the chapter on theocracy was Spinoza's reply to Calvinist political theory.

The secular signification of "theocracy"—divided sovereignty, checks and balances, and separation of powers—was the underlying one for Spinoza. The term "theocracy," though ill-chosen, filled a real need. For the realities of Dutch politics did not fit into the conventional classification of governmental forms, which assumed that total sovereignty was housed in a single man, in an aristocratic class, or in the masses. The Dutch Republic was a hybrid form in which sovereignty could not easily be localized. The Orange party especially scoffed at the notion that sovereignty could belong to burgomasters. "Who rules Holland?" asked one of their pamphleteers in 1650. His answer was that Marretye, a servant wench, rules the burgomaster's wife, the wife rules the burgomaster, the burgomaster rules Amsterdam, Amsterdam rules the whole of Holland. Therefore a servant wench rules Holland.[60] Spinoza, trying to adapt his terminology to realities, decided to apply the name "theocracy" to governments characterized by the separation of powers. Under this inaccurate heading, Spinoza wrote his pamphlet on contemporary Dutch politics in the guise of a discussion of the Hebrew confederation.

The commonwealth of the Hebrews, Spinoza stated, "might have lasted for ever." What were its characteristics which made for such stability?

In the first place, the judicial power among the Hebrews was separated from the executive. Evil rulers, Spinoza noted, try to assume the prerogatives of "sole interpreters of the law"; thereby they "try to surround their high-handed actions with a cloak of legality. . . ." But the Hebrew rulers were deprived of the judicial power, "the power of evil-doing was greatly curtailed for the Hebrew captains by the fact that the whole interpretation of the law was vested in the Levites who, on their part, had no share in the government, and depended for all their support and consideration on a correct interpretation of the laws entrusted to them." Calvinist leaders were thus reminded that the Levites "had no share in the government," though they could interpret the law, and would be supported by the people, if they did so correctly. Orange partisans were reminded that the Hebrew theocracy did not endow its rulers with absolute sovereignty, that the judiciary remained independent, and that captains themselves could be judged.

Secondly, Spinoza made the important point that the army of the Hebrew commonwealth was not composed of mercenaries; it was an army of citizen-soldiers. "There was another very important check on the unbridled license of the captains, in the fact, that the army was formed from the whole body of the citizens, between the ages of twenty and sixty, without exception, and that the captains were not able to hire any foreign soldiery. This I say was very important, for it is well known that princes can oppress their peoples with the single aid of the soldiery in their pay; while there is nothing more formidable to them than the freedom of citizen soldiers, who have established the freedom and glory of their country by their valour, their toil, and their blood." [61] The policy of De Witt and the Republican party was, as we have seen, to reduce the armed forces which were, indeed, composed mainly of mercenaries, whose loyalty, as the events of 1650 had amply shown, was not to the Republic but to the Prince of Orange.[62] The concentration of military power in the house of Orange, its command of the allegiance of the professional captains, was in the eyes of De Witt and Spinoza a perpetual threat to the stability and freedom of the Republic. De Witt's spokesman had written that "as to an armed State, it is held by all men of understanding for an infallible maxim, that he that is master of the soldiery . . . is likewise master of the state. . . . For the soldiers have always their officers whose commands they are daily accustomed to receive and obey. . . ; and lastly, seeing they have thereby also much more advantage in tumults and wars, than they can hope to gain in times of rest and peace; therefore he that can get to be their chief head and master, tho' by the greatest injustice of the world, may suddenly set on foot all manner of undutiful practices and undertakings against the lawful and unarmed rulers. . . ." By rousing the soldiery and "the rude rabble," a military commander, said Pieter, can seize power; ". . . the name and the right of that free republican government will likewise vanish," and the commander will become in reality the "sovereign monarch of that state. . . ." [63]

De Witt had throughout his years of rule tried persistently to reduce the power of the professional soldiers. As Sir William Temple, the English ambassador to the Netherlands, later described it: "The chief direction of their affairs had for eighteen years lain constantly in the hands of their Pensioner De Witt, a minister of the greatest authority and sufficiency, the greatest application and industry that was ever known in their State. In the course of his ministry, he and his party had reduced not only all the civil charges of the government in his Province, but in a manner all the military commands in the army, out of the hands of persons affectionate to the house of Orange, into those esteemed sure and fast to the interest of their more popular State." [64] Spinoza brought the practice of the Hebrew commonwealth to the support of De Witt's military policy; Scripture rebutted the militarism of the Orange-Calvinist party. It was part of the Republican philosophy which regarded monarchies as war-minded, and as adverse to the interests of peaceably-minded citizens and merchants, the philosophy which led Pieter de la Court to find "the true reason" of the Anglo-Dutch war in the militarist motivation of the house of Orange.[65]

The Dutch army of citizen soldiers had indeed astounded
Europe at the beginning of the seventeenth century and caused
a revolution in military science. With the feudal military art
in decline, Maurice of Nassau found an unexpected source of
strength in his citizen rank and file. He found he could maneuver
his infantry in flexible formation; the foot soldiers were no
longer a clumsy, rigid mass. The effect on Europe was much
like that produced by the raw soldiery of the French Revolution
at Valmy. Citizen soldiers, Spinoza therefore said, were men of
valor when their liberty was at stake.[66]

The Hebrew theocracy, moreover, was no unbridled clerical
or military dictatorship. If the Calvinist-Orange party meant to
emulate its ways, it must, according to Spinoza, take notice that
there was a God-given right to revolution in a theocracy which
would limit its authoritarian pretensions. "An additional check
may be found in the fear of a new prophet arising. . . . There
is no doubt that such an one would easily be able to enlist an
oppressed people in his cause, and by trifling signs persuade them
of anything he wished. . . ." Only "if affairs were well ordered"
would the captain be in a position to evaluate the claims and
proposals of the new prophet. In other words, an oppressed
people under a theocracy are not bound by the ruling high
priest and captain. An oppressed people, to take Spinoza's
contemporary parallel, would not be pledged to an immutable
allegiance to the captain-general, the Prince of Orange, and the
Calvinist luminaries. The ways of the Hebrew theocracy were no
sanction that a revolutionary prophet would not arise, authorized
by God to overthrow the existing order. The precedent of the
Hebrew commonwealth was no guarantee for undisturbed
Orangist-Calvinist hegemony.

The stability of the Hebrew state, furthermore, Spinoza
argued, was the outcome of its democratic character, not of
clerical hegemony. Its leadership was founded on ability, not on
birth in a hereditary caste. "Again, the captains were not
superior to the others in nobility or birth, but only administered
the government in virtue of their age and personal qualities."
The Hebrew theocracy, in Spinoza's description, conformed to the
previously mentioned principle of John de Witt that "the highest

dignities stand open to virtue; and that as much should never be deferred to possessions, family connections, qualities of ancestors, or other adjuncts of fortune, as to the piety, capacity, and merits of men themselves."

Like De Witt and Pieter de la Court, furthermore, Spinoza insisted on the basic principle of civilian supremacy in government. Rule by soldiers means a likelihood of war; only civilian rule guarantees that the pursuit of peace will be the ever-present aim of government. Civilian supremacy was a cardinal tenet, said Spinoza, of the Hebrew commonwealth. "Lastly, neither captains nor army had any reason for preferring war to peace. The army, as we have stated, consisted entirely of citizens, so that affairs were managed by the same persons both in peace and war. The man who was a soldier in the camp was a citizen in the marketplace, he who was a leader in the camp was a judge in the law courts, he who was a general in the camp was a ruler in the state. Thus no one could desire war for its own sake, but only for the sake of preserving peace and liberty. . . ." [67]

Peace was the great objective of the Republican party. Two centuries later, Herbert Spencer was to formulate as a general tendency of social evolution the rising ascendancy of the industrial over the military class. The English shopkeeper was to establish his primacy in world politics. In the seventeenth century, the Dutch merchants were trying to forge their conception of a government devoted to the arts of peace and to supplant in men's minds the image of government as devoted to war. Pieter had said pointedly "that the republican form of government is so acceptable to the merchants, and all wise and virtuous men, that the bare name, shadow, and appearance of freedom hath been able to encourage the traffick and navigation of Holland; . . . that we ought to expect many more good fruits from the thing itself, than from the appearance of it." The regents of Holland, Pieter had observed, "maintain themselves by the fisheries, manufactures, traffick and navigation," but these economic interests are not the aims of militarists or monarchists.[68] Peace and trade, said Pieter de la Court, flourished most under Republican governments.[69] Spinoza, the political philosopher of the Dutch Republican party, affirmed the direct relationship

between civilian rule and the pursuit of peace as a general
principle of political science.

The pursuit of peace was becoming a dominant theme
in the writings of the political and philosophical spokesmen of
the liberal merchants of the seventeenth century. Sir William
Temple observed in 1671 how the quest for commerce made for
peace. "The Hollanders," he wrote, "can have no interest to
offer at a war," but wish to continue the greatest advantage
that "their industry and address will gain them from all their
neighbours. And for these ends they will endeavor to preserve
the peace now in being, and band by leagues and negotiations
against any from whom they shall fear a breach of it." [70] No
wise state, Temple thought, "will ever begin a war," except for
sufficient design or defense, "for all other wars serve only to
exhaust forces and treasure, and end in untoward peaces."
Spinoza, De Witt, and Temple shared the high hope that
Europe was approaching an age of wisdom when men who believed that a policy of peace coincided with self-interest might
rule their governments. It was the working postulate of their
rational politics.

The Hebrew commonwealth, according to Spinoza, embodied a system of checks and balances against the arbitrary
power of captains and priests. Its stability, besides, was promoted
by "the very groundwork of the social fabric." The Hebrew state
"was so ordered as to inspire the most ardent patriotism in the
hearts of the citizens, so that the latter would be very hard to
persuade to betray their country, and be ready to endure anything rather than submit to a foreign yoke." Upon what was
this loyalty based? What was the social foundation which made
a people to whom "nothing would have been more abhorrent . . . than swearing allegiance to a foreigner, and promising
him obedience," a people which could not "conceive any greater
or more execrable crime than the betrayal of their country, the
kingdom of the God whom they adored"? What was the economic foundation which made disloyalty to the Hebrew commonwealth unthinkable for its citizens? Spinoza's answer was
one which joined him as a political theorist to contemporaries

like Harrington who were founding the economic interpretation of politics.

Spinoza wrote:

> There was one feature peculiar to this state and of great importance in retaining the affections of the citizens, and checking all thoughts of desertion, or abandonment of the country: namely, self-interest, the strength and life of all human action. This was peculiarly engaged in the Hebrew state, for nowhere else did citizens possess their goods so securely as did the subjects of this community, for the latter possessed as large a share in the lands and fields as did their chiefs, and were owners of their plots of ground in perpetuity, for if any man was compelled to sell by poverty his farm or his pasture, he received it back again intact at the year of jubilee: there were other similar enactments against the possibility of alienating real property.[71]

It matters little that we may find fault with Spinoza's sociology of the Bible. There is in fact no evidence that the communistic law of the jubilee was ever enforced among the ancient Hebrews. It remained a dream born in the minds of the poor who were overwhelmed with enclosures and foreclosures; the social protest in Amos and Isaiah against the land monopolists could look to no relief from the jubilee. What is striking, however, was Spinoza's daring assertion that national loyalty and patriotism are most securely founded on an equitable distribution of land, one in which the holdings of citizens are equal to those of their chiefs, and where there are guarantees against the loss of one's land. The social revolutionist in Spinoza spoke in the idiom of the Biblical sociologist. He admonished his Dutch contemporaries that the stability of their state depended on a solution to the problems of poverty and the conflict of social classes which beset the Netherlands. The true theocracy was not the Calvinist-Orange model of monarchist rule and class subservience; the true theocracy was a society which realized the ideal of the economic levelers.

Poverty and class inequality were still the rule in the Netherlands. When Temple compared the lot of the English yeoman to that of the Dutch peasant, he found the scales weighted far in favor of his own countrymen: "The yeomanry and commonalty of England are generally braver than in other countries, be- cause . . . they are so much better and fuller than those of their rank in any other nation. Their chief, and indeed, constant food, being of flesh" whereas meat in the Hollander's diet was a scarce item, "which the common people seldom do have above once a week. . . ." [72] Equality before the law was real in the Netherlands, but economic inequalities persisted.[73] And in Spinoza's estimation a real economic equality is required to elicit the deepest loyalty to the state; a formal legal equality would not suffice.

The class hierarchy of Holland in Spinoza's time consisted at the bottom of "the clowns or boors (as they call them) who cultivate the land," followed by "the mariners" and "the merchants or traders, who fill their towns," and finally, at the top, "the Renteeners, or men that live in all their chief cities upon the rents or interest of estates formerly acquired in their families, and the Gentlemen, and officers of their armies." The peasant class, the clowns, were described as "dull and slow of understanding," diligent people who lived upon "herbs, roots, and milks." The landlord class, on the other hand, was born to comfort and rule; the scions of the patrimonial estates, said Temple, "are generally bred up at schools, and at the universities of Leyden or Utrecht," and educated primarily for service in the government. Almost all the chief ministers came from the landlord class; they were "not men of mean or mechanic trades," as foreigners sardonically alleged. The merchants were content to leave government and administration to the landed gentry, so long as their own incomes and properties were safeguarded. Their daughters would marry their way into the genteel land- lords' families. Meanwhile, the landed gentry added to the in- come from their estates the dividends of shares in the Dutch East India Company.[74] The relations of the well-to-do classes were not unlike those which came to exist in England in the eighteenth and nineteenth centuries. And Spinoza, like the later liberal land reformers, like Jefferson who saw the strength of democracy in a land-holding yeomanry, criticized the economic landlordism by which the Dutch Republic was still dominated. The liberals of the Republican party were precursors of Adam Smith and Ricardo. The landed gentry was beginning to emerge as the "sinister interest," in Bentham's term, which subverted the stability of the republic. The commercial middle class, with its economic philosophy of free trade, was making its first self-assertion in the ideas of the Republican representatives.

The economic equality of its citizens, according to Spinoza, made poverty endurable in the Hebrew commonwealth. "Again, poverty was nowhere more endurable than in a country where duty towards one's neighbor, that is, one's fellow-citizen, was practised with the utmost piety, as a means of gaining the favour of God the King. Thus the Hebrew citizens would nowhere be so well off as in their own country; outside its limits they met with nothing but loss and disgrace." By such devices, says Spinoza, did the Hebrews succeed "in preventing civil war and removing causes of strife." [75] Spinoza's theory that civil war arises from an unequal distribution of land coincided with that which James Harrington, on the basis of the English experience, had set forth a few years earlier in the *Oceana*. His proposal for the avoidance of civil war is also similar: a society in which "no one was bound to serve his equal, but only to serve God, while charity and love towards fellow-citizens was accounted the highest piety. . . ."

Lastly, Spinoza reserved a jibe for the Calvinist way of life. Its austerity, he maintained, did not contribute to the stability of the state. Calvinist doctrine frowned on holidays and feasts; its morality was ascetic, it emphasized labor, thrift and frugality, it had no use for the saints' days and feast days which had characterized Catholic practice. But the Hebrew theocracy, Spinoza argued, was no fellow to the Calvinist way of life. The true theocracy promoted a life of joy and pleasure; therefore, it lived in the affections of its citizens. "Three times in the year they feasted before the Lord; on the seventh day of every week they were bidden to abstain from all work and to rest; besides these, there were other occasions when innocent rejoicing and feasting were not only allowed but enjoined. I do not think any better means of influencing men's minds could be devised;

for there is no more powerful attraction than joy springing from devotion, a mixture of admiration and love." The holidays of the Hebrew commonwealth were colorful and diverse: "It was not easy to be wearied by constant repetition, for the rites on the various festivals were varied and recurred seldom."

These, then, said Spinoza, were the "main features of the Hebrews' commonwealth." And if theirs was a theocracy, he was indeed prepared to learn from their statecraft and to apply their principles to the Dutch confederation. The Hebrew theocracy, in Spinoza's analysis, was a pilot state in the principles of the Republican party, a model in which were realized the separation of governmental powers, the supremacy of civilian over soldier, a citizens' army rather than one of mercenaries, a check upon tyranny in the right of prophets to arouse an oppressed population, a patriotic loyalty founded on an equal distribution of the land, and a national way of life which was one of rejoicing, of frank dedication to the pursuit of happiness. The Hebrew theocracy, as Spinoza portrays it, is kin to Rabelais's Abbey of Thélème, not to Calvin's Geneva.

But the Hebrew commonwealth declined and was finally destroyed. And from its decline, Spinoza likewise tried to deduce principles which would be applicable to the Dutch confederation. The Netherlands were then at the height of their power. "No country can be found either in this present age, or upon record of any story," wrote Temple admiringly, "where so vast a trade has been managed, as in the narrow compass of the four maritime Provinces of this commonwealth: nay, it is generally esteemed, that . . . more shipping belongs to them, than there does to the rest of all Europe." [76] Would Holland too decline necessarily as did the Hebrew commonwealth? What were the causes of the decline of states?

There is no immutable law of cyclical rise and fall in Spinoza's political theory. Spinoza's aim as a social scientist was to isolate those causal factors which have made for the decay of states. The wise statesman could then make use of this knowledge to preserve the Dutch Republic. The decline of a commonwealth, Spinoza insisted, arises from determinate social circumstances, not from any peculiar racial or psychological characteristics of its people. The character-structure of the Jews, as of peoples generally, was the outcome of social causes:

> Perhaps I shall be told that it [the complete destruction of their dominion] sprang from their hardness of heart; but this is childish, for why should this people be more hard of heart than others; was it by nature? But nature forms individuals, not peoples; the latter are only distinguishable by the difference of their language, their customs, and their laws; while from the two last—i.e., customs and laws—it may arise that they have a peculiar disposition, a peculiar manner of life, and peculiar prejudices. If then, the Hebrews were harder of heart than other nations, the fault lay with their laws or customs.

The Hebrew commonwealth declined, according to Spinoza, largely because it had a large, idle, contentious, meddling class of priests, who continually disturbed the peace of the polity and were a drain on its material resources. The contemporary moral for the Netherlands was obvious. The modern Levites were the Calvinist clergy, parasites and disrupters of the Dutch Republic. So Spinoza wrote:

> The gifts which the people were obliged to bestow on the Levites and the priests—the redemption of the first-born, the poll-tax due to the Levites, the privilege possessed by the latter of the sole performance of sacred rites—all these, I say, were a continual reproach to the people. . . . Moreover, we may be sure that the Levites were for ever heaping reproaches upon them; for among so many thousand there must have been many importunate dabblers in theology. Hence the people got into the way of watching the acts of the Levites who were but human; . . . and continually murmuring. Besides this, there was the obligation to keep in idleness men hateful to them, and connected by no ties of blood. Especially would this seem grievous when provisions are dear.[77]

The Calvinist clergy held an economic and political status in the Netherlands similar to that of the Levites in Spinoza's description. All the public churches were theirs, and they were wholly supported by the state. The Calvinist pastors preached boldly against "the vices, and sometimes the innocent entertainments, of persons most considerable in the government, as well as of the vulgar." Although the Republic paid their salaries, they were "in general, throughout the country, passionate friends to the house of Orange." [78]

Secondly, said Spinoza, the decline of the Hebrew commonwealth was abetted by the conflict of its organized priesthood with democratic, egalitarian principles. Spinoza, fellow traveler of Collegiants and Quakers, shared their dislike for any pastors claiming prerogatives above those of ordinary men. Under the Levite priesthood, said Spinoza, "the people began to wax cold, and at length to fall away from a worship, which, though Divine, was also humiliating, and even hostile, and to seek after something fresh." Tribal leaders, always adopting the "popular course," introduced new forms of worship, and thereby helped subvert the commonwealth. The claim of one tribe, the Levites, to a priestly monopoly destroyed the equality upon which the free, stable society was founded. The state, Spinoza wrote, should have kept firm the equality of all the tribes; "the tribes would thus have been united by a far closer bond, if all alike had possessed the right to the priesthood."

Korah, the Biblical prototype of the revolutionist, evoked Spinoza's sympathies. This rebel against Moses was, in Spinoza's eyes, a religious democrat: "certain men of no mean birth began to rebel against the choice of the Levites, and to make it a cause for believing that Moses had not acted by the commands of God, but for his own good pleasure. . . . They, therefore, stirred up a tumult, and came to him, crying out that all were equally sacred, and that he had exalted himself above his fellows wrongfully . . . ; but by the intervention of a miracle, in proof of the faith, they all perished. A fresh sedition then arose among the whole people, who believed that their champions had not been put to death by the judgement of God, but by the device of Moses. After a great slaughter, or pestilence, the rising subsided from inanition, but in such a manner that all preferred death to life under such conditions." Spinoza was frankly dubious of the Mosaic authority; his Republican allegiance for once brought him into conflict with the Biblical judgment, and he argued that the Mosaic victory over Korah failed to re-establish harmony. From this root betrayal of democracy sprang evils, which finally turned men from the republic, so that they wished to have a king. "Great changes, extreme licence, luxury, and hardness of heart grew up; things went from bad to worse, till at last the people, after being frequently conquered, came to an open rupture with the Divine right, and wished for a mortal king. . . ." [79]

The history of the Hebrews as Spinoza told it has at times only a tenuous relationship to the Biblical narrative. But it was the vehicle by which Spinoza's anti-monarchist feelings were fully projected. He inveighed against monarchy with all the bitterness which the prophet Samuel vented upon the Israelites who desired to be as other nations, to have a king. The Dutch Republican Spinoza described the evil consequences of the Jewish establishment of monarchy: "A vast material for new seditions was thus produced, eventually resulting in the ruin of the entire state. Kings are above all things jealous of a precarious rule, and can in nowise brook a dominion within their own." The kings schemed "to get all the sovereign rights into their own hands." Interminable conflicts with the Levites ensued, conflicts which took a religious form. Prophets arose against tyrannous kings. "Of discords and civil wars there was no end, for the causes for the violation of Divine right remained always the same, and could only be removed by a complete remodelling of the state." [80] Their abandonment of the republic was the third basic cause for the decline of the Hebrews' commonwealth. The corollary of Spinoza's political analysis was clear. He was warning the Dutch people against the blandishments of the house of Orange. In that direction were discord and civil war. He asked for the loyalty of all good men to the Republican government.

Spinoza did not propose that any effort be made to re-enact the Hebrew theocracy in the seventeenth century. Calvinist theologians spoke in that vein, but as a political scientist, Spinoza held that "it would be impossible to imitate it at the present day, nor would it be advisable so to do." The Hebrew commonwealth was especially designed for an autarchic society, "for those who desire to have no foreign relations, but to shut themselves up within their own frontiers, and to live apart from the rest of the world; it would be useless to men who must have dealings with other nations. . . ." In short, the Dutch commercial economy could not be managed with a political system adapted to a simple agricultural culture. Foreign trade, the problems of commerce and industry, the poverty of workmen—these posed problems which were not solved by an egalitarian distribution of landholdings. Spinoza was aware that a political form must be adapted to its economic foundation. Nevertheless, he insisted, there was much to be learned from the Hebrew experience: "though it could not be copied in its entirety, it possessed many excellent features which might be brought to our notice, and perhaps imitated with advantage." He set forth the universal principles of political science derived from this study which he regarded as his especial contribution to the discussion of Dutch political affairs.

First, said Spinoza, clericalism is contrary to a republic's welfare. The rule of clerics is always to be avoided. When the high priests gained political power in the second commonwealth, religion sank "into a degrading superstition," and Scripture was accommodated "to the very depraved current morals." Disputes and altercations multiplied, politics was commingled with religious quarrels. When magistrates "back up one side or another, they can never come to a compromise, but are bound to split into sects."

Secondly, said Spinoza, the institution of prophecy is incompatible with stable government. Prophets are too often overweening men, fanatics, who "rather irritated than reformed mankind by their freedom of warning, rebuke, and censure; . . ." prophets even reproached just governors. If prophets had had their way, "great civil wars would have resulted." Spinoza thus urged a scientific, secular politics; the age was not assisted by messianic Utopians or those who claimed to be the especial bearers of God's intervention in history.

Thirdly, declared Spinoza, democracy promotes peace, whereas monarchy is conducive to war. "It is remarkable that during all the period, during which the people held the reins of power, there was only one civil war. . . . But after the people, little accustomed to kings, changed its first form of government into a monarchy, civil war raged almost continuously. . . . Worn out with these and similar battles set forth at length in their histories, the Jews at length fell a prey to their enemies." [81] Kings fought for glory, not for peace and liberty; monarchy sapped the vitality of the Jewish state and made it vulnerable to its enemies.[82]

The people of the Netherlands, Spinoza finally argued, should avoid the intrusion of politics into intellectual questions; only tyrannies make crimes of opinions, "for everyone has inalienable right over his thoughts." The effort to control thoughts "leads to the rule of popular passion," and is usually prompted by selfish motives; "the Pharisees, in order to shake the position of men richer than themselves, began to set on foot questions of religion, and accused the Sadducees of impiety. . . ." The Calvinist clerics were to Spinoza the modern Pharisees who stirred the populace against the Republicans, modern counterpart to the freethinking Sadducees, "men whose unblemished character and distinguished virtue had excited the popular hatred. . . ." Piety and religion must "consist in acts only,— that is, in the practice of justice and charity, leaving everyone's judgement in other respects free." [83] Full sovereignty must lie in the secular government; and where a people has happily been spared a monarchy, it would be a disaster for it to enslave itself. Republican institutions must be safeguarded by the Dutch people, which must not allow itself to be misled by the monarchist partisans of Orange.

Such was the message which Spinoza, the political philosopher, addressed to the Dutch people. There was hope in the air, the springtime movement of freedom. The Dutch Republic was led by a wise man, and free men might give him their aid. The Dutch Republic could perhaps open a path in Europe for the freedom of the human spirit. Two years later, in 1672, came catastrophe. Wisdom knew its own impotence. "There is no individual thing in nature which is not surpassed in strength and power by some other thing, but any individual thing being given, another and a stronger is also given, by which the former can be destroyed." [84]

CHAPTER 5

Philosophic Liberal in a Reactionary Age

1672—Year of Catastrophe

In March 1672, without warning or provocation, Charles II, king of England, declared war upon the Dutch Republic. A few weeks later, Louis XIV of France followed his example. There had been reason to expect this step of the French king. For several months he had been complaining that the Dutch newspapers were hostile and that French goods imported into the Netherlands were subject to the duties. The ways of dictators conform to a recurrent pattern.

From all sides, enemies converged upon the Netherlands. At sea, the English fleet sailed to challenge the Dutch ships. On land, the French armies invaded Dutch soil. John de Witt had labored to prevent a two-front war. He had failed irreparably. The Dutch navy was ready for action, but the land forces were ill-trained and ill-equipped. Out of fear of the militarist house of Orange, De Witt had allowed the army to fall into neglect. He now tried to make up for lost time. He imposed new taxes on the people and began to mobilize an expanded army and navy. But fear spread throughout the land, and the terrified people began to turn for succor to the Prince of Orange, the youthful son of their great commanders. Despite De Witt's opposition, and though it was contrary to law, the prince was designated by the Estates-General as captain-general for one campaign.

Calamities awaited the Dutch. Within a month the French forces had overrun the provinces of Gelderland and Utrecht. Traitors surrendered Overyssel to the enemy. In June, Amsterdam made the fateful decision to open the dikes, and flood their Dutch soil to halt the French invasion. The people's suffering was great. In some districts, the peasants were reluctant to sacrifice their lands; force had to be used to overcome their resistance, and the sluices were strongly guarded to prevent their being secretly closed.[1] Panic spread among the Dutch people. A contemporary witness described those days:

> Everybody stood stunned and dumb; everybody found his house too small and fearsome and betook himself to the street where he encountered for his consolation nothing but lamentation and misery; everybody hung his head like a reed; everybody seemed to have received his sentence of death; the trades were at a standstill; the shops were shut; the courts were closed; colleges and schools took a vacation; the churches, on the other hand, were too small for the troubled hearts that groaned with anguish more than they could pray. . . . The government was without counsel, the people without reason, the country without rescue.[2]

The value of Dutch securities collapsed; shares of the Dutch East India Company fell from 572 to 250; there was a run on the Bank of Amsterdam.

Meanwhile, John de Witt returned from the sea, where a great but indecisive battle with the English fleet had been fought off the eastern coast of England. De Witt had participated courageously in the action by the side of the renowned Dutch Admiral De Ruyter. At The Hague, a first attempt on his life took place; he was stabbed, and severely wounded. De Witt still hoped to secure a negotiated peace, but Amsterdam took the lead in demanding a vigorous prosecution of the war, calling upon the provinces to defend themselves to their last drop of blood. The agitation, anger, and hatred against John de Witt was surging into violent flames. At Dordrecht, his own town, the mobs shouted "Up with Orange" and "Down with the De Witts." The States-General on July 8 overcame all constitutional scruples and, yielding to the clamor for military dictatorship, elected the Prince of Orange captain and admiral-general of the Netherlands Union.

But the hatred of the people for De Witt and his family was still unappeased. The mob sought its scapegoat. First, Cornelius de Witt, John's brother, was indicted on baseless charges, and, by vote of his judges, tortured on the rack. Cornelius steadfastly affirmed his innocence, but was none the less sentenced to exile and the loss of all his offices. John went to the prison to give comfort to his tortured brother. With the connivance of town councilors and officers, a company of militia broke its way into the jail. They found John de Witt reading the Bible to his sick brother. Cornelius was beaten and thrown down the stairs. The two brothers clasped each other's hands a last time. Then they were stabbed, clubbed, and shot to death. "At half-past four all was over and the madmen, drunk with bloodshed, danced on the bodies which were finally hung up by the feet to the lamp-post on the Groene Zoodje, horribly mutilated, even cut to pieces by desperadoes desirous of a bloody relic. Until late in the evening the rabble shrieked about the abused remains. . . ." [3]

The Trauma of Democracy: the People as Mob

Nearby, in a room upon the Pavilioengracht, the philosopher Benedict de Spinoza cried, in sorrow at the death of the statesman he admired, in bitterness with the mob, with the human race at its ugliest bestial worst. Were free men always to be destroyed by the vengeful slaves? Was this the outcome of the democracy he had extolled? "He shed tears when he saw his fellow-citizens rend to pieces one who was a father to them all, and, although he knew better than anybody what men are capable of, he could not but shudder at that cruel sight." [4] Four years later, the rising young German philosopher Leibniz visited Spinoza. The memory of the black day of the twentieth of August, 1672 was still poignant in Spinoza's mind. Leibniz set down his recollection: "After dinner I spent several hours with Spinoza. He told me that on the day of the murder of the De Witts he felt impelled to go out in the evening and exhibit in the neighborhood of the crime a poster with the words 'Lowest Barbarians!' But his landlord had locked the door to prevent his going out and incurring the risk of being torn to pieces." [5] "Ultimi barbarorum!"—that was a judgment which wound its way into Spinoza's philosophy of democracy. He would never again speak in optimistic tones of democracy and the city of Amsterdam. It is one thing to read and write of the atrocities which can spring from human nature. It is another to feel those atrocities directed against one's friends and one's self.

The cruelty of men can then never be denied, nor can one with sincerity plead circumstances of mitigation.

> On the one hand, he saw an act of parricide that had not its like, and extreme ingratitude; on the other hand, he saw himself deprived of an illustrious Maecenas, and of the sole support that was left to him. This was more than enough to overwhelm an ordinary soul, but a soul like his, accustomed to overcome inner troubles, was far from succumbing to it. As he was always master of himself, he soon got over this terrible incident; and when one of his friends who scarcely ever left him expressed his surprise thereat, our philosopher replied, "Of what use would wisdom be to us if after falling into the passions of the people we had not the strength to raise ourselves again by our own efforts?" [6]

Spinoza resumed his philosophic labors. But the sight of the people turned mob, the democratic trauma, left its impress on his thought. Henceforth, there was something pronouncedly of the suspicious recluse about him. The courageous political pamphleteer was gone; not the courage, but the impulse to persuade people to a rational polity, was diminished. The liberal philosopher adjusted himself to resigned existence in a time of reaction.

In 1674, the news probably reached Spinoza that his old teacher, Van dan Ende, had died on a gallows in France. Such was the end of the revolutionist. A generation had passed since those adventurous days when the young Spinoza, breaking through the ghetto confines, had learned of the world in the animated household of Van dan Ende, listening to philosophic speculation and political debate. Van dan Ende, with his ideals and impatience, was buried in the graveyard of revolutionary hopes. What was the way of wisdom?

Spinoza Withdraws Again

From this time on the image of Spinoza as the retired, solitary scholar, began to strike his contemporaries. His last landlord, Van der Spyjk, described him as living "an extremely lonely life." He was said to have "stayed at home for several whole

months at a time. For, being much too diligent, he devoted himself to his studies far into the night, and for the most part toiled
over his dark writings by lamplight from the tenth evening hour
until the third, and mostly abstained from human intercourse in
the daytime, so that not an hour be lost for the work of his own
undoing, and the perdition of others." And Kortholt adds in this
account written in 1700: "The accuracy of this is confirmed by
what Mr. Christ. Nic. von Greiffenerantz, Councillor to His
Serene Highness the Duke of Holstein, and who associated with
Spinoza in the Hague in the seventy-second year of this century,
said about him in his letter sent to my Father on the 6th of April,
1681, from Holm in Sweden: *he seemed,* says he, *to live all to
himself, always lonely, and as if buried in his study.*" Occasion-
ally Spinoza still talked politics, though evidently it was now the
observer and social forecaster rather than the participant who
was in the foreground; "he sometimes passed his spare hours in
conversing with learned and considerable men, whose company
he rather admitted than desired, and with whom he talked of
political affairs. For he loved the name of a Politician, and
sagaciously pierced into futurity, and foretold his friends several
events." [7] Jarig Jelles, the editor of Spinoza's posthumous works,
summed it up: "he withdrew himself entirely from the world and
hid himself." [8]

An attitude of suspicion became dominant in Spinoza's relation to his contemporaries. It was evident, for instance, in his
dealings with Leibniz. The German thinker had sought correspondence with Spinoza in a respectful manner. He was indeed
at this time something of a philosophic disciple of Spinoza. But
when an intermediary requested that Leibniz be permitted to
read the manuscript of the *Ethics,* Spinoza wrote mistrustfully in
1675: "I do not know why he has gone to France, when he was a
Councillor of Frankfurt. . . . I consider it imprudent to entrust
my writings to him so soon. I should like to know first what he
is doing in France, and to hear the opinion of our friend
Tschirnhaus, after he has associated with him longer, and knows
his character more intimately." [9] As a matter of fact, Spinoza's
political suspicion of Leibniz was ill-founded. Leibniz was a
perennial peacemaker, a conciliator of nations, religions, and

philosophic systems. What had taken him to Paris in 1672 was the hope of preventing a European war by a scheme which had all the logic and daring of a great metaphysical speculation. Leibniz wished to persuade Louis XIV not to declare war on Holland, but to seek his aggrandizement in the Mohammedan Near East, in Egypt and Turkey.[10] Expansion in the territories of the infidel, Leibniz argued, would indeed be worthy of a Christian monarch. Nothing came of Leibniz's scheme, and a few months later, the French armies were marching on Dutch territory.[11] Leibniz, however, persisted in diplomatic efforts at terminating the conflict, and participated in a London mission in 1673 for this purpose.

It was hard for Spinoza himself to refrain from amateur forays into diplomacy, and he too undertook what was evidently an unofficial mission on behalf of peace between France and the Netherlands. A lieutenant-colonel of the French Army, Stouppe, who was stationed in Utrecht in 1673, urged Spinoza to visit the French headquarters, and to talk with the commander-in-chief, the Prince de Condé. According to Colerus' account: "he writ several Letters to Spinoza, from whom he received several Answers; and at last he desired him to repair to Utrecht at a certain time. Monsieur Stoupe was so much the more desirous that he shou'd come thither, because the Prince of Condé, who took then possession of the Government of Utrecht, had a great mind to discourse with Spinoza: And it was confidently reported that his Highness was so well disposed to recommend him to the King, that he hoped to obtain easily a Pension for him, provided he wou'd be willing to dedicate one of his Books to his Majesty. He received that Letter with a Passport, and set out from the Hague a little while after he had received it." Evidently the proposed discussions were not consummated. Spinoza told his landlord "that he cou'd not see the Prince of Condé, because he set out from Utrecht some days before he arrived there. But that in the discourse he had with Monsieur Stoupe, that Officer had assured him, that he wou'd willingly use his Interest for him, and that he should not doubt to obtain a Pension from the King's Liberality, at his recommendation. Spinoza added that, because he did not design to dedicate any Book to the King of France, he had refused the offer that was made him, with all the civility he was capable of."

The citizens of The Hague, however, believed that there had been a political motive to Spinoza's visit to the French camp.

> After his return, the Mob at the Hague were extremely incensed against him, they look'd upon him as a Spy, and whispered in one another's Ears, that they ought to kill so dangerous a Man, who treated, without doubt of State affairs, keeping so publick a Correspondence with the Enemies. Spinoza's Landlord was alarm'd at it, and was afraid, not without reason, that the Mob wou'd break into the House, and perhaps plunder it, and then drag Spinoza out of it: But Spinoza put him in heart again, and remov'd his fears as well as he could. *Fear nothing,* said he to him, *upon my account, I can easily justify myself: There are people enough, and even some of the most considerable Persons of the State, who know very well what put me upon that Journey. But however, as soon as the Mob make the least noise at your Door, I'll go and meet 'em, tho' they were to treat me, as they treated poor Messieurs de Wit. I am a good Republican, and I always aimed at the Glory and Welfare of the State.*[12]

The various circumstances surrounding Spinoza's visit to the French headquarters indicate that the "mob" was probably correct in supposing that Spinoza had gone on some political mission. The whole story concerning Lieutenant-Colonel Stouppe's personal interest in obtaining Spinoza a pension from the French king was, in all likelihood, fabricated as the official version for the unofficial purpose of negotiation. Stouppe was hardly a person whom Spinoza could have regarded as a personal friend. Stouppe had a chameleonlike career behind him: pastor of a Walloon church, agent for Cromwell upon missions to Mazarin, and now, officer of the French Army. He had also completed in May, 1673, a book, *La Religion des Hollandais,* which defended those Netherlanders who were helping the French king in his war against their own country, in other words, an apology for Dutch collaborationists. To justify the latter, Stouppe belittled the significance of Calvinism in Dutch history. The Dutch rose against Spanish rule, he said, not because of their Calvinist religion but because they were attached to liberty's cause. Calvinism, he argued, was not really the religion of the Dutch; among them, said Stouppe, you also find Roman Catholics, Lutherans, Brownists, Independents, Arminians, Anabaptists, Socinians, Arians, Enthusiasts, Quakers, Tremblers, Seekers, Borrelists, Moscovites, Libertines, Jews, and Mennonites. Stouppe then added a sketch of Spinoza which no friend would have written. There is a man, he wrote, who has

> a great number of followers, . . . who was born a Jew, by the name of Spinoza, who has neither renounced Judaism nor embraced the Christian Religion; thus he's a very poor Jew and not a better Christian. He wrote several years ago a book in Latin entitled *Tractatus Theologico-Politicus* in which his intention seems to have been to destroy all Religions and particularly Judaism and Christianity, and to introduce Atheism, Libertinage, and the freedom of all religions. . . . This Spinoza lives in this country; he has resided for some time at the Hague, where he has been visited by all the curious Spirits and even by "de filles de qualité," who preen themselves for having more intelligence than others of their sex. His disciples don't dare to reveal themselves because his book absolutely overturns the foundations of all religions, and has been condemned by a public decree of the States. . . .

Stouppe also assailed Spinoza's effort to found liberalism on economic rationality. Spinoza, as we have seen, had commended the Dutch East India Company for prohibiting its representatives in Japan from practicing the Christian rituals. Stouppe wrote bitterly against this subordination of dogma to profit. "The action of the Hollanders in Japan, done with the support of public authority, must be indeed impious and detestable," he wrote, "if this Author, who professes atheism openly makes use of it for proving that the external rites of the Christian religion contribute nothing to salvation, that one can dispense with them, and not cease to be happy." Stouppe had read the *Tractatus Theologico-Politicus* well, saw the dangerous import of Spinoza's economic argument against Christian dogmatism, and falsely inveighed against him as an "atheist." [13]

Spinoza and Stouppe were thus scarcely cut out to be philosophical or personal associates. Besides being called an atheist, to have his friends threatened by indirection and to be referred to as a person frequented by bluestockings would have been enough to alienate Spinoza. Stouppe had written his accusations two months before Spinoza's arrival at Utrecht; they were not the aftermath of disappointment with Spinoza's mission. Spinoza, furthermore, was neither a pension-hunter nor a sycophant of the aristocratic class. When his friend De Vries, before his death in 1667, had wished to make Spinoza his general heir, "Spinoza wou'd never consent to it, and told him, that he shou'd not think to leave his Estate to any Body but to his Brother. . . ." When De Vries' brother desired to grant Spinoza an annuity of 500 florins, Spinoza insisted that "he would not accept, because he found it too considerable, so that he reduc'd it to 300 Florins. That Annuity was regularly paid him during his life. . . ." [14] It is scarcely to be believed that Spinoza, so careful of his integrity and independence in such matters, would toady to the French monarch and his representatives for a pension. This was a story designed to allay public suspicion, for, as Spinoza told his landlord, there were some statesmen who knew the real purpose of his mission. He continued, in his own hour of danger, to identify himself with the cause of De Witt.

As late as June 1672, John de Witt, despite strong opposition, had persisted in seeking a negotiated peace. He sent Pieter de Groot as a special envoy to Louis XIV to beseech peace. De Groot was empowered to offer great concessions to the French king—the surrender of Maestricht together with the so-called generality lands, and the payment of all the costs of the war. But De Witt's proposal was scornfully rejected, and the French demanded the humiliating payment of an enormous indemnity and a much larger cession of territory. The Dutch advocates of peace in the Republican party were prepared to go far for an end to hostilities, and they kept searching for some avenue of agreement; retirement from political activity was difficult for active Republicans to endure. [15] Spinoza, we may surmise, mindful of the Republican policy of seeking peace, made his journey to the French camp as an unofficial intermediary, with the knowledge, approval, and guidance of those peace advocates who still remained in high Dutch governing circles.[16] In 1673, at the time of Spinoza's mission, the peace party in Holland was gaining strength because of the suffering and pleas of the three provinces occupied by the enemy. The war party, headed by the Prince of Orange, was being obliged to make concessions to the desire for peace. When Sweden offered its mediation, the statesman Van Beuningen represented the States-General in negotiations at Cologne. He was joined by Pieter de Groot, formerly De Witt's personal envoy, who returned from Antwerp where he had been living with Pieter de la Court and other exiled Republican partisans.[17] It was during this time that Spinoza undertook to speak with the French commander. His mission was in all likelihood one incident in the concerted effort for peace which Republicans were making in the spring and summer of 1673.

Republican hopes for peace were, however, blasted once more. The war continued, and Spinoza's own retirement deepened. The intellectuals of the Republican party were dispersed. The economist Pieter de la Court, De Witt's collaborator, remained in Antwerp where he had fled after De Witt's murder.[18] Even Sir William Temple, the English ambassador who had labored fruitlessly with De Witt to construct a durable peace, was in retreat. A feeling of impotence and resignation came upon many European liberals with the murder of John de Witt. Temple wrote sadly to the Dutch historian De Wicquefort late in 1672 that he now "had no share at all in public affairs; but, on the contrary, I am wholly sunk in my gardening, and the quiet of a private life; which, I thank God, agrees with me as well as the splendor of the world. . . ." [19] De Wicquefort, unable to accommodate himself to political inactivity, was soon to spend several miserable years in various prisons.

Early in 1673, Spinoza received an offer of a professorship of philosophy from the University of Heidelberg. He was not, however, to be tempted from his retirement. This post might well have provided him with a public forum for his philosophy, but Spinoza declined the invitation. He replied that the duties of a professor would leave him no time for developing his philosophy. Moreover, he was dubious concerning an academic freedom which was contingent on his not disturbing the established religion. "I think I do not know," wrote Spinoza, "within what limits that freedom of philosophy ought to be confined in order to avoid the appearance of wishing to disturb the publicly established Religion. For Schisms arise not so much from an ardent love of religion as from men's various dispositions, or the love of contradiction, through which they are wont to distort and to condemn all things, even those that have been correctly stated." Then Spinoza stated his own personal experience: "I have already experienced these things while leading a private and solitary life, much more then are they to be feared after I shall have risen to this degree of dignity." His refusal of the offer, said Spinoza, was motivated by the "love of peace, which I believe I can obtain to a certain extent, merely by refraining from public lectures." [20] Peace, solitude, withdrawal were now the keynote of Spinoza's life.

The offer of the Heidelberg professorship was more than a routine academic proposal, for it had unusual political overtones. It was made on behalf of Karl Ludwig, the Elector Palatine. Karl Ludwig was no ordinary German princeling. He had spent the greater part of the twenty-seven years of his youth in Holland, where he had imbibed the most advanced political and philosophic ideas. Then Karl Ludwig returned to his native country to apply these ideas. In 1652 he made the first experiment in free trade and free industry in all German history at Mannheim. Tolls, rates, and guilds were abolished; wage regulation and restrictions on the hiring of labor were abrogated. The Palatinate had been devastated by the Thirty Years' War, and Karl Ludwig tried hard to attract Dutch capital, to revive trade, and to encourage immigration. Together with economic freedom, he brought religious freedom. Among his subjects Calvinists, Anabaptists, Lutherans, Catholics, and Jews dwelt amicably side by side, without hindrance. In 1652, Karl Ludwig reopened the University of Heidelberg.[21]

An English traveler, John Ray, has left us a description of the University of Heidelberg in the year 1672, together with a reprint of the catalogue of the university for that period. Among its faculty was a Jacob Israel, Professor Ordinarius of Physiology, who was elected Rector by a majority vote of the Senate.[22] To this distinction, a Jew could rise in the university supported by Karl Ludwig. The noted authority in international law, Samuel Puffendorf, was also among its faculty. There were sixteen professors, all of whom were appointed for life, with the exception of the professors of philosophy who held tenure only for one year. Presumably Spinoza's appointment would have been on the basis of annual tenure, not life. It was a small university, with an average student body of seventy-five. Spinoza's teaching duties would certainly not have been onerous. Karl Ludwig was a scholar, a master of six languages, and, as Ray testified, greatly beloved of his subjects.[23] Yet Spinoza chose to reject this proposed appointment.

The offer of the Heidelberg professorship, we thus perceive, came from a prince whose views on questions of economic and religious freedom coincided with those of John de Witt, Pieter de la Court, and Spinoza. Karl Ludwig would have made a good Dutch Republican. No doubt he shared the feelings of his fellow liberals upon the murder of John de Witt and the debacle of Dutch liberalism. The academic offer to Spinoza was made a few months after the shattering events of 1672. It was the gesture of comradeship of a liberal ruler to a distinguished liberal philosopher, the offer of a post as a refugee professor-in-exile to a Republican who like his fellows might soon be compelled to flee his native land. But Spinoza would not now surrender his solitary life. Was there much to look for from people? He could take an inventory of mass democracy in action: his own excommunication, Koerbagh dying broken in jail, De Witt lynched and torn to bits, the shrieking mob, men like Pieter de la Court in exile. He turned inward upon himself. As Colerus tells us: "Thus he spent the remaining part of his Life in the House of his last Landlord, which was somewhat above five years and a half. He was very careful to cast up his Accounts every quarter; which he did, that he might spend neither more nor less than what he could spend every year. And he would say sometimes to the people of the House that he was like the Serpent, who forms a Circle with his Tail in his Mouth; to denote that he had nothing left at the years end."[24] The closed circle, self-sufficient unto itself, had a strange significance for Spinoza. His seal, which he affixed to letters, was likewise an oval ring, containing a rose, the initials B.D.S., and the word "caute" [beware]. The image of the serpent, which in Spinoza spoke "beware," was the projective symbol of a man who had come to mistrust his fellow men, who stamped his mistrust and withdrawal upon his correspondence.

Meanwhile, Spinoza spent his days in completing the *Ethics*. Late in the summer of 1675, he was ready to send his book to the press. But Calvinist theologians made a stir against Spinoza before the Prince of Orange, and Spinoza chose to suppress his book. Reaction was in the ascendancy, the protective hand of John de Witt was gone, and silence seemed the way of prudence. As Spinoza wrote to Oldenburg, the Secretary of the English Royal Society, in September 1675:

> . . . I was setting out to Amsterdam with the intention of getting printed the work about which I had written to you. While I was engaged on this matter, a rumour was spread everywhere that a book of mine about God was in the press, and that in it I endeavored to show that there is no God. The rumour was believed by many. Therefore certain Theologians (perhaps the authors of this rumour) seized the opportunity of bringing complaints against me before the Prince and the Magistrates; moreover the dull-witted Cartesians, because they are believed to be in my favour, and in order to free themselves from this suspicion, continued and even now continue to denounce my opinions and writings everywhere. When I heard all this from certain trustworthy men, who also said that the Theologians were intriguing against me everywhere, I decided to postpone the publication I was preparing, until I saw how the matter turned out, and I also intended to inform you what plan I would then follow. But the business seems to grow daily worse, and I am yet uncertain what to do.

As the reaction persisted, the irenic motive in Spinoza diminished. He was less inclined to conciliate his readers or to seek a common denominator between his own philosophy and Christianity. He now affirmed bluntly that Christianity was just another superstition, founded on ignorance, and that he doubted whether monarchs would ever permit measures to eradicate superstition. The Prince of Orange, as monarchs generally, was the natural ally of theologians. Late in 1675 Spinoza wrote to Oldenburg:

> I regard it as the chief difference between Religion and Superstition, that the latter has ignorance, the former has wisdom, for its foundation. This, I believe, is the reason why Christians are distinguished from the rest of mankind, not by faith, or charity, or the other fruits of the Holy Spirit, but simply by their opinion. For, like all others, they make a stand on miracles alone, that is, on ignorance, which is the source of all wickedness; and so they turn their faith, even if it is true, into a superstition. I very much doubt whether Kings will ever allow the application of a remedy for this evil.

Spinoza, excommunicated by the Jews, had found no spiritual home among the Gentiles. Indeed, he remained spiritually excommunicate among the Christians. Their philosophies differed on ultimates: "I say, in the first place," he wrote, "that I hold an opinion about God and Nature very different from that which Modern Christians are wont to defend. For I maintain that God is, as they say, the immanent cause of all things, but not the transeunt cause. . . . Like Paul, and perhaps also like all ancient philosophers, though in another way, I assert that all things live and move in God; and I would dare to say that I agree also with all the ancient Hebrews as far as it is possible to surmise from their traditions, even if these have become corrupt in many ways." [25] When challenged to state plainly his "opinion of Jesus Christ, the Redeemer of the World, and the only Mediator for mankind, and of his Incarnation and Atonement," Spinoza replied that he found the doctrine of the Incarnation meaningless: "as to the doctrine which certain Churches add to these, namely, that God assumed human nature, I expressly warned them that I do not understand what they say. Indeed, to confess the truth, they seem to me to speak no less absurdly than if some one were to tell me that a circle assumed the nature of a square." [26] There was no supernaturalism in Spinoza's conception of Jesus, whom he regarded simply as a man in whom wisdom was most manifest. One could use the terminology of "the eternal son of

God," but it was a metaphorical way of referring to "the eternal wisdom of God," which is manifest in all human minds in proportion as their ideas are adequate, and, of all men, the most in Jesus.[27] In this sense, the knowledge of the nature of things was a participation in the Spirit of Christ.[28] But Spinoza made it clear that he was not among the Christians.

Why Did the Liberal Republic Fall?

The manuscript of the *Ethics* resided in his desk, awaiting some moment when it might be given to the world. Meanwhile, Spinoza meditated on the significance of the fall of John de Witt and the liberal Republicans. Why had the most scientific statesman of Europe failed? What were the weaknesses in the Dutch Republican form of government? And what could a political philosopher have to offer in an age of reaction? Could political science throw light on what was to be done to save the values of free men in an age of repression? It appeared likely in 1676 that a monarchy would be permanently established in the Netherlands. The advocate of democracy was no longer welcome in those times, and paeans concerning the liberalism of Holland could no longer come naturally to Spinoza's lips. Nevertheless, liberalism could still fight a rear-guard battle. It could endeavor to permeate any form of government, whether it was monarchy, aristocracy, or democracy. The problem was to safeguard the values of freedom by indicating the means whereby any governmental form might be imbued with a liberal spirit. Spinoza sought to apply his analysis, therefore, to every political form, and to solve the problem, under whatever given conditions, of how to maximize liberty. There was no use mourning the downfall of the liberal party, no use in bewailing the concrete demonstration that political Utopia was alien to the nature of men. The political scientist must work with the human animal as he finds him, and build his science accordingly. In Spinoza's scheme, sorrow was no virtue, scoffing was a weakness, and, whatever the fortunes of liberal statesmen, there was a God who never failed.

No longer was there any occasion for arraying Biblical texts against the Calvinist theologians. When the political propagandist of the *Tractatus Theologico-Politicus* perished with the murder of De Witt, the secular political scientist took his place, and Spinoza, dropping the theological idiom of popular persuasion, began his *Tractatus Politicus.* The prophets had used the theological idioms and metaphors of their time, Spinoza believed, because that was the only way in which they could reach the masses with their message. He too had used the Biblical idiom when he pleaded the cause of the Republic and John de Witt with masses who were enthralled by Calvinist doctrine. But now Spinoza's political analysis ceased to argue from Biblical precept. His authorities were henceforth realists, the men without illusions —Hobbes and Machiavelli.[29] Even his classification of governments was altered. It was straightforwardly an analysis of aristocracy, monarchy, and democracy; "theocracy," the "slogan-word" with which he had once tried to confute the Calvinist theologians out of their own mouths, faded from the scene. And Spinoza's whole discussion took the form of a dispassionate analysis of how to ensure a stable government, how to found a stable monarchy, democracy, or aristocracy.

During the year 1676, while Spinoza was at work on the *Tractatus Politicus,* he wrote to a friend: "Of this Treatise six chapters are already finished." The completed sixth chapter dealt with "the way in which a Monarchical Government ought to be constituted, so as not to sink into a Tyranny." [30] He was evidently writing with ease. During the next months, he finished the chapter on aristocracy. He had given his political testament to free men living in the age of monarchical despotism and had written his analysis of the failure of the Dutch aristocratic Republic. He began his chapter on democracy. Did he see his way through to a faith in the possibilities of democracy? Or did he come to a dead halt, unable to affirm that democratic faith which had animated the *Tractatus Theologico-Politicus?* Did he stop before an insoluble, insuperable problem, baffled by the mob, by the shadows of the slaves dancing around the mangled body of John de Witt? The fire that had burned within Spinoza had become private; the urge to enkindle others was overwhelmed; and he sought a freedom which was unassailable because it was purely intellectual. Only in strange glimmers, such as his painting of

himself in the mantle of the revolutionist Masaniello, did the
buried fire leap to the surface. Death intervened on February 21,
1677.

Spinoza's last treatise began with a note of disillusionment, a
farewell to Utopia. "Men," said Spinoza, "are of necessity liable
to passions," "prone to vengeance more than mercy": the power
of ethics and religion has little persuasion over the passions. "It
avails, indeed, in the hour of death, when disease has subdued
the very passions, and man lies inert, or in temples, where men
hold no traffic, but least of all, where it is most needed, in the
law-court or the palace." Reason can make a contribution toward
restraining the irrational impulses, but its road is "very steep."
No society of men will be enrolled under reason's aegis: "such as
persuade themselves, that the multitude or men distracted by
politics can ever be induced to live according to the bare dictate
of reason, must be dreaming of the poetic golden age, or of a
stage-play." There is no novel political form which reason can
discover which will bring order into men's lives. At the end,
Spinoza's weariness was akin to Ecclesiastes'—"The thing that
hath been, it is that which shall be; and that which is done is
that which shall be done: and there is no new thing under the
sun." So Spinoza wrote: ". . . I am fully persuaded that experience has revealed all conceivable sorts of commonwealth, which
are consistent with men's living in unity, and likewise the means
by which the multitude may be guided or kept within fixed
bounds. So that I do not believe we can by meditation discover in
this matter anything not yet tried and ascertained." Practical
politicians, he added, "are men of the utmost acuteness, or, if you
like of great cunning or craft," and it is extremely unlikely that
the political philosopher can conceive anything which has not
been long known to the political managers. Philosophers, said
Spinoza, "have never conceived a theory of politics, which could
be turned to use"; "chimera" or "Utopia" are the loci of their
doctrines. Statesmen, on the other hand, have written wisely concerning politics; "they had experience for their mistress, they
taught nothing that was inconsistent with practice." [31] Ideologues
may denounce the practical statesmen, but it is upon the latter's
experience that Spinoza would base his political philosophy.

Why, then, did John de Witt fail in his efforts to establish a stable, liberal aristocratic republic? The basic problem of aristocracy, according to Spinoza, was to constitute a governing class which would be numerous enough to provide a solid foundation —"to secure the stability of an aristocracy, it is necessary to consider the proportionate size of the actual dominion in order to determine the minimum number of patricians." According to Spinoza, De Witt failed to solve this problem of constitutional stability. De Witt did away with the monarchical aspects of the Dutch constitution, but did not realize that an aristocratic republican dominion requires its own firm foundation. Governmental forms are like organic systems; and if one part be changed, so likewise must its related parts be altered. From the failure of De Witt, Spinoza insisted, one cannot infer that the aristocratic republic is not a viable mode of government. De Witt's dominion collapsed because he had not provided his aristocratic republic with a sufficiently large governing class. Aristocracy is the rule of the few, but the few can be too few:

> But if any one retorts, that the dominion of the Dutch has not long endured without a count or one to fill his place, let him have this reply, that the Dutch thought, that to maintain their liberty it was enough to abandon their count, and to behead the body of their dominion, but never thought of remoulding it, and left its limbs, just as they had been first constituted, so that the country of Holland has remained without a count, and the actual dominion has lasted without the name. And it is no wonder that most of its subjects have not known, with whom the authority of the dominion lay. And even had this been otherwise, yet those who actually held dominion were too few to govern the multitude and suppress their powerful adversaries. Whence it has come to pass, that the latter have been able to plot against them with impunity, and at last to overthrow them. And so the sudden overthrow of the said republic has not arisen from a useless waste of time in debates, but from the misinformed state of the said dominion and the fewness of its rulers.[32]

This is a far cry from the Spinoza of the *Tractatus Theologico-Politicus* who had deprecated the role of the counts and had referred to the efforts of the last prince to usurp sovereignty. The history of the Netherlands seemed henceforth to Spinoza to testify to a monarchical bent. Now it turned out that the Prince of Orange was essentially a monarch, and that the Republic of the United Provinces was contrary to the traditions and history of its people. Apart from the ambiguity of tradition, however, there was "the fewness of its rulers" in the Dutch Republic, and this was evidently primary in the fall of De Witt. Spinoza and Sir William Temple, we may observe, shared similar views concerning the causes of the Republican failure. "Of instability and changes of government arrived by narrowing their bottoms, which are the consent and concurrence of the people's affections and interests," Temple wrote in his retirement, "all stories and ages afford continual example." [33] The base of the political system had to be kept broad if the superstructure was to be solid. "The two freshest examples" of this principle, said Temple, "may be drawn from the revolution of England in the year sixty, and of Holland in seventy-two." Holland had prospered for twenty years under the rule of the popular magistrates. There had been "a perpetual success of their affairs, by the growth of their trade, riches, and power at home. . . : yet the general humour of kindness in the people to their own form of government grew with the age and virtues of the young Prince, so as to raise the prospect of some unavoidable revolutions among them. . . . And . . . meeting with the conjunctive of a foreign invasion, it broke out into so curious a rage of the people . . . as ended in the blood of their chief ministers; in the displacing all that were suspected to be of their party throughout the government. . . ." [34]

The ruling class of the Dutch Republic, besides being few, had, in Spinoza's judgment, followed an unrealistic diplomacy. John de Witt had erred on the side of rationality. When Sir William Temple, scholar and lover of books, arrived at The Hague in January 1668 with orders to negotiate a treaty of alliance with John de Witt, he and the Dutch statesman were taken with each other. Both were free men, believers in reason, both hoped for the peace of Europe. From the efforts of these two friends was born the Triple Alliance, which they conceived to be the cornerstone of European concord.[35] Great Britain, Sweden, and the Netherlands were joined in 1668 in a pact of friendship and a defensive alliance against aggression by France. The plans for aggrandizement which the French king, Louis XIV, nourished, seemed checked once and for all by a treaty of collective security. To Temple, architect of peace, John de Witt addressed words of praise on April 27, 1668: "All Christendom owes you the glory of having first disposed the King of Great Britain's mind to so strict an alliance between His Majesty and this State, for the universal good and peace of Europe." [36]

The English ambassador doubted privately that diplomacy could halt the French drive toward war. Temple knew that an absolute state, which oppresses its people, often tries to direct their aggressive energies against foreign nations: "it may perhaps be necessary for France," he wrote in 1671, "(from respects within) to have some war or other in pursuit abroad, which may amuse the nation, and keep them from reflecting upon their condition at home, hard and uneasy to all but such as are in charge, or in pay from the court." He reflected that "the common people of France are as little considerable in the government as the children; so that the nobles and the soldiers may in a manner be esteemed the nation; whose interest and hopes carry them all to war." And Temple was aware that France would use every means "to break the confidence or force of that triple alliance, which alone seems to bound their prospect. . . ." But John de Witt and the Republican party placed their confidence in diplomatic security. They pursued their trade and commerce vigorously, kept their navy in good shape, and relied on English support. The Dutch Republicans tended to view politics as the outcome of calculations founded on economic self-interest. A commercial fallacy began to pervade their political foresight. France, they argued, would lose immensely if war came, "by the stop of their wines, salts, and other commodities." [37] Their strategy took on a purely defensive cast; they would in the last resort halt the enemy by opening the dikes, that terrible policy whereby, as Temple said, "the Dutch found no other way of saving their country but by losing it."

The Dutch Republicans, in their rational calculations, overlooked the irrational factor in human history. Charles II, king of

England, Catholic in his sympathies, was prepared to bargain his policy for money; he was amenable, moreover, to the persuasions of mistresses. The English monarch was induced by such means to forswear the Triple Alliance and enter into secret treaty with the French king. De Witt ignored the warnings of astute advisers and chose to rely upon the assurances of his fellow philosopher, the English ambassador, Sir William Temple. The latter himself was but an unknowing pawn in the pending war, an added means for deceiving De Witt. Then war came. As Temple said: "No clap of thunder in a fair frosty day could more astonish the world, than our declaration of war against Holland in 1672. . . . The Dutch could never be possessed with a belief that we were in earnest till the blow was given. . . . The Dutch had made no provision for their defence either at home or abroad. . . ." [38]

What was Spinoza's judgment of the diplomacy of John de Witt? The great statesman had placed an unswerving faith in a treaty, in a document. In Spinoza's eyes, this faith had been naive. De Witt had forgotten the first principles of international relations, that nations are each other's enemies, and that treaties bind them only so long as their self-interest dictates. To Spinoza, it could only seem that De Witt had been misled by his own lofty character to forget that no nation would consider itself bound by a scrap of paper. Spinoza wrote:

> . . . Two commonwealths are naturally enemies. For men in the state of nature are enemies. . . . Accordingly, if one commonwealth wishes to make war on another, and employ extreme measures to make that other dependent on itself, it may lawfully make the attempt. . . .
>
> . . . Every commonwealth has the right to break its contract, whenever it chooses, and cannot be said to act treacherously or perfidiously in breaking its word, as soon as the motive of hope or fear is removed. For every contracting party was on equal terms in this respect, that whichever could first free itself of fear should be independent, and make use of its independence after its own mind. . . . If then a commonwealth complains that it has been deceived, it cannot properly blame the bad faith of another contracting commonwealth, but only its own folly in having entrusted its own welfare to another party, that was independent, and had for its highest law the welfare of its own dominion.[39]

It had been De Witt's "own folly" that he entrusted the well-being of his country to another party. The realism of Spinoza's political judgment was not designed to satisfy a cynical mood or a sadistic bent for stripping things bare; it was the outcome of his conviction that a durable foundation for the values of free men can be founded only on realities.

The cataclysm of 1672 tended to make rational men into tempered political realists. Temple's political philosophy, for instance, went through an evolution much like Spinoza's. When Temple narrated the death of his friend, John de Witt, it was also his own story—the failure of a mission. As did Spinoza, Temple placed De Witt among the benefactors of humanity, who like the Gracchi of ancient Rome had been rewarded by his countrymen with ingratitude and death.[40] Like Spinoza, Temple was driven to ponder the cruelty of men, the "ultimi barbarorum." "Are the Dutch a people cruel by character?" Temple asked. Their barbarities in the East Indies were akin to their lynching of De Witt. But Temple, like Spinoza, came to terms with men's cruelty and saw human degradation as the inevitable outcome of causal laws and social circumstances. "But this action of that people may be attributed to the misfortune of their country; and is so unlike the appearance of their customs and dispositions, living, as I saw them, under the orders and laws of a quiet and settled state; that one must confess mankind to be a very various creature, and none to be known, that has not been seen in his rage, as well as his drink." [41] Much in Spinoza's fashion, Temple tried to reconcile himself to manifestations of human evil with the intellectual recognition that man was "a very various creature."

Spinoza, as the philosopher of political defeat, sought to transmute evil by an intellectual understanding of its necessary place in the infinite system of things. His *Tractatus Politicus* began with an affirmation: "I have looked upon passions, such as love, hatred, anger, envy, ambition, pity, and other perturbations of the mind, not in the light of vices of human nature, but as properties just as pertinent to it, as are heat, cold, storm, thunder, and the like to the nature of the atmosphere, which phenomena, though inconvenient, are yet necessary, and have fixed causes, by means of which we endeavor to understand their nature, and the mind has just as much pleasure in viewing them aright, as in knowing such things as flatter the senses." [42] Political science, for Spinoza and Temple alike, became a work of intellectual catharsis, in which evil, by being understood, was assimilated into divine necessity. As political scientists, they inquired into the necessities and uniformities of political phenomena and urged a political practice chastened in that understanding.[43] Temple, like Spinoza, made his farewell to Utopia: "The republic of Plato, the principality of Hobbes, the rotation of Oceana, have all been indicted and found guilty of many faults, or of great infirmities." For him, too, as for Spinoza, the old established ways were henceforth recognized as part of the inevitable scheme of things, in which it was the better part of wisdom to acquiesce: "The first safety of princes and states lies in avoiding all councils or designs of innovation, in ancient and established forms and laws, especially those concerning liberty, property, and religion. . . ." The differences between modes of government were now less important than the status of free men under them: "those are generally the best governments where the best men govern. . . ." [44] Political science was no longer a manual for reformers; it was a handbook for social technicians.

Theory of a Commercial Aristocracy

Spinoza's analysis of the problems of the Dutch Republic was set forth in detail in his chapter on aristocracy. There he elaborated on the conditions for stability of an aristocratic republic which De Witt had overlooked. To prepare himself for this analysis, Spinoza studied especially the constitutions of the Genoese and Venetian republics. This choice of background material was significant, for Genoa and Venice, like the United Provinces, were governments not of a landed aristocracy, but of a commercial aristocracy. John de Witt had himself proposed that the Dutch Republic should consider plans for constitutional reform based on the Venetian model. The conviction was widespread throughout the Netherlands and England that Venice had solved the problem of how to establish a stable aristocratic republic in which the commercial middle class held political power.

Writers like Harrington and James Howell believed that the Venetian constitution had lasted unchanged for a thousand years, without decay, that the Venetian republic was an "immortal Commonwealth," "forever incapable of corruption." Radical religious and political leaders in England disliked this adulation of the Venetian government. Baxter, for instance, in his *Holy Commonwealth* inveighed against Harrington for his admiration of Venice, "where Popery ruleth and whoredom abounds." [45] But Harrington was fascinated by the balanced or "equal" governmental system of the Venetian republic, and Spinoza was similarly impressed by the administrative devices of the Venetians. Spinoza especially admired the Venetian use of the secret ballot, with its contribution toward ensuring equality among all the members of the patrician class, as well as its promotion of efficiency. "But that all the patricians may have equal authority in making decrees and electing the ministers of the dominion, and that speed and expedition in all matters may be possible, the order observed by the Venetians is altogether to be approved, . . . every patrician signifies by ballot his opinion, approving or rejecting the candidate in question, so that it is not afterwards known, who voted in this or that sense."

Spinoza explicitly recognized that the wealthy were the ruling class in a stable aristocratic republic, "the patricians, who are always chosen from the rich, bear the largest share of the weight of the commonwealth." To preserve peace, to guarantee that the republic's rulers would never be misled into militarist aggressions, Spinoza proposed to tie the self-interest of the senators to the national commercial interest. "The emoluments of the senators should be of such a kind, that their profit is greater from peace than from war. And therefore let there be awarded to them a hundredth or a fiftieth part of the merchandise exported abroad from the dominion, or imported into it from abroad. For we cannot doubt, that by this means they will, as far as they can, preserve peace, and never desire to protract war. And from this duty not even the senators themselves, if any of them are merchants, ought to be exempt; for such an immunity cannot be granted without great risk to trade, as I think no one is ignorant."

Spinoza urged, furthermore, that the patricians, the governing class, should not be a hereditary caste. He was aware that a hereditary governing group would tend, as families died out, to grow ever smaller in numbers. He was concerned to avoid the contingency that "a few families hold the right of government in their hands." He therefore proposed that the patricians should be an open élite, that its proportion to the population at large should be fixed at the ratio of one to fifty, and then when vacancies in the patriciate occurred, they be filled by elective co-option of new persons into the patrician class. In this fashion, Spinoza felt that De Witt could have provided himself with a firmer and more numerous body of supporters.

Aristocracies decline, according to Spinoza, because of the workings of a tendency toward diminishing oligarchy. His reasoning was like that of Pareto and Mosca, theorists of the circulation of the élite, and his method for ensuring aristocratic stability was to keep an élite open in sufficient proportions to new talent. "For families often die out, and some persons are disqualified for their crimes, and a great many are driven by domestic poverty to neglect affairs of state, and meanwhile the more powerful aim at nothing else, but to govern alone; and thus the dominion is gradually limited to a few, and at length by faction to one." History is a graveyard of aristocracies, Pareto said, but Spinoza believed that social science could illumine the way to a stable aristocratic republic. "For a proportion ought to be maintained between the multitude and the patricians, so that with the increase of the former the number of the latter should be raised. And this proportion ought to be about fifty to one. . . . But there is no danger except in the smallness of their number." [46] If a state requires one hundred "first-rate men," able administrators, it should have a patrician class of five thousand, said Spinoza. For it is a psychological fact, he argued, that in a group of one hundred, only two or three will excel in vigor of mind, and he therefore made the ratio of one to fifty central in his political planning.

A sound aristocratic republic, Spinoza insisted, must rigorously exclude the lower classes from any share in the sovereignty. This was Spinoza's reply to a strong undercurrent of opinion at this time in the Netherlands which desired a reform of the aristocratic republic in a democratic direction. On September 7, 1673, this agitation reached an outspoken level of intensity. A meeting of citizens in Amsterdam, which took place under hectic circumstances, demanded the removal from office of all the friends of De Witt, the restoration of the "ancient rights" of citizens in the election of magistrates, the maintenance of the privileges of the guilds, and reforms in the government of the city and militia. In true democratic style, the citizens circulated a petition which embodied their demands. To appease the democratic agitation, some magistrates were deprived of office, but the Prince of Orange had no intention of abetting a democratic movement; the citizens' disaffection subsided after a few months. The democratic agitation was always prone to take a lawless, violent form; the people came near to plundering the house of Admiral De Ruyter, because he was De Witt's friend, and the bravest of the Dutch sea captains had to be taken into the prince's protective custody in order to safeguard his life.[47]

Spinoza now looked upon the democratic agitation with a saturnine eye. He was repelled by the mob, its cruelty, its irrationality, and was no longer carried away into moving phrases on behalf of democracy. The aristocratic republic, Spinoza held, should never consult with the multitude; "the latter is excluded from giving its advice or its vote." It is a defect in the dominion of the patricians if they yield to the political demands of workmen, commoners, and guildsmen: "we cannot doubt that the dominion rests the less with the patricians, the more rights the commons assert for themselves, such as those which the corporations of artisans in Lower Germany, commonly called Guilds, generally possess."[48] The struggle between burghers and guildsmen for the right to elect burgomasters and town councils had been for several hundred years the dominant fact in Dutch municipal life. The guilds were progressively shorn of their rights; they had created the office of burgomaster only to lose it to the encroachments of the rising wealthy class. As late as 1652, however, the guilds of Dordrecht, angered by their grievances, threw the town into an uproar.[49] But Spinoza refused to recognize the rights of the guildsmen.

The sovereignty of the patriciate should be absolute; the

foundations of an aristocracy, said Spinoza, "should rest on the sole will and power of the supreme council, so that it may be as independent as possible, and be in no danger from the multitude." The common people, Spinoza argued, need not fear oppression under such a dominion, for the patrician class would be so large that it would be immune to passions, and more amenable to the persuasive force of reason. Strangely enough, Spinoza seemed to overlook the self-interest and unreason which can enthrall the councils of aristocrats.

The Spinoza of the *Tractatus Theologico-Politicus* had spoken with fervor of Amsterdam as the city in which men of all peoples and creeds commingled; he had looked upon his native city as the cradle of liberty and equality. The Spinoza of the *Tractatus Politicus,* on the contrary, meditated soberly that the democratic spirit cannot withstand the passions that arise with the coming of foreigners. Democracy seemed to him now a tender plant, which required the soil of a frontier land and the seed of a homogenous people. Democracy and equality prevail "when a given multitude in search of fresh territories, has found and cultivated them," but the original pioneer "thinks it unfair, that the foreigners that join them should have equal right in the dominion with themselves, who sought it by their own toil, and won it at the price of their own blood." Democracy is thereby transformed into aristocracy. For as the waves of immigration continue, "the multitude is augmented by the influx of foreigners, who gradually acquire the national manners, until at last they are distinguished by no other difference than that of incapacity to get office; and while their number daily increases, that of the citizens, on the contrary, is by many causes diminished." Dutch democracy had been transformed into an aristocracy, Spinoza held, in accordance with the laws of political sociology. "I am fully persuaded," he wrote, "that most aristocracies were formerly democracies"; successive waves of immigration, in his opinion, were the causes which undermined democracy.

To guarantee, however, that all subjects, despite the aristocratic rule, should feel they have a stake in their country, Spinoza advocated a wide distribution of property. Otherwise, "the subjects having no part in the dominion would easily, in bad times, all forsake their cities, if they could carry where they pleased what goods they possess." The many small landowners should furthermore pay "every year an aliquot part of the year's produce, etc. as is done in Holland." [50] De Witt had been criticized by his political opponents for the high tax burden which he imposed on his countrymen, and, indeed, the excises were so severe that Temple remarked "that I heard it observed at Amsterdam, that, when in a tavern, a certain dish of fish is eaten with the usual sauce, above thirty several excises are paid for what is necessary to that small service." [51] To which Spinoza answered as befitted a Republican economist: "What nation," he asked rhetorically, "ever had to pay so many and so heavy taxes as the Dutch? Yet it not only has not been exhausted, but, on the contrary, has been so mighty by its wealth, that all envied its good fortune." [52] An aristocratic republic which was loyal to its people's economic interest could count, Spinoza believed, on the loyalty of its citizens.

Spinoza, however, with the wisdom of hindsight, parted company with the military policy of De Witt. The Grand Pensionary had been opposed to the hiring of mercenaries, and Spinoza indeed had agreed with him when he wrote the *Tractatus Theologico-Politicus*. As a consequence of De Witt's fear of militarism, the Dutch army had been allowed to fall into neglect. Now Spinoza, changing his mind upon this question, endorsed the enrollment of mercenaries; "it is certain," he wrote, "that it makes no difference to the laws or fundamental principles of this dominion, that the military be formed of others besides subjects." At the same time, Spinoza paid tribute to the policy of De Witt which had enabled men from the humblest social class to rise to the highest commands of the Netherlands forces. Admiral De Ruyter, for instance, had been born of working people, the son of a brewer's journeyman.[53] The commoners, Spinoza affirmed, give courage to the republic's arms, but it is worth while to have mercenaries at its disposal for unexpected events:

> For it is certain that those fight with peculiar valour who fight for altar and hearth. Whence, also, it is manifest that those are no less wrong, who lay down that military commanders, tribunes,

centurions, etc., should be chosen from among the patricians only.
For with what courage will those soldiers fight who are deprived
of all hope of gaining glory and advancement? But, on the other
hand, to establish a law forbidding the patricians to hire foreign
soldiers, when circumstances require it, whether to defend themselves and suppress seditions, or for any other reason, besides
being inconsiderate, would also be repugnant to the supreme
right of the patricians. . . .[54]

In effect, Spinoza affirmed that it was an error on De Witt's
part to have allowed the army to become weak and disorganized.

Constitution for the Dictatorship of the Commercial Aristocracy

Spinoza's outline of a constitution for an aristocratic republic was designed to safeguard the control of the patrician
class, and to provide checks against any monarchist or democratic
tendencies. The council of all patricians in the city was to be
assembled at fixed times to choose the ministers and to enact
laws. Among the patricians themselves, equality, he urged, was
to "be as far as possible maintained," and young men were to
be excluded from the patriciate in order to prevent a few
families from monopolizing political power. Spinoza specifically
disapproved of any effort "to create for the council a ruler or
prince, either for life, as the Venetians, or for a time, as the
Genoese," for with a royal executive, "we cannot doubt but that
the dominion thereby approaches the monarchical form. . . ."[55]
Spinoza thus gave his approval to the prolonged efforts of De
Witt to deprive the house of Orange of its traditional prerogatives. The Edict of Exclusion had been a sound attempt to
stabilize the structure of the Dutch Republic. Spinoza did not
attribute the downfall of De Witt to his actions against the
Prince of Orange, and, in this respect, he differed with contemporaries like Temple.[56] He was aware of the people's resentment against De Witt for his anti-Orangist outlook, but
believed that the Grand Pensionary should have pressed on
with further actions to consolidate the power of the patriciate.

To perform those supervisory functions customarily fulfilled by a prince, Spinoza proposed the formation of what he called a college of syndics—a group of patricians subordinate to the supreme council, "whose only duty should be to see that the constitution, as far as it concerns the councils and ministers of the dominion, be kept unbroken." Spinoza, moreover, urged that the syndics should have at their disposal their own security forces: "some portion of the soldiery must be assigned to it and be subject to its orders." The syndics were to be a fairly numerous body; once more Spinoza invoked the proportion which he regarded as psychologically sound—the syndics should be two per cent of the patricians, the same ratio which obtained between the patriciate and the multitude at large. Evidently Spinoza felt that the Liberal Republicans would have had a much better chance of retaining power if they had had such a guardian group over the constitution. It would have been the task of the syndics to make it treasonable for anyone to propose a change in the republican order: "if anyone in the supreme council raise a question about any fundamental law, as of prolonging the command of any general of an army, or of diminishing the number of patricians, or the like, he is guilty of treason, and not only is he to be condemned to death, and his goods confiscated, but some sign of his punishment is to remain visible in public for an eternal memorial of the event." In other words, a republican college of syndics would have punished as traitors those who moved and enacted the legislation which prolonged for life the command of the Prince of Orange over the Dutch forces. What Spinoza proposes in his constitution can be simply described: *it is a dictatorship of the commercial aristocracy*. All his constitutional safeguards, all his conditions for the stability of an aristocratic republic reduce themselves to this fact.

The syndics and the council of the patricians were to act, in Spinoza's plan, as bicameral legislative bodies; "no law can be repealed nor new law passed, unless first the college of syndics, and then three-fourths or four-fifths of the supreme council agree thereto." In addition, however, Spinoza proposed as a kind of permanent committee of public safety that a group of ten or more syndics sit every day "to hear the complaints and secret accusations of the commons against the ministers, and to look after the accusers, if circumstances require, and to summon the supreme council even before the appointed time, if any of them judge that there is danger in the delay." Lastly, Spinoza proposed the establishment of a senate, composed of four hundred members, that is, one-twelfth of the patricians, all of whom should be at least fifty years of age. The senate was not to have the power to impose new taxes, which was reserved to the supreme council. But foreign affairs, as with the United States Senate, were to be its especial province; the fortification of the cities, the conferring of military commissions, the decisions for foreign embassies were among its designated duties. But Spinoza was somewhat vague as to the senate's duties; at first he assigned it powers of taxation but then withdrew them, and he also denied to the senate the right to appoint ambassadors. The function of the senate was to be largely honorary, as were later European upper legislative chambers; the senate was to provide a goal to arouse men's ambitions, "so all the patricians will always have a great hope of gaining the rank of senator or syndic." In all ultimate decisions, Spinoza insisted, "all matters are to be referred to the supreme council, which in any way alter the existing state of things, as the deciding on peace and war." [57]

The Venetian constitution was undoubtedly the principal model for Spinoza's aristocratic republic.[58] The Great Council of Venice, like Spinoza's supreme council of patricians, was during most of its history a self-perpetuating oligarchy. Like Spinoza's patriciate, its membership included about two per cent of the population; as an aristocracy, therefore, it was relatively larger in proportion to the population than was, for instance, the French nobility, and it took care of Spinoza's fears concerning the fewness of rulers. The Great Council, like Spinoza's counterpart, had the right to appoint and elect officers, and in times of crisis, its vote determined public policy. The Venetian constitution, during its development, came to include a Council of Ten, which functioned as a permanent committee of public safety; it seems to have been the model for Spinoza's guardian committee of ten syndics. The Venetian Senate was an ancient, honored body; its members were elected for one year by the Great Council, and were nearly three hundred in number; the Senate's concerns were primarily with foreign policy, navigation, and commerce. The senate in Spinoza's scheme was likewise to be elected by the supreme council for one year, and its tasks were to be precisely those of the Venetian Senate. Even their numbers are similar if one makes allowances for the higher population of Holland. Venice, too, had in its earliest history been a democracy; its Great Council had at that time been elected by the population as a whole. Its history conformed to that evolutionary pattern which Spinoza discerned in the transition of democracies to aristocracies. The Venetian aristocracy had likewise tended to diminish in numbers, so that sovereignty came to be concentrated in the hands of a few families. The Council of Ten struggled to maintain the prestige of the patriciate and to prevent impoverished members from bringing it to dishonor among the common people. The Council of Ten acted as a secret police against the lower classes and suppressed any efforts on their part for political activity.[59] In short, Spinoza evidently believed that a reform of the Dutch Republic to conform to the Venetian Constitution—a reform, indeed, which De Witt had contemplated—would have been the salvation of his country.

The Constitution of Venice, however, was of that type of aristocracy which "takes its name from one city, which is the head of the whole dominion." Some emendations, therefore, were required in order to accommodate the proposed constitution to a dominion like that of Holland, "which is in the hands of more than one city, and which," said Spinoza, "I think preferable to the former." The modifications were not changes in principle. The proportion between the numbers of the patricians and the population was preserved, but, in addition, Spinoza proposed an inter-city senate which was the counterpart of the Provincial Estates of Holland. "But to manage the common business of the dominion, a senate is to be created on just the same footing as we described in the last chapter, so that there be between this senate and the former no difference, except that this has also authority to decide the disputes which may arise between cities." The existing legislative practice of the Provincial Estates was further approved by Spinoza; when a new measure was introduced "the question may first be discussed in the senate, and after the agreement of the senate in the matter, then let envoys next be sent to the cities by the senate itself, to inform the patricians of every city of the opinion of the senate, and lastly, if the majority of the cities follow that opinion, it shall then remain good, but otherwise be of no effect."

On two major questions, Spinoza once more assumed the role of the defender of Liberal Republicanism against the Orange party. He argued, in the first place, for the supremacy of the large cities like Amsterdam, and against disproportionate representation, and secondly, he opposed the policy of centralization advocated by the monarchical faction. At this time, the Provincial Estates of Holland were composed of nineteen voices, eighteen of which came from the cities, one from the nobility. "These cities," as Temple informs us, "were originally but six, Dort, Haerlem, Delf, Leyden, Amsterdam, and Tergou; but were increased by Prince William of Nassau, to the number of eighteen" when he gave to various small towns "an equal voice in the Provincial States with Amsterdam (which pays perhaps half of all charge of the Province)." A similar disproportionate representation prevailed in the States-General, where a small province such as Overyssel had a vote equal to that of Holland, which contributed more than half of the national budget. By such devices, the princes of Orange, who had a greater influence in the smaller towns, hoped to balance the power of the greater cities.[61] Spinoza was against this system of disproportionate representation which was used to whittle down the authority of liberal Amsterdam: "every city has so much right as against the dominion, as it exceeds the others in power. For he who seeks equality between unequals, seeks an absurdity. Citizens, indeed, are rightly esteemed equal, because the power of each, compared with that of the whole dominion, is of no account. But each city's power constitutes a large part of the power of the dominion itself, and so much the larger, as the city itself is greater. And, therefore, the cities cannot all be held equal." [62]

By 1674, the prestige of the Prince of Orange had grown immensely. His military victories had liberated almost all Dutch territory. It seemed highly possible that the whole sovereignty would be bestowed upon the Prince, and that the United Provinces would proclaim itself a monarchy. Influential statesmen were sympathetic to such a change, and governments by discussion and deliberation were in low esteem. The republican form of government was blamed for the initial Dutch defeat.[63] But Spinoza defended the deliberative procedures of the parliamentary republic against its critics; republican government may involve much time spent in discussion, but it has the high merit of preserving liberty. And talk is a small price to pay for the preservation of freedom. "Nor is it an objection," wrote Spinoza, "that while every city is consulting its own interest and suspecting the rest, they more often quarrel among themselves, and waste time in disputing. For if, while the Romans are debating, Saguntum is lost: on the other hand, while a few are deciding everything in conformity with their own passions only, liberty and the general good are lost. For men's natural abilities are too dull to see through everything at once; but by consulting, listening, and debating, they grow more acute, and while they are trying all means, they at last discover those which they want, which all approve, but no one would have thought of in the first instance." The Orange party pressed the advantages of centralization and efficiency. But Spinoza reminded the Dutch that decentralization of power had preserved their freedom against a monarchical usurper. In 1650, the city of Amsterdam had by its sturdy resistance frustrated a *coup d'état* by the Prince of Orange. With this incident still in men's memories, Spinoza remarked: "For where several cities enjoy liberty, it is not enough for him who is making ready his way to dominion, to seize one city, in order to hold dominion over the rest." [64] Among the main ingredients of the Dutch constitution, Temple had written, was "the freedom of the cities." [65] It is this ingredient which Spinoza, writing for once as a precursor of political pluralism, would exalt as a barrier against the growing authority of the Prince of Orange. The trend in Europe was toward centralized monarchy, toward so-called benevolent despotism. Spinoza's accents are those of the freedom which was born in the independent towns.

Aristocratic republics disintegrate, said Spinoza, because they lack an appropriate device for meeting crises. Partisans of Orange sometimes compared the authority of the prince to that of the old dictators of Rome who were brought to power in emergencies to safeguard the Republic. But Spinoza rejected the method of personal dictatorship as a solution for crisis, for, in his judgment, it endangered the republican constitutional structure. "And to be sure, as this authority of a dictator is quite royal, it is impossible for the dominion to change into a monarchy without great peril to the republic, although it happen for ever so short a time." To meet the contingencies of crisis, Spinoza would have relied exclusively on the council of syndics, which would wield dictatorial authority without tending to become an agency for personal rule: "the sword of the dictator should be permanent in the hands not of any natural person, but of a civil person, whose members are too numerous to divide the dominion amongst themselves, or to combine in any wickedness." [66] The syndics would not be paymasters of the soldiery; they would lack the dictator's Praetorian Guard. But they would be "sufficiently numerous to dare to accuse and condemn this or that influential man without fear of his enmity; especially as they vote by ballot, and the sentence is pronounced in the name of the entire council." Here again Spinoza followed the guidance of the Venetian Constitution, which he had mastered in Machiavelli's analysis.[67] Spinoza presumably believed that the mandates of a council of syndics would have enabled De Witt and his friends to enforce their authority during the crisis of 1672 and survive.

No republic is stable if it is founded on the proposition that men are rational. Spinoza made no such assumption. He recognized that most men are moved by passions. What passions, he therefore asked, could be harnessed on behalf of the stability of the republic? The passion of avarice, he answered, the passion for the accumulation of capital. Encourage this passion, and make the successfully avaricious the ruling class. Then the foundations of the republic will be secure. The dominion should be so constituted, Spinoza wrote, "that the majority, I do not say are anxious to live wisely (for that is impossible), but are guided by those passions whence the republic has most advantage. And therefore the chief point to be studied is, that the rich may be, if not thrifty, yet avaricious. For there is no doubt, that, if this passion of avarice, which is general and lasting, be encouraged by the desire of glory, most people would set their chief affection upon increasing their property without disgrace, in order to acquire honors. . . ." Matters would stand well. For the governing class would be numerous and loyal— "most of the rich have access to government and to the offices of the dominion open to them." [68] It is to a realistic economic interpretation of politics that Spinoza at the end adhered—a recognition that men are both selfish and irrational. Molière, his contemporary, wrote *L'Avare* in contempt of the money-mad men who were rising with the new middle class. Spinoza, however, his days as a radical over, saw no alternative for the stability of the Dutch Republic but to entrust the powers of government to *L'Avare*.

No constitution can provide safeguards against the unforeseen, the unpredictable, and Spinoza was too wise to claim for his republic an eternal equilibrium. In times of terror and insecurity, men will turn like frightened children to some dominant personality; constitutions are then brushed aside like fences against which animals stampede: "In whatever degree, therefore, a commonwealth is rightly ordered," he wrote, "and its laws well made; yet in the extreme difficulties of a dominion, when all, as sometimes happens, are seized by a sort of panic terror, all, without regard to the future or the laws, approve only that which their actual fear suggests, all turn towards the man who is renowned for his victories, and set him free from the laws, and (establishing thereby the worst of precedents), continue him in command, and entrust to his fidelity all affairs of state: and this was, in fact, the cause of the destruction of the Roman dominion." [69] With that last thrust against the

Orange party, Spinoza concluded his analysis of aristocracy. The Republic was warned against blindly running into personal dictatorship.

As Spinoza was writing this last portion of the *Tractatus Politicus,* there were signs that the tide toward monarchy and personal dictatorship was beginning to recede. People were becoming dissatisfied with the prince, with his restless desire for military glory. Pamphlets against the prince began to issue from the presses. The friends of De Witt were beginning to return to active political life. Van den Bosch, formerly secretary to De Witt, became pensionary of Amsterdam in 1677 and entered into secret negotiations for peace. Statesmen who were counted among the prince's friends were beginning to speak their mind for a peace policy. Amsterdam was inclining openly against the prince's warlike, anti-French obsession.[70] Spinoza's analysis of aristocracy took on an unforeseen relevance; perhaps the new architects of the Dutch Republic would profit from the tragic failure of John de Witt.

Spinoza felt that republican leaders in the future should be more mindful of political psychology. They should lend to their government something of the glamour, pageantry, and drama which the masses enjoy. For republics tend to be drab affairs compared to monarchies; they lack the legend and the color that surround crowned persons. Spinoza advised the aristocratic republic to cultivate the appeal of costumery.[71] He proposed that men who were candidates for the patriciate "be allowed to wear a particular ornament only permitted to them, to distinguish them and make them to be had in honour by the rest. . . ." De Witt and his burghers had lived with simplicity, without ostentation, but the masses usually adore conspicuous consumption when it occurs among their social superiors. De Witt's habit was "grave, and plain, and popular; . . ." he had only one servant, and "upon his visits of ceremony" wore a plain cloak; "upon other occasions, he was seen usually in the streets on foot, and alone, like the commonest burgher of the town." The burgomasters of Amsterdam likewise appeared "in all places with the simplicity and modesty of other private citizens." [72] But the masses, Spinoza felt, longed for colorful appurtenances in their sovereigns. Therefore, Spinoza added as a matter of "great importance" that "the patricians, when they walk, should be distinguished by some special garment, or dress, and be saluted by some special title; and that every man of the commons should give way to them; and that, if any patrician has lost his property by some unavoidable misfortune, he should be restored to his old condition at the public expense. . . ." An aristocratic republic, in Spinoza's view, rests on the deference of the masses. Walter Bagehot, two hundred years later, regarded this principle of deference as the key to the workings of the English constitution, and said: "The fancy of the mass of men is incredibly weak; it can see nothing without a visible symbol, and there is much that it can scarcely make out with a symbol." [73] This same perception of the power of symbols led Spinoza to criticize the rationalist fallacy in the everyday practices of De Witt the politician. Reason holds sway in political science, but in political action, reason bids you to take allegiance to the irrational. The principle is a familiar one to propagandists, public-relations counselors, and president-makers. Each polity has its own symbols which the would-be practitioner of the political art must respect.

An aristocratic republic in the future, Spinoza also advised, should keep itself immune to the charges of nepotism which had been hurled against De Witt. Holland, the commercial center, was free from the corrupt domination of noblemen found frequently in the rural provinces. But Holland had its own form of corruption, a commercial, bourgeois one—the easy sacrifice of the social welfare to family interests, the distribution of lucrative offices to friends and relatives, the misuse of public funds. De Witt himself had filled the posts of government with friends and relatives and was not altogether dissociated from their profitable, sometimes dubious, commercial ventures. No one dared accuse De Witt of corruption or bribery; the fact still remained, however, that he had been instrumental in securing political appointments for his father, brother, and numerous cousins.[74] De Witt's nepotism had brought an immense influence to his own family in the government of Holland. To prevent such practice, Spinoza proposed, as we have seen, that young men be ineligible for the patriciate so that "it will never happen that a few families hold the right of government in their hands." To keep the judiciary free from family interest, Spinoza urged that "two related by blood should not sit on the same bench together." Lastly, by way of pointed criticism of De Witt's nepotism, Spinoza advocated that kinsmen should not sit in the same councils, and that a special law for the supreme council should provide "that in elections no man may nominate a relation, nor vote upon his nomination by another, and also that two relations may not draw lots from the urn for the nomination of any minister of the dominion." [75] Spinoza stopped short of a law excluding from the supreme council the relatives of patricians, because the enforcement of such a law would have had to lie in the hands of the commoners, and divided sovereignty, in Spinoza's view, was inimical to the aristocratic republic.

Spinoza also warned against the tendency of legislative bodies to allow power to devolve upon the administrative officials. John de Witt had concentrated an immense power in himself as Grand Pensionary of Holland. Throughout the towns of the Netherlands, the pensionaries were becoming shapers of policy as well as administrators. The pensionary, in principle, was simply "a civil lawyer, versed in the customs, and records, and privileges of the town, . . . a servant of the Senate and the Burgomasters. . . ." [76] The office of the pensionary, however, had grown in its significance, until in Holland, it became virtually the prime ministry of the province.[77] A kind of managerial assumption of power had taken place. To Spinoza, this development was one which tended to undermine the aristocratic republic. He therefore proposed that "in every council the secretaries and other officials of this kind, as they have not the right of voting, should be chosen from the commons." Spinoza, in other words, aimed to underscore the subservience of the administrative officials to the patriciate; power would be less likely to devolve upon officials who were commoners. He stated explicitly the grounds of his fear of administrative encroachments upon sovereignty: "But as these [the secretaries], by their long practice of business, are the most conversant with the affairs to be transacted, it often arises that more deference than right is shown to their advice, and that the state of the whole dominion depends chiefly on their guidance: which thing has been fatal to the Dutch." If the senate is allowed to become dependent on the officials rather than its members, it then deteriorates as a legislative body and ends as a meeting place for "the sluggish." The patricians cease to be concerned with defending the foundations of the republic. They avoid risks, and "the liberty of a dominion is never defended without risk." In a crisis, they appoint "ambitious ministers, who are slaughtered as victims to appease the wrath of those, who are plotting against liberty." The tragedy of De Witt was that of a scapegoat offered up by a patrician class which had lost its fiber, its devotion to liberty, as it abdicated its responsibilities.

The Impasse of Authoritarian Liberalism

To ensure its stability, the aristocratic republic, Spinoza held, must protect the values of free men. All the patricians, therefore, "must be of the same religion, that is of that most simple and general religion which in that treatise we describe." [78] The *Tractatus Theologico-Politicus* had set forth the basic principles of the "universal religion"—that there exists a God, and that "the worship of this Being consists in the practice of justice and love towards one's neighbor." This was the content of religion as far as Spinoza was concerned. It coincided with the enlightened rationalism of the Liberal Republicans. Religion, for Spinoza, was not metaphysics. The religious man, according to Spinoza, may be theist or pantheist, subscribe to determinism or free will; he may adhere to an ethics with either a natural or supernatural ground. "Everyone may think on such questions as he likes," says Spinoza; "I will go further," he adds, "and maintain that every man is bound to adapt these dogmas to his own way of thinking . . . so that he may the more easily obey God with his whole heart." [79] All patricians, however, according to Spinoza, should be religious liberals, men who believe that the practice of justice and charity is the worship of God. Beyond this universal religion, no patrician should venture into the byways of dogma. "For it is above all to be avoided, that the patricians themselves should be divided into sects, and show favour, some to this, and others to that, and thence become mastered by superstition, and try to deprive the subjects of the liberty of speaking out their opinions." To enforce the dominance of the liberal universal religion, Spinoza, strangely enough, was prepared to restrict the freedom of assembly and association. Men may speak as they wish, "yet great conventicles are to be forbidden." The followers of other religions may build temples, "yet these are to be small, and limited to a certain standard of size, and on sites at some little distance one from another." By contrast, the temples of the "natural religion should be large and costly," and the patricians themselves would be the sole administrators of its principal rites, the authoritative interpreters of the natural religion, to whom preachers, chosen from the commoners, would be accountable.[80] In this fashion, Spinoza proposed to make the religion of justice and charity into the national worship. The Liberal Republicans, indeed, had become associated in Holland with the notion of a national liberal religion. De Witt had been rebuked by his critics for what they believed to be his desire: to establish out of the many creeds one common religion, which they satirized as the De Witt religion.

What shall we think of Spinoza's final version of religious liberalism? As a theory of liberty, it is at the opposite pole to Adam Smith's famous analysis of the conditions for religious freedom. A proliferation of sects, in Smith's opinion, was the effective guarantee for religious toleration; zeal becomes innocent, he wrote, where the society is divided into a "thousand small sects," none of which is too strong to hurt anybody. The religious leader would then have to learn the qualities of candor and moderation seldom found among the great state-supported churches. "The teachers of each little sect, finding themselves almost alone, would be obliged to respect those of almost every other sect," and by mutual concessions would gradually approximate to "that pure and rational religion, free from every mixture of absurdity, imposture, or fanaticism, such as wise men have in all ages of the world wished to see established. . . ."[81] By contrast, Spinoza would have the aristo-

cratic republic enact the rational religion into the positive law
of the nation.

Spinoza's animus against the Calvinist clerics gave an authoritarian aspect to his liberal philosophy. He hated the synods
and the consistories, the conventicles, the whole apparatus of religious intolerance and dogmatism. "Enlightened persons," he
had written, "who know the reasons for the convoking of
councils, or synods," would be sceptical of such assemblages.[82]
The liberal philosophy, however, can become self-destroying
when it is imposed upon others with the repressive devices of
illiberalism. With what conviction can liberalism, the philosophy
of the free rivalry of ideas, confront the citizens if its first
practical act is to exclude its opponents from an open hearing
before public opinion? Can liberalism preserve the liberal spirit
if it takes on the attitudes of intolerance?

Spinoza's proposal for a national rational religion was indeed
identical with the policy which Robespierre was to follow during
the French Revolution. On the seventh of May, 1794, the
National Convention established the Worship of the Supreme
Being; the opening clauses of the decree of the 18th Floréal of
the Year II averred: "(1) The French people recognize the existence of the Supreme Being and the immortality of the soul;
(2) They declare that the best service of the Supreme Being is
the practice of the duties of man. . . ."[83] During the time that
followed, the temples of the national religion were indeed the
largest and costliest; Saint-Merry was the Temple of Commerce,
Sainte-Marguerite became the Temple of Liberty and Equality,
and Notre Dame was transformed into the Temple of the
Supreme Being. Robespierre proclaimed the republican character of the rational universal religion: "The idea of the Supreme
Being and the immortality of the soul is a continual reminder
of justice: therefore it is social and republican." Robespierre
drew his intellectual inspiration from Rousseau, but during the
years of ideological ferment which preceded the revolutionary
era in France, Spinoza's ideas had provided the greatest single
stimulus to articulate discontent. The French police were as-
siduous in arresting the copyists of Spinoza manuscripts which,
nevertheless, circulated briskly throughout France in the first

part of the eighteenth century. Spinoza might well have regarded the religious innovations of the French Revolution as an
application of his political doctrine.[84]

The French effort to establish a national religion of "universal morality" was terminated by the Concordat of Napoleon
with Pope Pius VII in 1802. Its heritage remained, however,
in the notion of a secular state founded on lay education.
Rationalism and clericalism confronted each other as standing
enemies in the French Republic. English liberalism, by contrast,
arose in the climate of many sects; despite its advanced ag-
nosticism, English liberalism was under no compulsion to make
anticlericalism a cardinal tenet. The pluralism of associations,
the abundance of self-organized, democratic churches provided
the setting for a never-ending debate among a variety of religious alternatives. The clash of beliefs led to a fission of associations. English liberalism grew naturally from a soil which
was diversified in its intellectual seed. Its standpoint was far
different from that of Continental liberalism which from its
beginnings had to struggle for its existence against powerful,
monolithic state churches. There is consequently a gulf between
John Stuart Mill and Auguste Comte, between the liberalism
of open-mindedness and that which is doctrinaire, between a
readiness to question all so-called "inarticulate major premises"
and the rigidity which transforms itself as Comtism did into
a Catholicism minus the pope. The liberalism of Spinoza's
aristocratic republic, it must be avowed, was not free from the
authoritarian response.

But Spinoza hoped that the authoritarian patricians would
respect the values of free men. He recalled how Koerbagh and
Cornelius de Witt had been broken in prison, and he asked
that the patrician judiciary "never compel anyone to confess
by torture." He hoped that the patrician judges would transcend
class interest and be at once fair to the commoners and unafraid
of their equals. He hoped that the syndics, despite their high
social status, would like Roman tribunes "be most popular with
the commons, whose applause they will try as far as they can
to bid for," and that they would stand as a court of last appeal
against the bias of patrician judges.[85] He struggled with his

geometrical diagram for the aristocratic republic, trying to circumscribe the values of a free man within a stable constitution. He was debarred from the ranks of political participants, but he understood his impotence, and, understanding it, pursued the high vocation of political science, bringing wisdom to those with power who might perhaps be wise enough to use it.

Academic Freedom and Public Education

The reaction of 1672 had dispelled whatever faith Spinoza may have had in the freedom of the state universities of the Netherlands. Free thought, Spinoza came to believe, would flourish best in private universities, competing on the free market of ideas, and relatively immune to the pressure of state authorities. In this respect, his opinion resembled that which Adam Smith later forcefully expressed. Spinoza wrote flatly in *Tractatus Politicus:* "Academies that are founded at the public expense, are instituted not so much to cultivate men's natural abilities as to restrain them. But in a free commonwealth arts and sciences will be best cultivated to the full, if everyone that asks leave is allowed to teach publicly and that at his own cost and risk. But these and like points I reserve for another place." [86]

Death prevented Spinoza from fulfilling his promise to discuss further the restraints which public universities placed upon freedom. What would have been the first full discussion of academic freedom thus remained unwritten. The experience of the universities in the Netherlands certainly lent weight to Spinoza's position; their annals would have stirred a seventeenth-century Thorstein Veblen into writing a *Higher Learning in the Netherlands*. Freedom at the universities fluctuated with political changes. Liberal Republican rule brought a comparative liberty of thought to the state's academic institutions. The political dominance of the Calvinist party brought a recrudescence of anti-intellectualism. Spinoza after 1672 was too disillusioned to put his faith in public universities.

The Dutch universities were founded during the period when Calvinist loyalties were at their highest, in the atmosphere of the War of Independence against Spain, the Catholic imperial power. In 1575, William of Orange persuaded the Estates of Holland to provide for a complete university at Leyden. The towns of Groningen and Utrecht founded their universities respectively in the years 1614 and 1634. The statutes of Leyden, as framed by William, were most liberal; they imposed no restrictions of a religious or philosophical character. But the forces against academic freedom were strong. The statutes of Utrecht and Groningen soon outlawed liberty of thought and prohibited departures from Aristotle's philosophy; the so-called absurd paradoxes and new dogmas were barred from the academic halls.

The Dutch universities, too, had their boards of trustees, curators, as they were called, who were appointed by the Provincial Estates or the respective civic authorities. The curators were not themselves members of their universities; they acted solely as delegates of the sovereign. Sometimes they resisted clerical dictation, but the Calvinist clergy, unflagging in its struggle for influence, gained hegemony when political conditions were opportune. The approved official philosophy was a modified version of scholasticism; "ethics was commonly regarded with some suspicion on account of its heathenish tendencies." [87] The governing authorities supervised the workings of their universities closely. Textbooks were prepared in accordance with their desires. The *Institutiones Logicae,* for instance, a text which Spinoza used, was written by Professor Burgersdijck of Leyden at the behest of the Provincial Estates of Holland.[88]

The Cartesian philosophy raised the issue of academic freedom within the universities in its sharpest form, for it began with universal doubt and provoked questions, even when it gave answers, concerning the attributes of God. The Calvinist clergy were suspicious of the heresies latent in the Cartesian method; they cast a cold eye upon such a professor as Adrian Heerebord, who in 1641 dared to introduce his students at Leyden, Europe's leading university, to the works of Descartes.[89] They prevailed upon the curators to import a new professor, Adam Stuart, to bring Heerebord to terms. The furore against his philosophy became so vehement that the great Descartes himself complained to the curators in 1647. But matters did not improve, and in 1656, the year Spinoza was excommunicated, the curators prohibited all mention of Descartes's theories at their university. Intolerance was rampant, even in Holland, the citadel of freedom, the province where John de Witt, brilliant student of Cartesian mathematics, held the prerogatives of Grand Pensionary. De Witt himself deemed it wise to moderate the aggressive Cartesians, and on his initiative the Provincial Estates of Holland resolved on September 30, 1656, that the curators of Leyden were to see that professors of philosophy and theology did not encroach upon each other's domain. Moreover, it was decreed that, for the sake of tranquillity, the philosophemes of Cartesians were not to be taught in the classrooms. Academic freedom in the provincial universities was rendered hollow by the persistent lobbying and exhortation of the Calvinist clergy.

Republican tolerance, however, gradually made itself felt during the later years of John de Witt's tenure of office. Those were the happy years in which Spinoza was writing the *Tractatus Theologico-Politicus,* when pride in the progress of Dutch freedom spoke through his pages. In those years, from 1665 to 1669, the able Cartesian Arnold Geulincx was professor at Leyden, to the annoyance of his contemporaries. By 1669, the climate had become free enough to affect the balance of power between philosophic parties; in that year two pronounced Cartesians were appointed to professorships. The year 1672, however, brought debacle to Republican freedom; with political reaction came intellectual reaction. William III became the sovereign of Holland, and all Cartesians were dismissed from the University of Leyden. The Calvinist clergy, in the full glow of their victory, prevailed upon the curators to promulgate a syllabus of errors, which no professor would be allowed to defend—such errors, for instance, as: "all philosophy is independent of religion, and man's highest good is to be content with his condition." A Cartesian teacher, Heidanus, protested against such infringements on his freedom. He was an old man, in his eightieth year, but, nevertheless, was peremptorily ousted from his post.[90] The University of Utrecht went through a similar experience. The new ideas, banished from the halls of higher learning, led a subterranean existence among little groups of thinkers in Amsterdam. It was an age when free thought could survive only in "invisible colleges." The academic philosophy of the Dutch universities decayed; its product was a dull, sterile scholasticism. But the higher learning was made safe for Calvinist orthodoxy.

With such experiences in mind, Spinoza became convinced that public university education could never be free education. The "impudent theologians," he felt, could best be fought on a market of ideas which was free and competitive.

A Republican Conceives the Theory of Limited Monarchy

The aristocratic Republic of the Netherlands, as we have seen, had been shaken by the events of 1672. As Spinoza wrote his *Tractatus Politicus,* he was aware that the hegemony of the Prince of Orange might be transformed into the sovereignty of a monarch. If the Netherlands were to become a monarchy, the practical question for the political scientist then was: What sort of monarchy should it be? Should it be an absolute monarchy or a limited monarchy? Under which of these forms of monarchy would the values of free men be least endangered? To this problem Spinoza addressed himself in his chapters on monarchy.

Spinoza opened a new chapter in political thought by coming forth as the theorist of limited, constitutional monarchy. Thomas Hobbes in his *Leviathan* in 1651 had stated the case for absolute monarchy in magisterial terms. There was a strong trend in Europe toward centralized, absolutist states; it was to receive its culminating formulation the following century in the doctrine of benevolent despotism. Spinoza set himself against this trend. He mustered powerful arguments against absolute monarchy and replied systematically to Hobbes. He called for a monarchy in which there would be no mercenaries, no standing army to menace the liberties of the people. He hoped to maintain the rights of the people by arming its citizens in a people's militia. Aware that landed classes have found their political expression in absolute monarchy, Spinoza called forthrightly for the nationalized ownership of all lands and houses, with the payment of rents as the commonwealth's single tax. He proposed the establishment of a great council, drawn from all classes of citizens, to whose majority decisions the monarch should acquiesce. He asked for a commonwealth in which all citizens would join in trade and commerce, in which the pursuit of peace would be the primary objective. He urged a liberal policy in the welcoming of immigrants and proposed to facilitate their naturalization as citizens. He denied to the monarch the authority to enact or repeal laws and virtually conferred sovereignty on the great council. He proposed that there be no established state religion. To buttress his argument, Spinoza turned to the history of Spain, Europe's leading example of an absolutist state, and affirmed with telling power that the years of Aragon's greatness were those in which it enjoyed democratic, constitutional monarchy. He had read the passages in which Hobbes advocated absolute rule on the ground that the masses of men are such miserable creatures. With an outburst of strong emotion, Spinoza, for once, defended the masses. All men are alike, he said, and if the masses are miserable, it is because they have been broken and corrupted by the denial to them of the opportunity to govern themselves. He acknowledged that power corrupts the powerful, but just as much so does the lack of power corrupt the powerless, the impotent. And in words which foreshadow Locke, he justified the right of subjects to resist the violence of an absolute monarch with violence. He concluded that "the multitude may preserve under a king an ample enough liberty; if it contrive that the king's power be determined by the sole power, and preserved by the defence of the multitude itself." [91] Spinoza, confronted as a Republican by the probable foundation of a monarchy in the Netherlands, responded as a Republican; he formulated the theory of limited, constitutional monarchy, the monarchy which would be a republic in disguise.

The basis of government according to Hobbes is fear; the final cause, he says, which induces men to accept the restraints of government is their "getting themselves out from that miserable condition of War, which is necessarily consequent to the natural passions of men, when there is no visible Power to keep

them in awe, and tie them by fear of punishment. . . ." [92]
But the best dominion, Spinoza replies, is not founded on fear.
We may cite again his relevant words: "For a free multitude is
guided more by hope than fear; a conquered one, more by fear
than hope: inasmuch as the former aims at making use of life,
the latter but at escaping death. The former, I say, aims at living for its own ends, the latter is forced to belong to the
conqueror; and so we say that this is enslaved, but that free." [93]
Hobbes declares that "the Common Peace and Safety" could
be guaranteed only by the conferring of all power upon one
Man (or one Assembly, as an afterthought). Spinoza answers
that there is no real peace among men in a government based
on terror. The numb, the intimidated, the suppressed, may
make no overt movements of violence, but they are not at peace.
"Of a commonwealth, whose subjects are but hindered by terror
from taking arms, it should rather be said, that it is free from
war, than that it has peace. For peace is not absence of war,
but is a virtue that springs from force of character. . . . Besides, that commonwealth, whose peace depends on the sluggish-
ness of its subjects, that are led about like sheep, to learn but
slavery, may more properly be called a desert than a commonwealth." Spinoza concedes that a despotism like that of the
Turks has lasted longer without change than any other
government, whereas popular or democratic governments have
been the least perduring. But an unchanging slavish existence
is scarcely the end of government. "Yet if slavery, barbarism,
and desolation are to be called peace, men can have no worse
misfortune. . . . Slavery then, not peace, is furthered by hand-
ing over to one man the whole authority. For peace, as we said
before, consists not in mere absence of war, but in a union or
agreement of minds."

It is noteworthy that Spinoza's discussion of the Turkish
despotism led him to abandon stability as the primary criterion of
the superiority of a mode of government. Stability, permanence
were the values which smacked of substance, and an unchanging
type of dominion won the admiration of the seventeenth-century
political metaphysicians. [94] But Spinoza recognized that the happiness of men is the touchstone of governments in the eyes of

those who know their own values, who are not slaves. To refute Hobbes's defense of absolutism, Spinoza undertook a more profound psychological analysis of peace. Peace does not characterize the submissive, the terror-stricken; conflict and repressed anger rage within slaves, and one must not mistake the acquiescence of the slave for the peace which comes with free expression.

Spinoza furthermore denied that a Hobbesian absolute monarchy was ever founded by any people. In the Hobbesian myth, all men conferred all their power, strength, and will upon one man, without reservations, and thereby instituted the great Leviathan, the Mortal God.[95] Spinoza replied that "nowhere, as far as I know, is a monarch chosen absolutely without any conditions expressed." Ministers, he said, are justified "in refusing to execute his orders" when the latter contravene the fundamental law of the dominion, for the constitution is constituted, in effect, of "eternal decrees of the king" which bear against any contrary edict. By this legal fiction, Spinoza prepared the groundwork for the defense of constitutional monarchy. For a monarchy to be stable, he said, every law must be an explicit will of the king, "but not every will of the king a law."

A monarchy, according to Spinoza, requires the support of the masses much more than an aristocracy does. Only a popular democratic monarchy can be stable. Effective sovereignty in Spinoza's proposed monarchy would lie with the great council, a parliamentary body of members elected for not more than four years. The council, he proposed, would be numerous, three or four or five members being chosen from constituencies which might reach six hundred in number. A short term of office, in Spinoza's judgment, would make it possible for many citizens to aspire to election, and, moreover, prevent the councilors from assuming "great licence." Its large membership would make the council less vulnerable to corruption and crime. Even the king, Spinoza argued, would feel safer with a larger council. "The fewer counsellors, then, there are, and the more powerful they consequently are, the more the king is in danger of their transferring the dominion to another." Furthermore, Spinoza stipu-

lated that "from every sort of class of citizens a certain number
be chosen" so that "what has most votes in such a council will
be to the interest of the greater part of the subjects." The
council would thus represent all classes, and its will would
express the will of the majority. The king was to respect and
accept that will. "The king, then, whether he is induced by
fear of the multitude, or aims at binding to himself the majority
of an armed multitude, or is guided by a generous spirit, a wish
that is, to consult the public interest, will always confirm that
opinion, which has gained most votes, that is, which is to the
interest of the greater part of the dominion. . . ." The king,
moreover, was not to decide any matter without first consulting
the council, and no citizens would be able to deal with the king
save through the council. The one significant monarchical prerogative would be the king's right to select the councilors himself—
a prerogative limited, however, in its exercise to lists of eligible
candidates presented by the constituencies themselves. The great
council, Spinoza proposed, should meet at least four times a year
to receive an accounting from the ministers. During the intervals,
a sub-council of at least fifty men would meet daily to supervise
the national affairs.

Although Spinoza was prepared to allow the aristocratic
republic to hire mercenaries, he was strongly opposed to such a
practice under a monarchy. The house of Orange had used its
control of the mercenaries in the Dutch Army as a lever of political influence. Spinoza shared a common purpose with the Liberal
Republicans in proposing to eradicate this avenue of monarchist
subversion. "The militia must be formed out of citizens alone,
none being exempt, and of no others." An army of mercenaries is
a threat to the liberties of the citizenry, and its presence is a perpetual incitement to war; "citizens are altogether subdued, and
are laying the foundations of eternal war, from the moment that
they suffer mercenaries to be levied whose trade is war, and who
have most power in strifes and seditions." A people's militia is a
restraint on monarchs, a professional army encourages their worst
propensities: "kings usually are fonder of exciting their soldiery
than restraining their soldiery, and shut their eyes more to their
vices than to their virtues, and generally, to hold under the best

of them, seek out, distinguish, and assist with money or favour the idle, and those who have ruined themselves by debauchery, and shake hands with them, and throw them kisses, and for the sake of mastery stoop to every servile action." This was the powerful argument of the Republicans that monarchy meant the hegemony of the army and a policy of war. To the many Dutch citizens who by 1676 were becoming weary of the militarist frame of mind of the Prince of Orange and his entourage, Spinoza's words were laden with the meanings of their own experiences.

Peace and liberty were to be safeguarded, in Spinoza's plan, by a parliamentary council and people's militia. "But it cannot be doubted," he wrote, "that the majority of this council will never be minded to wage war, but rather always pursue and love peace." Kings are often chosen, he observed, because wars are more efficiently conducted by them, and their rule is often justified by apologists as a necessity of war. To this Spinoza replied: "it is manifest folly, I say, that men should choose slavery in time of peace for the sake of better fortune in war," and "democracy has this advantage, that its excellence is greater in peace than war." A people's militia helps preserve democracy: "that the citizens may continue independent, and defend their liberty, the militia ought to be composed of the citizens only, and none of them to be exempted. For an armed man is more independent than an unarmed. . . ." A standing professional army is a menace to liberty; professional soldiers, Spinoza maintained, become debauched in time of peace, "from excess of leisure," and "meditate nothing but rapine, civil discord, and wars." A monarchy with a professional army is one in which "only the soldiery enjoy liberty, but the rest are slaves." Spinoza warned the Dutch people that if a monarchy were instituted, they must hedge their king with democratic sanctions. The maintenance of liberties depends on an equal distribution of military power throughout the whole citizenry; a monopoly of military power in the hands of a small group means despotism. In short, the militarist policy, the professional army, and the hiring of mercenaries advocated by the Orange party were incompatible, in Spinoza's opinion, with the freedom of the Netherlands' citizens.

Attachment to peace, in Spinoza's judgment, was most firmly

rooted in a state which was founded on the pursuits of trade and commerce. Consequently, Spinoza advocated the abolition of private landed property in his monarchy. In a proposal which echoed the English Diggers and his own early radical associations, Spinoza urged that "the soil, therefore, and whatever adheres to it in the way we have mentioned, must be quite common property of the commonwealth." This communistic principle, wrote Spinoza, is an "accession to the cause of peace and concord . . . of great weight." According to his plan, "the fields, and the whole soil, and, if it can be managed, the houses should be public property, that is, the property of him, who holds the right of the commonwealth: and let him let them at a yearly rent to the citizens, whether townsmen or countrymen, and with this exception let them all be free or exempt from every kind of taxation in time of peace." [96] Spinoza, with these proposals for the nationalization of the land and a single tax, looms as a forerunner of Henry George.[97] All citizens were to have a stake in the defense of their land because all would be engaged in commerce. Without a landed gentry, and through a widespread participation in trade, a real measure of economic equality would obtain among the people. "Hence all will have nearly an equal risk in war. For all will be obliged, for the sake of gain, to practice trade, or lend money to one another, if as formerly by the Athenians, a law be passed, forbidding to lend money at interest to any but inhabitants; and thus they will be engaged in business, which either is mutually involved, one man's with another's, or needs the same means for its furtherance. And thus the greatest part of this council will generally have one and the same mind about their common affairs and the arts of peace." [98]

Spinoza reiterated the thesis of the Liberal Republicans, of De Witt and Pieter de la Court, that there is an indissoluble relation between the pursuit of trade and the desire for peace. The commercial classes regarded war as an excrescence of feudalism, of lords and kings; trade, they felt, necessarily unites men, and makes for peace. "For besides that war will always cause them fear of losing their property and liberty, it is to be added, that war requires fresh expenditure, which they must meet, and also that their own children and relatives, though intent on their domestic cares, will be forced to turn their attention to war and go a-soldiering, whence they will never bring back anything but unpaid-for scars." Thus, in the midst of the third Anglo-Dutch war and the struggle with France, Spinoza incorporated a tract against war and militarism in his *Tractactus Politicus*. To Dutch tradesmen, he repeated in effect, unweariedly: "De-militarize the monarchy, if that turns out to be your form of government, and establish within its framework the supremacy of your own economic interest."

To reduce provocations to war, Spinoza proposed a restriction on the marital diplomacy of monarchs. "The king must not be allowed to contract a foreign marriage, but only to take to wife one of his kindred, or of the citizens. . . ." For, as Spinoza says, "it is very much to be avoided that war should be stirred up, on account of the king's domestic affairs. . . ." [99] The marriage, for instance, of Louis XIV of France to the daughter of Philip IV, king of Spain, "was the seed of a fresh war." Other examples were at hand in contemporary Dutch history, though as a wise political scientist Spinoza forbore from too pointed a reference to the marital projects of the house of Orange. The marriage of the young Prince of Orange, William II, to the Princess Maria Stuart of England in 1642 was still fresh in people's memories; it had embroiled the Dutch Republic in schemes to restore the throne to the Stuart family. The Orange royalists had been prepared to plunge their country into war for a foreign monarch, and to sacrifice their country's trade, commerce, and citizens in a foreign adventure. And as Spinoza wrote the *Tractatus Politicus* in 1677, the story was being repeated. Negotiations were afoot between Charles II, king of England, and the Prince of Orange to marry William to Charles's oldest niece Mary, daughter of the Catholic Duke of York.[100] Before the year's end, this marriage was indeed consummated. Spinoza's injunction against a foreign marriage by a king was an explicit warning that the house of Orange with its schemes for aggrandizement through diplomatic marriages might involve the Dutch people in needless troubles.

Spinoza, in addition, provided that "the care of the education of the king's sons should also fall on this council, and the guardianship, where a king has died, leaving as his successor an infant or boy." [101] With this proposal, Spinoza endorsed the course of action which John de Witt had taken with respect to the education of the young Prince of Orange. The Orange party tried hard to have the prince educated under their own auspices at Leyden, a center of monarchist influence. John de Witt, however, persuaded the Provincial Estates of Holland to guide the prince's education "as an instrument of great hope for the service of the high commissions and employments" which awaited him. De Witt himself was later included in the commission for the prince's education. He desired to have the prince live at The Hague "in the house and under the eyes" of the States-General. In 1661, when the prince's mother died, Charles II of England took her place as guardian. The authorized guardians quarreled with the States-General, and the upshot was that the Orange party undertook the prince's upbringing. Naturally, the young prince was inculcated with hostility to the Republican cause and animosity for John de Witt. His education was not the kind that prepared him to be a constitutional monarch; he was taught to claim privileges against the Republic. It was astounding, besides, that a foreign potentate shared in the decision for an anti-Republican education for a Dutch prince. Therefore, Spinoza, as a safeguard for constitutional monarchy, asked that the great council assume the responsibility for the king's education, and his guardianship as well, if need be.

The Orange party had tried to reduce the influence of the large towns in favor of the small ones. Amsterdam had been in the forefront of opposition to monarchical designs. To give a voice to the larger centers of population proportionate to their numbers, Spinoza proposed that "the larger towns . . . have, in proportion to the number of their citizens, a greater number of counsellors, and be able, as is equitable, to contribute more votes." [102] The Calvinist party demanded that "there may be only one religion in the State; all heretics must be driven out; for better is a desolate city than a trafficking city full of sectarians." [103] But Spinoza felt that liberty under a monarchy was best preserved by the presence of a variety of sectarians: "As for religion, no temples whatever ought to be built at the public expense; nor ought laws to be established about opinions. . . . And so let such as are allowed the public exercise of their religion build a temple at their own expense." [104] Under the aristocratic republic, as we have seen, Spinoza urged the maintenance of a national liberal religion with its appropriate temples. A constitutional monarchy, on the contrary, has no place for a state religion; Spinoza is saying to the Dutch people: "If you are to have a monarchy, by all means keep it clear of established clerical interference with religious ideas and observances, if you wish to preserve your liberties."

The Liberal Republican party of John de Witt had welcomed foreigners to Holland. Like the Athens of Pericles, which drew to itself the enterprise of free-minded immigrants, it regarded liberality to the outsider as a token of greatness. Pieter de la Court had argued "that freedom or toleration in, and about the service or worship of God, is a powerful means to preserve many inhabitants in Holland, and allure foreigners to dwell amongst us." [105] The attraction of aliens to the free soil of Holland was part of the liberal creed. But the issue of naturalization and citizenship remained a live one in Dutch politics. Protestant craftsmen, on the whole, enjoyed a welcome in Amsterdam, and were allowed to purchase the "poortersrecht" (right of citizenship). The guilds, however, resisted this liberal policy which increased competition among the laborers. The Jews had been placed under definite disabilities. Only merchants of importance were allowed to buy the "poortersrecht," and they were granted a "lesser citizenship" only. They could not transmit their status to their children, while the crafts and retail trades still remained generally closed to them. Eastern European Jews, as peddlers, were debarred from citizenship. Spinoza, as a Liberal Republican, would have the constitutional monarchy adopt the most liberal policy toward the newcomers from other lands. The refugee was to find a welcome road to citizenship. "If a foreigner takes to wife the daughter of a citizen, his children are to be counted citizens. . . . But those who are born and bred within the dominion of foreign parents should be allowed to purchase at a fixed price the right of citizenship. . . . For no harm can arise thence to the dominion, even though the captain of thousands, for a bribe, admit a foreigner into the number of their citizens for less than the fixed price; but, on the contrary, means should be devised for more easily increasing the number of citizens, and producing a large confluence of men." [106]

The Masses: Free Men or Slaves?

Advocates of absolute monarchy, whether Calvinist or Hobbist, tend to emphasize the radical evil in men, their lusts, their incapacity for self-government, their need for a rigorous authority to curb their impulses and guide them in their own best interest. The image of mankind as cursed with original sin was strong in the political theory of the seventeenth century. Proverbs were used, as Spinoza noted, to justify such attitudes: " 'the mob, if it is not frightened, inspires no little fear.' " [107] Spinoza was moved for the last time to defend the people against those who scorned them in order to dominate them. His defense of the masses strikes at the heart of every doctrine of dictatorship, because every apologist for dictatorship finally insists that the masses, inherently incompetent, must be led by their masters. The psychological essence of every authoritarian ideology is to disguise the sadism of the masters as a benevolence toward the slaves. The populace, however, said Spinoza, does not differ from other mortals; "all have one common nature." The rulers, the men of the upper classes, have the same vices as the ruled, the men of the lower classes, but the former are absolved, the latter are condemned, "not because the deed, but because the doer is different." The arrogance of rulers "is glossed over with importance, luxury, profusion, and a kind of harmony of vices, and a certain cultivated folly, and elegant villany, so that vices, each of which looked at separately is foul and vile, because it is then most conspicuous, appear to the inexperienced and untaught honorable and becoming." The emotion of the radical spoke in these words, the resurgence within Spinoza of the feelings which linked him in his youth to Mennonites and Quakers, a hostility to the ways of ruling classes.

If the masses are miserable, Spinoza continued, it is because they have been made so by the policy of their rulers. "Lastly, as for the populace being devoid of truth and judgment, that is nothing wonderful, since the chief business of the dominion is transacted behind its back, and it can but make conjectures from the little, which cannot be hidden. For it is an uncommon virtue to suspend one's judgment." The masses, if not conditioned to govern themselves, will naturally be incapable of self-rule; and the secret processes of absolute monarchy obviously do not prepare the masses to govern themselves. Hobbes had argued that the secrecy of its procedures was an advantage of monarchy over both aristocracy and democracy, "a Monarch receiveth counsel of whom, when, and where he pleaseth, . . . and with as much secrecy as he will. . . . Nor is there any place, or time, wherein an Assemblie can receive Counsel with secrecie, because of their own Multitude." [108] To which Spinoza replied that secrecy in government may make for security against foreign enemies, but it also becomes an instrument against the domestic liberties. A great good is exchanged for a small benefit: "to entrust affairs of state absolutely to any man is quite incompatible with the maintenance of liberty; and so it is folly to avoid a small loss by means of the greatest of evils." Hobbes had envisaged a garrison state in which all values were subordinated to military security. Spinoza countered that the basic ends of government are sacrificed in the garrison state, and that the garrison minded have forgotten the aims of human happiness.

Secrecy has its uses, but no one will ever prove, Spinoza held, that a state cannot exist without it. The counsels of a parliamentary dominion, which seeks "to avoid war and preserve peace," said Spinoza, "can hardly be concealed. But everyone will also admit with me that it is far better for the right counsels of a dominion to be known to its enemies, than for the evil secrets of tyrants to be concealed from the citizens. They who can treat secretly of the affairs of a dominion have it absolutely under their authority, and, as they plot against the enemy in time of war, so do they against the citizens in time of peace." Those who lust for absolute rule insist that the commonwealth's interest requires "that its business be secretly transacted"; the more they clothe their arguments "with a show of utility," thereby they contribute to "the more hateful a slavery." This is Spinoza's reply to the seventeenth-century version of totalitarian ideology which like its later versions tried to justify its domestic repressions by the specter of foreign encirclements.

There is no absolute transfer of rights to the monarch in Spinoza's constitution. Again, Spinoza was the precursor of Locke rather than the disciple of Hobbes: "the multitude does not, if it is free, transfer to the king anything but that, which it cannot itself have absolutely within its authority, namely, the ending of controversies and the using despatch in decisions." Against Hobbes, Spinoza said that it would be "manifest folly" for men to "choose slavery in time of peace for the sake of better fortune in war." Citizens in Spinoza's monarchy delegate only limited rights; therefore, "the king's utmost right is but to choose one of the opinions offered by the council, not to decree anything, or offer any opinion contrary to the mind of all the council at once." Hobbes had maintained that the decision as to his successor was in "the Judgment and Will of the present Possessor," that this right was inherent in the nature of monarchy. But Spinoza affirmed that a king "cannot hand the dominion over to another, unless with the concurrence of the multitude or its stronger part." When a king dies, sovereignty reverts "to the multitude, which can, therefore, lawfully lay down new and abolish old laws." There is no political myth for Spinoza by which the people can be regarded as having permanently surrendered all their right. And where Hobbes denies any right to revolution against the absolute monarch, "they that are subjects to a Monarch, cannot without his leave cast off Monarchy . . . ," Spinoza allows his own aversion to despotism to take on a revolutionary hue: "a king can be deprived of the power of ruling, not by the civil law, but by the law of war, in other words, the subjects may resist his violence with violence."

Thomas Hobbes had blamed the bad example of the Dutch Republic for inciting Englishmen to rise against their monarch. "And I doubt not," he wrote, "but many men, have been contented to see the late troubles in England, out of an imitation of the Low Countries. . . ." Spinoza's reply to Hobbes was founded on the notion that Dutch political experience had something to teach Europe—the lesson once more of the supreme value of human liberty.

There was one monarchy, wrote Spinoza, which came close to realizing the conditions of his proposed constitution—that of Aragon, whose subjects were singularly loyal to their kings and whose constitution was for long preserved. In Aragon, the sovereignty was in the hands of a council, the so-called Seventeen, and "every citizen had the right to summon the king himself before this council." This constitutional monarchy endured in Aragon, and its subjects retained their liberties, "until the reign of Philip II, who oppressed them with better luck, but no less cruelty, than he did the United Provinces." For the narrative of these events, Spinoza evidently relied on Antonio Perez, whose observation he cited: "an absolute dominion is to the prince very dangerous, to the subjects very hateful, and to the institutes of God and man alike opposed. . . ." [109]

Who was this Antonio Perez, whose analysis of monarchy Spinoza found more congenial than Hobbes's? A strange, melodramatic sequence of events turned Antonio Perez, Secretary of State to the King of Spain, Philip II, into an advocate of constitutional monarchy and the rights of the individual. Perez lived at a time when the *Fueros,* the "Liberties" of Aragon, the last survival of free institutions in Spain, were under attack. The Aragonese had kept their home rule, but the trend of Spanish political evolution was toward centralization and absolutism. The precarious *Fueros* were unable to withstand the assault of the Spanish king and the Inquisition. Antonio Perez emerged as the head of a movement in their defense called the "caballeros de la libertad." The Holy Inquisition, faithful servants of absolutism, accused Perez of holding that God was corporeal, and on this pretext, tried to imprison him. Theological heresy was presumably the handmaiden to its political sister. But a multitude of workmen (*labradores*) and shopkeepers, shouting, "Long live freedom! Long live Antonio Perez!" intervened to frustrate the Inquisition. Perez then threatened a revolt which would make Aragon a free republic like Venice. When the Inquisition persisted in its efforts to seize Perez, the populace forcefully freed him. Then the king's army marched on Saragossa. The workmen and shopkeepers fought the king's troops, but were suppressed with great bloodshed in 1591. Perez himself escaped across the snows of the Pyrenees to France. In his person, he had come to represent the principle of autonomy and liberty in its struggle against centralization and authority.[110] Thenceforth, however, his life was the melancholy one of a political exile, plotting in foreign countries for the freedom of his own, and driven, more and more, into machinations in the twilight zone between treason and liberation. During these years, Perez wrote his *Relaciones,* a work of political autobiography, which affected many readers with its story of the Spaniards' struggle to preserve their freedoms against their king. Spinoza had in his library a copy of *Las Obras de Perez,* published in 1644, a volume which included the *Relaciones.*[111] Spanish was the language in which Spinoza was most at home, and Perez's history was one to impress a thinker whose Jewish ancestors had known the tyranny of the Spanish Inquisition, and whose countrymen had fought a War of Independence against Philip II.

Neither heritage nor environment inclined Spinoza toward the absolutist doctrine of Hobbes. His heroes, apart from De Witt, were men like Masaniello and Perez who shared one quality—they had been fighters for the freedom of man against tyranny.

Finally Spinoza turned to the writing of his chapter on democracy, "the third and perfectly absolute dominion." He wrote only a few paragraphs, enough to set down a definition of the kind of democracy which he proposed to discuss, one "wherein all, without exception, who owe allegiance to the laws of the country only, and are further independent and of respectable life, have the right of voting in the supreme council and of filling the offices of the dominion." A few lines later the manuscript closes. Was it death which prevented its completion? Or had Spinoza come up against an impasse? There was an ambivalence in Spinoza toward the masses, the mob, the multitude. He would defend the masses against those phrase-makers who said that "the mob, if it is not frightened, inspires no little fear." But he himself in the *Ethics* affirmed: "the multitude becomes a thing to be feared if it has nothing to fear." The radical pamphleteer and the disillusioned follower of De Witt were two poles of ambivalent feeling in Spinoza.[112] When Spinoza was writing on aristocracy, the memory of De Witt's fate made him hostile to the participation of the masses in their government. When, however, he was discussing monarchy, his fear of tyranny awakened his democratic impulses, and with a revived optimism, he defended the masses' moral and political capacity.

The man who felt himself one with Masaniello and Perez defended the common people against those who mocked and railed at them. This was the Spinoza in whom William Ames, Quaker agitator, had perceived a kindred soul, the Spinoza who had defied the mighty of the Jewish community and had chosen excommunication, the Spinoza who questioned the institution of private property. The Spinoza who had seen the mob on the day they lynched the brothers De Witt, however, spoke with aversion and contempt for the multitude, who were the puppets of passions and superstition. How was one to build democracy upon the foundation of such human nature? Montesquieu was later to write that a republic, unlike a monarchy, required to be founded on the virtue of its citizens.[113] Was there an anxiety in Spinoza that the character of men as he saw them was an unstable basis for the perfect dominion, democracy? The democratic aspiration and the trauma of the mob struggled within his thought. The political thinker found himself divided within as did the philosopher, meditating on man and the universe. Not all the resources of the geometrical method could resolve the conflict within Spinoza himself.

CHAPTER 6

A Free Man's Philosophy

When he felt death approaching, Spinoza became concerned for the manuscript of the *Ethics* on which he had labored for many years. He entrusted, as we have seen, his letters and papers to the publisher John Rieuwertsz, one of his oldest Collegiant friends. Spinoza died on the twenty-first of February, 1677. Rieuwertsz supervised the arrangements for his friend's burial, and a few months later printed the *Opera Posthuma* of Spinoza. It was a dangerous enterprise: "the Printer's name and the place wherein that Book was Printed, are not mention'd in the Title-page." The next year, the Provincial Estates of Holland and West Friesland decreed that Spinoza's works "vilipended the authority of miracles." The statesmen affirmed their "highest indignation" with this profane and atheistic book, and prohibited its sale and publication.[1] The decrees of statesmen are not, however, the decrees of God; Spinoza's ideas became part of the liberal heritage.

Mystic and Scientist: The Incompatible Components of Spinoza's Metaphysics

The *Ethics* of Spinoza is a vision of man and his relation to the universe. Its conception has an impersonal grandeur, its man-made words seem to reach beyond language, trying to encompass an endless universe, and to surmount time and its human instance. The *Ethics* was not another tome written to take its place on a shelf of treatises on metaphysics. It was a book which issued from a man's intense experience, the world-perspective of a man immersed in the social and political conflicts of his time. It was not a footnote to other books; its breath was that of a man struggling to come to terms with a world in crisis. It lives as a human document because its writer sought, with transcendent honesty, to speak the truths which were deepest within him.

The *Ethics* is set down in accordance with the geometrical method. Its structure seems impeccable and dispassionate; theorems and demonstrations follow on the axioms with impressive order. But a mathematical façade may conceal an inner being which is riven with deep conflict. A logical surface may enclose seething, warring impulses of a thinker who is striving for self-mastery. The mathematical method was for Spinoza, as it is for Bertrand Russell, an expression of an emotional longing toward realities beyond formulae. The geometrical method was an over-compensation for an inner nonlogical world of emotional turmoil.[2] Its significance was peripheral, not essential.

The young Spinoza, as we have seen, was drawn to the mysticism and social radicalism of the Quakers and Collegiants; in mature manhood he was enrolled among the Liberal Republicans associated with John de Witt, the advocate of mathematics and scientific law. These two components of Spinoza's personality permeate the *Ethics,* unreconciled, unsynthesized. There is the Spinoza who believes that nature is governed by scientific law, that its language is that of mathematics; and there is the mystic Spinoza who holds that God transcends mathematical description, that the word "one" does not apply to substance. There is the Spinoza who writes the ethics of the free man, who seeks his happiness in accordance with the best available psychological, medical, and social knowledge, but then there is also the Spinoza who seeks the highest beatitude in the intellectual love of God, a mystic union between man's mind and God's. The Liberal Republican Spinoza was deeply convinced that man's freedom was dependent on the conditions of his social existence; to the mystic Spinoza, political realities would suddenly seem unimportant beside the eternal being of man's intellect. "Whatever be the social state a man finds himself in, he may be free." [3]

The "free man" is the central conception of Spinoza's *Ethics.* Classical philosophers had tried to define the "wise man" or "the philosopher," and philosophic wisdom was presumed to be the especial province of the pure philosopher. But the "free man" for Spinoza expresses his belief in man's capacity to find happiness in a liberal social world; the "free man" uses his reason not to frustrate his bodily desires but to bring them to their highest satisfaction. What were the social roots of the ethics of the free man?

The Ethics of the Free Man as a Critique of the Calvinist Ethics

Spinoza's ethics of the free man is a point-by-point criticism of the ethics of the Calvinist party. The great struggle in the Netherlands between the Calvinist, pro-Orange group and the Liberal Republicans was not only political; it expressed itself in the divergence of two ways of life. The free man, says Spinoza, "does the will of no one but himself, and does those things only which he knows are of greatest importance in life, and which he therefore desires above all things," whereas the slave, "whether he wills it or not, does those things of which he is entirely igno- rant." [4] The free man knows his own values, and is not a puppet maneuvered through his unconscious by other people's wills. The free man in everyday life pursues happiness:

> It is the part of a wise man, I say, to refresh and invigorate him- self with moderate and pleasant eating and drinking, with sweet scents and the beauty of green plants, with ornament, with music, with sports, with the theatre, and with all things of this kind which one man can enjoy without hurting another. For the human body is composed of a great number of parts of diverse nature, which constantly need new and varied nourishment, in order that the whole of the body may be equally fit for everything which can follow from its nature. . . .[5]

These illustrations may seem trivial. But in each of them Spinoza, as a matter of fact, takes his stand upon a point of con- tention between the Calvinists and the hedonistic Liberal Repub- licans. The theater, for instance, was an important moral and political issue at that time. John de Witt, as a young man, trans- lated Corneille's *Horace,* but did not dare to sign his work. For he aspired to public life, and therefore deemed it expedient to conform to the prejudices of the presbytery of Dordrecht, which

had severely condemned the theater.[6] The authoritative synod
of Dort in 1619 had had a deleterious effect upon the stage, literature, and the arts generally. Strict Calvinist preachers inveighed
against the "sinful vanity and unfruitful works of darkness" of the
theater. They held the devil was the father of plays and poetry,
and they remembered that the poets had never sided with them
against the Remonstrants. "Amsterdam was the chief scene of a
fierce contest between theology and art, between theatre and consistory, because the drama was flourishing there just at that
time." [7] The government was compelled by clerical pressure to
reprimand poets and playwrights from time to time.[8]

The ties of personal friendship, furthermore, linked Spinoza
to a concern for the theater. Lodewijk Meyer was the close friend
who, at Spinoza's own request, edited *The Principles of Descartes'
Philosophy*. Meyer was the physician for whom Spinoza sent in
the last hours of his life. But Lodewijk Meyer was also the foremost personage in the Dutch theater; he was indeed the first
director of the Amsterdam theater, and the founder in 1669 of
the society *Nil volentibus arduum* which introduced into the
Dutch drama a new classicism more in keeping with the Liberal
Republican philosophy.[9] Legend furthermore had it that an attempt upon Spinoza's life was made as he was leaving after the
performance at an Amsterdam playhouse.[10] The free man delighted in the arts. During the hours before he went to his death,
Cornelius de Witt was reading the plays of Molière—*L'Avare* and
Tartuffe.[11] Greed and hypocrisy, the two forces which had overwhelmed him and his brother, were read in comedy before they
fulfilled their tragic reality.

The Calvinist theologians were on guard against the new
scientific philosophy and its corollary, the ethics of human happiness. Spinoza remembered how Descartes had been maligned by
the rector of the University of Utrecht, Voetius, a zealous Calvinist.[12] The errors of the day, according to Voetius, were playgoing
and dancing (apart from the private dances of husband and wife).
Teachers of dancing, Voetius held, should be banished from the
land, and those who held dances prosecuted; smoking and feasting were likewise denounced; serious theological discourse was to
supplant them.[13] The brothers De Witt had, however, learned

dancing in their teens. In his maturity John still retained a love
for the joys of life.[14] The charming Countess Sophie-Marguerite
van Nassau sought him out for her soirées and as a companion at
the carnival. He was, indeed, well known as an accomplished
dancer and musician. The admired ladies of the salons vied for
his presence, but it was the lovely Baroness of Slavata who won
De Witt for membership in "L'Ordre de l'Union et de la Joye."
In 1653, De Witt and kindred blithe spirits at The Hague used to
meet in this kind of "underground" circle under the stimulating
guidance of the Baroness. Its ruling proverb was that of
Rabelais's Abbey of Thélème—"Do what thou wilt"—and its purpose was to promote the good life, that is, dancing, music, versify-
ing, and, as a correspondent of De Witt stated, to chase away

> Dame Mélancolie
> Qui ne fit jamais en sa vie,
> Que des maux de coeur et de teste,
> Et troubla mainte belle feste.
> [Lady Melancholy
> Who never in her life made
> Anything but trouble for the heart and head
> And was a killjoy at many a fine party.]

On February 23, 1653, the young Grand Pensionary received a
commission from the Baroness as "Chevalier de L'Ordre de
l'Union et de la Joye." It read:

> Amelia, by the gifts of nature sole protectress of joy, to those
> whom it concerns. . . .
> Having known the intention of Monsieur de Witt to laugh,
> dance, frolic, and have fun, . . . we have well desired to gratify
> him with membership in our Union. . . .[15]

In the atmosphere of this hedonistic society, the youthful Liberal
Republicans had a meeting place in which they could speak their
minds freely, laugh and be gay; here was an oasis in the gloom of
the Calvinist desert where the heterodox ideas of human happiness and liberties could flourish.

The thought of death had preoccupied men's minds greatly

at the end of the Middle Ages, and the fear and anxiety of death permeated the outlook of Calvinism.[16] But, with increasing prosperity, the rise of standards of living, and the emergence of a well-to-do middle class, the Calvinist ethics, with its asceticism, frugality, hatred of the body, was more and more scrutinized and rejected. Not the fear of death but the joy of life became the guiding principle of ethical philosophies. This pattern of ethical evolution was repeated in England during the eighteenth century and America in its revolutionary era. Adam Smith, a later critic of Calvinist austerity, observed that the strict morality prevails among the common people, for the poor workmen, who cannot afford the excesses of gaiety, are driven to abhor that which they cannot have. To combat the austere morality, Smith proposed measures very much in accord with Spinoza's ethics of the free man—the cultivation of science as an antidote to superstition, frequent and gay public diversions, and the encouragement of those who "amuse and divert the people by painting, poetry, music, dancing; by all sorts of dramatic representations and exhibitions." [17] Jeremy Bentham added his philosophic criticism of the principle of asceticism. Unlike the principle of utility which aimed at the pleasure of the person and the community, asceticism, said Bentham, was the doctrine of those who "think it meritorious to fall in love with pain." [18] Asceticism had somehow inverted the normal biological workings of human nature. Thus the English thinkers carried out the hedonistic criticism of the stern Calvinist morality in their country.

American thought later made a similar rejection of the Calvinist doctrine. The Puritan ethic had fulfilled a unique function in the pioneer setting. Life in the wilderness was one of scarcity, and the Puritan virtues—thrift, abstemiousness, hostility to ornament and frivolity—were well suited to an economy in which the first accumulations were to be made with hard labor. But the pioneer economy of scarcity gave way to the mature economy of abundance. When plentiful goods were available, the harsh self-denial of the Puritan virtues lost the validation of objective fact. Virtues lose their biological ground, though not their tenacity, when they emanate from internal decree rather than external necessity. And the Calvinist ethic was again perceived to be, under the conditions of prosperity, an obstacle to human happiness. Men like Jefferson and Franklin began to criticize the Calvinist morality and the Calvinist God, and to aver themselves hedonists and Epicureans. Spinoza's ethics of the free man is the precursor of this movement, the classical psychological criticism of the Calvinist ethics.

The Calvinist ethic made the fact of death central in life; men were to brood upon salvation, damnation, and predestination.[19] Like existentialism in one mood, it enjoined men to dwell in their thoughts on the imminence of life's end. To this, Spinoza replied: "A free man thinks of nothing less than of death, and his wisdom is not a meditation upon death but upon life." There was a streak of hatred, of sadism, in the Calvinist ethic, and Spinoza declared: "Hatred can never be good." To the Calvinist passion against joy, he replied:

> Nothing but a gloomy and sad superstition forbids enjoyment. For why is it more seemly to extinguish hunger and thirst than to drive away melancholy. My reasons and my conclusions are these: —No God and no human being, except an envious one, is delighted by my impotence or my trouble, or esteems as any virtue in us tears, sighs, fears, and other things of this kind, which are signs of mental impotence; on the contrary, the greater the joy with which we are affected, the greater the perfection to which we pass thereby, that is to say, the more do we necessarily partake of the divine nature.

The Calvinist ethic taught men to regard themselves as tainted with original sin, with guilt; its ethical injunctions were suffused with a commandment to man that he hate himself. But the ethic of the free man regarded self-hatred as a disease. Spinoza declared that, instead of making man despise himself, "self-satisfaction is indeed the highest thing for which we can hope." Reason, indeed, said Spinoza, demands "that every person should love himself, should seek his own profit,—what is truly profitable to him,—should desire everything that really leads man to greater perfection." [20] Humility and repentance are not virtues; neither of them springs from reason; "on the contrary, the man who repents of what he has done is doubly wretched or impotent." The doctrine of original sin, the notion that sin began with Adam's free choice to commit evil, made no sense to Spinoza: "Nor do divines remove this difficulty, at least not by deciding, that the cause of this want of power is a vice or sin in human nature, deriving its origin from our first parents' fall." [21]

Fortitude is the primary characteristic of the free man, that is, his "strength of mind and generosity" which are an expression of true liberty. The man with fortitude rises above any passion in which there is a component of hatred: "its possessor can hate no one, be angry with no one, can neither envy, be indignant with, nor despise anybody, and can least of all be proud." The aim of Spinoza's ethics is to expel every component in man's emotional life which is the product, not of the fulfillment of desire, but of its frustration. The morality of fear, humility, and repentance may be a second-best concession to the weakness of the multitude, but it is scarcely fit for the free man, who lives in accordance with reason. When the free man acts to achieve social reforms, it is not because he is swayed by pity for the underdog. "Pity is sorrow, and therefore is in itself evil." "Pity in a man who lives according to the guidance of reason is in itself evil and unprofitable." The free man desires a happy social community because it is his emotional desire to "do well . . . and to rejoice." His emotions are friendly to his fellow men. Frustrated men hate other human beings; men whose emotional lives are lives of fulfillment and satisfaction are not driven to hatred of either others or themselves. Therefore, "whatever conduces to the universal fellowship of men, that is to say, whatever causes men to live in harmony with one another is profitable, and, on the contrary, whatever brings discord into the State is evil." And this is the basis for Spinoza's social philosophy: "A man who is guided by reason is freer in a State where he lives according to the common laws than he is in solitude, where he obeys himself alone." [22]

The Calvinist metaphysic held that only a minority of humanity might hope to be among the elect, the fortunate recipients of salvation through God's grace.[23] Even today this tenet is used by members of the Dutch Reformed Church in South Africa against the Negroes among whom they live.[24] Spinoza replied to this doctrine: "The highest good of those who follow after virtue is common to all, and all may equally enjoy it." [25] Spinoza was aware that only a few men could be free in his sense. "All are able to obey, whereas there are but very few, compared with the aggregate of humanity, who can acquire the habit of virtue under the unaided guidance of reason." [26] For the masses of men, a universal theology or religion whose basic principles are consistent with reason will be the path of salvation. But virtue and salvation, in any case, are open to all men who seek them.

The economic ethics of capitalist accumulation was likewise subjected by Spinoza to psychological criticism. In the *Tractatus Theologico-Politicus* he had ridiculed those "who think supreme salvation consists in . . . gloating over their money-bags," and he returned to the passion for money-making in the *Ethics*. "As money has presented us with an abstract of everything, it has come to pass that its image above every other usually occupies the mind of the multitude because they can imagine hardly any kind of joy without the accompanying idea of money as its cause." The accumulation of wealth was not an end in itself, but was only justified by actual needs and consumption. "Those, however, who know the true use of money, and regulate the measure of wealth according to their needs, live contented with a few things." [27] The Calvinist ethic, by Spinoza's time, was considerably interwoven with an ideology of capital accumulation.[28] Calvin's doctrine, in the abstract, as R. H. Tawney has pointed out, could have been developed in the direction of either an intense individualism or a rigorous Christian socialism.[29] Indeed, during the first half of the seventeenth century, an influential segment of Calvinist opinion still retained a bias against capitalist banking.[30] Whatever the scruples that had to be overcome concerning interest on bank loans, there were no such scruples concerning dividends and profits in industry and trade. The Calvinist ministers during the seventeenth century had nothing but praise for the activities of the great monopolies, the Dutch East India and West India Companies.[31] And when Sir William Petty in Spinoza's time described the Dutch as "thinking, sober and patient men, and such as believe that labour and industry is their duty towards God," he was indeed describing the coalescence of the Calvinist ethic with the ideals of industry, frugality, and saving.[32] The

Calvinist doctrine of election, the Calvinist antipathy to consumer's joys, the Calvinist hostility to pleasure—all these lent themselves to the notion that the good man indefinitely postponed his pleasures and accumulated capital instead. Capital accumulation signified abstinence, and abstinence was cherished by the Calvinist ethics.[33] But the ethic of abstinence was not the way of the free man, who was not obsessed by the anxiety for accumulation.

The Mystic Rejection of Libertine Hedonism

The ethics of Spinoza is straightforwardly hedonistic. "All those things which bring joy are good," he wrote, whereas "superstition, on the contrary, seems to affirm that what brings sorrow is good, and, on the contrary, that what brings joy is evil."[34] As such, Spinoza's ethics was linked to the general revival of Epicurean ethical ideas in Europe during the middle of the seventeenth century. *An Apologie for Epicurus,* published by an Englishman, Charleton, in 1656 described the ancient sage as "a great Master of Temperances, Sobriety, Continence, Fortitude, and all other Vertues," and in another work, *Epicurus' Morals,* the same author declared his hedonistic creed: "Forasmuch as it's sweet, or pleasant, for a man to live without pain; and sweet, or pleasant, likewise, to enjoy good things and be recreated by them: it is an evident truth that without both these sweetnesses or Pleasures, or one of them at least, Felicity cannot be understood." Pierre Gassendi made it his task to revive the philosophy of Epicurus in all its amplitude, its physics and its ethics. He published a large treatise in 1647 on the life, customs, and writings of Epicurus, and he defended Epicurus' conception of happiness as consisting of "the ease of the Body and the Tranquillity of the Mind."[35] Sir William Temple, in his political retirement, writing essays on gardening and the cure of the gout, paid the homage of a disciple to Epicurus.[36] And Saint-Evremond, the celebrated French *libertin* who visited Spinoza declared: "je me fais une sagesse . . . de rejeter ce qui me déplaît et de recevoir ce qui me contente. [I consider it wise . . . to reject what gives me displeasure and to accept what pleases me.]" Contemporaries

like Stouppe associated the philosophic standpoint of the Epicurean *libertins* with Spinoza's in essential respects.[37]

There was one basic difference, however, between Spinoza
and the Epicurean libertines of his time. It arose from the divergence in their social outlooks. The *libertins* were essentially
a movement of the aristocratic classes of France and England.[38]
They were sceptics who emphasized the uncertainty of the
knowledge that comes to us through the senses and who doubted
the powers of reason.[39] They were indeed precursors of the vogue
which Hume's scepticism had among the English upper class in
the second half of the eighteenth century. They used Epicurean
hedonism to justify the moral laxity of their fellow members of
the aristocratic leisure class. At the courts of the French and
English kings, the systematic pursuit of adultery, for instance, was
among the chief delights.[40] Saint-Evremond therefore found the
Dutch mores with regard to marriage unusually staid; the men he
deemed ungallant, and the women prudish. Holland, he observed,
was the country of long engagements, where the parties reluctantly married each other through the compulsion of habit or
some silly conception of honor, and where absolute fidelity was
the rule after the nuptials. The Dutch world was not one in
which Saint-Evremond could feel at ease; it lacked grace and
sprightliness. Spinoza, on the other hand, did not look upon the
institution of marriage with levity: "With regard to marriage, it
is plain that it is in accordance with reason, if the desire of connection is engendered not merely by external form, but by a love
of begetting children and wisely educating them; and if, in addition, the love both of the husband and wife has for its cause not
external form merely, but chiefly liberty of mind." [41] At the
Court of Louis XIV, it was customary for the husband to knock
before entering his wife's boudoir in order not to discomfit her
lover. Such unions were alien to Spinoza's standpoint, which, on
such matters, reflected traditional Jewish mores.

The Epicurean libertines, furthermore, were basically sceptical concerning the destiny of man. They did not believe he could
attain the "supreme felicity." [42] Saint-Evremond, a thorough
gentleman, thought it was more important to enjoy the world
than to know it, "for, to speak wisely, we are more concerned

with enjoying the world rather than with understanding it." [43]
Knowledge was no source of man's supreme happiness for the
French *libertin*. At most, man could hope to spend his days
pleasantly, but there was no blessedness, no eternal joy. Saint-
Evremond thought that there was one source of human sadness
which was uneliminable—a man could never have the assurance
that there was a life beyond the grave.[44] But Spinoza was no
sceptic. He believed that reason brought certain knowledge. He
was a hedonist, but the greatest joy of all was the knowledge of
God that reason could bring to man. The polished pleasures of
the leisure class were empty frivolities to Spinoza; they were titilla-
tions of one part of the body which did not involve the whole
organism, the whole personality. Cheerfulness, said Spinoza, can
never be excessive, but pleasurable excitement can be overdone;
for "cheerfulness is joy, which, in so far as it is related to the
body, consists in this, that all the parts of the body are equally
affected," whereas in the case of pleasurable excitement, "one or
some of the parts of the body are affected more than others, . . .
and so hold the mind down to the contemplation of one object
alone, that it can think about nothing else. . . ." [45] False values
could never bring joy to the total man; the sexual quest of the *libertin,* the pecuniary drive of the money-maker, the power hunt of the
political man were passions, inadequate ideas: "Nor are those
believed to be less mad who are inflamed by love, dreaming about
nothing but a mistress or harlot day and night, for they excite
our laughter. But the avaricious man who thinks of nothing else
but gain or money, and the ambitious man who thinks of nothing
but glory, inasmuch as they do harm, and are therefore, thought
worthy of hatred, are not believed to be mad. In truth, avarice,
ambition, lust, etc. are a kind of madness, although they are not
reckoned amongst diseases." There was a highest value for
Spinoza, the supreme happiness, the most intense love, in which
there was no admixture of pain or uncertainty, and which came
when reason brought man to God. "It is therefore most profitable
to us in life to make perfect the intellect or reason as far as possible, and in this one thing consists the highest happiness or
blessedness of man; for blessedness is nothing but the peace of
mind which springs from the intuitive knowledge of God, and to

perfect the intellect is nothing but to understand God, together with the attributes and actions of God, which flow from the necessity of His nature." Spinoza and the libertines shared an admiration for Epicurus; happiness, however, as conceived by a man molded in the democratic and Republican movements was filled with a high seriousness, idealism, and aspiration, which was unintelligible to the sophisticated courtiers who distilled cynical wisdom amidst their flattery of kings.[46] The belief in man's union with God, which Spinoza shared with the Collegiants and Quakers, with tradesmen and workpeople, gave to his hedonism a culmination unknown to the aristocratic libertines, this union with God—"what a union! what a love!" [47]

The Therapy of Self-understanding: Precursor to Freud

The great contribution of Spinoza to ethical philosophy was not his hedonism. That, after all, he shared with many of his contemporaries, Hobbes, Locke, and the *libertins*. What made his *Ethics* a landmark in man's achievement of self-understanding was Spinoza's discovery of the distinction between conscious and unconscious forces in man's psychological life. The free man, indeed, is the man who is fully conscious of himself, who knows his own desires, and whose will is not the slave of unconscious anxieties, the concealed wills of others acting against his own. Spinoza's hedonism differs from his contemporaries' in so far as it is a *therapeutic* hedonism. The values of the free man are not set down as arbitrary postulates by Spinoza. He believes that these values are common to all men, that they are intrinsic to human nature. Some men deny these values, but their denial does not issue from their own desires, but from unconscious fears which have been instilled within them. Such men have only an "inadequate idea" concerning themselves; their emotions are passions, not actions, for passions are the affective states which accompany frustration, when a person's behavior is not an expression of his own desires. Passions are the outcome of the repression of desires under the compulsion of external forces. Actions, on the contrary, are those feelings which fulfill the person's nature, without frustration or repression. The consciousness of our behavior, when it is free of any component of repression, is called by Spinoza an "adequate idea."

> The desires which follow from our nature in such a manner that they can be understood through it alone, are those which are related to the mind, in so far as it is conceived to consist of adequate ideas. The remaining desires are not related to the mind, unless in so far as it conceives of things inadequately, whose power and increase cannot be determined by human power, but by the power of objects which are without us. The first kind of desires, therefore, are properly called actions, but the latter passions; for the first always indicate our power, and the latter, on the contrary, indicate our impotence and imperfect knowledge.[48]

What, then, is the technique of therapy which Spinoza proposes to those who are slaves to forces of which they are unconscious? His therapy is the same as that which Freud has made known in our time.[49] Spinoza proposes that the unconscious determinants of our behavior should be brought into clear consciousness; when we know the causes of our irrational behavior, the irrational motives themselves lose their force, and we can then act rationally in accordance with our desires as we now clearly apprehend them. "A passion ceases to be a passion as soon as we form a clear and distinct idea of it."

The basic ethical contrast for Spinoza is between true virtue and impotence. But "virtue" and "impotence" are not for Spinoza terms of an irreducible moralistic mode. Ethics to Spinoza is a branch of applied psychology, and ethical terms can be fully defined in psychological language. The impotent man, the follower of false values, suffers from a species of mental disease: "impotence therefore consists in this alone—that a man allows himself to be led by things which are outside himself, and by them to be determined to such actions as the common constitution of external things demands, and not to such as his own nature considered in itself alone demands." The impotent man is dominated through his unconscious by forces external to him; his own character, his own desires, are lost to his view: "the man, therefore, who is ignorant of himself, is ignorant of the foundation of all the virtues, and consequently is ignorant of all the virtues." The virtuous man for Spinoza is not one who lives up to commandments which emanate from some source other than his own body and mind. People usually regard the virtuous man as one endowed with a conscience stern and unbending in the restrictions it imposes on his desires. The virtuous man is taken as the man with a strong superego, to use Freud's language. But Spinoza would regard this "virtuous" man as a slave. The foundation of virtue for Spinoza is the fulfillment of our desires, the fulfillment of our being. "The endeavor after self-preservation is the primary and only foundation of virtue." "Virtue means nothing but acting according to the laws of our own nature, . . . and happiness consists in this— that a man can preserve his own being." "The more each person strives and is able to seek his own profit, that is to say, to preserve his being, the more virtue does he possess; on the other hand, in so far as each person neglects his own profit, that is to say, neglects to preserve his own being is he impotent."

In Freud, man's efforts to achieve happiness are opposed by the obstacles of unconscious influences, fears, anxieties; these must be surmounted by understanding, and psychoanalysis is a sustained effort to understand the sources of these anxieties. In the same way for Spinoza, "this effort to understand is the primary and sole foundation of virtue. . . . The virtuous man is the one who acts with full conscious awareness of his desires. "A man cannot be absolutely said to act in conformity with virtue, in so far as he is determined to any action because he has inadequate ideas, but only in so far as he is determined because he understands." [50] When desires are channeled by fears and anxieties, they fail to fulfill man's being; but when they are guided by understanding to maximal expression, they are a fulfillment of ourselves; "all the appetites or desires are passions only in so far as they arise from inadequate ideas, and are classed among the virtues whenever they are excited or begotten by adequate ideas. . . ."

Moralists, when psychoanalyzed, turn out to be disguised immoralists. Beneath the manifest, apparent content of men's moralizings, Spinoza finds the real content of their words, the symptoms of "disease of mind." Those who disparage men are precisely those who within themselves are most dependent on the world's good opinion; those who profess themselves cynics are those who have been most hurt by ideals to which their emotions cling, and their bitterness is that of a betrayed lover. "Indeed it is certain that those covet glory the most who are loudest in declaiming against its abuse and the vanity of the world. . . . So also a man who has not been well received by his mistress thinks of nothing but the fickleness of women, their faithlessness, and their oft-proclaimed failings,—all of which he forgets as soon as he is taken into favour by his mistress again." [51] Freud's explorations into the unconscious showed the coincidence of contraries in the life of the anxiety-ridden, where latent reality and manifest content are in apparent opposition. And Spinoza's analysis uncovers the same pattern in the relationship between underlying emotional realities and men's words. For instance, "although despondency is contrary to pride, the despondent man is closely akin to the proud man"; each longs to be above others, and to find fault with his fellow men. "Those who have the most credit for being abject and humble are generally the most ambitious and envious." The man who commits suicide is the agent of external aggressive forces against himself; "all persons who kill themselves are impotent in mind, and have been thoroughly overcome by external causes opposed to their nature." [52]

Spinoza's method resembles Freud's procedure in the earlier years of the great analyst's work, when therapeutic motives were dominant. But in his later years, Freud became a philosophic pessimist; he came to believe that a death instinct is innate to man, and that an aggressive tendency acts against man's self unless it is diverted to external objects. During this latter phase, Freud became sceptical concerning the therapeutic value of psychoanalysis.[53] Spinoza would regard the belief in a death instinct as an "inadequate idea." "A very little reflection will show," says Spinoza, "that it is as impossible that a man, from the necessity of his nature, should endeavour not to exist, or to be changed into some other form, as it is that something should be begotten from nothing." The drives of man are his essence, the forces in which man asserts his existence, and a drive to self-annihilation is, for Spinoza, a self-contradiction. "Desire is the essence itself of man in so far as it is conceived as determined to any action by one of his affections." [54] A more basic category, indeed, than desire is appetite, which Spinoza also defines as "nothing but the very essence of man." Desire denotes those appetites of which we are conscious, but sheer appetition, conscious or unconscious, is the ultimate in man; "there is no difference between appetite and desire, unless in this particular, that desire is generally related to men in so far as they are conscious of their appetites, and it may therefore be defined as appetite of which we are conscious." Medieval philosophers had spoken of reason as the essence of man. Spinoza, in that sense, is no rationalist. Appetite is the essence of man; man is a mode of those restless, surging forces of motion and rest, of feeling and idea, which constitute the extension and thought of nature.[55] The good is not an edict from man's conscience or supernatural power; "we neither strive for, wish, seek, nor desire anything because we think it to be good, but, on the contrary, we adjudge a thing to be good because we strive for, wish, seek, or desire it." [56] The ethics of the free man is an endeavor to restore to consciousness, under the conditions of civilized society, an awareness of our own appetites, our own selves, which have become so beclouded and repressed that we are deprived of adequate ideas concerning them.

The Calvinist ethic, like the neo-orthodoxy of our own time, made anxieties the stuff of ethical experience. The aim of Spinoza was to help eradicate anxieties, to remove the burden of guilt from men. In one of Spinoza's dialogues, to which we have already referred, "Love" speaks of the persecutions of "the two archenemies of the human race, namely, Hatred and Remorse." [57] The churches, said Spinoza, had become theaters in which ministers played the demagogue. "Verily, if they had but one spark of light from on High, they would not insolently rave, but would learn to worship God more wisely, and would be as marked among their fellows for mercy as they now are for malice; . . . they would no longer fiercely persecute, but rather be filled with pity and compassion." [58] Those who would instill in men the conviction of guilt, would make them brood on their impotence; they are not ethical teachers: such preachers who "know how to revile men, to denounce vices rather than to teach virtues, and not to strengthen men's minds but to weaken them, are injurious both to themselves and others. . . ." [59]

To achieve a therapy of understanding, Spinoza is concerned with the analysis of anxiety, with ambivalence and fear. That emotion which disposes a man "as not to will the thing he wills, and to will that which he does not will, is called *fear*." Place this emotional configuration against an unconscious background, and we have what Freud calls *anxiety*. And Spinoza tries to unravel the components which enter into ambivalences, the mixtures of love and hatred for the same object, the "vacillations of the mind," as he calls them.[60] The aim is always the same: to enable the emotions of love and joy to fill the life of the personality, to conquer hatred and sorrow by understanding, which finally terminates in the knowledge and joy in God. "The mind acts only in so far as it understands. . . . To understand, therefore, is the absolute virtue of the mind. But the highest thing which the mind can understand is God. . . ." [61]

Intellectual Love of God and Intellectual Hatred

Spinoza, the ethically-minded psychiatrist, merged into Spinoza, the mystic lover of God. All the emotions of the body, all our images and conceptions of things, says Spinoza, can be related to the idea of God, for "whatever is, is in God, and nothing can either be or be conceived without God." With the clear understanding of the necessity of things comes joy, peace of mind, and love for God occupies the mind above all things. This is a love, furthermore, which cannot be contaminated by either envy or jealousy. "Our sorrows and misfortunes," says Spinoza, "mainly proceed from too much love towards an object which is subject to many changes, and which we can never possess." But our love for God is "towards an immutable and eternal object," "a love therefore which cannot be vitiated by the defects which are in common love. . . ." It is a strange love indeed, for it is eternally unrequited; "God loves no one and hates no one," for as a perfect being, He can neither increase nor decrease his relative perfection. And "he who loves God cannot strive that God should love him in return." [62]

And yet we can ask once more: Is not Spinoza's theory of the intellectual love of God a colossal example of an "inadequate idea"? Is there not a streak of masochism that runs through this doctrine which insists that we love God though He never love us? We are asked to love this substance without feeling, this entity of geometrical perfection and indifference. How would this "love of God" have fared if Spinoza the psychiatrist had placed it under analytic scrutiny? Would not the first act of the free man have been to affirm his independence of this nonmoral geometrical entity, this whole which, by definition, contains all things? Why, indeed, worship a logical tautology?

Again, we may ask: Why should men not hate God? A doctrine of the intellectual hatred of God would seem to be far more justified than one of love. For God is the cause of sorrow, on Spinoza's ground, and we should hate Him as an idea associated with all our pain. A philosophy similar to Schopenhauer's would then be our conclusion. Man's highest good would not be to persevere in his being; rather, his virtue would lie in a denial of his essence, in escape from his will. Escape from reality, withdrawal from nature, rather than union with it, would be our aim. To this metaphysics of Byronic defiance, Spinoza replies: "No one can hate God." Why? Because "in so far as we understand the causes of sorrow, it ceases to be a passion, that is to say, it ceases to be sorrow; and therefore in so far as we understand God to be the cause of sorrow do we rejoice." [94] Once more we are confronted by Spinoza's view that a pain, a passion when understood loses its painful character. But, we may persist in asking, does understanding possess this magical efficacy? Does understanding transmute suffering into joy? Does a hungry man suffer the less because he has a clear and distinct idea of the laws of physiology? We may study the laws of societies and come to a partial understanding of the causes of poverty and war; does that knowledge give us occasion to rejoice in the infinite power of God?

A passion ceases to be one when understood only if its cause was lack of understanding, but there are countless passions which arise, not because of our lack of understanding, but because of our lack of power. We may understand why men go to war and not be able to do anything about it. Freud, after all his psychoanalytical labors, remained an unhappy man. He had come to the conclusion that an instinct for aggression was part of man, and he despaired of human efforts toward world peace and community. Understanding, in such cases, heightens sorrow by making us feel that it is irremediable. We have already cited Spinoza's classical summation of the place of the individual in the scheme of things: "There is no individual thing in nature which is not surpassed in strength and power by some other thing, but any individual thing being given, another and a stronger is also given, by which the former can be destroyed." If our basic aim is to persevere in our being, will not our sorrow be unending as we contemplate the infinite number of things that can destroy us? The thought of our finitude then must pain and torment us. Will our understanding of Spinoza's axiom eradicate this pain? No, for it will only remind us of the infinite ways in which our existence can be destroyed. It requires again a masochist frame of mind to delight in the fact that we can be destroyed in an infinite rather than a finite number of ways. We are called on by Spinoza to admire "the power and workmanship of nature," "to conceive things as they are in themselves," not "in a disturbed, mutilated, and confused fashion," but in the manner in which "the brave man will consider above everything that all things follow from the necessity of the divine nature," for then, "in so far as we understand, we cannot desire anything except what is necessary."

This is gallows humor written into a metaphysics. The human race is asked to admire the power of nature which may destroy it and to take delight in the beauty of the mathematical laws which threaten it with annihilation. The soldier killed by a bullet is asked to rejoice in the laws of motion which govern the bullet's trajectory. And it is false to say that with knowledge, we can only desire what is necessary; for we can long for a more just order of things even when the powers of injustice and indifference overwhelm us. Behind Spinoza's metaphysics lies an injunction to love that which is necessary, a cosmic acquiescence. To love that which destroys you, however, is a sign of a "disease of the mind." The masochist hates himself, and Spinoza has abundantly said that reason demands "that every person should love himself." [63] The intellectual love of God, as a form of self-hatred, is a neurotic manifestation or, as Spinoza would say, an "inadequate idea."

This strain of masochism manifests itself likewise in Spinoza's definition of love. Descartes, whose *Passions of the Soul* was studied closely by Spinoza, defined love as an emotion which stimulated one to union with another object. "Love is an emotion of the soul caused by the movement of the spirits which incites it to join itself willingly to objects which appear to it to be agreeable." [64] Love, for Descartes, is close to its physical, sexual basis. But Spinoza sublimates sexuality in metaphysics. It can hardly escape one's attention that almost every reference of his to the love between the sexes is in terms of some revulsion. There is praise for the man "who is not moved by the gifts of a harlot to serve her lust"; there is "the love of a harlot, that is to say, the lust of sexual intercourse, which arises from mere external form," which "easily passes into hatred, unless, which is worse, it becomes a species of delirium"; there are the obsessed men "who are inflamed by love, dreaming about nothing but a mistress or harlot day and night," [65] "the lascivious man" who does not cease to be lascivious when he is too timid to "gratify his desire," the man whose disillusionment with all women disappears when his mistress reinstates him to his lost status. Jealousy and detestable images, according to Spinoza, stalk the lover of a woman: "This feeling is generally excited when the love is love towards a woman. The man who imagines that the woman he loves prostitutes herself to another is not merely troubled because his appetite is restrained, but he turns away from her because he is obliged to connect the image of a beloved object with the privy parts and with what is excremental in another man." [66] Physical, sexual love to Spinoza partook of a bestial, degrading character; the women who appear in the *Ethics* are almost always harlots who wish to reduce the being of men, harlots who make men play the fool. Physical love, Spinoza further reasoned, divides men; when two men love the same person, one will have to think of his beloved as someone he has lost. Sorrow comes inevitably in the wake of love, to add to jealousy, that "vacillation of the mind," that ambivalence which is experienced when "love and hatred are both felt together." The harlot looms with a power in Spinoza's writing which his rarer references to the love of a wife scarcely have.[67] Whatever the personal experiences which led to his attitude, there was an abhorrent quality about sexual love to Spinoza.[68] It seemed to him a passion quite different from the love which arises from "the freedom of the mind." And the definition of love which Spinoza proposed reflects this hatred of the body; he is indeed driving the harlot out of his images of love. Love for him is dissociated from the idea of union with the beloved object; love is rarefied, spiritualized, sublimated. "Love is joy with the accompanying idea of an external cause." Authors like Descartes, said Spinoza, "who define love to be the will of the lover to unite himself to the beloved object" have not perceived its essence. Love, continued Spinoza, can be conceived without either the lover's desire for union with his absent beloved, or his desire for continued union with the beloved whom he possesses.[69] Love can be conceived, Spinoza held, without either of these desires; it is simply the joy that arises from the idea of the beloved.

According to Freud, eros, love or *libido,* though it pervades all living things, always involves the longing for union.[70] To Spinoza, however, love became dissociated from its biological aim—there is the fulfillment without the bodily taint. Love is not only sublimated but maimed. The erotic component in life seems somehow to have been twisted by the personal circumstances of Spinoza's life. Baruch's mother died when the child was six years old. She was his father's second wife. Shortly afterward, the father, Michael D'Espinoza, married for the third time. Baruch grew up under his stepmother's care. A child of six, seeing another woman trying to fill his real mother's role, might well be embittered, resentful. How much love was there in the D'Espinoza household? The wives replaced themselves as death took them away. The children of the different marriages seem to have had little love for each other. Spinoza was still a member of the Jewish community when his father died. Nevertheless, his siblings tried to deprive him of any share in inheritance. As Colerus tells us: "His Father's Succession was to be divided between him and his Sisters, to which they were condemned in Law, tho they had left no Stone unturn'd to exclude him from it. Yet instead of dividing that Succession, he gave them his share, and kept only for himself a good Bed, with its furniture." His sister, Rebekah, was prepared to present herself as Spinoza's heir when it seemed that there might be some estate, but she retired from the scene when Spinoza's debts came into the picture.[71] We do not get the impression of a family whose members were strong in their affections for one another. And distrust in persons, mutable creatures, is most deeply ingrained when the formative years are spent in an atmosphere where proximity is the occasion for hostility.

External circumstances, moreover, in his maturity, made it virtually impossible for Spinoza to have a normal emotional life. In manhood, Spinoza evidently loved Clara Maria van dan Ende, daughter of his teacher. "Spinosa having often occasion to see and speak to her, grew in Love with her, and has often confest that he design'd to marry her." She was a girl quite unlike those whom he had known in the Jewish quarter. She was witty, knew Latin and music, and could fill her father's place as a teacher in his absence.

In advanced Dutch circles, a "new woman" was beginning to appear, who claimed the right to participate in learning and social movements. There was the celebrated Anna Maria van Schurman, known as "the Sappho of Europe," who amazed scholars with her command of many languages and zeal for learning, and with whom Descartes frequently enjoyed discussion.[72] Antoinette Bourignon was still another woman with a remarkable capacity for religious leadership, and with a considerable influence in Amsterdam. And Clara Maria van dan Ende, teacher in her father's school, was similarly no ordinary Dutchwoman, preoccupied with domestic duties. She had been touched by the new learning and the new movements. Was marriage, however, a possibility between her and Spinoza? When Clara married, she insisted upon a ceremony within the Roman

Catholic church. Her involvement in modern modes of thought had not emancipated her from loyalty to her church. Spinoza had left the Jewish community, but he never became a Christian. He spoke of the Christians as an outsider would, and rejected the claims of Roman Catholicism in the strongest terms.[73] Of one thing we may be reasonably certain; Spinoza would never have submitted to the marriage ritual of a Catholic priest, let alone convert to Catholicism, as his rival for Clara's hand felt constrained to do.[74]

As an excommunicate Jew who remained excommunicate from all organized religion, Spinoza's life had an enforced solitariness. Whom could he ask to share his existence? Clara, apart from her Catholic devoutness, had preferred another man. Spinoza reassured himself that the human love denied him was petty and paltry compared to his eternal philosophic love. He meditated on the slavery of men to harlots and mistresses. He evolved a new, unusual conception of love. Did its sweeping grandeur issue from the repressed longings of one whom social circumstances debarred from the free man's life? Had Spinoza, a man of intense emotions, tried to find in union with God the surrogate consummation of his desires? Early educational influences might well have helped to warp his idea of love. Jewish tradition regarded woman as an inferior, and looked upon sexual relations as a familial duty rather than an erotic joy; the study of the Torah, not love, was taken as man's great end.[75] Spinoza's theory of love, we may venture to say, was not conceived by a free mind, aware of itself; there was a component of enslavement here, of whose causes he was ignorant; he too was doing not his own will but the will of others.

The Eternity of the Human Mind: Spinoza's Leap Beyond the Geometrical Method

The free man might hope to understand the causes of his human frustration; he might then apply the remedies of social science, of medical science, of psychology. The free man would try to raise standards of living and build the basis for cooperative human relationships. Epicureans and social utilitarians could meet with Spinoza on the platform of this common philosophy. They shared what we would call the humanism of the free man. But in Spinoza, who had met with Quakers and Collegiants and had lived with Mennonites, something remained which was not quite satisfied by the medical, psychiatric approach. The desire within him for the eternal life that the inner light brings was strong. This yearning, which had united him to Pieter Balling, William Ames, and Jarig Jelles, took him out of the familiar coordinates of political science and political action. Spinoza's character always retained an element foreign to De Witt, Machiavelli, or Hobbes. The analytical political philosopher talked of constitutions realistically, and refused to indulge in Utopian luxuries. But the mystic metaphysician, writing the last book of the *Ethics*, sought for a more ultimate meaning in life than the labors of the political reformer. A Utopian metaphysic broke through the confines of his scientific system to project upon the universe the eternity of the human mind.

In the last part of the *Ethics*, Spinoza passes to the consideration of those matters which pertain "to the duration of the mind without relation to the body." He was undertaking to do something which was impossible within the framework of his system. He wished to prove that part of the human mind is eternal, that part, namely, which we call the intellect, "through which alone we are said to act"; on the other hand, that part of the human mind which is composed of passions and inadequate ideas, namely, the imagination, he argued, perishes. The mind, then, in so far as it understands is an eternal mode of thought, and all such modes "taken together form the eternal and infinite intellect of God." The more scientific knowledge we have, the more our minds are eternal: "death is by so much the less injurious to us as the clear and distinct knowledge of the mind is greater. . . ." [76]

The knowledge of the laws of nature is not for Spinoza the highest kind of knowledge. There is a direct, "intuitive" insight, which gives one a direct knowledge of God, and Spinoza undertakes to explain "how much more potent it is than the universal knowledge, which I have called knowledge of the second kind." Our everyday knowledge, based on sensation and hearsay, is an inferior variety called the first kind; it is the source of error, "opinion or imagination," as Spinoza classifies it. Our scientific knowledge, on the other hand, consists of adequate ideas; it is based on common notions, that is, the properties in which "all bodies agree," and such universal laws of nature are understood clearly and distinctly.[77] Scientific knowledge is the achievement of what Spinoza calls reason. Spinoza indeed accepts Descartes' account of scientific knowledge. Bodies, Descartes had said, "are not properly speaking known by the senses or by the faculty of imagination, but by the understanding only." [78] A piece of wax when heated, Descartes observed in his famous example, changes its color, taste, shape, size, state, smell, but is still apprehended as the same wax by the understanding, which provides us with the universal laws of physical things. But Spinoza does not rest content with the formulations of science. His mystical aspiration seeks a higher kind of knowledge than the scientist's labor of reason. The free man, the hedonist, regards fortitude as his highest achievement; it is that strength of mind and generosity which makes its possessor rise above all anger, hatred, or envy. But the mystic wishes not ordinary fortitude, but blessedness, that love which is "called Glory in the sacred writings," a salvation, which consists "in a constant and eternal love towards God." And it is the third kind of knowledge, the mystic insight, which gives rise to the "highest possible peace," and which makes it "possible for the human mind to be of such a nature that that part of it which perishes with its body, in comparison with the part of it which remains, is of no consequence." It is from this knowledge, as well, that there springs "the intellectual love of God," our joy in God as the direct source of our highest insight.

Can the human mind have an eternal part? If we accept Spinoza's standpoint in its scientific aspect, the answer is no. Spinoza rejects the ordinary theory of personal immortality. "The mind," he affirms, "can imagine nothing, nor can it recollect anything that is past except while the body exists." [79] There is a strict parallelism, in his system, between the order of thoughts and the order of physical things; each physical object has its corresponding mental mode. But what happens to this parallelism when Spinoza discusses the eternity of the human mind? Spinoza the mystic simply abandons the structural order of his metaphysics. He argues that there is "a certain mode of thought which pertains to the essence of the human mind and is necessarily eternal." To what mode of extension, to what type of physical existence would this eternal mode of thought correspond? There can be none to fulfill the requirement. If there were, it would have to consist in the physiological organization of our body which corresponds to the mystic insight, and that organization is certainly not eternal. And on the physiological level, the brain-states which correspond to our highest insights are no more privileged than those which correspond to our lowest errors in perception; they are all physiological states which perish.

Spinoza is mindful that his structure of proof is near tottering at this stage. For in the midst of an argument, presumably of a strictly geometrical kind, he appeals to our feelings on the matter as proof for the eternity of the human mind. "Nevertheless we feel and know by experience that we are eternal." What part has feeling in a treatise written according to the geometrical method?

This eternity of the human mind which Spinoza claimed we feel is not to be confused, he insists, with anything having to do with time or duration. "Eternity cannot be defined by time, or have any relationship to it." Duration, he writes, can be ascribed to the mind only so long as the body exists; we have no recollection of having existed before our bodies' existence. Yet, says Spinoza, "we feel that our mind, in so far as it involves the essence of the body under the form of eternity, is eternal, and that this existence of the mind cannot be limited by time nor manifested through duration." It would be one thing to acknowledge with Spinoza that in God's intellect "there necessarily exists an idea which expresses the essence of this or that human body under the form of eternity." That would be true of all bodies, each electron, each star, each animal, and would only imply that the whole of nature, as a unified physical system, had its corresponding mental mode.[80] But we would have no more personal status in such a system than the consciousness of a white blood corpuscle within us has in our consciousness; the corpuscle's life is a transient episode, together with its consciousness, which perishes in itself completely, though the consciousness of the total person continues to exist.[81] If God's mind is eternal, our minds still remain transient, in each and every one of their components, the God-like as well as the bestial.

Spinoza's theory of the mind's eternity was indeed a residue from his early thinking which fitted ill with his mature *Ethics*. When he first formulated this conception, it was linked to the belief that the highest reality of God was incorporeal. Spinoza's first philosophic writings did not hold that extension was an attribute equivalent in status to God's thought. In the *Short Treatise*, Spinoza explained how our "Regeneration," our being "born again," was achieved through love and union with an eternal incorporeal. He wrote that "our second birth will take place when we become aware in us of entirely different effects of love, commensurate with the knowledge of the incorporeal object, and as different from the first as the corporeal is different from the incorporeal, spirit from flesh." We come to embrace, said Spinoza, "that without which we can neither be nor be understood, and which is in no way corporeal." [82]

Much of Spinoza's later intellectual struggle arose from an effort to graft the doctrine of the intellectual love of God onto the more scientific conception of God and nature of his later years. A speculation which was directly connected with a belief in God's incorporeality was, however, flagrantly inconsistent with his later view that the modes of extension corresponded to those of thought. Spinoza's early philosophy indeed showed a theological cast of mind which grew less pronounced in his mature years. When he renounced Talmudical Judaism, the concepts of Collegiant pantheist theology had at first preoccupied him. He tried to translate traditional theological notions into more philosophic terms. The "son of God," for instance, he interpreted as the infinite understanding which exists in nature from all eternity. In those early years, also, Spinoza believed that intuition gave us many truths; the Jews, he wrote, "apprehended the Ten Commandments by pure intuition; to this

opinion I myself once inclined. . . ." [83] When he completed the
Ethics, however, the deliverances of intuition had become confined to a narrow domain; besides God, we could know by
intuition the ratios of the "simplest numbers," and, evidently,
nothing more.[84] Intuition, as an organon of knowledge, over
and above reason and perception, thus declined in its significance
during the course of Spinoza's evolution. But all the stages of
Spinoza's thought left their impress on the *Ethics,* and in its
successive books the pantheist mystic alternated in ascendancy
with the scientific hedonist.

The mystic in Spinoza tried to break through the bonds
which his psychology and physiology placed upon the mind.
This longing to transcend time through seeing things "under
the aspect of eternity" recurs often in changing forms in the
human spirit. The novelist Proust, for instance, believed that
the artist, by fixing the content of the passing moment, could
stop time's flux; all could thus be transfigured, "under the
aspect of eternity, which is that of art." Man could thereby
find an absolute outside time, and art would be the mystic
conquest of duration.[85] Bertrand Russell similarly believed that
the study of mathematics brought a liberation from time. Art,
mathematics, intellectual love of God, thoughts of eternal objects—these remain activities of the human organism, and the
intense experience of human selves in these activities cannot
be known to give us access to a realm outside time. The
protestants against the human status, the great rebels against the
givenness of what man is, have been too proud to stoop to vulgar
devices of personal immortality. They have tried to define a
more Olympian eternity. But to what reality does this word
"eternity" correspond? Does it not remain a linguistic surd, the
projection of an emotion in which the projection fails to
complete itself because the existent materials at hand cannot
be combined into the desired arrangement? Eternity is a longing which cannot project itself upon reality, a longing for a
dream which cannot even be dreamt. How does Spinoza define
"eternity"? "By eternity, I understand existence itself, so far
as it is conceived necessarily to follow from the definition alone
of the eternal thing." And what is "duration"? "Duration

is the indefinite continuance of existence." [86] Eternity, in other words, is necessary existence and, in the last analysis, the necessary existence of God. But even that which necessarily exists continues to exist. Its continuance is limitless, its duration, we may say, is necessary and without terminus. "Existence itself" is Spinoza's undefined term, but even his imaginative power does not liberate the meaning of that term from its durational quality. The moral of the history of these brave efforts at transcendent projection is clear. As men we may long to see things "sub specie aeternitatis," but as men we shall hopelessly fail, and our intellect and imagination will both remain thoroughly world-bound; try as we may, our vision is always "sub specie aetatis," or in rare moments perhaps "sub specie saeculorum."

Ultimate Uncertainty: the Failure of the Geometrical Method

Spinoza himself seems at the end to have become doubtful about the human ability to see things "under the aspect of eternity"; he seems to have become uncertain concerning his own philosophy of the eternity of the human mind. The next to the last proposition of his *Ethics* reads: "Even if we did not know that our mind is eternal, we should still consider as of primary importance Piety and Religion, and absolutely everything which in the Fourth Part we have shown to be related to strength of mind and generosity." How amazing is this proposition! What would we think of the geometer who asserted as a theorem of importance that doubt concerning one section of his geometry should not be taken to impugn the validity of proofs in the previous sections? We should obviously conclude that our geometer was honestly doubtful concerning the proofs he had been offering in the section in question, and was hastening to admonish the reader not to extend these doubts to those demonstrations which were more reliable and well grounded. And this is, indeed, what Spinoza does at the close of the *Ethics*. He reminds us that the philosophy of the free man remains valid even if we abandon our hope for eternity. Fortitude, that is, strength of mind and generosity, is still the ideal

character of the free man, even if we can never achieve blessedness or glory. The values of the free man are grounded in man's
biological nature and are clarified by the sciences of man—
psychology and medicine. They provide the basis of our political and social life. And they remain valid even if the mystic
longing for eternity is inevitably frustrated. "But in order to
determine what reason prescribes as profitable, we had no regard
to the eternity of the mind, which we did not recognise till we
come to the Fifth Part."

The commands of reason are of primary importance, says
Spinoza, "even if we were now ignorant of the eternity of the
mind." The creed of the multitude, Spinoza continues, regards
piety as a burden which is endured simply because of hope for
a reward after death or because of fear of dreadful punishments
in the hereafter. If the multitude disbelieved in immortality,
they would prefer to follow their passions and lusts. To this
creed, Spinoza replies: "This seems to me as absurd as if a man,
because he does not believe that he will be able to feed his
body with good food to all eternity, should desire to satiate
himself with poisonous and deadly drugs; or as if, because he
sees that the mind is not eternal or immortal, he should therefore prefer to be mad, and to live without reason,—absurdities
so great that they scarcely deserve to be repeated." [87] We may
ask, however: Are such devices by which men would repress the
sorrow of death, absurd? If the fact of death is an ever-present
reminder of man's impotence, a persistent cause of sorrow, and
if as free men we refuse to be ignorant of our sorrow's cause,
and avail ourselves of any easy device for repressing the un-
pleasant, shall we know any unalloyed joy in our lives? And
if men seek oblivion, even madness, to escape the reminder of
death, we usually say that it is regrettable that life's affections
and activities were not absorbing enough to leave them untroubled, but we cannot assuage the longing for eternity itself.
Men who are consumed with the intellectual hatred of God,
who feel the void between the universe and their longings, finally
turn their hatred inward against themselves, because the universe is cosmically indifferent to their hostility. We can see the
futility of such hatred, but can we ever transform it to love?

Can we love this nature as a whole with sincerity? Can we love it without hating ourselves, offering ourselves in masochist self-immolation to the God who does not love us?

The doubt as to immortality which had entered the last pages of his *Ethics* went to the heart of Spinoza's life and philosophy. The young Spinoza, the friend of Collegiants and Quakers, had written a rhapsody to the wonderful love for God which suffused the human mind with eternity. It was now almost a generation since Spinoza and his friends used to gather together in their circle; there had been youth, friendship, and hope in those days as they went forth to do battle with superstition.[88] Some of the circle were now dead, and meanwhile political reaction had triumphed. The philosopher statesman De Witt, the father-image to the young radicals, was murdered. Defeat and melancholy replaced the buoyancy of youth. In a later age, young Europeans, after the failure of the Revolution of 1848, turned from philosophies of social reconstruction to the pessimism of Schopenhauer. Spinoza lived through the crisis-experience and wondered which of his youthful principles had survived the test of history, how much of youthful vision would withstand the revision of experience. His politics had once been a hymn to the martyrs of liberty. The poetry of politics was gone in his middle age. Was his youthful dedication to God to go too? Was he to take leave of that all-embracing God whose spirit was in all nature, the God he had shared with left Republicans and Quaker mystics? Was the eternity of the human mind another illusion with which the tired philosophic liberal must come to terms?

Spinoza as a Left Cartesian

Two streams of feeling and thought had converged in Spinoza's experience; his personality gave to their union a distinctive form of finite staccato propositions, which strained themselves to tell of an incommensurable nature. There was first the Quaker-Collegiant affiliation to pantheism, the philosophy of social radicals like Winstanley, to which the youthful Spinoza was early drawn. His own teacher, Van dan Ende, had been a disciple of Cesare Vanini, the Neopolitan priest who earlier in the century had refused to acknowledge any God but nature. This mystic pantheist longing Spinoza shared with his personal friend, Pieter Balling, who spoke of the light as Spinoza spoke of the intellectual love of God, the light "which leads Man in Truth, unto the way of God, . . . giving him Peace in his Conscience, yea, brings him Union with God, wherein all Happiness and Salvation do Consist." Union with the all-encompassing God was for every man to achieve, and Balling availed himself of Cartesian terminology to utter his vision; this "light is a clear and distinct Knowledge of Truth in the Understanding of every Man, by which he is so convinced of the Being and Quality of things that he cannot possibly doubt thereof." [89]

Alongside the mystic religious longing, however, Cartesian thought in Holland was also tending toward a pantheist outcome. Every philosophic system is capable of development in various directions. For a philosophic system is a vocabulary for expression which youth acquires, and when it begins to grope for its own ideas, even its own fresh vision is first stated in the only language which it has learned to speak. The traditional language is the mold in which even rebellion is cast, and its resources are strained in the effort to speak the new. We must speak with the words we know, till a new vocabulary gradually emerges, more adequate to our thought. As Hegel's philosophy, for instance, was transformed in fission to left Hegelianism and right Hegelianism, so likewise was Cartesianism transformed in Holland. Spinoza, we might say, was the most thoroughgoing of the left Cartesians.

It was in Holland, not France, that the philosophy and mathematics of Descartes had their greatest impact.[90] French universities, under strict ecclesiastical control, had no welcome for the ideas of a thinker whose works to this day are on the *Index Librorum Prohibitorum*. But daring spirits in the newer Dutch universities were receptive to Cartesian modes of thought. They began to develop Descartes' ideas in novel directions.

In the history of thought, extralogical factors are decisive in determining in which direction, among the many alternatives

possible, a philosophy will be developed.[91] Philosophic systems
have open historical potentialities. The currents of the social
environment impinge upon the personality of the philosopher;
his response to the changing world takes the form of a changing
philosophic perspective. As a philosopher, however, he undertakes to present his new philosophy as the product of an "internal
criticism" of his predecessor's system. The motive power of the
extralogical factors, their generative drive, falls out of view in the
"formal" statement of the philosophy. We have seen the power
of these extralogical factors in the shaping of Spinoza's pantheism;
their impact was to impel the Cartesian ideas by a process of
internal self-criticism toward a pantheist conclusion. The
emotional longing wrought its systematic expression from the
notions given at hand.

When Spinoza began his discussions with his circle of
Cartesian friends, the process of development toward pantheism
had already progressed far within Cartesian ranks. Descartes
himself had verged on a complete identification of God with
nature; "by nature, considered in general," he wrote, "I now
understand no other thing than either God Himself or else the
order and disposition which God has established in created
things." [92] But Descartes, however, had not developed a pantheistic conception of substance. Created substance was distinguished by him from uncreated substance; God, he held,
was "the uncreated and independent thinking substance." In
addition, according to Descartes, two kinds of created substance
are known to us clearly and distinctly—that which thinks, and,
secondly, corporeal substance: mind and body. This theory of
three substances was an unstable one; Descartes himself observed
that given the definition of substance as an "existent thing
which requires nothing but itself in order to exist," that "to
speak truth, nothing but God answers to this description as
being that which is absolutely self-sustaining, for we perceive
that there is no other created thing which can exist without being
sustained by his power."

The pantheist, determinist criticism of Descartes was especially the work in Holland of Regius, a professor of medicine
at Utrecht during the years 1638 to 1679. When Darwin

published his *Origin of Species* in 1859, the kindly fates gave him Thomas Henry Huxley to act as his "bulldog" in controversy. Regius was Descartes' bulldog in the Netherlands; he fought a bitter polemic on behalf of the new philosophy with Voetius, the Aristotelian theologian. With a man like Regius taking up the cudgels on his behalf, Descartes could write in 1631 during his long sojourn at Amsterdam: "What other country where you can enjoy such perfect liberty. . . ." But Regius came to be dissatisfied with his master's philosophic compromises. He doubted that human error was to be explained by the notion of the free will running away with the understanding; against the Cartesian theory, Regius held to the determinist view that "every untimely judgment depends upon the acquired and inborn temperament of the body." A species of medical materialism was taking root at Utrecht. One of Regius' pupils was so bold as to carry the criticism against the doctrine of substance itself. If man is composed of two heterogeneous components—thinking and extension—then man cannot be regarded as a substance *per se,* but only as a substance *per accidens.*[93] Or, as Spinoza would have put it, man is not a substance but a mode of that which exists in and is conceived through substance.[94] The orthodox party was furious with Regius for such speculations; Descartes advised him to repudiate this doctrine, but Regius' departures from his master were now pronounced.[95] Thus, the generation that followed Descartes began to push his system toward a pantheist culmination. At the same time, Collegiant mystics were using the Cartesian vocabulary to convey their "clear and distinct idea" of union with God. Both modes of thought, scientific and mystic, converged in Spinoza. Thought and extension were recognized by Spinoza, following Descartes, as attributes of substance, but now the argument emerged frankly, without Descartes' hesitation, that there was only one substance, and that men, like other objects, were modes of this one substance.

To the conception of God, Spinoza contributed three unique innovations; God was for him absolutely infinite being, the wholeness of living Nature, and the Necessity of all things. Spinoza defined God as a being absolutely infinite, that is, God possessed an infinite number of attributes, "each one of which ex-

presses eternal and infinite essence." [96] Of these attributes, only
two are known to man—thought and extension—but there are
infinite unknown realities.[97] Secondly, all God (or Nature) was
conceived by Spinoza as living, as animate; there are no objects
in his system without their corresponding mentality, and his nature, in all its details, is panpsychist. Lastly, the laws of God or
nature are logical necessities which apply to every event, every
object. Each of these three innovations was related to current
scientific speculation in the seventeenth century concerning nature.

The Infinity of God: the Discovery of the Plurality of Attributes

The seventeenth century was the one which discovered
infinity. It was an age of geographic exploration and conquest;
new lands, new peoples, new ways, and an infinite variety of lives
were unfolded to hitherto Europe-bound imaginations. Hobbes,
Locke, Spinoza, and Leibniz wrote about the customs of American
Indians, Turks, Japanese, Chinese.[98] The invention of the telescope had revealed the endlessness of the stellar macrocosm; the
invention of the microscope was bringing to human eyes the
infinitude of the microcosm. In mathematics, the infinite took
its place in the conceptions of calculus as the domain of numbers
was extended to embrace the world of motion. Spinoza's visionary
declaration that God is a being with infinite attributes, unknown
to us, is part of the tendency in the seventeenth century to conceive of an infinite plurality of worlds, unbeknown to man.
There was an infinity-intoxication during those years; these notions were heady, and carried the imagination to undreamed of
realms.[99] The century in which Cyrano de Bergerac speculated
on voyages to the moon was not dissimilar to ours in which
children read of space ships and cadets. A new world had been
opened up, in its infinite immensity, and as Spinoza forms his
image of God, it projects the wonderments of the time with endless vistas.

From the "supreme power of God," Spinoza reiterated, "or
from His infinite nature, infinite things in infinite ways, that is
to say, all things have necessarily flowed, or continually follow by

the same necessity, in the same way as it follows from the nature of a triangle, from eternity and to eternity, that its three angles are equal to two right angles." [100] An infinity of modes follows from an infinity of attributes, but human beings can know only thought and extension because "the essence of mind consists only in this, that it is the idea of a Body actually existing." [101] But we know there are infinite other attributes, because God has maximal reality, and Spinoza assumes that "the more reality or being a thing possesses, the more attributes belong to it." [102] We do possess one bit of information concerning the unknown infinite attributes, namely, that the order of their modes corresponds to the order of our known mental and physical occurrences.[103] As men, we are composed of minds and bodies, but according to Spinoza we are at the same time, unbeknown to ourselves, modes of infinite other attributes. It is an unexplained metaphysical accident in his system that our minds know only our bodies, and not the infinite other modes of the infinite other attributes. Without evidence, however, Spinoza was still motivated to assert the existence of infinite other attributes.

His acquaintance and fellow optician, the great scientist, Christian Huygens, was led to not dissimilar speculations within astronomy concerning an infinity of unknown worlds. Huygens' best known work, the *Cosmotheoros,* was published posthumously in 1698. Its theme was the possible plurality of worlds. As translated into English, its title was *The Celestial Worlds Discovered, or Conjectures Concerning the Inhabitants, Plants and Productions of the Worlds in the Planets.* In this book, Huygens raised the question: "why may not every one of these stars or suns have as great a retinue as our Sun. . . . ? For if with our bare eyes we can observe above a thousand, and with a telescope can discover ten or twenty times as many, what bounds of number must we set to those which are out of the reach of even these assistances! especially if we consider the infinite power of God? Really, when I have been reflecting thus with myself, methought all our arithmetic was nothing. . . . Indeed, it seems to me certain that the Universe is infinitely extended; but what God has been pleased to place beyond the region of the stars is as much above our knowledge as it is beyond our habitation." Huygens was moved as other men in the seventeenth century were by the spectacle of infinite variety of being. "What a wonderful and amazing scheme have we here of the magnificent vastness of the Universe! So many suns, so many earths, and every one of them stocked with so many herbs, trees, and animals, and adorned with so many seas and mountains! And how must our wonder and admiration be increased when we consider the prodigious distance and multitude of the stars?" He speculated that on other planets " 'tis not improbable that those great and noble bodies have somewhat or other growing and living upon them, though very different from what we see and enjoy here." "There's no hopes of our going such a journey," Huygens said, to see the diversities of things, but the speculative intellect could take one on interplanetary travels.[104]

God, for Spinoza, was likewise a being who must command our infinite "wonder and admiration." Spinoza did not venture with telescope into infinite unknown astronomical worlds. He believed he could discover his plurality of worlds by purely logical means, using his geometrical method to prove at least their existence. As a metaphysician, he was prompted to bring tidings of a God infinite in attributes. His metaphysics was a projection of the adoration of the infinite. The "proof" that he provided was a flimsy scaffolding for his vision. Why take for granted that the more reality a thing has, the more attributes it possesses? We can imagine a complex structure, an intricate magnificent building, but it will happen not to exist, whereas a weak, straw-thatched hut will be real, quite real. What is real can be bare and impoverished, colorless and characterless. What is beautiful and rich in conception can be unreal, and live only on paper. Reality, Spinoza assumed, is proportional to the number of attributes, but this axiom was nothing but the geometrized form of a longing for infinite deity.

All Things Live in God: Spinoza's Panpsychism

The living spirit of God, men like Winstanley had said, is omnipresent throughout every particle of the universe; the visible world is but the outer garment of God's ubiquitous life. For

Spinoza, this belief that the universe is permeated by the living spirit of God became the doctrine of the parallelism of God's attributes; "substance thinking and substance extended are one and the same substance, which is now comprehended under this attribute and now under that. Thus, also, a mode of extension and the idea of that mode are one and the same thing expressed in two different ways." [105] It followed that "the order and connection of ideas is the same as the order and connection of things." Everything in nature is alive for Spinoza; not only is matter not inert, but every object is genuinely alive, a mode of thought as well as of extension, "for those things which we have proved hitherto are altogether general, nor do they refer more to man than to other individuals, all of which are animate, although in different degrees. For of everything there necessarily exists in God an idea of which He is the cause, in the same way as the idea of the human body exists in Him." [106]

Panpsychism, the notion that everything is alive, was born as a mystical, social revolutionary doctrine in the seventeenth century, but it was remarkably reinforced by the science of the time. The last half of the seventeenth century was the age of microscopy; men were going about with their new-fashioned microscopes, magnifying everything. There was the usual delight in an unusual device, and microscopomania prevailed as scientists wrote memoirs as to how all sorts of objects, private and public, looked in the microscopic image. The great microscopists, Leeuwenhoek and Swammerdam, began to exert a significant influence on philosophic ideas. It was to their observations that a thoroughgoing panpsychist like Leibniz could appeal for the empirical support for his doctrine that "every portion of matter may be conceived as like a garden full of plants, and like a pond full of fish." [107]

Spinoza was indeed one of the Dutch microscopists, reveling in the magnifications which revealed the variety of minute living things, and fitting his observations into his philosophy. As Colerus narrates: "He observed also, with a Microscope, the different parts of the smallest Insects, from whence he drew such Consequences as seem'd to him to agree best with his Discoveries." His famous countryman Leeuwenhoek was engaged in similar work with insects. It was Leeuwenhoek's close observation of the structure and metamorphosis of the flea through all its stages which had upset the popular myths concerning the origin and propagation of this "minute and despised creature." In terminology which was akin to Spinoza's, Leeuwenhoek averred the flea to be "endowed with as great perfection in its kind as any large animal." [108] When Leeuwenhoek accumulated evidence to show that every living organism reproduces its like, he came closer to Spinoza's view of causation than did the notion of spontaneous generation.[109] And Spinoza, as we have seen, in explicating his grounds for believing that "each part of Nature accords with the whole of it" made full and explicit use of the new physiology and microscopy of blood and its constituents.[110]

There is, in fact, ground for believing that Leeuwenhoek and his fellow microscopist, Spinoza, were members of at least one common scientific circle of friends. When many members of the Royal Society, including Huygens, indicated their scepticism concerning Leeuwenhoek's reports on "little globules," the Dutch microscopist gathered together in 1677 a committee of eight gentlemen who sent testimonials of confirmation. Among these eight scientific witnesses was Henricus Cordes, Lutheran pastor at The Hague.[111] Spinoza was an attendant at Cordes' sermons, for which he avowed a high admiration.[112] Leeuwenhoek and Spinoza thus shared a personal association in addition to their microscopical enthusiasm. Above all, Spinoza, admiring the perfection of God in the infinite variety of the modes which were the outcome of his power, felt as did Leeuwenhoek, who, observing his animalcules, exclaimed: "And who can discover all the farther perfections with which so minute and (to us) insignificant a creature may be endowed?"

Microscopy at its birth had a relevance to economics and the understanding of human races as well as to theology. When Leeuwenhoek argued that there was no spontaneous generation among the corn-beetle, the issue was of practical interest to those who ran granaries, for, as he said, the corn-beetle is "a very noxious insect, well-known to corn dealers and bakers in this country." [113] The fact and problem of colored races was impressing itself upon the Dutch in the seventeenth century, in Java,

Japan, and in Brazil. Spinoza recorded a nightmare in which there came "the image of a certain black and scabby Brazilian whom I had never seen before." [114] Leeuwenhoek, pondering on the causes of color differences, "took from the arm of a Negro girl [also from Brazil] thirteen years of age, a small portion of the upper skin," and decided against the theory that the blackness of Negroes is produced by their bodies being rubbed with an oil in their infancy.[115] Microscopy and entomology had a practical purview in the eyes of the Dutch East India Company. Leeuwenhoek was asked to study how nutmegs, newly arrived by the East India Fleet, might be preserved from injury by insects. But the same commercial interests do not seem to have regarded Spinoza with favor. Cornelis Bontekoe, a prominent physician at The Hague, published a book which maintained that tea-drinking was a panacea for all disease. Bontekoe was widely held to be in the pay of the Dutch tea merchants. It is astonishing that in this work on behalf of tea-drinking, Bontekoe felt impelled to assail "the godless works of Spinoza." Spinoza, the Liberal Republican, was still condemned in the advertising tracts of the East India Company.[116]

The world that microscopy was opening to men's eyes was one which had been especially pioneered by Dutchmen. A Dutch spectacle-maker in 1590 was probably the inventor of the compound microscope. Another Dutch spectacle-maker in 1608 was the inventor of the telescope. The making of lenses for spectacles, like the arts of polishing and cutting precious stones, was an established and lucrative skilled trade in the Netherlands.[117] The demand for lenses was brisk in Spinoza's time. Three lens-grinders were brought to Leyden to teach the art to its students. Leibniz asked Leeuwenhoek why he didn't educate a school of young men in his skill, whereupon Leeuwenhoek, more the lover of pure knowledge, replied that "most students go there to make money out of science, or to get a reputation in the learned world." [118] He declined to impart his art to the devotees of vulgar goals. It was a wise choice of occupation which Spinoza had made, for it provided him with a good livelihood and linked him with a select community of investigators at the border of human knowledge. And it was a remarkable new world of what

Leeuwenhoek called "living atoms," which was replacing the cold mechanism which Descartes had imputed to the nonhuman world.[119] The infinite diversity of living things, the omnipresence of life, the desire which animated the whole world—this was the vision which Spinoza felt confirmed by the new science of the small.[120]

Scientific Determinism and Enslavement to God: a Masochist Projection

"Spinoza begins where Descartes ended, in *Naturalism*." [121] This was Leibniz's judgment, and it undoubtedly applies to Spinoza's universal determinism. "An individual thing, or a thing which is finite and which has a determinate existence unless it be determined to existence and action by another cause which is also finite and has a determinate existence; and again, this cause cannot exist nor be determined to action unless by another cause which is also finite and determined to existence and action, and so on *ad infinitum*." [122] The sources of Spinoza's determinism were manifold. It had, oddly enough, affinities with the Calvinist doctrine of predestination. Analysts of Marxian social determinism have been struck by its similarity in form and function to the metaphysical theory of predestination. The same can be said with assurance of Spinoza's theory. For his first discussion of determinism occurs in a chapter in the *Short Treatise* entitled "On Divine Predestination." [123] Spinoza at this time, like Leibniz later, aimed to take the traditional concepts of theology and infuse them with a novel scientific content. His early argument for determinism, or "divine predestination," states the core of his standpoint: "Now that there are no accidental things we prove thus: That which has no cause to exist cannot possibly exist; that which is accidental has no cause: therefore. . . ." The initial terminology of Spinoza's determinism was Calvinist, but this was shed in his more mature writings. The scientific movement was leading Spinoza's contemporaries to a conception of determinism like his own. Thomas Hobbes, for instance, affirmed that man's behavior was a segment in a causal series: "every act of mans will, and every desire, and inclination proceedeth from some cause, and that from another cause, in a continuall chain, (whose first link is in the hand of God the first of all causes,) they proceed from *necessity*. So that to him that could see the connexion of those causes, the *necessity* of all mens voluntary actions, would appear manifest." [124]

Above all, the rise and growing vogue of the mathematical method made the conception of determinism seem axiomatic. Whenever a new "method" has been proposed in the history of thought, its converts and proponents have seen in it the promise of a new age. Bacon with his inductive method, Descartes with his geometrical method, Hegel's dialectical method, Spencer's evolutionary method, Russell's mathematical logic, the logical empiricists with their semantical analysis all have been regarded as prophets whose insight when extended to social and human issues would bring the final solutions. Every method has had its methodological madness, and among the young Cartesians, of the left and right wings, in the seventeenth century, the mathematical method augured tremendous conquests. So Spinoza said that theological superstition "would have been sufficient to keep the human race in darkness to all eternity, if mathematics, which does not deal with ends, but with the essences and properties of forms, had not placed before us another rule of truth."

There were other causes, said Spinoza, which were contributing to the conception of a determinist world order and were "tending to make men reflect upon these universal prejudices, and leading them to a true knowledge of things." Among them, no doubt, was the fact that the new method offered the hope of guidance in forming a social order in which human liberty and happiness would be achieved. Determinism was, as we have seen, a guide to "the advantage of common society," "to the welfare of our social existence." It was the basis on which a science of psychology could be constructed to alleviate men's anxieties; it provided the foundation for social science. Social radicalism has often had a propensity toward determinist social theory; Mill, Marx, Veblen, the French Encyclopaedists illustrate this tendency, and Spinoza too was drawn toward the causal analysis of human behavior.

The idea of free will, the pillar of conventional theology, was therefore abandoned by Spinoza. It was a fiction of the human mind, a popular fallacy: "Their idea of liberty therefore is this —that they know no cause for their own actions; for as to saying that their actions depend upon their will, these are words to which no idea is attached." Again, he argues: "men believe themselves to be free simply because they are conscious of their own actions, knowing nothing of the causes by which they are determined. . . ." [125] Free will was thus for Spinoza a concept scientifically meaningless.[126] It was founded on our ignorance as to underlying psychological and physical causes, on our unconsciousness, in other words, of our minds and bodies. Free will was an inadequate idea, a confused one, which vanished when we understood all the causes of human behavior. Free will, we might say, was the projection in metaphysics of men whose lives were slavish, whose lives were moved by uncomprehended powers in their unconscious.

Again, however, we cannot but wonder whether there was not a strong, unconscious compulsion in Spinoza himself to renounce free will. How much of this argument was once more a covert appeal to masochist feelings, the outcome of his drive to humble himself before God? How much of it was extralogical in character, extramathematical? The language which Spinoza used to describe the advantages of determinism in his earliest writing was laden with self-immolation. From this doctrine, Spinoza says, "it follows therefrom that we are truly servants, aye, slaves, of God, and that it is our greatest perfection to be such necessarily." This knowledge of God brings us "our own eternal happiness and bliss. For the sole perfection and the final end of a slave and of a tool is this, that they duly fulfill the task imposed on them." If God should say, writes Spinoza, "that man should serve him no more, that would be equivalent to . . . annihilating him; because all that he is consists in this, that he serves God." [127] A slave is a slave even if it is to God, not man, and a slave is a slave even if he is a metaphysical, rather than a political, one. Spinoza was exceedingly aware that men projected their emotional needs into the gods whom they would worship, "each man has devised for himself, out of his own brain, a different mode of worshipping God, so that God might love him above others, and direct all nature to the service of his blind cupidity and insatiable avarice." [128] In Spinoza himself, however, there was a component of self-abnegation, a longing to be beyond all emotions, to look at things neutrally, dispassionately, to deny his own feelings, and, finally, to prostrate himself before nature. The vocabulary of the despot was adapted to describing this relentless mathematical God, who geometrized with sadistic indifference to human beings. Human beings were to take joy in their status as theorems in the flow of consequences; some of them were to be especially joyful because they were more important theorems, that is, propositions with greater generality than others. We should, according to Spinoza, be blissful in our role as servants of the Lord. In his vision of the infinite God, Spinoza had forgotten the clear courage of the free man: "Humility is not a virtue, that is to say, it does not spring from reason."

The Mathematical Method: the Language of Artisans and Merchants

The God of Spinoza, mathematical, scientific, had much that was congenial to the scientifically-minded merchants and artisans in the seventeenth century. The language of theology, men were beginning to urge, should be the sober language of mathematics. Bacon, Descartes, and Hobbes had led the way. Bacon had urged that inquirers into nature should follow "the use and wisdom of the Mathematicians," and reduce arguments "by means of definitions" to order, thereby avoiding "the high and formal discussions of learned men [which] end oftentimes in disputes about words and names"; Hobbes had attributed the absurdities of philosophers to the fact that "there is not one of them that begins his ratiocination from the Definitions, or Explications of the names they are to use; which is a method that hath been used only in Geometry; whose conclusions have hereby been made indisputable." The mathematical method alone, said Hobbes, "is free from controversy and dispute, because it consisteth in comparing figure and motion only, in which things truth and the interest of men oppose not each other." [129] When Thomas Sprat in 1667 published his *History of the Royal Society in London,* he stated the case for the mathematical method as it was conceived by a commercial civilization rising to greatness. The nation of shopkeepers would be a nation of scientists; it had had enough of "extravagances" and that pulpit "eloquence" which "ought to be banish'd out of all civil Societies, as a thing fatal to Peace and good Manners." [130] What the natural scientists of the Royal Society wished to do, said Sprat, was "to return back to the primitive purity and shortness, when men deliver'd so many things almost in an equal number of *words*. They have exacted from all their members a close, naked, natural way of speaking, positive expressions, clear senses, a native easiness, bringing all things as near the Mathematical plainness as they can, and preferring the language of Artizans, Countrymen, and Merchants, before that of Wits or Scholars." Philosophy will "attain to Perfection, when either the Mechanic Labourers shall have Philosophical Heads or the Philosophers shall have Mechanical Hands." The Platonic aristocratic tradition had alienated thinking from men's doings with their hands, but the seventeenth-century scientific spokesmen linked mathematics with plain speech concerning things which could be seen and handled. They worked to undo the repression and hatred of the senses which was a legacy from antiquity.

Men with a Calvinist turn of mind did not think science was a way to God. Sprat took notice of such antiscientists: "And here the Men of a retir'd and severe Devotion are the loudest: For they tell us, that we cannot conquer and despise the World while we study it so Much; that we cannot have sufficient leisure to reflect on another Life, while we are so taken up about the curiosities of this; . . . and that it is vain to strive after the Purity and Holiness of our Minds, while we suffer them to spend so much Time on the Labours of our Senses." To the austere, otherworldly antiscientists, Sprat replied very much as Spinoza did. The scientist's concern with material things does not lead him to atheism. Rather, when the scientist's experiments enable him to perceive the numberless particles that move in the blood, he becomes all the readier to believe in the eternal power. "He has always before his Eyes the Beauty, Contrivance, and Order of God's works." It would behoove the clerics, Sprat indicates, to take heed of the trend of the times, "the universal Disposition of this Age is bent upon a rational Religion"; "If our Church should be an enemy to Commerce, Intelligence, Discovery, Navigation, or any sort of Mechanicks: how could it be fit for the present Genius of this Nation? What greater Advantage could its Adversaries have against it?" [131]

Spinoza likewise conceived of his mathematical method as a way toward truth not found among the harangues from pulpits. Whilst the preachers dwell on the "vice of human nature, which they therefore bewail, laugh at, mock, or, as is more generally the case, detest; whilst he who knows how to revile most eloquently or subtilly the weakness of the mind is looked upon as divine," Spinoza preferred to understand the human emotions by making use of the dispassionate mathematical method. Spinoza expected that the clerics would cry out that he was endeavoring "to treat by a geometrical method the vices and follies of men." He was ready to reply with his cosmic doctrine that nothing in nature is vicious. "Nothing happens in nature which can be attributed to any vice of Nature, for she is always the same and everywhere one." To the antiscientists, Spinoza asserts that scientific knowledge is a path to God: "the more we understand individual objects, the more we understand God." [132] Like Sprat, he held that there is more understanding of God in the knowledge of blood physiology than in the exhortations of theological censors.

The calculations of merchants, the technical skills of mechanics, the new respect for the human body and its senses—all these were associated with the conception of mathematical method in the seventeenth century. The very example that came to Spinoza's mind when he wished to illustrate his theory of knowledge was one commonplace in the experience of Dutch commercial men: the rule for finding the fourth number in a proportion where the other three numbers were given.[133] "A merchant," Spinoza remarked, "does not hesitate to multiply the second and third together and divide the product by the first." The merchant, observed Spinoza, will justify his procedure either by appealing to a schoolmaster's authority, his own experience, a logical demonstration, or lastly, intuition. The Rule of Three was known in the seventeenth century as the Merchants' Key or

Merchants' Rule; it was the primary principle in the textbooks on arithmetic which Dutch commercial expansion had called forth. The Rule of Three was the example one might expect from the philosopher who, in his youth, as Bento D'Espinosa, had sold spices on Amsterdam markets.

"Mathematical" and "geometrical" acquired in the seventeenth century what we might call "slogan-value." *The Philosophical Transactions of the Royal Society* published articles and announcements of books which introduced these terms into their titles. The volume for 1668 told of Steno's treatise on the muscle, *Nic Stenonis Musculi Descriptio Geometrica,* in which

> The Author of this Book declareth, that his design in composing it was to show, that in a Muscle neither the Parts of it can be distinctly named, nor its Motion duly considered, unless the Doctrine thereof become a part of the Mathematicks. And He is of the opinion, that there is no other cause of the many Errors which spoil the History concerning the Humane Body, than that Anatomy hath hitherto disdained the Laws of the Mathematicks: and therefore . . . to consider, that our Body is an Engine made up of a thousand subordinate Engines, whose true knowledge whoever thinks it that it can be investigated without mathematical alliance must also think that there is matter without Extension, and Body without Figure.[134]

There was the Tractatus of the Jesuit Honoratus Faber where "all the Propositions are ranged according to a Geometrical method," Samuel Parker's *Tentamina Physico-Theologica de Deo,* and accounts of writings of those such as Joseph Glanvill who advocated the new methods for the advancement of knowledge.[135]

With these currents of thought, Spinoza was in close touch. Steno, the brilliant mathematical anatomist and an old friend of Spinoza's, had converted, in personal despair, to Roman Catholicism.[136] Their friendship was so close that he presumed to urge Spinoza toward a similar salvation, "for I am persuaded," he wrote, "that the memory of an old companionship still preserves a mutual love." The society of young philosophers with whom Spinoza was friendly studied the geometrical method as expounded by Borelli, who some years later made a classic application of the method in his *De Motu Animalium,* a work in which, *more geometrico,* the system of human movement was constructed. Spinoza disagreed with Borelli's analysis of definition, and conveyed his doubts to his friend, Simon De Vries.[137] There was a general agreement, however, among the young thinkers in 1663 concerning the utility and power of the geometrical method.

The mathematical method had come in the second half of the seventeenth century to be associated with the vague democratic political aspirations of the lower classes. It had about it something of the subversive. John Webster, chaplain in Cromwell's army, wrote of the "many valiant champions" who "have stood up to maintain truth against the impetuous torrent of antiquity, authority, and universality of opinion," "strong men, who fight not with the plumbeous weapons of notions, syllogism, and putation, but with the steely instruments of demonstration, observation, and experimental induction." "Syllogistic sophistry," said Webster, led only to a "civil war of words," which mathematical method would help obviate. The defenders of the old order regarded Aristotelian logic and scholastic metaphysics as mainstays of absolute monarchy. Henry Stubbe, critic of the Royal Society, attacked the "mechanical education" as a philosophy subservient to Cromwell, a regicide. Baconians were assailed in 1671 as linked with the Commonwealth and the "Olivarian adversaries." Casaubon at Cambridge in 1669 held that the new philosophy would lead to atheism and the overthrow of the social order.[138] Descartes during his years in Holland had liked to talk mathematics and astronomy with the shoemaker, Rembrantz, a self-taught geometer.[139] Mathematics with a shoemaker! The genteel could well stamp this as treason to the lofty tradition of Plato and Aristotle and suspect that a motive of revolt lurked behind the enthusiasm for geometrical demonstration.

Thus, the language of merchants and mechanics, their ways of talking and arguing, obtruded themselves into philosophy. The God of Spinoza was no product of aristocratic aloofness. He was no purified being, nor was Spinoza fearful as Plato was of sullying the divine idea by admitting its presence in the lowliest natural objects. This God was all nature, and his laws were those which the ordinary mechanic met in everyday life. And if there was a strange cruelty about this God, let us remember that this was a revolutionary age, when men were trying to be applied social scientists, and the God of a revolutionary age is neither gentle nor kind.

The Final Disunity of Spinoza's Thought: Linguistic Nonsense or Linguistic Transfiguration?

Mystic and scientist struggled within Spinoza as he labored to achieve a coherent system which would be pantheist and religious, in which God's infinite necessity would coexist with the life of free men. His great contemporary Hobbes said bluntly that no pantheist philosophy could keep from atheism: "to say the World is God, is to say, there is no cause of it, that is, no God." [140] And it must be acknowledged that Spinoza's effort to weld together mysticism and logic breaks apart; his speculative power was immense, but the problem he had posed for himself was beyond all human power.

The contradiction between Spinoza the scientist and Spinoza the mystic is one which cannot be resolved. The scientist worships a mathematical God; the laws of mathematics are for him the standard of truth, and he declares that "it follows with the greatest clearness, firstly, that God is one, that is to say, in nature there is but one substance, and it is absolutely infinite." [141] But Spinoza the mystic thinker holds that "Measure, Time and Number are nothing but Modes of thought or imagination. Therefore it is not to be wondered at that all who have tried to understand the course of Nature by such notions . . . could not extricate themselves except by breaking up everything and committing even the most absurd absurdities." How can we say then that God is one? For one itself is a number, an aid to the imagination, and not a symbol which can refer to reality. We clearly apprehend that the number one applies to God, but we also clearly apprehend, according to Spinoza, that all numerical conceptions lead to contradiction. "God is one," says Spinoza in the *Ethics,* but he also says in a letter that "it is certain that he who calls God one or single has no true idea of God or is speaking of him inappropriately." [142]

And how shall we say that mathematics is the standard of truth if number, and all theorems of numbers, lead to absurdities? What laws of nature shall we formulate if mathematical ideas are held to be self-contradictory? Mathematical physics would thus be reduced to a set of confused ideas concerning extension, and Spinoza's philosophy would lead to a rejection of the intellect not unlike Bergson's. Moreover, how shall mathematics be taken as an adequate basis for the understanding of God if it consists of inadequate ideas? What laws of nature can be regarded as "adequate ideas" if time itself is regarded as only an "aid to the imagination"? For the laws of nature employ the concept "time" as defined by the movements of instruments, processes, or recurrent events.[143] Time, however, is regarded by Spinoza as a distortion of duration.[144] But neither duration nor eternity has a place, however, in the system of natural science, which is ineluctably bound to ordinary time.[145]

The effort to wed determinism to an infinite God is likewise one which ends in a verbal quagmire. The particular world order that we know exhibits certain causal relations, but we can imagine all sorts of worlds in which events would succeed each other in improbable patterns. It is a peculiar consequence of belief in Spinoza's God that we must accept as a theorem that whatever infinite system of modes is self-consistent must necessarily exist. For, as Spinoza says, "Whatever we conceive to be in God's power necessarily exists." To assert that there is a system of entities in the actual intellect of God which does not necessarily exist would be a limitation of God's power. It would follow therefore, according to Spinoza, that whatever is possible must exist. The flood-gates of existence would be opened to all the infinite unlikely worlds that we can imagine. For we can conceive an infinitude of self-consistent worlds, all the variety of possible universes, according to the laws of chance. Charles Peirce once remarked that universes were not as plentiful as blackberries, but for Spinoza's God they would be plenteous without limitation, for "from the necessity of the divine nature infinite things in infinite ways (that is to say, all things which can be conceived by the infinite intellect) must follow." [146] Therefore all the varieties of noncausal universes, all the varieties of worlds of random aggregates, should likewise "have necessarily flowed," from God's existence. God's omnipotence reaches out to all the modes of indeterminist worlds as well as to all conceivable determinist world orders. From an absolutely infinite God, anything may "follow" just as the most improbable distribution of events is, none the less, a conceivable occurrence in accordance with a law of probability. And yet, there is a determinist anthropomorphism in Spinoza. He would limit the power of God to one set of determinist laws, forgetting that God's infinite power is not confined to one set of physical laws. If God is a geometer, then he would, if he had infinite power, geometrize in non-Euclidean as well as Euclidean worlds. He would actualize in physical space all the geometries which the pure mathematician could possibly conceive.

The contingency of this world is something which Spinoza denies. From the idea of God, "infinite numbers of things follow in infinite ways," but it should be observed that "follow" does not mean "deducible from." Spinoza deduces no laws of physics from the idea of God; he introduces them as axioms and lemmas. And we have seen that every possible world "follows" from the idea of God, in the sense that God's infinite power actualizes every possible system. But there was an ambiguous conviction in Spinoza that there is a mathematical sense in which all things are deducible from God. "Things," he says, "are conceived by us as actual in two ways; either as we conceive them to exist with relation to a fixed time and place, or in so far as we conceive them to be contained in God, and to follow from the necessity of the divine nature." [147] The object of science, according to Spinoza, would be to show how all spatio-temporal things "follow" from the idea of God. Evidently there is a tremendous confusion here in the notion of "contained in God." The phrase is used in two different senses by Spinoza. At times, "God or Nature" is taken to be the whole, that is, the class of all events, the class of all existent things. The whole obviously contains its parts, but we could never deduce the parts from the whole unless we already knew, to begin with, that it was a whole made up precisely of those parts.[148] To define a class of all events does not enable us to infer what events have actually occurred. The other sense of "God or Nature" is something which is more than a class of existents—an immanent, functioning cause from which events are, through a hierarchy of attributes and infinite modes, deducible. This is the God in which all things are and through which all things must be conceived. Here there is clearly a mystical use of "in God" and "contained in God." For we would not say that a class of objects is the "immanent cause" of its members, nor would we say that a whole is the "immanent cause" of its parts. A logical relation of class-inclusion is not a causal determination. If God is nature, that is, the totality of things, then it is wrong for Spinoza to say "in nature, there is nothing contingent, but all things are determined from the necessity of the divine nature to exist and act in a certain manner." [149] The class of all events could well be a class of contingent events; from membership in a universe-class, nothing follows, and if there were nothing, there would still be a whole. As the logicians say, the null-class is included in the universe-class. God, in his infinite power, would presumably have a nihilist streak, a component of null being. A universe-class may necessarily exist, but it would be austere, indeed, to accumulate intellectual love for this logical truism.

The intellectual love of God can only be maintained by Spinoza by devices which reduce his God to a legerdemain of words. William van Blyenbergh, grain merchant of Dordrecht, studied theology in his spare time. This God of Spinoza's, in which everything is contained and which is the cause of all things, perturbed Blyenbergh. Was not evil then caused by God? Were not all men of all characters partakers of God with equal necessity? "Do not the ungodly, then, with their little perfection, serve God as much as the godly? . . . What reasons are there, then," he queried, "why I should not eagerly commit all villainies (if only I can escape the condemnation of the judge)?" [150] Why should one, we might add, love the God who is the author of evil?

Spinoza replied to the grain merchant's challenge with devices of terminological definition. God, he argued, is the cause of all things which express essence, but villainy, evil and error contain no essence; therefore, God is not their cause.[151] What Spinoza means is that no negative predicate expresses essence; negative predicates signify no reality, they mean nothing; "things which agree in negation only, or in that which they have not, really agree in nothing." [152] If a black object and a white one have in common the fact solely that neither of them is red, this only affirms, says Spinoza, "that black and white agree in nothing." Nero's matricide, Spinoza acknowledges, proved that the Roman was "ungrateful, unmerciful, and disobedient. And it is certain that none of these things expresses any essence, and therefore God was not the cause of them, although He was the cause of the act and the intention of Nero." [153] God, according to Spinoza, is not the cause of negations; He is the cause of what is, not of what is not. But, we can answer, if God was the cause of Nero's character, he was clearly the cause of Nero's being a hating rather than a loving person. We can call the loving person a nonhating one, and the hating person a nonloving one. It is an arbitrary matter as to which group we assign a negative predicate. It would be just as valid to argue that God was not the cause of such negative traits as "uncruel, unharsh, unmean." An accident of language, the use of negative prefixes, is Spinoza's device for maintaining the stature of his God. But the God who is the cause of everything cannot escape his involvedness in evil by the verbal dodge that hatred and evil are nothing.

The deepest psychological sources of Spinoza's thought cannot, of course, be known. Why was Spinoza so intensely committed to the intellectual love of God? What was the origin of this yearning which filled his life? We can only venture conjectures on the basis of such biographical facts as we have. Spinoza's mother died, as we have noted when he was six years old. The mother in the traditional Jewish family was the wellspring of love for the children, whereas the father was much more the embodiment of authority. Did the loss of his mother at the age of six, when the anxieties of authority are beginning to be felt, so affect Spinoza that his overwhelming unconscious aim was to return somehow to a union which brings peace? Was the longing for God the unstilled longing of a child for a vanished mother-love? Or did Spinoza's austerity, his readiness to love a God which did not love him represent an unconscious effort to reconcile himself to the childhood aspect of a stern, unloving father? We cannot know. It is striking, however, that when Spinoza searches in debate for a classical instance of evil what comes to his mind for illustration is Nero's matricide, which "in so far as it contained something positive, was not a crime: for Orestes too did the same outward deed and had the same intention of killing his Mother, and yet he is not blamed, at least not in the same degree as Nero." Perhaps this choice of illustration sprang from an unhappy memory of boyhood years with the stepmother Esther. Did resentments against her or guilt feelings associated with his mother's death lurk behind this illustration? At times, we are disquieted by the anxiety symptoms which break through his self-reserve: "when he had a mind to divert himself somewhat longer, he look'd for some Spiders, and made 'em fight together, or he threw some Flies into the Cobweb, and was so well pleased with that Battel, that he wou'd sometimes break into Laughter." [154] The frustrated love of a child, its repressed impulses, can issue in strange forms of self-hatred and sadism. Perhaps such were the deepest roots of the awe-inspiring aspiration of the intellectual love of God. The nightmare, in which Spinoza saw a terrifying image of a black Brazilian, may have been the record of his anxieties of fear of the communal authority, even as his longing for union with God may have expressed his deprivation of a mother's love.[155]

Descartes told how the foundations of his philosophy were revealed to him in three dreams which came to him in 1619. Spinoza's nightmare, on the other hand, suggests a nameless fear which festered in the heart of his philosophy. The innermost history of men's ideas remains inscrutable, and we are left, at the end, only with surmises as to those causes which are most important in the making of philosophies.

So Spinoza struggled with words to convey his great imaginative conception of the universe. The words failed him, never saying exactly what he would have said. For he never meant by his words what men mean. When he said that God and nature are the same, he did not mean by nature the material world as it is experienced by us.[156] Nature was expressed in an infinity of unexperienced attributes; it was, with the exception of thought and extension, an immense agnostic unknowable. When he spoke of infinity, it was of a reality which fell outside the range and language of mathematics altogether.[157] When he spoke of substance as the "cause of itself," he strained at the notion of causation in trying to describe reality which necessarily existed, that is, a reality without cause. When he spoke lastly of "existence," the word did not have its everyday signification. God necessarily exists, said Spinoza, because there can be no external cause which could hinder God from existing. But a metaphor of struggle for existence already assumes the existence of the struggling objects, and their existence is a contingent, brute fact. The infinity of imaginable, nonexistent worlds are not hindered from existence by something more powerful; they simply happen not to exist. And if only finite things existed, it would not follow that the finite was more powerful than the infinite. "Inability to exist is impotence," Spinoza said, but if an infinite God never existed, it would not be because He had proved himself impotent. The nonexistent are beyond all power and weakness. "It is not of the nature of reason to consider things as contingent but as necessary," Spinoza held. Would man, only partially free, and holding fast to that freedom which he possesses, finally affirm that it is the nature of reason to recognize the contingency in things, the recalcitrance of realities to any all-inclusive human system?

Never had so encompassing a vision of God been recorded as on that manuscript which Spinoza left in his desk for his Collegiant friends to publish after his death. Some would say that he had exceeded the limits of language, others that he had taken the sense-bound words of science and filled them with a content through which one could glimpse the greatness of God.[158] Was his vision an emotion which persisted in outraging the rules of grammar, or had the power of Spinoza's imagination transfigured the words of men into the intellect of the living God?

Epilogue

Spinoza's philosophy was not contrived with threads of thoroughgoing consistency. Only those immune to the toil and turmoil of their times can manufacture systems of unruffled unity. Spinoza's ideas were resilient to the impressions and traumas of experience. He was no detached, serene metaphysician, stereotyped in copybooks, but rather a man immersed in the hopes and tragedies of his time, with emotions which moved him to stand against mobs and princes. His philosophy was an effort at wisdom and understanding in a revolutionary age.

Spinoza's thought was most mystical, most theological, in his early years. At that time, he was drawn to groups like the Quakers and Collegiants whose way of life combined mysticism with Utopian political aspiration. The later direction of his intellectual evolution was toward a scientific world view, an ethics founded on medical psychology, and a political science which shed Utopian hope in favor of a mastery over realities. There was an unresolved conflict in Spinoza between the scientist and the mystic, between the social reformer and the political acquiescent. Unlike his great contemporaries, however, Spinoza's thought was tending toward secularism.

Great thinkers in an age of crisis rarely follow a single path. Their very sensitivity to the deepest questions and crucial alternatives makes of their own lives an endless search. Spinoza's friend Steno, the anatomist, abandoned science to become a Catholic, and became a bishop and organizer of Catholic propaganda for North Germany. Jan Swammerdam, born like Spinoza in Amsterdam, was a genius in entomology, a founder of that science. In 1673, he underwent an intense spiritual crisis, the outcome of years of personal difficulty and struggle. Swammerdam left science and exchanged his hours with the microscope for membership in the mystic communal society led by Antoinette Bourignon. This was the century in which Pascal

254

forsook mathematics for Jansenist contemplation, and in which Isaac Newton wrote more than a million words on such subjects as Apocalyptic literature and the Sibylline Oracles.[1] But Spinoza's intellectual evolution was in the opposite direction. It was said by some who knew him, according to Bayle, "that he fell into atheism only unconsciously, and that he was very far from it in the year 1663." [2] To describe Spinoza as having evolved into an atheist is a simple mistake, but it is true that the character of his thought became more secular and scientific in the years after 1663.

The decade of Spinoza's political participation, before the murder of John de Witt, brought to the fore an emphasis on the ethics of the free man and the scientific foundations of politics. For propagandist purposes, Spinoza would still play at the game of translating theological symbols into scientific terms. "By the help of God," he wrote, "I mean the fixed and unchangeable order of nature or the chain of natural events." [3] Theological symbols were still so powerful in people's minds that as a practitioner of the political art Spinoza sought to enlist their attractive influence in the Liberal Republican cause. With the death of De Witt and the collapse of Republican liberalism, the theological mantle was dropped. Spinoza's tone became more secular; it was a *Political Treatise* he now undertook, and the omission of "Theological" from the title signified a radical change in his spirit. The next to the last proposition of the *Ethics* confessed his doubts concerning the eternity of the human mind, but insisted that the ethics of the free man, founded on psychological science, was, none the less, validly demonstrated. Spinoza had undertaken a translation of the Old Testament into Dutch. He discussed it with various scholars and "had finished the five Books of Moses, a great while ago, when some few days before he died he burnt the whole Work in his Chamber." [4] It is said that when he committed a book of his to the fire in the year of his death, Spinoza remarked with jesting bitterness: "I have devoted prolonged and much study to the thinking out and writing down of things which now certainly no one will read." Was there a symbol of emancipation in this act, the last thrusting aside of his starting point, an assertion of freedom from theology, sect, and all its works? Was this a rite of rebirth of the free man?

Leibniz, a powerful thinker but obsequious man, writing a generation after Spinoza's death, warned against the spread of Spinoza's philosophy. He said that the diffusion of such ideas, "insinuating themselves little by little into the minds of men of high life who rule others and upon whom affairs depend, and slipping into the books in fashion, dispose all things to the general revolution with which Europe is threatened." The disciples of such ideas as Spinoza's, said Leibniz, would "be capable, for their pleasure or advancement, of setting on fire the four corners of the earth, as I have known from the character of some whom death has swept away." [5] The philosophy of Spinoza had been born in an atmosphere which savored of the underground; Spinoza had admonished his friends when he sent them his writings to remember "the character of the age in which we live." [6] There were circumstances in which he felt that prudence justified the dissimulation of one's opinions.[7] He was rebellious, from time to time, against such self-imposed restraint; "as far as I am concerned," he once wrote, "I openly and unambiguously confess that I do not understand Holy Scripture although I have spent some years in the study of it. . . ." [8]

Spinoza died as his philosophy was being condemned by churches, consistories, magistrates, and synods. Death saved him perhaps from the tortures which had been meted out to his friend Koerbagh. "For," as his earliest biographer wrote, "although he did not have the good fortune to see the end of the late wars, when the States are resuming the government of their Empire half lost either through the fortune of arms, or as the result of an unfortunate choice, still it is no small happiness to have escaped the storm which his enemies were preparing for him." [9] But Spinoza's ideas survived in the subterranean channels to which free thought is driven in a repressive society. Bayle describes that Spinoza had a "great number of followers" who "do not dare to reveal themselves." [10] To found a sect had been far from Spinoza's intention; there was no longing in him for disciples, no craving for the reassurance of admirers. The free man who wishes to assist other people, Spinoza had written, will "not draw them into admiration, so that a doctrine may be named after him. . . ." [11] But the power of his free thought impressed many men after his death and moved circles of handicraftsmen, clergymen, philosophers to the standpoint of freedom. The publisher in 1690 of a pamphlet against Spinoza wrote: "Everywhere Spinoza's works are offered for sale; to an age thirsting for innovation they are recommended by their folly; they allure the reader by their godlessness. . . . Also Spinoza has left behind no less abundant a crop of disciples than some Greek sophist or disputant. But these, with a wantonness peculiar to them, labour with the sole object of making known and diffusing far and wide the previous doctrines of the new master. In this rash enterprise they have succeeded." Another writer in Holland averred, "they run after Spinoza by shoals." Men like Jacob Bril of Leyden, the shoemaker of Middleburk, Marinus Adriansz Brooms, the preacher Van Hattem of Zealand spread the knowledge of Spinoza's thought.[12] Dissenting and rebellious spirits of the laboring class were drawn to Spinoza's ideas, so that the conscientious historian Basnage, in trying to belittle the significance of his followers, remarked: "We must reckon those for nothing, who gave him the Title of Blessed, after his death, since they were Mechanicks. . . ." [13]

But there were others besides humble workmen who came under Spinoza's influence. John Locke, the future philosopher of the Glorious Revolution of 1688, lived in the circles which had partaken of Spinoza's ideas. When Locke arrived at Amsterdam in 1684, a fugitive from academic espionage at Oxford and persecution by King James II, he became a friend of J. G. Graevius and Philipp Limborch. These men had known Spinoza personally and, though they believed him too extreme, shared with him common liberal views.[14] For two years, Locke lived with the Quaker merchant of Rotterdam, Benjamin Furly, where a club of Collegiants and Spinozists known as the "Lantern" gathered regularly.[15] Locke's close friend, Jean Le Clerc, had been much influenced by Spinoza's historical method, Biblical criticism, and advocacy of freedom of thought.[16] It was in this atmosphere that Locke wrote his famed *Epistola de Tolerantia* in 1685.[17] And the creed which Locke drew up in 1689 for the small "society of Pacific Christians" which he and some friends had formed, corresponded exactly to the principles of universal religion which Spinoza advocated.[18]

There was, indeed, as Leibniz feared, a revolution in the making to which the ideas of Spinoza contributed.[19] The precursors of the French Revolution drew sustenance from this philosophy which was a hymn to freedom. Spinoza's work suffered the fate of political classics; men were influenced by writings which were unread, so that Voltaire could say: "As for Spinoza, everybody talks of him and nobody reads him." And like all revolutionary thinkers, he attracted the efforts of refuters who wrote competent refutations, and who never touched the tremendous truths which he had spoken for his time.[20] A revolution came, and still another. Leibniz, though he feared them, had dared to believe that good would come forth out of evil. "Providence itself will correct men by the revolution itself which must spring therefrom." But the free society for which Spinoza worked still remained a dream hidden somewhere in the infinite understanding of God. Perhaps Spinoza would now add: Until the multitude are free, and free men the multitude, men cannot know God or love Him.

NOTES

1. The Excommunication of Baruch Spinoza

References to Spinoza's *Ethics, On the Improvement of the Under-standing, Tractatus Theologico-Politicus,* and *Tractatus Politicus* are to the translation of R. H. M. Elwes, *The Chief Works of Benedict de Spinoza,* Volumes I and II, Revised Edition, London, 1919. Use has also been made of the translation by William Hale White, *Ethic,* New York, 1883, reprinted in the *Spinoza Selections,* edited by John Wild, New York, 1930. All references to Spinoza's correspondence are to *The Correspondence of Spinoza,* translated and edited by A. Wolf, London, 1928. Citations of the *Short Treatise* are to Spinoza's *Short Treatise on God, Man, and His Well-Being,* translated and edited by A. Wolf, London, 1910.

1. Sir Frederick Pollock, *Spinoza: His Life and Philosophy* (2nd ed.; London, 1899), pp. 17-18. This version is translated from the original Portuguese document.

2. *Diary and Correspondence of John Evelyn,* ed. William Bray (London, 1883), I, 24.

3. Cecil Roth, *A Life of Menasseh ben Israel* (Philadelphia, 1934), pp. 62-63, 71, 146-147. There was no difference whatever according to M. Kayserling between Menasseh's methods of scholarship and those of his Dutch contemporaries. Cf. M. Kayserling, *The Life and Labours of Manasseh ben Israel* (London, 1877), trans. F. de Sola Mendes, p. 11. Also cf. Rev. Dr. Adler, "A Homage to Menasseh ben Israel," *Transactions of the Jewish Historical Society of England,* I (1893-94), 30. Abraham Yaari, *Mebet Defuso shel Menasseh ben Israel* (Jerusalem, 1946).

4. Franz Landsberger, "Rembrandt's Synagogue," *Historia Judaica,* VI (1944), 70.

5. Arthur E. Kuhn, "Hugo Grotius and the Emancipation of the Jews in Holland," *Publications of the American Jewish Historical Society,* XXXI (1938), 176. The Amsterdam government in 1616 prohibited the Jews from marrying or having sexual relations with any Christian women. Cf. Herbert I. Bloom, *The Economic Activities of the Jews of Amsterdam in the Seventeenth and Eighteenth Centuries* (Williamsport, 1937), p. 20. But Evelyn as late as 1641 found in Leyden a Burgundian Jew married to an apostate Kentish woman. *John Evelyn, op. cit.,* p. 30.

6. Alexander Marx, *Studies in Jewish History and Booklore* (New York, 1944), pp. 210-211.

7. Mr. Basnage, *The History of the Jews from Jesus Christ to the Present Time,* trans. Tho. Taylor (London, 1708), p. 740.

8. When Haham (Chief Rabbi) David Nieto a half-century later in 1703 was accused of having affirmed the Spinozist heresy that God and nature were one, the vast majority of the London Synagogue came to his defense. His principal attacker was excommunicated, but a reconciliation was effected on the Day of Atonement. It is noteworthy, however, that the Amsterdam Synagogue, made sensitive by its experience with Spinoza, was prepared to render an advisory judgment against Nieto. Cf. Moses Gaster, *History of the Ancient Synagogue of the Spanish and Portuguese Jews* (London, 1901), pp. 106-108. Leon Roth, "David Nieto and the Orthodoxy of Spinozism," *Chronicon Spinozanum*, I (1921), 278. Israel Abrahams, "Heresy," *Encyclopaedia of Religion and Ethics* (New York, 1914), VI, 622-624. Jacob J. Petuchowski, *The Theology of Haham David Nieto* (New York, 1954), pp. 9-10, 47-48, 120-121.

9. John Colerus, *The Life of Benedict de Spinosa*, trans. from the French (London, 1706), reprinted in Sir Frederick Pollock, *op. cit.*, p. 390. The value of a Dutch florin, or guilder, was at this time probably half a crown in English money. Cf. William Sewel, *A Compleat Dictionary, Dutch and English* (Amsterdam, 1756), II, 303.

10. Cf. Jacob S. Raisin, *The Haskalah Movement in Russia* (Philadelphia, 1913), pp. 131, 255-257. A. L. Patkin, *The Origins of the Russian-Jewish Labour Movement* (Melbourne, 1947), pp. 76-94. Isaac Levitats, *The Jewish Community in Russia, 1772-1844* (New York, 1943), pp. 81, 134, 174.

11. Herbert I. Bloom, *op. cit.*, pp. 18, 41. Also cf. Violet Barbour, *Capitalism in Amsterdam in the Seventeenth Century* (Baltimore, 1950), p. 25. Salo Baron, *A Social and Religious History of the Jews* (New York, 1937), III, 132-133. The Jewish printer Joseph Athias wrote in 1667 that he had for several years printed more than a million Bibles for England and Scotland. "There is no plough boy or servant girl without one," he declared. In 1670 the Dutch Republic gave him a monopoly for the publication of English Bibles. Cf. Albert Hyma, *The Dutch in the Far East* (Ann Arbor, 1942), p. 30.

12. *Menasseh ben Israel's Mission to Oliver Cromwell*, ed. Lucien Wolf (London, 1901), p. 139.

13. Cf. E. Slijper, "Netherlands," *Jewish Encyclopaedia* (New York, 1916), IX, 229. Also, H. I. Bloom, *op. cit.*, p. 23.

14. Lucien Wolf, *op. cit.*, p. 88. In 1656, there were seven Jewish names out of 167 shareholders in the Dutch West India Company, but these four per cent of the owners probably held a much higher proportion of the stock. Cf., Herbert I. Bloom, "A Study of Brazilian Jewish History 1623-1654, Based Chiefly Upon the Findings of the late Samuel Oppenheim," *Publications of the American Jewish Historical Society*, XXXIII (1934), 50.

15. It should not be inferred that Jewish interests were predominant in Amsterdam capitalism. In 1631, when no Jew was worth more than 50,000 guilders, there were 160 Gentiles who possessed more than that amount. The tax returns of 1674 likewise indicate that the wealth of Christian burghers far exceeded that of the richest of the Jews. Cf. H. I.

Bloom, *The Economic Activities of the Jews of Amsterdam*, pp. 11-12, Salo Baron, *op. cit.*, pp. 132-133. Also, cf. A. M. Vaz Dias, "De Deelname der Marranen in Het Oprichtingskapital der Oost-Indische Compagnie," *Drie en Dertigste Jaarboek van Het Genootschape Amstelodamum* (Amsterdam, 1936), pp. 43-44.

16. Cecil Roth, *A Life of Menasseh ben Israel*, pp. 53, 94-95. Albert M. Hyamson, *A History of the Jews in England* (2nd ed.; London, 1928), p. 147. Menasseh's book had a distinctly realistic note; the length of human life, he argued, was not predetermined by God, but was dependent on constitutional, temperamental, and geographical circumstances.

17. *The Conciliator of R. Manasseh ben Israel: A Reconcilement of the Apparent Contradictions in Holy Scripture*, trans. E. H. Lindo (London, 1842), I, iii, 35-36, 69, 113, 117; II, 240-241, 249. Menasseh's work abounds in references to the most diverse sources—churchmen such as Aquinas and Augustine, pagans such as Lucretius, Suetonius, and Virgil. Unlike Maimonides, Menasseh held that the universe was created by God with man as the final end.

18. Moses Bensabat Amzalak, "Joseph Da Veiga and Stock Exchange Operations in the Seventeenth Century," *Essays Presented to J. H. Hertz*, ed. I. Epstein, E. Levine, and C. Roth (London, 1944), pp. 35, 40, 42-44. The tulip mania which swept the Netherlands in 1636 and 1637 showed how bizarre the money madness could become. It was a great speculative boom, perhaps the earliest in capitalist civilization. Members of all classes tried to make an easy florin. Then came collapse and catastrophe. The workingmen and poor people lost all they had. Fifty pamphlets were published arguing the pros and cons of the tulip mania. Vague images of men seized by the money madness may well have been among Spinoza's earliest memories. Cf. N. W. Posthumus, "The Tulip Mania in Holland in the Years 1636 and 1637," *Journal of Economic and Business History*, I (1928-29), 439-442.

19. "In the political struggle between the stadtholders and the anti-Orange party, they [the Jews] almost always took the part of the former." Cf. John Lothrop Motley, *The Rise of the Dutch Republic*, ed. William Elliot Griffis (New York, 1898), pp. 853-854. Cecil Roth, *op. cit.*, pp. 59, 66-67. E. Slijper, *op. cit.*, p. 228. Cecil Roth, *A History of the Marranos* (Philadelphia, 1932), p. 336. A. M. Hyamson, *op. cit.*, p. 147. Heinrich Graetz, *History of the Jews* (Philadelphia, 1897), IV, 678. Mr. Basnage, *op. cit.*, p. 739.

20. Cecil Roth, *History of the Marranos*, p. 244. *Menasseh ben Israel*, p. 63. Moritz Kayserling, "Isaac de Fonseca Aboab," *Jewish Encyclopaedia*, I, 74. H. I. Bloom, *The Economic Activities of the Jews of Amsterdam*, p. 30.

21. Moses Gaster, *op. cit.*, pp. 14-16. Also cf. Albert M. Hyamson, *The Sephardim of England* (London, 1951), pp. 26-28. The original constitution of the Amsterdam Synagogue is available in B. H. de Castro, *De Synagoge der Portugeesch-Israelietische Gemeente te Amsterdam* ('S Gravenhage, 1875), p. xxi ff. Also cf. *El Libro de los Acuerdos*, trans. Lionel

D. Barnett (Oxford, 1931), pp. 3-4. The Synagogue's governing council, the "govierno politico," was described by De Barrios as consisting of "7 Juezes que se llaman en Hebreo los seis Parnasim, y el Septimo Gabay. Exercen sobre la General congregación su oficio un Año, y eligen de seis en seis meses, a las benemeritas personas que entran en su lugar. Una vez tres en Ros a Sana o Principio de Año, y otra con Gabay en Sabat a Gadol que se interpreta el Sábado Grande. [Seven judges who are called in Hebrew the six Parnasim, and the seventh Gabay. They fulfill their office over the general congregation for one year, and every six months they choose the most deserving persons to replace them. Those of them are selected on Rosh Hashonah, or the New Year's Dày, and the rest with the Treasurer on the Sabbath Hagadol which means the Great Sabbath.]" Daniel Levi de Barrios, *Govierno Popular Judayco* (Amsterdam, 1683 [?]), p. 24. Also cf. Sigmund Seeligman, "Amsterdam," *Jewish Encyclopaedia*, I, 538. H. Graetz, *op. cit.*, IV, 684.

22. Maurice Aron, *Histoire de l'Excommunication Juive* (Nimes, 1882), pp. 79, 82, 107-108.

23. Cf. B. H. de Castro, *op. cit.*, Bijlage, C, pp. xliv-xlvi.

24. H. Graetz, *History of the Jews*, III, 489, 501, 529, 527, 536, 542.

25. Maurice Aron, *Histoire de l'Excommunication Juive*, pp. 90-91. *The Code of Maimonides, Book Fourteen, The Book of Judges*, trans. Abraham H. Hershman (New Haven, 1949), p. 75.

26. C. Roth, *Menasseh ben Israel*, pp. 52-57. B. H. de Castro, *op. cit.*, pp. 16-17.

27. C. Roth, *op. cit.*, pp. 59-60.

28. Philipp Limborch, *The Remarkable Life of Uriel Acosta, to which is added, Mr. Limborch's Defence of Christianity, with Memoirs of Mr. Limborch's Life* (London, 1740), pp. 3, 21, 26, 29-30, 37, 42. For secondary accounts, cf. Israel Abrahams, "Acosta," *Encyclopaedia of Religion and Ethics*, I, 74-75. Frederick de Sola Mendes, "Uriel Acosta," *Jewish Encyclopaedia*, I, 167-168. For Spinoza's similiar views, cf. *Tractatus Theologico-Politicus*, p. 187; *Ethics*, Part Four, Prop. XXXVII, Scholium; *Correspondence*, p. 290.

29. N. Porges, "Gebhardt's Book on Uriel Da Costa," *The Jewish Quarterly Review*, XIX (1928), 46. C. Roth, *Menasseh ben Israel*, pp. 92-93. Moritz Kayserling, "Moses Raphael de Aguilar," *Jewish Encyclopedia*, I, 275. Cecil Roth, "The Strange Case of Hector Mendes Bravo," *Hebrew Union College Annual*, XVIII (1943-44), 237.

30. Philipp Limborch, *op. cit.*, pp. 15, 17-18, 32-33, 43.

31. *Ibid.*, p. 23.

32. I. Sonne, "Da Costa Studies," *The Jewish Quarterly Review*, XXII (1932), 263.

33. A. M. Vaz Dias, *Spinoza Mercator & Autodidactus* (The Hague, 1932), p. 55. Albert Rivaud, "Documents Inédits sur la Vie de Spinoza," *Revue de Métaphysique et de Morale*, XLI (1934), 255-257.

34. H. I. Bloom, *The Economic Activities of the Jews of Amsterdam*, p. 75.

35. *On the Improvement of the Understanding*, pp. 4-5. *Ethics*, Part Four, Appendix, Par. XXIX.

36. *The Oldest Biography of Spinoza*, ed. A. Wolf (London, 1927), pp. 67-68. H. I. Bloom, *The Economic Activities of the Jews of Amsterdam*, p. 17.

37. K. O. Meinsma, *Spinoza und Sein Kreis*, trans. Lina Schneider (Berlin, 1909), p. 216 ff. Madeleine Francès, *Spinoza dans les Pays Néerlandais de la seconde moitié du XVIIᵉ Siècle* (Paris, 1937), pp. 41, 123, 244-245.

38. Colerus, *op. cit.*, p. 388.

39. A. Wolf, *The Oldest Biography of Spinoza*, p. 52.

40. Pierre Clément, *Trois Drames Historiques* (Paris, 1857), pp. 416-418. "Le Chevalier de Rohan," *Episodes de l'Histoire de France* (Deuxième Edition, Paris, 1859), pp. 236-237. *La Police de Louis XIV* (Paris, 1866), p. 158. G. Pariset, "Sieyès et Spinoza," *Revue de synthèse historique*, XII (1906), 320.

41. Of a Lucianist book, it was said in 1619: "Qui est un lucianisme, qui mérite d'estre jeté au feu avec l'auteur s'il était vivant. [Whatever is a lucianism, that deserves to be thrown into the fire with the author if he were living.]" Bayle, more mild and just in his judgment, felt that Lucianist scepticism was motivated less by a desire to help men than by a delight in mocking at their foibles, "puisqu'au lieu de faire cela par un bon motif, il n'a cherché qu'à contenter son humeur moqueuse, . . . et qu'il n'a point temoigné moins d'indifférence, ou moins d'aversion pour la vérité que pour le mensonge. [Since instead of doing it because of a good motive, it has only sought to satisfy its mocking humor, . . . and that it hasn't shown less indifference, or less aversion, to truth than to falsehood.]" Rabelais, for example, was considered a Lucianist. *Dictionnaire Historique et Critique de Pierre Bayle* (Nouvelle Edition, Paris, 1820), XI, 625, 627-628. Also, Howard Robinson, *Bayle the Sceptic* (New York, 1931), p. 217.

42. *Ethics*, Part Three, Preface. Also, see Spinoza's criticism of "the Derider," *Short Treatise*, p. 95.

43. *Tractatus Politicus*, p. 360. A. J. Servaas van Rooijen, *Inventaire des Livres Formant la Bibliothèque de Benedict Spinoza* (The Hague, 1888), pp. 142, 174.

44. De Witt, in revising Pieter's book for its second edition in 1661, added two chapters, XXIX and XXX, entitled: "Of the Reasons why Liberty has not brought with it more Advantages since the Death of the Prince of Orange," and "Of the Good Fruits produced by the Beginnings of Good Government." Jean de la Court was the original "Van den Hove," but Pieter allowed his brother's work to be attributed to himself. The phraseology of Spinoza's reference seems to imply that V. H. was alive at the time. In that case, since Jean had died more than a decade previously, Spinoza was referring directly to the surviving brother, Pieter. The frankness of Pieter's book later caused political embarrassment for De Witt, who had obtained approval for its publication during an almost empty session of the Estates. The assembly subsequently suppressed the book.

Cf. M. Antonin Lefèvre-Pontalis, *John de Witt*, trans. S. S. E. and A. Stephenson (Boston, 1885), I, 300-302; II, 75.

45. John de Witt, *Political Maxims of the State of Holland*, trans. from the Dutch (London, 1743), pp. 70-73. Pieter de la Court's book, published as the *Mémoires de M. de Witt*, was ascribed popularly to John de Witt's authorship. J. M. Robertson's verdict on the Dutch trading companies had the sharp clarity of an English liberal: "The capitalist monopolists and 'imperialists' of the republic were thus the means of artificially limiting its economic basis, and later of subverting its republican constitution." Cf. *The Evolution of States* (London, 1912), p. 317. Also cf. James Edwin Thorold Rogers, *Holland* (London, 1888), p. 245.

46. Colerus, *op. cit.*, pp. 391-392. Spinoza's reply to the Synagogue was entitled *Apologia para justificarse de su abdicacion de la synagoga* [*Apology to justify himself for his withdrawal from the synagogue*]. Cf., M. Kayserling, *Biblioteca Española-Portugueza-Judaica* (Strasbourg, 1890), p. 105.

47. A. Wolf, *The Oldest Biography of Spinoza*, p. 51.

48. Colerus, *op. cit.*, p. 399.

49. *Tractatus Theologico-Politicus*, pp. 55-56. The hatred of Turks against Jews and Christians, of Jews against Christians and Turks, and of Christians against Jews and Turks is derived, says Spinoza, from ignorance and hearsay; the latter is the lowest grade of knowledge. *Short Treatise*, pp. 72-73. Also cf. *Correspondence*, p. 259.

50. *Tractatus Theologico-Politicus*, p. 56. Spinoza's explanation of the tenacity of Portuguese Jews is doubtful. As Cecil Roth observes, the latter were for a long time spared the rigors of the Inquisition. Physical compulsion and intimidation, persistently used, seem to have been the principal causes for the assimilation of most Spanish New Christians. Cecil Roth, *A History of the Marranos*, pp. 62, 85.

51. *Tractatus Theologico-Politicus*, p. 56.

52. *Ibid.*, p. 56.

53. *Ibid.*, pp. 139-140. Menasseh had also accepted the fantasy-world of the neo-Kabbalists. Cf. C. Roth, *Menasseh ben Israel*, p. 99.

54. *Tractatus Theologico-Politicus*, pp. 238, 252-253. Spinoza's argument against the Jewish community's right to excommunicate was adopted by Moses Mendelssohn. Cf., the latter's *Jerusalem: A Treatise on Ecclesiastical Authority and Judaism*, trans. M. Samuels (London, 1838), I, pp. 103-114.

55. The membership of the Mahamad in the summer of 1656 is given in Carl Gebhardt, "Juan de Prado," *Chronicon Spinozanum*, III (1923), 275. The list of the chief Jewish shareholders in the Dutch West India Company is provided by Samuel Oppenheim, "The Early History of the Jews in New York, 1654-1664," *Publications of the American Jewish Historical Society*, XVIII (1909), 15. The identity of Councilor David Osorio with the shareholder Bento Osorio is established by the document in E. N. Adler, "The Jews of Amsterdam in 1655," *Transactions of the Jewish Historical Society of England*, IV (1899-1901), 226. For Osorio's Levantine activities, cf. H. I. Bloom, *The Economic Activities of the Jews of Amsterdam*, pp. 86-87. For

Pereira's economic importance, *ibid.*, pp. 38-39. The identification of "Dionnis Jennis" with Rabbi Isaac Aboab is likewise provided by H. I. Bloom, *op. cit.*, p. 90. The frequency of pseudonyms among the Dutch Jewish merchants makes it impossible to identify all the Jewish shareholders in the India companies. Aliases were used, often several by one person, in order not to endanger the lives of relatives and correspondents in Spanish territory. Cf. E. N. Adler, *op. cit.*, p. 225; H. I. Bloom, *op. cit.*, pp. 90, 207. For Usselinx's remark, *ibid.*, p. 206. For the list of Jewish shareholders in the Dutch East India Company, cf. Herman Watjen, *Das Judentum und die Anfânge der modernen Kolonisation* (Berlin, 1914), p. 12. The tax estimates of Jewish fortunes in 1631 are in H. I. Bloom, *op. cit.*, p. 11. On Pharar, Musaphia, Bueno, and Abrabanel, cf. M. Kayserling, *Biblioteca Española-Portugueza-Judaica* (Strasbourg, 1890), pp. 7, 31, 44, 75. Jacob J. Petuchowski, *op. cit.*, p. 46. Cecil Roth, *A Life of Menasseh ben Israel*, pp. 52, 66-67, 116-119. On Ishac Belmonte and Henriques, cf. M. Kayserling, *Sephardim* (Leipzig, 1859), pp. 289, 290-291. Also, M. Kayserling, *Biblioteca Española*, p. 27. H. I. Bloom, *op. cit.*, p. 204.

56. Samuel Oppenheim, "Early History of the Jews in New York," *Publications of the American Jewish Historical Society*, XVIII (1909), 8. Lee M. Friedman, *Jewish Pioneers and Patriots* (New York, 1943), pp. 134-136. All was not well, however, between the rich and poor Jews. In 1655, the Rev. Megapolensis wrote his superiors in Amsterdam that poverty-stricken Jews had come to him several times weeping that their coreligionists, the Jewish merchants, "would not even lend them a few stivers." The good reverend proposed to remove "the obstinate and immovable Jews" entirely from the colony of New Amsterdam. Cf. *Ecclesiastical Records of State of New York* (Albany, 1901), I, 335. Also cf. H. I. Bloom, *op. cit.*, p. 143. David and Tamar de Sola Pool, *An Old Faith in the New World: Portrait of Shearith Israel 1654-1954* (New York, 1955), p. 17.

57. Arnold Wiznitzer, "The Number of Jews in Dutch Brazil (1630-1654)," *Jewish Social Studies*, XVI (1954), 113. C. Roth, *Menasseh ben Israel*, pp. 52-53.

58. M. Kayserling, "Isaac Aboab: the First Jewish Author in America," *Publications of the American Jewish Historical Society*, 1897, No. 5, p. 128. Also cf. "Isaac de Fonseca Aboab," *Jewish Encyclopaedia*, I, 74. H. Graetz, *op. cit.*, IV, 694.

59. Arnold Wiznitzer, *The Records of the Earliest Jewish Community in the New World* (New York, 1954), p. 56.

60. A. Wolf, *op. cit.*, p. 48.

61. Aboab envisaged the hegemony of Israel with the advent of the Messiah. The doctrine of the chosen people was central in his writing. Isaac Aboab, *Compendio de diferentes materias dignas de se lerem para ter a noticias do que ellas contem* [*Compendium of different matters worthy of being read so that one may know what they contain*], Anno 5442, pp. 16, 18. For the story of the response of Amsterdam Jewry to the Messianic claim of Sabbatai Zvi, cf. Heinrich Graetz, *History of the Jews*, V, 139-155.

62. Cf. David Kaufmann, "L'Elégie de Mose Zacut sur Saul Morteira," *Revue des Etudes Juives*, XXXVII (1898), 12. S. Mannheimer, "Saul Levi Morteira," *Jewish Encyclopaedia*, IX, 37. M. Kayserling, "Zacuto," *ibid.*, XII, 627.

63. Cecil Roth, *The History of the Jews of Italy* (Philadelphia, 1946); pp. 402-403.

64. Zacuto was also the author of the first play written in the Hebrew language in modern times. His *Yesod Olam* (the Foundation of the World) is a drama built around Abraham's persecutions and steadfast loyalty to God. Abraham is the exemplar of Israel faithful to the Lord despite the malevolent powers of the Inquisition. Cf. Israel Abrahams, *Jewish Life in the Middle Ages* (2nd ed., London, 1932), pp. 290-294.

65. Cf. the manuscript entitled *Providencia de dios con israel verdad y heternidad de la lei de moseh compuesto. Por el cientisimo y mui docto sabio el señor H. Saul Levi Mortera Morenu a Rab ab bet din Y Ros Yesiba de el K. K. de talmud tora en Amsterdam.* [*On the providence of God for Israel, and the truth and eternity of the Law of Moses. By the most sage and learned master, the Señor, Saul Levi Mortera, our teacher, and Rabbi of the Court, and head of the school for Talmud Torah of the K. K. in Amsterdam.*] At the close of the manuscript there is the notation: "Este libro fue copiado de su original por Abraham y dana, correcto el eno de 1683: siendo el dicho dehedad de 60 [This book was copied from its original by Abraham y dana, and corrected in the year 1683: the aforesaid being 60 years of age]." The manuscript had been in circulation, however, as early as 1664. Cf. M. Kayserling, *Biblioteca Española-Portugueza-Judaica*, p. 74. Also cf. E. H. Lindo, *The History of the Jews of Spain and Portugal* (London, 1848), p. 368.

66. A. Wolf, *op. cit.*, p. 50.

67. George Alexander Kohut, "Jewish Martyrs of the Inquisition in South America," *Publications of the American Jewish Historical Society*, IV (1894), 132-134.

68. M. Kayserling, "Une Histoire de la Littérature Juive de Daniel Lévi de Barrios," *Revue des Études Juives*, XVIII (1889), 280. Daniel Lévi de Barrios, *La Corona de Ley*, p. 2. Daniel Levi de Barrios, *Arbol de las Vidas del Kahal Kados Amstelodamo*, pp. 69, 70, 76, 85, 86, 101, 102. Also, M. Kayserling, *op. cit.*, p. 286. In the community's memory, Spinoza became the shadowy figure of the "atheist," and Isaac Orobio was praised for confuting him:

> "Ishac Orobio Medico eminente
> Con sus libros da envidia a la sapiente
> Y en lo que escrivio contra el Atheista
> Espinosa, mas clara haze la vista.

> "[Ishac Orobio, eminent physician,
> With his books makes envious the learned,
> And what he wrote against the Atheist
> Espinosa, clarifies the perception.]"

69. Lucien Wolf, *op. cit.,* pp. xxii, xli, lxviii.

70. Moses Gaster, *op. cit.,* p. 88. In 1792, the London Jewish community reacted with similar timidity to the hysteria which swept England with the onset of the French Revolution. That year an alien bill was enacted by Parliament for the control of the movements of foreigners on British soil. The wardens of the Portuguese Synagogue, concerned with removing any suspicion of Jacobinism which might attach to the Jews, instructed their rabbi to remind the congregation of their duty to king and constitution. Nevertheless, several Jews were deported from England presumably as "security risks." The protests of the great English liberal leader Charles James Fox were of no avail. Cf. James Picciotto, *Sketches of Anglo-Jewish History* (London, 1875), pp. 221-222.

71. Cf. Carl Gebhardt, "Juan de Prado," *Chronicon Spinozanum* (The Hague), III (1923), 283-284. Leon Dujovne, *Spinoza* (Buenos Aires, 1941), I, 95.

72. A. Wolf, *op. cit.,* pp. 44-49.

73. Isaiah Sonne, "Leon Modena and the Da Costa Circle in Amsterdam," *Hebrew Union College Annual,* XXI (1948), 14.

74. *Tractatus Theologico-Politicus,* pp. 108, 147. *Correspondence,* p. 353. Even in his *Hebrew Grammar,* Spinoza refers to the "Phareisaei superstitione," a strong expression for a chapter on the Hebrew alphabet. Cf., "Compendium Grammatices Linguae Hebraeae," *Benedicti de Spinoza Opera,* ed. J. Van Vloten and J. P. N. Land (The Hague, 1883), II, 529.

75. *Tractatus Theologico-Politicus,* pp. 17, 80, 116, 118. The great Isaac Newton, on the other hand, found Maimonides' method congenial to his own scriptural divagations. Cf. Sir Isaac Newton, *Theological Manuscripts,* ed. H. McLachlan (Liverpool, 1950), pp. 12, 16-17.

76. *Tractatus Theologico-Politicus,* pp. 120-121, 149.

77. It was for this reason that Spinoza took his excommunication with such finality. Excommunications could otherwise be almost inconsequential. At the sister synagogue in London, within a few years, "they had become very much accustomed to the application of the Herem, and did not pay much attention to the infliction. A slight repentance, an open avowal of regret, the ready payment of the fine, was sufficient to obliterate all the evil consequences resulting therefrom." Moses Gaster, *op. cit.,* pp. 168-170. Shortly after Spinoza's death, Jacob de Andrade Velosino wrote a reply to him entitled *Theologo Religioso o Theologo Politico de Bento de Espinosa que de Judeo se fez Atheista* [*Religious and Political Theology of Bento de Espinosa who from a Jew made himself into an Atheist*]. Velosino was born in the Brazilian Jewish colony but came to Holland after the Portuguese conquest. He edited one of Morteira's works, and his criticism of Spinoza was evidently in Morteira's spirit. Cf. George Alexander Kohut, "Early Jewish Literature in America," *Publications of the American Jewish Historical Society,* III (1895), 109. M. Kayserling, *Biblioteca Española-Portugueza-Judaica,* p. 12. Also, M. Kayserling, "Jacob de Andrade Velosino," *Hebraeische Bibliographie,* III (1860), 58-59.

2. *Revolutionist in Mystic Withdrawal*

1. John Colerus, *The Life of Benedict de Spinosa*, trans. from the French (London, 1706), reprinted in Sir Frederick Pollock, *Spinoza: His Life and Philosophy* (2nd ed.; London, 1899), p. 392.

2. Roger Bigelow Merriman, *Six Contemporaneous Revolutions* (Oxford, 1938), pp. 19-26. Masaniello's name was still a fearful symbol to colonial conservatives on the eve of the American Revolution. Cf. Carl Becker, *The Eve of the Revolution* (New Haven, 1918), p. 173.

3. William Sewel, *The History of the Rise, Increase, and Progress of the Christian People Called Quakers* (Philadelphia, 1811), I, 180, 222-223.

4. James Geddes, *History of the Administration of John de Witt: Grand Pensionary of Holland* (The Hague, 1879), I, 319-320.

5. Albert Hyma, *The Dutch in the Far East* (Ann Arbor, 1942), pp. 67-68.

6. Colerus placed the date at which Spinoza began to reside in Rijnsburg as 1664, but Spinoza's first letter to Oldenburg was written from Rijnsburg in 1661. Evidently he had been in residence there for some time. Cf. Colerus, *op. cit.*, p. 392. *Correspondence*, p. 78.

7. W. A., Fellow of the Royal Society, *The Present State of the United Provinces* (London, 1671), pp. 343-344. The author said the Collegiant assembly was held "ten or twelve times a year." He added that "there are many others that sit at home reading the Scripture, and never come to any Church, except it be out of curiosity. The Arianisme has those that profess it. . . . There are Atheists enough too."

8. Preserved Smith, *Age of the Reformation* (New York, 1920), p. 154.

9. Many of the Anabaptists followed Michael Servetus in denying the dogmas of the Trinity and the divinity of Jesus. Amsterdam itself had been an Anabaptist stronghold during the 1530's. Its lower classes were infused with revolutionary ideas, and during the Anabaptist uprising of 1535 they seized the Amsterdam city hall. "Not a known Anabaptist in the city was spared. Thus Amsterdam was saved." As the social crisis of the sixteenth century ended, and the struggle for national independence with Spain took the foreground, many of the Anabaptists became Calvinists and joined the Reformed Church. Once they had outnumbered the Calvinists, but now their numbers diminished. Almost all the survivors of the sect who remained after the defection to the Calvinists became Mennonites. The two names, "Anabaptist" and "Mennonite," tended to become practically synonymous. Cf. Henry Elias Dosker, *The Dutch Anabaptists* (Philadelphia, 1921), pp. 88, 91. Three-fourths of the Dutch martyrs in the War of Independence against Spain are said to have been Anabaptists. Cf. *ibid.*, p. 141. Also cf. C. Henry Smith, *The Story of the Mennonites* (Berne, Indiana, 1941), pp. 84, 207-208, 211. E. Belfort Bax, *The Rise and Fall of the Anabaptists* (London, 1903), pp. 31, 327, 363. R. J. Smithson, *The Anabaptists* (London, 1935), p. 102. Roland H. Bainton, "The Left Wing of the Reformation," *The Journal of*

Religion, XXI (1941), 124-134. John Horsch, "Menno Simons' Attitude Toward the Anabaptists of Münster," *The Mennonite Quarterly Review*, X (1936), 55-72.

10. J. Winfield Fretz, "Mutual Aid among the Mennonites," *The Mennonite Quarterly Review*, XIII (1939), 34. For communistic ideas among the Mennonites, also cf. C. Henry Smith, *The Story of the Mennonites*, pp. 207-208. H. E. Dosker, *The Dutch Anabaptists*, pp. 135, 215. As late as 1695, it was charged that the Collegiants, Mennonites, and Quakers "taught that in this life all things should be owned in common." They were also accused of nourishing hopes for violent revolution and free love. Cf. Lambertus Hortensius, *Histoire des Anabaptistes* (Paris, 1695), pp. 1-2.

11. J. Winfield Fretz, *op. cit.*, p. 30.

12. H. E. Dosker, *The Dutch Anabaptists*, pp. 207-208.

13. Cf. Hugo Grotius, *De Jure Belli Ac Pacis*, Introduction by James Brown Scott (Oxford, 1925), II, Bk. I, xix.

14. Hugo Grotius, *The Jurisprudence of Holland*, trans. R. W. Lee (Oxford, 1926), I, 81. The law of nature provided Grotius with a basis for acquiescence to the social status quo: "the law of nature further teaches that everyone must be content with what is his, not only because it is otherwise impossible to maintain friendship among men." *Ibid.*, p. 81. Also cf. W. S. M. Knight, *The Life and Works of Hugo Grotius* (London, 1925), p. 246. Spinoza possessed in his library two works of Grotius, *De Satisfacione* and *De Imperio Summarum Potestatum*. The first was an attack on so-called "socinian" principles. Cf. A. J. Servaas van Rooijen, *Inventaire des Livres Formant la Bibliothèque de Benedict Spinoza* (The Hague, 1888), pp. 147, 183.

15. Robert Barclay, *The Inner Life of the Religious Societies of the Commonwealth* (2nd ed.; London, 1877), pp. 89-90. A contemporary described them as follows: "Il y en a aussi qu'on appelle Collegiens, parce qu'ils s'assemblent separément, où chacun a la liberté de parler, d'expliquer l'Ecriture, et de prier ou de chanter. Ceux qui sont veritablement Collegiens, sont unitaires. Ils ne communient jamais dans leur College, mais ils s'assemblent deux fois l'an, de toutes les parties de la Holande, à Rijnsbourg, qui est un village environ à deux lieues de Leide, . . . on y reçoit toutes les sectes, même les Catholiques Romains, lors qu'ils s'y présentent. [There are also those called Collegiants, because they have separate assemblies, where each one has the liberty to speak, explain Scripture, pray or sing. Those who are truly Collegiants are unitarians. They never have a general meeting in their College, but they gather twice a year from all parts of Holland, at Rijnsbourg, which is a village about two leagues from Leyden, . . . there they receive persons of all sects, even Roman Catholics, when they present themselves.]" Cf. Lambertus Hortensius, *Histoire des Anabaptistes* (Paris, 1695), p. 160. Also cf. M. Diderot, *Encyclopédie* (Paris, 1753), III, 638. Rufus M. Jones, *Spiritual Reformers in the Sixteenth and Seventeenth Centuries* (London, 1914), pp. 117-123. William C. Braithwaite, *The Beginnings of Quakerism* (London, 1912), p. 406.

16. Spinoza "learned a Mechanical Art," says Colerus, "before he embrac'd a quiet and retir'd life, as he was resolved to do. He learned therefore to make Glasses for Telescopes, and for some other uses, and succeeded so well therein, that People came to him from all Parts to buy them; which did sufficiently afford him wherewith to live and maintain himself." Colerus, *op. cit.*, pp. 391-392.

17. *Correspondence*, pp. 52-53. *The Oldest Biography of Spinoza*, ed. A. Wolf (London, 1927), pp. 188-189. According to Bayle, Jelles submitted his *Confession of Faith* for Spinoza's judgment. "Spinoza replied to him that he had read it with pleasure, and that he had not found anything in it which could be altered." Cf. *Correspondence*, pp. 442-443; also pp. 267-268.

18. *Improvement of the Understanding*, pp. 3-7.

19. *Correspondence*, pp. 98-99.

20. *Ibid.*, pp. 138-139.

21. Cf. William Sewel, *The History of the Rise, Increase, and Progress of the Christian People called Quakers*, written originally in Low-Dutch by William Sewel, and by himself translated into English (London, 1722). Balling's "The Light upon the Candlestick" is included as an Addendum in this book. Cf. pp. 717, 719. William Sewel was a noted early Quaker historian and missionary. The religious search common among so many young men in those years was typically expressed in Charles Marshall's account of the Seeker Society of Bristol: "Now as I advanced in years, I grew more and more dissatisfied with lifeless, empty professions and professors, feeling the burden of the nature of sin. . . . And seeing that I could not find the living among the dead professions, I spent much time in retirements alone. . . . And in those times viz. about the year 1654, there were many (in these parts) who were seeking after the Lord. . . ." Cf. Rufus M. Jones, *Studies in Mystical Religion* (New York, 1936), pp. 130, 464.

22. *Correspondence*, p. 123. Rufus M. Jones, *op. cit.*, p. 117.

23. Colerus, *op. cit.*, pp. 403-404. *Correspondence*, p. 455. *The Oldest Biography of Spinoza*, p. 139.

24. *Correspondence*, p. 410.

25. *Ibid.*, pp. 260-261. The saying that "the possessions of friends are common" was enunciated by Pythagoras. Cf. Iamblichus, *Life of Pythagoras*, trans. Thomas Taylor (London, 1818), p. 68.

26. For Overton's intrigues, cf. *The Nicholas Papers: Correspondence of Sir Edward Nicholas, Secretary of State*, ed. George F. Warner (Westminster, 1897), III, 44. On the millenarian discussion which was evoked by the question of the admission of the Jews into Britain, cf., Cecil Roth, *A Life of Menasseh ben Israel* (Philadelphia, 1934), pp. 186, 255. Louise Fargo Brown, *The Political Activities of the Baptists and Fifth Monarchy Men in England during the Interregnum* (Washington, 1912), pp. 15, 24-25, 33. Isabel Ross, *Margaret Fell: Mother of Quakerism* (London, 1949), p. 95. Also, Don Patinkin, "Mercantilism and the Readmission of the Jews to England," *Jewish Social Studies*, VIII (1946), 164. On English radicals, Cromwell, and the Jews, cf. Thomas Carlyle, *Oliver Cromwell's Letters and Speeches* (The

Sterling Edition, Boston), XVII, 428; XVIII, 409. *Menasseh ben Israel's Mission to Oliver Cromwell*, ed. Lucien Wolf (London, 1901), pp. xvii, xxi, xxix. Wolf mistakenly assigns 1651 as the date of Cromwell's speech against the Judaisers. Also cf. Cecil Roth, *op. cit.*, pp. 194, 332. Lucien Wolf, "Cromwell's Jewish Intelligencers," *Essays in Jewish History* (London, 1934) p. 91 ff. Some wealthy Jews gave financial support to the Royalists. Cf. Lucien Wolf, "Crypto-Jews under the Commonwealth," *Transactions of the Jewish Historical Society of England,* I (1893-4), 71.

27. William I. Hull, *The Rise of Quakerism in Amsterdam 1655-1665* (Swarthmore, 1938), p. 205. Also cf. Isabel Ross, *Margaret Fell*, pp. 93-95. When Ames described Spinoza as "tender," he was using the word with a distinctive Quaker connotation. "Tender" was a favorite word of George Fox. "It means," as Rufus Jones states, "that the persons to whom it is applied are religiously inclined, serious, and earnest in their search for spiritual realities." Cf. George Fox, *An Autobiography*, ed. Rufus M. Jones (Philadelphia, 1919), p. 70. With respect to the relation between the Quakers and Mennonites, Robert Barclay observed that George Fox was "the unconscious exponent of the doctrine, practice, and discipline of the ancient and stricter party of the Dutch Mennonites." Cf. *The Inner Life of the Religious Societies of the Commonwealth* (London, 1876), p. 77.

28. As G. P. Gooch wrote, the Quaker apostles who went to Holland caused the greatest excitement by preaching that all goods should be held in common. According to him, furthermore, the Amsterdam Quakers put this maxim into practice. G. P. Gooch, *The History of English Democratic Ideas in the Seventeenth Century* (Cambridge, 1898), p. 276.

29. William I. Hull, *Benjamin Furly and Quakerism in Rotterdam* (Swarthmore, 1941), pp. 189-190.

30. *Ibid.*, p. 196.

31. William I. Hull, *The Rise of Quakerism in Amsterdam*, pp. 221, 226, 255.

32. *Ibid.*, p. 298. An English letter writer in 1663 or 1664 thus described the Dutch Mennonites and Quakers: "Both they and many sepatists are against fighting, not a few of them believe ye fifth monarchy shall be set up in ye world & administered by a miraculous power." *Ibid.*, p. 14.

33. W. I. Hull, *The Rise of Quakerism in Amsterdam*, pp. 27, 214-215, 234, 267. W. I. Hull, *Benjamin Furly*, pp. 10-11. *Correspondence*, pp. 131, 138, 196, 198, 207.

34. W. I. Hull, *Benjamin Furly*, pp. 166, 189. An agent of Charles II wrote in 1666 from Rotterdam: "Colonel Sidney is in great esteem with De Witt and often in consultation with Benjamin Furly the quaker, being resolved to shape some designe for Ingland, . . . I desired to know the quakers name who ye phanatiques do so confide in and he answered me that the quakers name is benjamin Furly." *Ibid.*, p. 54.

35. *Short Treatise*, pp. cxxv, 71-72.

36. *Ethics*, Part Four, Appendix, Par. XIII.

37. *Correspondence*, pp. 205-206.

38. Rufus M. Jones, *Studies in Mythical Religion*, p. 478. Not only Spinoza's pantheism but also his views on good and evil would have fallen under this act. For Spinoza had written: "Now good and evil are neither things nor actions. Therefore good and evil do not exist in nature." *Short Treatise*, p. 60.

39. Cf. Robert Barclay, *The Inner Life of the Religious Societies of the Commonwealth* (London, 1876), pp. 417-419. "They were not, strictly speaking, sects; they were more or less contagious movements or tendencies of thought which affected groups . . . without producing any unifying, cementing organization." Rufus M. Jones, *Studies in Mystical Religion*, pp. 452, 467.

40. *Ibid.*, pp. 468-469.

41. "There was," as Rufus M. Jones has written, "a strong wave of pantheistical sentiment abroad, both on the Continent and in England." Cf. *Mysticism and Democracy in the English Commonwealth* (Cambridge, Mass., 1932), p. 16.

42. Cf. *The Works of Gerrard Winstanley*, ed. George H. Sabine (Ithaca, 1941), pp. 105, 109. David W. Petegorsky, *Left Wing Democracy in the English Civil War: A Study of the Social Philosophy of Gerrard Winstanley* (London, 1940), pp. 136, 231. Also cf. Winthrop S. Hudson, "Economic and Social Thought of Gerrard Winstanley: Was He a Seventeenth-Century Marxist?" *The Journal of Modern History*, XVIII (1946), 1-21. Winthrop S. Hudson, "Gerrard Winstanley and the Early Quakers," *Church History*, XIII (1943), 183.

43. D. W. Petegorsky, *op. cit.*, pp. 132, 179.

44. *Ethics*, Part Five, Prop. XXIV.

45. Thomas Franklin Mayo, *Epicurus in England (1650-1725)* (Dallas, Tex., 1934), p. 27. D. W. Petegorsky, *op. cit.*, p. 73. Eduard Bernstein believed that the Amsterdam imprint was probably a device to conceal the pamphlet's publication in London from the English censorship. Cf. Eduard Bernstein, *Cromwell and Communism*, trans. H. J. Stenning (London, 1930), p. 91. Amsterdam was, however, a center for the publication of English books, and there is no real ground for Bernstein's conjecture.

46. W. Schenk has questioned the materialist character of Overton's thought; cf. *The Concern for Social Justice in the Puritan Revolution* (London, 1948), pp. 168-171. But this interpretation seems to me belied by the actual argument of Overton. Cf. Eduard Bernstein, *op. cit.*, pp. 91-92.

47. *Correspondence*, p. 290. *Tractatus Theologico-Politicus*, Preface, p. 7. Spinoza, furthermore, regarded Plato's theory of ideas and Aristotle's theory of universals as nonsense. Spinoza was a thorough-going nominalist. "For it is precisely the particular things, and they alone, that have a cause, and not the general, because they are nothing." *Short Treatise*, p. 50.

48. T. F. Mayo, *op. cit.*, pp. 43, 51.

49. *Correspondence*, p. 99. *Ethics*, Part Four, Preface; Part One, Prop. XV. For the hostile critic of 1673, cf. Jean Baptiste Stouppe, *La Religion des Hollandois* (Cologne, 1673), pp. 62-63.

50. *The Diary of Robert Hooke (1672-1680)*, ed. H. W. Robinson and

W. Adams (London, 1935), p. 368. Robert F. Horton, *John Howe* (London, 1895), pp. 32, 114.

51. The pamphlet was written by a physician, J. Rodenpoort, and printed at Bois-le-Duc. Cf. Servaas van Rooijen, *Inventaire des Livres,* pp. 20-21. It charged Spinoza with abetting sexual immorality among the youth: "Il les excite à ne plus respecter les femmes et à se livrer à la débauche, car suivant sa doctrine, le bien et le mal ne sont que des idéalités. [He excites them to respect women no more and to give themselves to debauchery, for according to his doctrine, good and evil are only ideas in the mind.]" It mourned the times and declared that new "infernal ideas" were rising in that century which rejected all the restraints of the sovereign power. The earlier attacks of Frans Kuyper were directed against both Spinozists and Quakers. Spinoza's name was also associated with that of Jean de Labadie, a preacher of great force, whose doctrine, a blend of free love, communism, and the light within, caused a great stir in Holland during 1666 to 1669. Labadie converted a burgomaster of Amsterdam, Conrad van Beuningen, and was said to have had 60,000 adherents in the Netherlands. Seven synods were convened to consider his heresy. A *History of the Anabaptists* published at this time evidently coupled Spinoza with him as subversive influences. Cf. William I. Hull, *William Penn and the Dutch Quaker Migration to Pennsylvania* (Swarthmore, 1935), pp. 3-4, 13. Una Birch, *Anna von Schurman* (New York, 1909), pp. 149-150, and for a good account of Labadie, *Journal of Jasper Danckaerts, 1679-1680,* ed. B. B. James and J. F. Jameson (New York, 1913), pp. xxi, xxii. Also, "Sects," *Encyclopaedia of Religion and Ethics,* XI, 323.

Both William Penn and John Locke visited the Labadist communist colony during their sojourns in Holland. Locke made perhaps the first liberal analysis in modern history of the psychology of communism. He wrote in his diary on August 21, 1684: "Here . . . is the church of the Labadists; they receive all ages, sexes, and degrees upon approbation, after trial. They live all in common; . . . they seemed to expect that a man should come there disposed to desire and court admittance into their society, without inquiring into their ways; . . . which signs of grace seem to me to be, at last, a perfect submission to the will and rules of their pastor, M. Yonn; who, if I mistake not, has established to himself a perfect empire over them. . . . He is *dominus factotum;* and though I believe they are . . . generally speaking, people of very good and exemplary lives, yet the tone of voice, manner, and fashion, of those I conversed with, seemed to make one suspect a little of Tartouf." Lord King, *The Life and Letters of John Locke* (London, 1884), p. 162.

52. Rufus M. Jones, a great successor of the seventeenth-century mystics, held that "a true and genuine democracy is intrinsically and inherently mystical in character." Democratic mysticism, he said, makes of the individual an over-individual, linking him with the blessed community as the totemic bond unites the primitive tribe. Cf. *Mysticism and Democracy in the English Commonwealth,* pp. 25-26.

53. D. W. Petegorsky, *op. cit.,* p. 235.

54. Octavius Brooks Frothingham, *Transcendentalism in New England* (New York, 1876), pp. vi, 136, 143. For Spinoza's influence on the New England transcendentalists, cf., Octavius Brooks Frothingham, *George Ripley* (Boston, 1899), pp. 98, 102-104. Ralph Waldo Emerson in his lecture on "Character" in 1864 said: "Spinoza has come to be revered."

55. D. W. Petegorsky, *op. cit.*, p. 128. D. W. Robertson, *The Religious Foundations of Leveller Democracy* (New York, 1951), p. 15. Also cf. Jerald C. Brauer, "Puritan Mysticism and the Development of Liberalism," *Church History*, XVIII (1950), 161-162.

56. Brand Blanshard, "Early Thought on the Internal Light," *By-Ways in Quaker History*, ed. Howard W. Brinton (Pendle Hill, Penn., 1944), p. 160.

57. *Ethics*, Part Four, Prop. XXXVI.

58. "In the mysticism of both Everard and Saltmarsh, in the free grace of John Eaton, in the 'sufficiencie of the spirit' doctrine of How and Spencer, the effect had been to establish the claims of the multitude to be heard and to receive justice from those in power." D. W. Robertson, *The Religious Foundations of Leveller Democracy*, p. 44.

59. *Tractatus Politicus*, p. 369.

60. Colerus, *op. cit.*, p. 394. At the same time, Spinoza felt that "it is not untidy and neglected appearance that makes us scholars," and that "affectation of negligence is the mark of an inferior mind." Lucas states that he tried to dress like a gentleman, not like a pedant. Cf. A. Wolf, *The Oldest Biography of Spinoza*, p. 64. *Short Treatise*, p. 97.

61. Robert Barclay, *The Inner Life of the Religious Societies of the Commonwealth*, p. 84. William I. Hull, *Benjamin Furly and Quakerism in Rotterdam*, p. 13.

62. John Cunningham, *The Quakers* (Edinburgh, 1868), p. 45.

63. A. Wolf, *The Oldest Biography of Spinoza*, p. 157. *Ethics*, Part Three, The Affects, Definition XLIV.

3. Political Scientist in the Cause of Human Liberation

1. This tension between political participation and mystic withdrawal becomes especially acute in a post-revolutionary age. It led Lilburne from Levelling agitation to Quaker contemplation. "There had been two men in Lilburne, the warrior and the mystic. Once cut off from the battle of politics, the warrior was displaced by the mystic, and John Lilburne, the crusader, became a Quaker. Perhaps as years of imprisonment broke down his bodily vigor, he lost his old faith in his ability to force the world into justice and righteousness; in such a mood he would welcome the Quaker belief in the power of patience and long suffering." Theodore Calvin Pease, *The Leveller Movement: A Study in the History and Political Theory of the English Great Civil War* (Washington, 1916), pp. 355-356. In our time, this

evolution has once more become familiar as we have observed Marxists and Communists find their way to religious faith and mysticism.

2. *Tractatus Theologico-Politicus*, p. 249. "Les Mennonites," said a critic in the seventeenth century, "s'excusèrent d'etre enrolés dans ces Compagnies [de milices], disant qu'ils ne croyoient pas, qu'un Chrétien pût en bonne conscience porter les armes pour quelque sujet que ce soit. [The Mennonites excused themselves from being enrolled in these companies of militia, saying that they didn't believe that a Christian could in good conscience carry arms for any cause whatsoever.]" Jean Baptiste Stouppe, *La Religion des Hollandois* (Cologne, 1673), p. 86. Madeleine Francès, *Spinoza dans les Pays Néerlandais* (Paris, 1937), p. 132.

3. A. J. Servaas van Rooijen, *Inventaire des Livres Formant la Bibliothèque de Benedict Spinoza* (The Hague, 1888), p. 142. Paul-Louis Couchoud, *Benoît de Spinoza* (Paris, 1902), p. 131.

4. *Correspondence*, p. 123.

5. John Colerus, *The Life of Benedict de Spinosa*, trans. from the French (London, 1706), reprinted in Sir Frederick Pollock, *Spinoza: His Life and Philosophy* (2nd ed., London, 1899), pp. 392–393. Lucas confirms the abundance of Spinoza's social relationships at this period. "The real men of learning," he tells, "overwhelmed" Spinoza with their visits and persuaded him to leave the country and settle in the city. Cf. *The Oldest Biography of Spinoza*, ed. A. Wolf (London, 1927), p. 59.

6. *Correspondence*, pp. 181, 202, 206.

7. *Ibid.*, p. 206.

8. As Motley said: "The Netherlands drifted into a confederacy of aristocratic republics, not because they had planned a republic, but because they could not get a king, foreign or native." John Lothrop Motley, *The Life and Death of John of Barneveld* (New York, 1874), I, 24.

9. During his visit to the Netherlands, St. Evremond became friendly with John de Witt and exchanged ideas with Spinoza. His observations on the precarious character of the Dutch Republican experiment were keen: "I remember that I have often said in Holland, and even to the Pensioner himself, that Men were mistaken as to the temper of the Hollanders. The World believes, that the Hollanders love Liberty; whereas they only hate Oppression. There are amongst them a few proud haughty Spirits, and 'tis Pride and Haughtiness that makes the true Republican. . . . If they love the Republick, 'tis for the Benefit of their Trade; more than for any Satisfaction they find in being Free. The Magistrates love to be Independent, to govern those that depend on them: As for the People, they would more easily acknowledge the Authority of the Prince, than that of the Magistrate. 'Tis true, that when a Prince of Orange had a Design to surprise Amsterdam, all declared for the Burgomasters; but that was rather out of a Hatred of Violence, than Love of Liberty. When another opposed a Peace, after a long expensive War, a Peace was made in spite of him: But it was done through a Sense of the present Misery; and the Respect they had naturally for him, was only

suspended, not destroy'd. When their extraordinary strokes were over, they returned to the Prince of Orange. The Republicans have the Dissatisfaction to see the People take up their first Affections, and they apprehend a Monarchical government. . . . Holland, says Grotius, is a Republick made by Chance, which is kept up by their Fear of the Spaniards. . . . The Apprehension which France now gives them, produces the same Effects. . . . But to judge of Things by themselves, the Hollanders are neither Free, nor Slaves. . . ." St. Evremond spoke pleasantly of the impression Spinoza made on him, though he found him guarded concerning his philosophic views: "The latter, . . . was of a middle stature, and pleasing countenance: his learning, modesty, and disinterestedness made him esteem'd and courted by all the ingenious persons then at the Hague. . . . Spinoza did not lay himself open all at once. He still us'd some caution. . . ." Cf. *The Works of Monsieur de St. Evremond,* trans. Mr. Des Maizeaux (London, 1728), I, lvi; II, 141-142.

10. Sir William Temple, "Observations on the United Provinces of the Netherlands," *The Works of Sir William Temple* (London, 1770), I, 113.

11. James Geddes, *History of the Administration of John de Witt* (London, 1879), p. 105. Also, *ibid.,* pp. 117-118, 145-147, 155, 197-198, 202, 364.

12. *Ibid.,* pp. 382, 408, 434-435. Also cf. G. N. Clark, "P. Geyl: Oranje en Stuart, 1641-1672," *The English Historical Review,* LVII (1942), 140.

13. *Tractatus Theologico-Politicus,* pp. 6, 264. Sir Josiah Child, who rose to become governor of the English East India Company, similarly explained in 1668 that Holland was prosperous in part because of its liberalism: "their toleration of different opinions in matters of religion: by reason of which many industrious people of other countries . . . resort to them with their families and estates." *A New Discourse of Trade* (5th ed.; London, 1751), p. 4.

14. W. A., Fellow of the Royal Society, *The Present State of the United Provinces* (London, 1671), pp. 352-353.

15. *The English Works of Thomas Hobbes,* ed. Sir William Molesworth (London, 1840), VI, 168. As David Hume observed in his *History of England,* the influence of the Dutch example became considerable with the outbreak of civil war: "the commercial part of the nation desired to see a like form of government established in England" (Edition of Boston, 1849), V, 228. When the Long Parliament excluded the bishops from a voice in the House of Lords, it found a precedent in the exclusion of the clergy from the Estates of Holland. Parliament's demand that it, and not the king, should control the armed forces, likewise followed the constitutional path of the Dutch Republic. Prominent Independent leaders, who had imbibed ideas of toleration during their exile in Holland, held seats in Parliament. The committee on law reform was especially influenced by such Dutch practices as civil marriage. Cf. Douglas Campbell, *The Puritan in Holland, England and America* (New York, 1892), II, 379.

16. Hobbes' remarks on Spinoza are found in *John Aubrey's Brief Lives (1669-1696),* ed. Andrew Clark (Oxford, 1898), I, 357. The usual rendition has been as follows: "When Spinoza's *Tractatus Theologico-Politicus* first came

out, Mr. Edmund Waller sent it to my lord of Devonshire, and desired him to send word what Mr. Hobbes said of it. Mr. H. told his lordship: —Ne judicate ne judicemini. He told me he had cut through him a barre's length, for he durst not write so boldly." A recent, careful study of the original manuscript, however, indicates that the editor misread the handwriting of Aubrey. The reading I have cited is given by V. de S. Pinto in his "A Note by Aubrey," *The Times Literary Supplement*, September 15, 1951, p. 581. As Mr. Pinto writes: "This makes perfectly good sense. The reference is to the old game of throwing the bar: a trial of strength, the players contending which of them could throw or pitch it farthest." Also cf. *English Biography in the Seventeenth Century*, ed. Vivian de Sola Pinto (London, 1951), pp. 223-224.

17. Pieter de la Court, in John de Witt, *Political Maxims of the State of Holland*, trans. from the Dutch (London, 1743), pp. 44, 49.

18. *Ibid.*, p. 356.

19. Albert Hyma, *Christianity, Capitalism, and Communism* (Ann Arbor, 1937), p. 148.

20. Bernard H. M. Vlekke, *Nusantara: A History of the East Indian Archipelago* (Cambridge, Mass., 1944), p. 132.

21. Albert Hyma, *The Dutch in the Far East* (Ann Arbor, 1942), pp. 159, 161.

22. *Tractatus Theologico-Politicus*, pp. 76, 212-213.

23. Immanuel Kant, *Perpetual Peace* (New York, 1939), p. 37.

24. *Short Treatise*, pp. 72-73. The great thinkers of the seventeenth century broke through European provincialism to consider the ways of other races and cultures. Locke, Hobbes, and Leibniz referred extensively to the reports of travelers concerning primitive peoples, and Spinoza's writings allude to the Chinese, Japanese, Turks, and Indians. Amsterdam, the great port which harbored ships from many seas, was a school in the variety of men's patterns of life. Cf. Geoffrey Atkinson, *Les Relations de Voyage du XVIIᵉ Siècle et L'Evolution des Idées* (Paris, 1924), pp. 110-111, 184, 212.

25. *Short Treatise*, p. 33.

26. *Tractatus Theologico-Politicus*, p. 264.

27. Henri Pirenne, *Belgian Democracy: Its Early History*, trans. J. V. Saunders (London, 1915), pp. 225-226.

28. *Ibid.*, pp. 228-235.

29. Margaret Mann Phillips, "Erasmus and Propaganda," *The Modern Language Review*, XXXVII (1942), 7. Adriaan Jacob Barnouw, *Vondel* (New York, 1925), p. 36. Petrus Johannes Blok, *History of the People of the Netherlands*, trans. Ruth Putnam (New York, 1900), III, 398.

30. *Short Treatise*, pp. 36-40.

31. M. M. Phillips, *op. cit.*, p. 7.

32. As Oliver Wendell Holmes judiciously observed: "the wave of protest which stormed the dikes of Dutch orthodoxy in the seventeenth century, stole gently through the bars of New England puritanism in the

eighteenth." Cf. *John Lothrop Motley: A Memoir* (Boston, 1881), p. 202. Also cf. p. 194.

33. John Lothrop Motley, *The Life and Death of John of Barneveld*, I, 45. P. J. Blok, *op. cit.*, III, 399.

34. "In burghers' mansions, peasants' cottages, mechanics' back-parlours, on board herring smacks, canal boats, and East Indiamen, . . . there was ever to be found the fierce wrangle of Remonstrant and Contra-Remonstrant, the hissing of red-hot theological rhetoric, the pelting of hostile texts . . . each paused to hold high converse with friend or foe on fate, free will, or absolute foreknowledge. . . . Province against province, city against city, family against family; it was one vast scene of bickering, denunciation, heartburnings, mutual excommunication and hatred." J. L. Motley, *op. cit.*, I, 338-339.

35. J. L. Motley, *op. cit.*, p. 346. Blok, *op. cit.*, III, 428. George Edmundson, *History of Holland* (Cambridge, England, 1922), p. 130.

36. *The Works of Sir William Temple, op. cit.*, I, 179. Temple adds that the Arminians, though "but few in number," are "considerable by the persons, who are of the better quality, the more learned and intelligent men, and many of them in the government."

37. Herbert D. Foster, "Liberal Calvinism: The Remonstrants at the Synod of Dort in 1618," *Collected Papers* (New York, 1929), p. 142.

38. A. J. Barnouw, *Vondel*, p. 74.

39. Herbert D. Foster said pointedly: "Fundamental differences of doctrine were not the real ground for the excommunication and banishment of the Remonstrants," *op. cit.*, p. 143.

40. Motley's judgment on the interrelations of economics and theology at the trial of Oldenbarnevelt is striking: "There is no doubt however that the disapprobation with which Barneveldt regarded the West India Company, the seat of which was at Amsterdam, was a leading cause of the deadly hostility entertained for him by the great commercial metropolis. It was bad enough for the Advocate to oppose unconditional predestination and the damnation of infants, but to frustrate a magnificent system of privateering on the Spaniards in time of truce was an unpardonable crime." J. L. Motley, *op. cit.*, II, 345; also pp. 107-108.

41. P. J. Blok, *op. cit.*, pp. 484-485.

42. M. Antonin Lefèvre-Pontalis, *John de Witt*, trans. S. S. E. and A. Stephenson (Boston, 1885), II, 660.

43. *Ibid.*, I, 85.

44. James Geddes, *op. cit.*, pp. 35-36.

45. I. Todhunter, *A History of the Mathematical Theory of Probability* (London, 1865), pp. 38-39. Phyllis Allen, "Scientific Studies in 17th Century English Universities," *Journal of the History of Ideas*, X (1949), 248.

46. *Ethics*, Part Three, Preface. Part One, Appendix.

47. Robert Gibbes Barnwell, *A Sketch of the Life and Times of John de Witt* (New York, 1856), p. 56.

48. *Ethics*, Part Three, Preface.

49. Frederick Hendricks, "Contributions to the History of Insurance and of the Theory of Life Contingencies, with a Restoration of the Grand Pensionary De Witt's Treatise on Life Annuities," *The Assurance Magazine* (London, 1852), II, 231, 250, 258. Also cf. I. Todhunter, *op. cit.*, p. 407. De Witt's work on the theory of probability was "his most important contribution to mathematics," and "a very commendable performance for a man deeply involved in the affairs of state," according to Julian Lowell Coolidge, *The Mathematics of Great Amateurs* (Oxford, 1949), p. 131. •

50. Pieter Geyl, "Johan de Witt, Grand Pensionary of Holland, 1653-72," *History*, XX (1936), 307, 319.

51. Pieter de la Court, *op. cit.*, p. 314. James Geddes, *op. cit.*, p. 457.

52. Lefèvre-Pontalis, *op. cit.*, I, 191.

53. James Geddes, *op. cit.*, pp. 443-446.

54. *Tractatus Theologico-Politicus*, pp. 5, 11.

55. *Ethics*, Part Four, Prop. LXX.

56. Cf. Karl Marx, *Capital*, trans. Eden and Cedar Paul (London, 1928), p. 865. Marx prefaced his book with a jibe at public opinion, and Dante's lines were his final words: "Follow your own bent, no matter what people say." As a scientific socialist, however, he awaited the day when the acceptance of his doctrine by the public would constitute its supreme verification.

57. *Tractatus Theologico-Politicus*, p. 7.

58. *Ethics*, Part Two, Prop. XLIX, Scholium; Prop. XLVIII.

59. *Tractatus Theologico-Politicus*, p. 5.

60. *Ethics*, Part Five, Prop. XXV, XXVII, Coroll. XXXII, Part One, Appendix.

4. The Promise and Anguish of Democracy

1. *Ethics*, Part Four, Prop. XXXVI, LIV.

2. Cf. Thomas Hobbes, *Leviathan* (Everyman's Edition), (London, 1914), pp. 65, 71, 87.

3. Cf. Albert Hyma, *Christianity, Capitalism, and Communism* (Ann Arbor, 1937), p. 144. Why were the lower classes so intensely Calvinist? John Lothrop Motley's answer is worth pondering: "the majority of the humbler classes . . . found in membership of the oligarchy of Heaven a substitute for those democratic aspirations on earth which were effectually suppressed between the two millstones of burgher aristocracy and military discipline. . . ." Cf. *The Life and Death of John of Barneveld* (New York, 1874), II, 114-115. To be a member in spirit of the "aristocracy of God's elect" compensated for one's bodily existence as God's neglected.

4. A. J. Barnouw, *Vondel* (New York, 1925), p. 73.

5. George Edmundson, *History of Holland* (Cambridge, England, 1922), p. 184. P. J. Blok, *History of the People of the Netherlands* (New York, 1900), IV, pp. 263, 270-271.

6. Cf. G. N. Clark, *The Seventeenth Century* (Oxford, 1929), pp. 79-80. For the contrast between the soldier Maurice and the statesman Barneveld, cf. Motley, *op. cit.,* I, 23-31.

7. M. Antonin Léfèvre-Pontalis, *John de Witt,* trans. S. S. E. and A. Stephenson (Boston, 1885), I, 409.

8. Cf. *A Defence of Liberty against Tyrants,* ed. H. J. Laski (London, 1924), p. 22.

9. Blok, *op. cit.,* III, 403, 422, 427.

10. A. J. Servaas van Rooijen, *Inventaire des Livres Formant la Bibliothèque de Benedict Spinoza* (The Hague, 1888), p. 198.

11. James Geddes, *History of the Administration of John de Witt* (New York, 1880), I, 78. George Edmundson, *op. cit.,* p. 204.

12. Geddes, *op. cit.,* p. 92.

13. *Ibid.,* pp. 122, 292, 396.

14. Blok, *op. cit.,* IV, 296-297.

15. *Tractatus Theologico-Politicus,* pp. 242-243.

16. ". . . This new monarch could only consolidate his power by . . . disturbing with war and peace which might encourage discontent, in order that the populace might be engrossed with novelties and divert its mind from brooding over the slaughter of the king." *Ibid.,* p. 243.

17. *Ibid.,* p. 244. Spinoza was following Grotius in his interpretation of Dutch history. The eminent jurist had in his *Annals and History of the Netherlands* argued that the representative assemblies were as old as the nation itself, and that their Princes had been delegated authority by the States, and not the other way around. Cf. Bernard H. M. Vlekke, "Historiography," in *The Contribution of Holland to the Sciences,* ed. A. J. Barnouw and B. Landheer (New York, 1943), p. 100. Also, M. de Burigny, *The Life of Hugo Grotius* (London, 1754), pp. 256-259. W. S. M. Knight, *The Life and Works of Hugo Grotius* (London, 1925), pp. 123-125.

18. *Tractatus Theologico-Politicus,* pp. 248-249.

19. *Ibid.,* p. 251. When the Quakers William Penn and George Keith argued for five hours in 1677 with the Dutch Mennonite leader, Galenus Abrahams, his reply too was that "nobody nowadays could be accepted as a messenger of God unless he confirmed the same by miracle." This was precisely Spinoza's ground. Cf. George Fox, *An Autobiography,* p. 556.

20. *Tractatus Theologico-Politicus,* pp. 248-249.

21. As G. N. Clark observes: "Democratic ideas in the modern sense play a very small part in the seventeenth century. Few men seriously proposed to extend any sort of franchise to artisans or labourers, and no such proposal had any more influence on events than to create a temporary disturbance." *The Seventeenth Century,* p. 85.

22. *Tractatus Theologico-Politicus,* pp. 253-254.

23. Thomas Hobbes, *Behemoth, Works,* VI, 190. The history of the English Bible as a revolutionary tract abundantly confirms Hobbes's judgment. The course of the revolution can be traced from 1543, when Parliament forbade laborers the right to read the Bible by themselves, to

1643, when Cromwell's army carried pocket "Soldiers' Bibles." Cf. *The Bible in Its Ancient and English Versions,* ed. H. Wheeler Robinson (Oxford, 1941), pp. 179, 224.

24. *Tractatus Theologico-Politicus,* pp. 209, 256.

25. *Ibid.,* pp. 252-255.

26. George Macaulay Trevelyan, *England under the Stuarts* (16th ed.; London, 1933), p. 340.

27. Spinoza returned to the theme of the futility of revolution in the *Tractatus Politicus,* p. 315. It is pointless, he says, to try to remove a tyrant, "thereby the causes which make the prince a tyrant can in no wise be removed, but, on the contrary, are so much the more established, as the prince is given more cause to fear, which happens when the multitude has made an example of its prince, and glories in the parricide as in a thing well done."

28. *Tractatus Theologico-Politicus,* p. 252. *Ethics,* Part Four, Appendix, XVII.

29. *Tractatus Theologico-Politicus,* p. 239.

30. *Leviathan,* p. 89.

31. *Ethics,* Part Four, Prop. LXIII.

32. *Tractatus Politicus,* pp. 314-315.

33. *Tractatus Theologico-Politicus,* pp. 206, 259, 276.

34. *Tractatus Theologico-Politicus,* p. 207. Spinoza repeats this conviction: "such is the best system of government and open to the fewest objections, since it is the one most in harmony with human nature. In a democracy (the most natural form of government, as we have shown in Chapter XVI) everyone submits to the control of authority over his actions, but not over his judgment and reason; that is, seeing that all cannot think alike, the voice of the majority has the force of law, subject to repeal if circumstances bring about a change of opinion. In proportion as the power of free judgment is withheld we depart from the natural condition of mankind, and consequently the government becomes more tyrannical." *Ibid.,* pp. 263-264.

35. Sir William Temple, in Spinoza's time, described it well: "The sovereign authority of the city of Amsterdam consists in the decrees or results of their Senate, which is composed of six and thirty men, by whom the justice is administered, according to ancient forms, in the names of officers and places of judicature. . . . These Senators are for their lives, and the Senate was anciently chosen by the voices of the richer burghers, or freemen of the city, who upon the death of a Senator met together, either in a church, a market, or some other place spacious enough to receive their numbers; and there made an election of the person to succeed, by the majority of voices. But about a hundred and thirty or forty years ago, when the towns of Holland began to increase in circuit, and in people, so as these frequent assemblies grew into danger of tumult, and disorder upon every occasion, by reason of their numbers and contention; this election of Senators came, by the resolution of the burghers in one of

their general assemblies, to be developed for ever upon the standing Senate at that time; so as ever since, when any one of their number dies, a new one is chosen by the rest of the Senate, without any intervention of the other burghers; which makes the government a sort of Oligarchy, and very different from a popular government, as it is generally esteemed by those, who, passing or living in the countries, content themselves with common observations or inquiries." Sir William Temple, "Observations upon the United Provinces of the Netherlands," *The Works of Sir William Temple* (London, 1770), I, 116-117.

36. *Tractatus Theologico-Politicus*, pp. 205, 247.

37. "The motto of a Radical politician should be Government by means of the middle for the working classes." John Stuart Mill, "A Letter to the Earl of Durham on Reform in Parliament," *The Westminster Review*, 1839, No. LXIII, p. 262. Mill advocated universal suffrage, but was apprehensive of the forces it would release. The workmen's leaders, he wrote, must realize "the mass of brutish ignorance which is behind them, . . . the barbarians whom Universal Suffrage would let in. . . . Can they wonder that the middle classes, who know all these things,—who do not know them, should tremble at the idea of entrusting political power to such hands?"

38. *Tractatus Theologico-Politicus*, pp. 257-259.

39. Cf. K. O. Meinsma, *Spinoza und sein Kreis*, trans. Lina Schneider (Berlin, 1909), pp. 351-368. For similarities in Spinoza's views cf. *Tractatus Theologico-Politicus*, p. 131; *Ethics*, Part Four, Prop. XXXV, Scholium.

40. "Adrian Coerbagh, jurist and doctor of medicine of Amsterdam, thirty-five years of age, asked whether he had not composed a small book entitled *Bloemhof*, says, 'Yes.' Asked whether he had written it alone, he says: 'Yes,' and that he had the help of no one. Asked whether anyone agrees with him in his views, he replies: 'No one but himself, according to his knowledge.' He asserts that he was not involved with either Berckel or anybody else on this matter. He affirms that he never spoke of this matter to either Spinoza or his brother. He says that he had social relations with Spinoza, and visited him several times, but had never discussed this matter and this problem with him. . . . Asked whether he understands the Hebrew language, he replies: 'Only with the help of a dictionary.' Asked what the Hebrew word 'schabinot' (schechinat) means, he answers that he doesn't know, but would have to look it up in Buxtorf's Lexicon. He asserts that he never discussed this doctrine with Spinoza. Questioned concerning the words in his dictionary about the middle of p. 664 which begins with, 'Who really was the father of Jesus,' as to whether he had come to an agreement with Spinoza with respect to this doctrine, he answers: 'No.' He states that he had visited Van Den Ende once or twice five or six years ago."

Thus reads the entry in the Book of Testimony of the Municipal Archives of Amsterdam for the twentieth of July, 1668. And the magistrates signed their names: Schulzen, Van Waveren, Hans Bontemantel, Capelle,

Hulst, Corver, Hudde. On the margin of the court report, a further statement is inscribed: "Ten years' imprisonment and afterwards to be banished for ten years from Holland, Zealand and Westvriesland." The name of the statesman Van Beuningen was added to the last entry: "The magistrates sentence the prisoner to a fine of 4000 florins, half for the Officer and half for the poor, besides another fine of 2000 florins for prison costs and expenses; the books which will be found are to be suppressed." Trans. from J. Freudenthal, *Die Lebensgeschichte Spinoza's* (Leipzig, 1899), pp. 119-121. Van Beuningen at this time was in opposition to De Witt's policies. Cf. Lefèvre-Pontalis, *op. cit.*, II, 77.

41. Cf. Rev. Dr. A. Cohen, *Everyman's Talmud* (New York, 1949), p. 42 ff.

42. ". . . Nor do I know what ought to be thought of a man who hangs himself," *Ethics*, Part Two, Prop. XLIX, Scholium.

43. *Tractatus Theologico-Politicus*, p. 263.

44. *Ibid.*, p. 200.

45. *Job* 23:3, 4, 5, 6.

46. *Tractatus Theologico-Politicus*, pp. 261-263.

47. *Schenck* v. *U. S.*, 249 U. S. 47 (1919), *Abrams et al.* v. *U. S.*, 250 U. S. 616 (1919).

48. *Tractatus Theologico-Politicus*, p. 260.

49. *Correspondence*, p. 255.

50. *Tractatus Theologico-Politicus*, pp. 259-260, 265-266.

51. Historical scholarship tends often to forget the complex emotional strains in a great thinker's work. The spirits of revolution and resignation, of defiance and acquiescence dwelled side by side in Spinoza's thought. The conflicts of his time were mirrored in his own emotional struggles; his greatness was his effort to bring some unifying clarity to otherwise discordant drives. It is an error to portray Spinoza as either a revolutionist or a conservative. He was neither exclusively, as he was both in different strands of his personality and thought. Pollock, for instance, depicted Spinoza as a model Tory: "I submit that any view which would make out Spinoza to be a progressive social reformer is clearly ruled out by Spinoza himself," whereas Professor Wolfson, writing in the midst of America's depression and the resurgence of radical ideas, affirmed: "Made of sterner stuff and living a few centuries later, Spinoza would have perhaps demanded the overthrow of the old order with its effete institutions so as to build upon its ruins a new society of a new generation raised on his new philosophy. He would then perhaps have become one of the first apostles of rebellion." In a different mood, however, Professor Wolfson later declares that Spinoza "would have become a substantial, respectable and public-spirited burgher and a pillar of society." Cf. Frederick Pollock, "Review of Robert A. Duff, Spinoza's Political and Ethical Philosophy," *Mind*, N. S., XII (1903), 402. Harry Austryn Wolfson, *The Philosophy of Spinoza* (Cambridge, Mass.), 1934, II, 330, 351.

52. *Tractatus Theologico-Politicus*, pp. 261-262.

53. *Correspondence,* p. 260.

54. Two such catalogues linked Spinoza to the protective interest of John de Witt. The first, falsely attributed to *Nil Volentibus Arduum,* was entitled: *Sleutel Ontsluytende de Boecke-kas van de Witte Bibliotheck.* [Key to the Bookcase of De Witt's Library]. Cf. p. 15. The second catalogue was called *Appendix Van't Catalogus van de Boecken van Mr. Ian de Wit, Bestaende in een partye Curieux en Secrete Manuscripten.* Cf. p. 7.

55. *Ethics,* Part Four, Prop. LXIX, Scholium.

56. *Tractatus Theologico-Politicus,* p. 224.

57. *Ibid.,* pp. 182, 225-226.

58. De Witt held that the United Provinces were a confederation of independent republics, each of which had surrendered only a limited portion of its sovereignty. The selection of their respective stadtholders, and the choice of a captain-general had, for instance, never been delegated to the States-General. Cf. James Geddes, *op. cit.,* p. 443.

59. *The Works of Flavius Josephus,* trans. William Whiston (Philadelphia, 1872), Vol. II, Against Apion, Bk. II, Par. 17, p. 512. Spinoza's indebtedness to Josephus with respect to his classification of governments seems to have escaped the attention of the various commentators.

60. Geddes, *op. cit.,* p. 120.

61. *Tractatus Theologico-Politicus,* pp. 226, 227, 237.

62. Cf. James Geddes, *op. cit.,* pp. 200-202. De Witt failed to alter the mercenary composition of the Dutch Army. As Sir William Temple observed, "the main of all their forces and body of their army has been composed, and continually supplied out of their neighbor-nations." *The Works of Sir William Temple,* I, 165.

63. Pieter de la Court, in John de Witt, *Political Maxims of the State of Holland,* trans. from the Dutch (London, 1743), pp. 314-315.

64. Sir William Temple, "An Essay upon the Original and Nature of Government," *The Works of Sir William Temple,* I, 56.

65. Pieter de la Court, *op. cit.,* pp. 391-393, 415-417. "Yet those that conceived themselves bound as slaves to the house of Orange, did not only oppose the concluding of the said foresaid desirable treaty, but also sent away those ambassadors with all manner of reproach and dishonors. . . ," p. 392.

66. Cf. E. M. Lloyd, *A Review of the History of Infantry* (London, 1908), p. 102. Ferdinand Foch, "Army," *Encyclopaedia Britannica* (London, 1941), II, 402.

67. *Tractatus Theologico-Politicus,* p. 228.

68. Pieter de la Court, *op. cit.,* pp. 313, 318.

69. Pieter de la Court, *op. cit.,* pp. 356, 415-417. Also, see the contrast between soldiers and merchants which Temple depicted. "The soldier thinks of a short life, and a merry. The trader reckons upon a long, and a painful. One intends to make his fortunes suddenly by his courage, by victory and spoil; the other slower, but surer, by craft, by treaty, and by industry." "Observations upon the United Provinces," *op. cit.,* p. 165.

70. Sir William Temple, "A Survey of the Constitutions and Interests of the Empire, Sweden, Denmark, Spain, Holland, France, and Flanders with Their Relation to England in the Year 1671," *The Works*, II, 220.

71. *Tractatus Theologico-Politicus*, pp. 228-230.

72. Temple, "Observations upon the United Provinces," pp. 166-167.

73. Grotius in 1631 described the equality before the law which obtained in the Netherlands: "The distinction between noble and un-noble (to say nothing of the conduct of public affairs, of which we shall speak when we treat of public law) was formerly very great: killing or other outrage committed upon a nobleman was more highly taxed than in the case of a commoner: in many matters a commoner might not testify against a noble or be his judge: besides, the nobles were free from contribution. All of these differences are now obsolete; the first because legal process has been made the same for all, not merely by custom, but also by charter; the last, because the contribution is obsolete, and the public taxes are imposed upon noble and un-noble alike." *The Jurisprudence of Holland*, trans. R. W. Lee (Oxford, 1926), p. 59. The middle classes in Holland had written equality into the law long before the French Revolution achieved it in France.

74. Temple, "Observations upon the United Provinces," pp. 153-156.

75. *Tractatus Theologico-Politicus*, p. 231.

76. Temple, "Observations upon the United Provinces," p. 182.

77. *Tractatus Theologico-Politicus*, pp. 232, 233.

78. Temple, "Observations upon the United Provinces," pp. 179-180.

79. *Tractatus Theologico-Politicus*, pp. 233-235. It is noteworthy that Spinoza's interpretation of Korah's rebellion follows the account of Josephus, not that of the Pentateuch. Cf. Flavius Josephus, *Antiquities of the Jews*, Bk. IV. Chap. II.

80. *Tractatus Theologico-Politicus*, p. 236. As Pieter warned: "all persons, who for their particular interest do willingly introduce such a monarchical government into our native country, will commit a crime which afterwards can never be remedied, but like Adam's original sin be derived from father to son to perpetuity. . . ." *Op. cit.*, p. 415.

81. *Tractatus Theologico-Politicus*, pp. 237-240.

82. As Pieter said: "It is evident, that monarchies of themselves are more subject to wars than republicks, whether by inheritances, or to secure their relations, or to assist them in the conquest of foreign countries. And moreover, these princes and captains-general are much more inclined to war than republicks; insomuch that they often are the aggressors . . . ," *op. cit.*, p. 352.

83. *Tractatus Theologico-Politicus*, pp. 241, 242.

84. *Ethics*, Part Four, Axiom.

5. Philosophic Liberal in a Reactionary Age

1. Petrus Johannes Blok, *History of the People of the Netherlands*, trans. Oscar A. Bierstadt (New York, 1907), IV, 380.
2. Quoted from Valckenier, Blok, *ibid.*, p. 381.
3. Blok, *ibid.*, p. 396.
4. *The Oldest Biography of Spinoza*, ed. A. Wolf (London, 1927), p. 65.
5. Foucher de Careil, *Réfutation inédite de Spinoza par Leibniz* (Paris, 1854), p. lxiv. *The Oldest Biography of Spinoza*, p. 180. J. Freudenthal, *Die Lebensgeschichte Spinoza's* (Leipzig, 1899), p. 201. Leibniz recognized Spinoza's close affiliation with the Republican party and its theorists. This is evident from a passage written in 1710 in which he disputes with Colerus and Bayle the alleged authorship by Spinoza of a certain book, *On the Right of Ecclesiastics*. The book was indeed written by Lodewijk Meyer, Spinoza's close personal friend, along lines similar to Spinoza's own thought, and was designed to confute the enemies of De Witt. Leibniz, however, believed that its author was Pieter de la Court, the economist spokesman of the Republican party and collaborator of John de Witt. Leibniz had discussed politics with Pieter as well as Spinoza during his visit to Holland, and he joined their names together. "Les lettres initiales, L. A. C., me font juger, que l'auteur de ce Livre a été Monsier de la Court, ou Van den Hoof, fameux par l'Intérêt de la Hollande, la Balance Politique et quantité d'autre Livres, qu'il a publiés (en partie s'appelant V. D. H.), contre la puissance du Gouverneur de Hollande, qu'on croyoit alors dangereux à la République, la mémoire de l'entreprise du Prince Guillaume II sur la ville d'Amsterdam étant encore toute fraiche. . . . Je vis Monsieur de la Court, aussi bien que Spinoza, à mon retour de France par L'Angleterre et par la Hollande, et j'appris d'eux quelques bonnes anecdotes sur les affaires de ce tems-là. . . . [The initial letters, L. A. C., made me think that the author of this book was Monsieur de la Court, or Van den Hoof, famous for the interest of Holland, the Political Balance and a number of other books, which he published (some of them under the name V. D. H.), against the power of the Ruler of Holland which was then believed to be dangerous to the Republic, since the memory of Prince William II's enterprise against the City of Amsterdam was very fresh . . . I saw Monsieur de la Court, as well as Spinoza, on my return from France through England and Holland, and I learned from them several good anecdotes on the affairs of that time.]" Freudenthal, *op. cit.*, p. 236. Also, *The Correspondence of Spinoza*, p. 50; Wolf, *The Oldest Biography*, p. 140. The Republican theorists knew and quoted each other's works. Pieter de la Court referred to the *De jure ecclesiasticorum* of Lodewijk Meyer to buttress his argument that liberty of religion was not to be expected under a monarchy. Cf. John de Witt, *The Political Maxims of the State of Holland* (London, 1743), p. 341. Pieter also made reference to the *Political Balance* of V. H., the same V. H.

whom Spinoza cited with approval. Cf. *The Political Maxims of the State of Holland*, p. 339, and *Tractatus Politicus*, p. 360. Sir Frederick Pollock identified V. H. as Pieter de la Court himself. Cf. *Spinoza: His Life and Philosophy* (2nd ed.; London, 1899), p. 315. But it seems more likely that V. H. was, rather, Pieter's brother, Jean de la Court, author in 1661 of the *Polityke Weeghschael*. Cf. A. J. Servaas Van Rooijen, *Inventaire des Livres Formant la Bibliothèque de Benedict Spinoza* (The Hague, 1888), p. 174.

6. Wolf, *The Oldest Biography*, pp. 65-66. The Dutch historian Japikse found no evidence among De Witt's papers that he had ever assisted Spinoza with financial means. It is probable therefore that Lucas overstated the extent of the purely personal relationship between Spinoza and De Witt. Cf. N. Japikse, *John de Witt* (Amsterdam, 1928), pp. 286-288.

7. Cf. Sebastian Kortholt's Preface to Christian Kortholt's book, *On Three Great Impostors* (Hamburg, 1700), in Freudenthal, *op. cit.*, pp. 26-28, trans. in Wolf, *The Oldest Biography*, pp. 166-167. I have, however, preferred the translation given in *Selections from Bayle's Dictionary*, ed. A. E. Beller and M. du P. Lee, Jr. (Princeton, 1952), p. 307.

8. Wolf, *The Oldest Biography*, p. 155.

9. *Correspondence*, p. 341.

10. Leibniz wrote in his memorial to the king of France: "The conquest of Egypt, that Holland of the East, is infinitely easier than that of the United Provinces. . . . War with Holland will ruin the new Indian companies as well as the colonies and commerce lately revived by France, and will increase the burdens of the people while diminishing their resources. The Dutch will retire into their maritime towns, stand there on the defensive in perfect safety, and assume the offensive on the sea with great chance of success. . . . The possession of Egypt opens the way to conquests worthy of Alexander. . . . Whoever has Egypt will have all the coasts and islands of the Indian Ocean. It is in Egypt that Holland will be conquered; it is there she will be despoiled of what alone renders her prosperous, the treasures of the East." Cf. A. T. Mahan, *The Influence of Sea Power upon History* (5th ed.; Boston, 1894), p. 142. Also, John Theodore Merz, *Leibniz* (Philadelphia), pp. 39-40.

11. Needless to say, Leibniz's warning that a war against the Dutch would ruin the French trading companies was confirmed by subsequent events. Colbert's efforts at reform were nullified by the war of 1672. Cf. Charles Woolsey Cole, *Colbert and a Century of French Mercantilism* (New York, 1939), II, 551. Leibniz had all the experience in this regard of a seventeenth-century Norman Angell; proofs by rationalists that war is a great illusion scarcely affect the irrational will to illusion.

12. John Colerus, *The Life of Benedict de Spinosa* (London, 1706), reprinted in Pollock, *op. cit.*, p. 398.

13. Jean Baptiste Stouppe, *La Religion des Hollandois* (Cologne, 1673), pp. 32, 49-64, 65-66, 108-109, trans. by the writer.

14. Colerus, *op. cit.*, p. 396.

15. Abraham de Wicquefort, who had been commissioned through De Witt's influence to write a contemporary history of the Dutch Republic with a Republican interpretation, engaged in secret diplomatic intrigues with English agents. For these activities, Wicquefort was finally convicted of treason. Blok, *op. cit.*, IV, 428, 548-549.

16. Pollock doubted that Spinoza's journey to the French headquarters was on behalf of "a secret political errand." He remarks that "if the thing had happened while the De Witts were alive and in power, the supposition would have been plausible enough." What Pollock fails to notice is the resurgence of the peace party in 1673 and the renewed political participation at that time of De Witt's friends. Cf. Pollock, *op. cit.*, p. 35. Wolf, on the other hand, attributed Spinoza's mission to his desire to help terminate the war between France and Holland. Cf. A. Wolf, *The Oldest Biography*, p. 179.

17. Blok, *op. cit.*, IV, 407-408.

18. Van Rooijen, *op. cit.*, p. 143.

19. "Letters of Sir William Temple," *The Works of Sir William Temple* (London, 1770), II, 182.

20. *Correspondence*, p. 267.

21. J. H. Clapham, "Charles Louis, Elector Palatine, 1617-1680," *Economica*, III (1940), 384-391.

22. John Ray, *Observations Topographical, Moral, and Physiological; Made in a Journey Through part of the Low-countries, Germany, Italy, and France* (London, 1673), p. 87.

23. It is noteworthy that John Wilkins, the precursor of philosophic linguistics, was for a time chaplain to Karl Ludwig, and, as Aubrey tells us, "was well preferred there by his highnesse." Cf. *John Aubrey's Brief Lives*, ed. Andrew Clark (Oxford, 1898), II, 300.

24. Colerus, *op. cit.*, pp. 393-394.

25. *Correspondence*, pp. 303, 334, 343, 441.

26. *Ibid.*, pp. 340, 344. Those who attested to the resurrection of Christ's body, said Spinoza, were simply deceived. *Ibid.*, pp. 358-359.

27. *Ibid.*, p. 344. Whereas the prophets had only an inadequate knowledge of God, Jesus, on the contrary, in Spinoza's opinion, had an adequate intuitive comprehension of God, which he formulated in a way "common to the whole human race." *Tractatus Theologico-Politicus*, pp. 64, 70.

28. Also cf. *Ethics*, Part Four, Prop. LXVII, Scholium: "the spirit of Christ, that is to say, by the Idea of God, which alone can make a man free. . . ."

29. *Tractatus Politicus*, pp. 315, 378. *Correspondence*, p. 269.

30. *Correspondence*, p. 366.

31. *Tractatus Politicus*, pp. 287-289.

32. *Ibid.*, pp. 345, 376. Pieter de la Court observed: "in governments where so few are rulers, as in the cities of Holland," cf. *Political Maxims of the State of Holland*, p. 305.

33. Sir William Temple, "An Essay upon the Original and Nature of Government," *Works* I, 54.

34. *Ibid.*, p. 57. Even before the collapse of the Dutch Republic in 1672, other liberal Englishmen had questioned the stability of any government which, in a crisis, would have to rest on the good-will of the multitude. The classical republicans were aristocratic in their philosophy and as uneasy with the problem of mass allegiance as was De Witt. When, for example, Algernon Sidney, a member of England's Council of State, left his country because he disapproved of Cromwell's assumption of power, to find at The Hague a close personal friend in John de Witt, he could not aver any respect for democracy. "As to popular government," Sidney wrote, "that is pure democracy where the people perform all that belongs to government; I know of no such thing, and if it be in the world, have nothing to say for it." Alex. Charles Ewald, *The Life and Times of the Hon. Algernon Sydney*, 1622-1683 (London, 1873), p. 256.

35. "Letters of Sir William Temple," *Works*, I, 361, 397. The quarrels of the English and Dutch East India Companies were a major problem in the negotiations between De Witt and Temple. The English, as newcomers into the Asian trade, demanded an open-door policy, which the Dutch, as masters of the best and most trading stations, resisted. Cf. Homer E. Woodbridge, *Sir William Temple* (New York, 1940), pp. 98-100.

36. Sir William Temple, *Works*, I, 514.

37. Sir William Temple, "A Survey of the Constitutions and Interests," *Works*, II, 221, 224, 225.

38. Sir William Temple, "Memoirs from 1672 and 1679," *Works*, II, 255, 256.

39. *Tractatus Politicus*, pp. 306-307.

40. Temple, *ibid.*, pp. 257-258. "In the mean time, the State and the government of Holland took a new form, and with it a new heart. Monsieur De Witt and his brother had been massacred by the sudden fury of the people at the Hague, and by the fate of ministers that govern by a party or faction, who are usually sacrificed to the first great misfortunes abroad that fall in to aggravate or inflame the general discontents at home. . . . They were both presently laid dead upon the place, then dragged about the town by the fury of the people, and torn in pieces. Thus ended one of the greatest lives of any subject in our age, about the 47th year of his own; after having served, or rather administered, that State, as Pensioner of Holland, for about eighteen years with great honour to his country and himself." Also cf. "Of Popular Discontents," *op. cit.*, III, 36. Temple paid a further tribute to De Witt: "a person that deserved another fate, and a better return from his country, after eighteen years spent in their ministry, without any care of his entertainments or ease, and little of his fortune. A man of unwearied industry, inflexible constancy, sound, clear, and deep understanding, and untainted integrity; so that, whenever he was blinded, it was by the passion he had for that which he esteemed the good and interest of his State. This

testimony is justly due to him from all that practised him; and is the more willingly paid, since there can be as little interest to flatter, as honour to reproach the dead." "Observations upon the United Provinces," *op. cit.*, I, 168.

41. *Ibid.*, p. 168.

42. *Tractatus Politicus*, pp. 288-289.

43. C. B. MacPherson, "Sir William Temple, Political Scientist?" *The Canadian Journal of Economics and Political Science*, IX (1943), 44-45.

44. Sir William Temple, "Of Popular Discontents," *op. cit.*, pp. 39, 41, 46.

45. Z. S. Fink, "Venice and English Political Thought in the Seventeenth Century," *Modern Philology*, XXXVIII (1940), 160, 164.

46. *Tractatus Politicus*, pp. 351, 352, 357, 359.

47. Blok, *op. cit.*, IV, 405. Blok, *The Life of Admiral De Ruyter*, trans. G. J. Renier (London, 1933), p. 321.

48. *Tractatus Politicus*, pp. 347, 348.

49. Cf. James Geddes, *History of the Administration of John de Witt* (New York, 1880), p. 22.

50. *Tractatus Politicus*, p. 348, 350, 351.

51. Sir William Temple, "Observations upon the United Provinces," *op. cit.*, I, 206. Also cf. M. Antonin Lefèvre-Pontalis, *John de Witt*, trans. S. S. E. and A. Stephenson (Boston, 1885), I, 27.

52. *Tractatus Politicus*, pp. 349, 360.

53. Lefèvre-Pontalis, *op. cit.*, I, 337. P. Blok, *The Life of Admiral De Ruyter, op. cit.*, p. 11.

54. *Tractatus Politicus*, p. 349.

55. *Ibid.*, p. 353.

56. William Sewel, the early historian of Quakerism, also attributed De Witt's fall to his attempt by the Perpetual Edict to exclude William of Orange from the Stadtholdership: "But how strong soever this Edict was sworn to, yet Heaven brought it to nought, and broke the Ties of it by the Refuse of the Nation: for Women, and many others of the Mob, forced the Magistrates, when the French were come into the Province of Utrecht, and all seem'd to run into Confusion, to break their Oaths, and to restore that young and magnanimous Prince to the Honour and Dignity of his renowned Ancestors. The miserable fate of the two Brethren, John and Cornelius de Wit, who had been chief Instruments in making the said Perpetual Edict, and were killed and butchered in a most abominable Manner by the Inhabitants of the Hague, was not without good Reason disapproved by grave and serious People. 'Tis true, it was a great Mistake that they acted so, that they seemed to set Limits to the Almighty; tho' I do not believe their Intent was such, but rather what they did in making void the Stadtholdership they judged conducive to the Benefit of their Country." William Sewel, *The History of the Rise, Increase and Progress of the Christian People called Quakers* (London, 1722), p. 511.

57. *Tractatus Politicus*, pp. 354-358.

58. For the significance of Venice as a model for political theory in the seventeenth century, cf. especially Zera S. Fink, *The Classical Republicans:*

An Essay in the Recovery of a Pattern of Thought in Seventeenth Century England (Evanston, Ill., 1945), p. 28 ff. The Venetian Constitution had been celebrated by the famous Jewish statesman Abravanel, who found a welcome under Venice's freedom after the Jews were driven from Spain. Cf. B. Netanyahu, *Don Isaac Abravanel* (Philadelphia, 1953), pp. 169-170.

59. For various points concerning the Venetian constitution cf. William Roscoe Thayer, *A Short History of Venice*, pp. 97-98, 104-105, 116, 213, 216-217, 306-307. Horatio F. Brown, *Studies in the History of Venice* (New York, 1907), p. 297 ff. Paolo Sarpi early in the seventeenth century had analyzed the Venetian constitution as the expression of mercantile interests. "The Spaniards," he wrote, "who have so little kindness for the Venetian Government have not a more odious name than to call it, A Republick of Merchants." Cf. Paolo Sarpi, *Advice Given to the Republick of Venice. How they ought to Govern themselves both at Home and abroad, to have perpetual Dominion*, trans. Dr. Aglionby (London, 1693), p. 25. Sarpi, like Spinoza, warned that democratic tendencies were deleterious to a merchants' aristocratic republic. "But all Assemblies of numerous Bodies are to be avoided as the Plague, because nothing can sooner overturn the Commonwealth, than the Facility the People may meet with in getting together to confer or debate about their Grievances. . . ." *Ibid.*, p. 13. Sarpi's philosophy of government was a forerunner of Spinoza's realism; the heroic Italian held "that all is just which is any ways necessary for the maintaining of the Government," and he advised always feeding the people cheaply, "For the nature of the rabble is so malicious. . . ." *Ibid.*, pp. 3, 22. The worldly-wise and struggle-weary political scientists of the seventeenth century could not muster much enthusiasm for the common man. Sarpi, furthermore, felt that a common bond of economic interest and hostility to Spain joined the Venetian and Dutch Republics. "It is greatly for the interest of the Republick, to cultivate a strict Friendship with the seven united Provinces of the Netherlands. . . ." He urged more trade with the Dutch, and felt that the wills of both commonwealths would easily be united because "they are eager Pursuers of Merchandize." Cf. *The Maxims of the Government of Venice* (London, 1707), pp. 125-126.

60. *Tractatus Politicus*, pp. 370-372.

61. Sir William Temple, "Observations upon the United Provinces," *op. cit.*, I, 121-122.

62. *Tractatus Politicus*, p. 371.

63. Cf. Blok, *op. cit.*, IV, 419.

64. *Tractatus Politicus*, pp. 376-377.

65. Sir William Temple, *ibid.*, p. 115.

66. *Tractatus Politicus*, pp. 379-380.

67. "And therefore all republics should have some institution similar to the dictatorship. The republic of Venice, which is pre-eminent amongst modern ones, had reserved to a small number of citizens the power of deciding all urgent matters without referring their decisions to a larger council. And when a republic lacks some such system, a strict observance of the

established laws will expose her to ruin. . . ." Niccolo Machiavelli, *The Prince and the Discourses on the First Ten Books of Titus Livius*, trans. Christian E. Detmold (New York, 1940), p. 203.

68. *Tractatus Politicus*, pp. 381-382. The experience of Venice once more seemed to confirm Spinoza's theory that a stable aristocratic republic must be founded on the pursuit of wealth as its ideal end. Machiavelli had affirmed that "a republic cannot be established where there are gentlemen," that is, persons not engaged in the accumulation of capital. The government of Venice was composed of gentlemen, but as Machiavelli answered, "the gentlemen of Venice are so more in name than in fact; for they have no great revenues from estates, their riches being founded upon commerce and movable property, and moreover none of them have castles or jurisdiction over subjects, but the name of gentlemen is only a title of dignity and respect, and is in no way based upon the things that gentlemen enjoy in other countries." Cf. Machiavelli, *Discourses, op. cit.*, pp. 256-257.

69. *Tractatus Politicus*, p. 383.

70. Blok, *op. cit.*, IV, 435, 437-438, 448.

71. *Tractatus Politicus*, p. 356.

72. Sir William Temple, "Observations upon the United Provinces," *op. cit.*, pp. 118, 136. On De Witt's temperance, cf. Temple, "Of the Cure of the Gout," *op. cit.*, III, 244.

73. Walter Bagehot, *The English Constitution* (London, 1928), p. 79.

74. Blok, *op. cit.*, IV, 221, 353, 445.

75. *Tractatus Politicus*, pp. 352, 364.

76. Sir William Temple, "Observations upon the United Provinces," *op. cit.*, p. 119.

77. James Geddes, *History of the Administration of John de Witt* (New York, 1880), pp. 130-131.

78. *Tractatus Politicus*, pp. 367-368.

79. *Tractatus Theologico-Politicus*, pp. 186, 188. Sir William Temple at the same time was proposing similar distinctions with respect to religion and society. On matters of dogma concerning "our future happiness," said Temple, controversies are futile. "For belief is no more in a man's power, than his stature or his feature. . . ." On the other hand, "The other great end of religion, which is our happiness here, has been generally agreed on by all mankind, as appears in the records of all their laws, as well as all their religions. . . . For all agree in teaching and commanding, in planting and improving, not only those moral virtues which conduce to the felicity and tranquillity of every man's private life, but also those manners and disposi- tions that tend to the peace, order, and safety of all civil societies and govern- ments among men." *Religious men*, says Temple, are not those who empha- size points of dogma, concerning which men have never agreed, but are, rather, those who follow virtue and morality, upon which men usually agree. This conception coincides with Spinoza's universal religion. Cf. Temple, "Observations upon the United Provinces," *op. cit.*, pp. 172-174.

80. *Tractatus Politicus,* p. 368.

81. Adam Smith, *An Inquiry into the Nature and Causes of the Wealth of Nations* (New York, 1937), p. 745.

82. *Tractatus Theologico-Politicus,* p. 275.

83. A. Aulard, *Christianity and the French Revolution,* trans. Lady Frazer (London, 1927), pp. 125, 126, 154.

84. "The greatest single influence exerted upon the writers of the period is that of Spinoza. So great is his influence, in fact, that one is tempted to see in the whole movement a gigantic manifestation of spinozism triumphant over other forms of thought. It evidenced itself in various ways. The translation of the Tractatus, though incomplete, brought the biblical critic Spinoza to the attention of the treatise writers. . . ." ". . . The negative Spinoza of the Tractatus became far more influential than the positive Spinoza of the Ethics. . . ." Ira Wade, *The Clandestine Organization and Diffusion of Philosophic Ideas in France* (Princeton, 1938), pp. 269-270. Also pp. 3-4, 111.

85. *Tractatus Politicus,* pp. 365, 366.

86. *Ibid.,* p. 369.

87. J. P. N. Land, "Philosophy in the Dutch Universities," *Mind,* III (1878), 90.

88. *Short Treatise,* pp. 190-191.

89. Spinoza subsequently criticized the Cartesian doctrine of "Professor Heereboordius of Leyden" in his "Cogitata Metaphysica," Appendix to *The Principles of Descartes' Philosophy,* trans. H. H. Britan (La Salle, 1943), p. 175.

90. Heidanus had in previous years sought the friendship of John de Witt. Cf. Lefèvre-Pontalis, *op. cit.,* I, 108.

91. *Tractatus Politicus,* p. 344. Hobbes denied that a "mixed monarchy" (a limited monarchy, as we would say) could possibly exist. Cf. Thomas Hobbes, *De Cive,* ed. Sterling P. Lamprecht (New York, 1949), pp. 89-90.

92. Thomas Hobbes, *Leviathan* (London, 1914), pp. 87, 89.

93. *Tractatus Politicus,* pp. 314-315, 317.

94. The great admiration in the seventeenth century for the Venetian Constitution was founded on the mistaken idea that it had lasted unchanged for twelve centuries. Political philosophers were led to speculate as to what sort of constitution would enable a dominion to endure without impairment, without decay, till the end of time. It was, in other words, a quest for an unchanging, incorruptible political substance which inspired a species of political metaphysics. Cf. Z. S. Fink, "The Political Implications of Paradise Regained," *The Journal of English and Germanic Philology,* XL (1941), 483, 486.

95. *Leviathan,* pp. 89-90. Leibniz later elaborated with detail on Spinoza's observation that pure absolute monarchy is not to be found. Even in Turkey, said Leibniz, the Sultan had been called to defend himself before a sacred court, and when he refused to do so, his subjects were released from their allegiance. The Estates in France were, in his opinion, another example of

the constitutional restraints on monarchy. Cf. A. J. Carlyle, *Political Liberty: A History of the Conception in the Middle Ages and Modern Times* (Oxford, 1941), pp. 108-109.

96. *Tractatus Politicus*, pp. 319-338.

97. The central importance of the distribution of land in determining the mode of government was becoming a recognized principle among political scientists in the seventeenth century. Apart from Harrington, there was Temple who argued with Charles II that England could never accommodate itself to an absolute government; in France, "the peasants having no land, were as insignificant as the women and children are here: that, on the contrary, the great bulk of land in England lies in the hands of the yeomanry or lower gentry, and their hearts are high by ease and plenty, as those of the French peasantry are wholly dispirited by labour and want. . . ." Temple, "Memoirs from 1672 to 1679," *op. cit.*, II, 263.

98. *Tractatus Politicus*, p. 331. A great controversy as to whether the taking of interest was justified had raged in the Netherlands during the middle of the seventeenth century. Shortly before 1640, there was a huge increase in the number of writings which vehemently defended interest. The publications of Salmasius were especially influential in persuading people that interest was consonant with natural law, and would be helpful to agriculture and commerce. By 1658, the advocates of interest had largely won their case. Cf. Eugen von Bohm-Bawerk, *Capital and Interest*, trans. William Smart (London, 1890), p. 35. Spinoza takes the standpoint of the commercial and trading classes and fully accepts the contribution of interest to the economic life.

99. *Tractatus Politicus*, pp. 326, 331, 338.

100. Cf. James Geddes, *A History of the Administration of John de Witt* (New York, 1880), pp. 78-79, 83-84, 112-114. Blok, *op. cit.*, IV, 436-437.

101. *Tractatus Politicus*, p. 321.

102. *Ibid.*, p. 336.

103. Barnouw, *Vondel*, p. 74.

104. *Tractatus Politicus*, p. 326.

105. Pieter de la Court, *Political Maxims of the State of Holland*, p. 49. Violet Barbour, *Capitalism in Amsterdam in the Seventeenth Century* (Baltimore, 1950), pp. 16-17. H. I. Bloom, *The Economic Activities of the Jews of Amsterdam* (Williamsport, 1937), pp. 22-23.

106. *Tractatus Politicus*, p. 325.

107. *Ibid.*, p. 341.

108. *Leviathan*, pp. 90, 98, 102.

109. *Tractatus Politicus*, pp. 329-330, 334, 339, 342, 343.

110. Cf. Julia Fitzmaurice-Kelly, *Antonio Perez* (Oxford, 1922), pp. 41-49, 58, 92. Also cf. Roger Bigelow Merriman, *The Rise of the Spanish Empire* (New York, 1934), IV, 578 ff. For a less sympathetic portrayal of Perez, cf. Gregorio Marañon, *Antonio Perez, "Spanish Traitor,"* trans. Charles David Ley (London, 1954). Also cf. James Anthony Froude, "Antonio Perez: An

Unsolved Historical Riddle," *The Spanish Story of the Armada* (New York, 1905), pp. 139, 145.

111. Van Rooijen, *op. cit.*, p. 117. Also, *Las Obras y Relaciones de Antonio Perez* (Geneva, 1676). There is an error in the Spinoza literature concerning the identity of Antonio Perez. R. H. M. Elwes in his *Works of Spinoza,* I, 334, mistakenly identified him as a Belgian professor of law, and this inaccuracy was repeated by A. G. A. Balz in his edition of Spinoza's *Writings on Political Philosophy* (New York, 1937), p. 135.

112. *Tractatus Politicus,* pp. 341, 386. *Ethics,* Book IV, Prop. LIV, Scholium.

113. Cf. Baron de Montesquieu, *The Spirit of Laws,* trans. Thomas Nugent (London, 1878), I, 21, 43.

6. A Free Man's Philosophy

1. John Colerus, *The Life of Benedict de Spinosa,* trans. from the French (London, 1706), reprinted in Sir Frederick Pollock, *Spinoza: His Life and Philosophy* (2nd ed.; London, 1899), pp. 403-404, 416.

2. As Nietzsche remarked acutely but with his characteristic overstatement: "the hocus-pocus in mathematical form, by means of which Spinoza has, as it were, clad his philosophy in mail and mask— . . . in order thereby to strike terror at once into the heart of the assailant who should dare to cast a glance on that invincible maiden, that Pallas Athene:—how much of personal timidity and vulnerability does this masquerade of a sickly recluse betray!" *Beyond Good and Evil,* trans. Helen Zimmern (London, 1909), p. 10.

3. *Tractatus Theologico-Politicus,* p. 276.

4. *Ethics,* Part Four, Prop. LXVI, Scholium. Spinoza's definition is in accord with that of Hobbes: "A Free-Man, is he, that in those things, which by his strength and wit he is able to do, is not hindred to doe what he has a will to." *Leviathan* (London, 1914), p. 110.

5. *Ethics,* Part Four, Prop. XLV, Scholium.

6. M. Antonin Lefèvre-Pontalis, *John de Witt,* trans. S. S. E. and A. Stephenson (Boston, 1885), I, 88-89.

7. Petrus Johannes Blok, *History of the People of the Netherlands,* trans. Ruth Putnam (New York, 1900), III, 488. Also cf. A. J. Barnouw, *Vondel* (New York, 1925), pp. 20-21.

8. The Quakers and other heretical sects were blamed by the Calvinist consistories for the "stage-players" at the annual fairs. Cf. William I. Hull, *The Rise of Quakerism in Amsterdam* (Swarthmore, 1938), pp. 153-154.

9. Lodewijk Meyer was a remarkable man who undertook the task of creating a new, live theater in the Netherlands. Meyer, a disciple of Spinoza, believed in a universal Christianity founded on reason; this view brought him many enemies. He felt that the Biblical themes of traditional Dutch drama provided plays suitable for pastors, but the theater's vocation, in Meyer's out-

look, was something higher. Like De Witt, he admired Corneille, whose *Le Menteur* he translated in 1658. He became the chief innovator of classicism in the Dutch theater; the aim of drama, according to Meyer, was the analysis of passions and ideas. In 1665 he became regent of the new theater of Amsterdam, but his policies brought his replacement in 1668. Thereupon, in 1669, Meyer became the leading founder of the famous society *Nil Volentibus Arduum*, the "niets gewichtigs betrachtende" [they who like nothing serious]. The N.V.A. was the combative spokesman for the new classicism. It refused to pander to vulgar tastes or strong language, and it preferred themes such as that of *Cinna*, in which patriotism triumphs over sexual love. Very much as Bernard Shaw tried to create a new Fabian drama to supersede Victorian romanticism, Lodewijk Meyer might be characterized as the apostle of a Liberal Republican theater in Holland. The war of 1672 closed the Dutch theater for five years, but in 1677, Meyer returned to office and high influence as regent of the Amsterdam theater. Cf. J. Bauwens, *La Tragédie Française et le Théâtre Hollandais au Dix-Septième Siècle* (Amsterdam, 1921), pp. 40, 111-116, 243-250.

10. "Monsieur Bayle tells us, That he happen'd one day to be assaulted by a Jew, as he was coming out of the Playhouse, who wounded him in the Face with a Knife, and that Spinosa knew that the Jew design'd to kill him, tho his wound was not dangerous." Colerus, *op. cit.*, p. 390.

11. Lefèvre-Pontalis, *op. cit.*, II, 461.

12. *Correspondence*, p. 255.

13. Elizabeth Sanderson Haldane, *Descartes: His Life and Times* (London, 1905), p. 246.

14. Lefèvre-Pontalis, *op. cit.*, I, 88. James Geddes, *History of the Administration of John de Witt* (New York, 1880), pp. 37, 302.

15. J. A. Dijkshoorn, *L'Influence Française dans les Moeurs et les Salons des Provinces Unies* (Paris, 1925), pp. 203, 205, 210-212, 219-225. Gustave Cohen, "Le Séjour de Saint-Evrémond en Hollande (1665-1670)," *Revue de Littérature Comparée*, XI (1926), 56-57, 73-75.

16. Cf. Johan Huizinga, *The Waning of the Middle Ages* (London, 1927), p. 124.

17. Adam Smith, *The Wealth of Nations* (New York, 1937), p. 748.

18. Jeremy Bentham, *Principles of Morals and Legislation in Works* (Edinburgh, 1843), I, 6.

19. Barneveld, who hated the Calvinist creed, once argued with the Stadtholder Maurice: "You hold then," said Barneveld, "that the Almighty has created one child for damnation, and another for salvation, and you wish this doctrine to be publicly preached." After his initial surprise that this cruel doctrine was part of the reformed faith, the soldier said: "And suppose our ministers do preach this doctrine, is there anything strange in it, any reason why they should not do so?" John Lothrop Motley, *The Life and Death of John of Barneveld* (New York, 1874), II, 120-121.

20. *Ethics*, Part Four, Prop. LXVII, XLV, LII, XVIII.

21. *Tractatus Politicus*, p. 293.

22. *Ethics*, Part Four, Prop. LXIII, LIV, L, XL, LXIII.

23. The hold which the doctrine of predestination acquired among the lower classes was the measure of their hatred for the Spanish oppressor and their own rich. It was taken for granted that the lowly would be God's elect, that the oppressors would be damned. "Against the oligarchy of commercial and juridical corporations there stood the most terrible aristocracy of all, the aristocracy of God's elect, predestined from all time and all eternity to take precedence of and to look down upon their inferior and lost fellow creatures." Cf. Motley, *op. cit.*, I, 331.

24. The decrees of the Synod of Dordrecht of 1618 still bind the Dutch Reformed Church in South Africa. As far as the Negro is concerned, the stern Calvinists remember that the descendants of Ham were cursed in the Scriptures: "Cursed be Canaan. A servant of servants shall he be. . . ." Cf. Stuart Cloete, *Against These Three* (New York, 1947), p. 35.

25. *Ethics*, Part Four, Prop. XXXVI.

26. *Tractatus Theologico-Politicus*, pp. 199, 262.

27. *Ethics*, Part Four, Appendix, Par. XXVIII, XXIX.

28. The linkage in Holland between the Calvinist ethics and capitalistic values has continued down to our own time. A Dutch novelist tells in his autobiography: "A business failure in the minds of most respectable Dutchmen is tantamount to the most unpardonable sin. . . . It is unmentionable. One can't even pray to one's Calvinist God to be forgiven for having failed in one's business." The sense of guilt is part of the Calvinist child's inalienable heritage: "I was named after her father, a most austere and inflexible Calvinist, who from my birth saw nothing but evil in me." David Cornel De Jong, *With a Dutch Accent* (New York, 1944), pp. 4, 5.

29. R. H. Tawney, *Religion and the Rise of Capitalism* (Middlesex, England, 1938), p. 112.

30. Voetius at Utrecht was against allowing bankers to take communion; his opinion conformed to the decision of the early provincial synod at Dordrecht in 1574 that a banker could not partake of Holy Supper. In 1656, the theological faculty at Utrecht still advised a church that a banker's widow could not join their congregation unless she gave prior restitution of interest to the poor. The tide of opinion, however, became strong for social approval of capitalist banking. The Estates of Holland and West Friesland in 1658 resolved that the question of bank loans was outside the jurisdiction of churches or synods. Two years later, the Walloon Reformed Churches in the Netherlands decided that any person employed in a bank would be admitted to communion provided the magistrates enforced a rate of interest which did not exceed the bounds which the pastors thought proper. Cf. Albert Hyma, "Calvinism and Capitalism in the Netherlands, 1555-1700," *The Journal of Modern History*, X (1938), 327, 330, 331, 334, 335.

31. Ernst Beins, *Die Wirtschaftsethik der Calvinistischen Kirche der Niederlande 1565-1650* ('s Gravenhage, 1931), p. 16. The career of Willem

Usselinx, devout Calvinist and upbuilder of capitalist enterprise in the New World, was a model example of the union between Calvinist doctrine and economic motive. Cf. J. F. Jameson, "Willem Usselinx, Founder of the Dutch and Swedish West India Companies," *Papers of the American Historical Association*, Vol. II, No. 3, New York, 1887. The Charter of the Dutch West India Company in 1640 provided that "no other religion shall be publicly admitted in New Netherland, except the Reformed." The Company contributed toward the salaries of ministers, who were nominated on the recommendation of the classis of Amsterdam.

32. *The Economic Writings of Sir William Petty*, ed. Charles Henry Hull (Cambridge, England, 1899), I, 262.

33. Cf. the contrary opinion in H. M. Robertson, *Aspects of the Rise of Economic Individualism* (Cambridge, England, 1935), p. 172.

34. *Ethics*, Part Four, Appendix, Pars. XXX, XXXI.

35. Cf. Clara Marburg, *Sir William Temple, A Seventeenth Century "Libertin"* (New Haven, 1932), pp. 22-23. Joseph Bougerel, *Vie de Pierre Gassendi* (Paris, 1737), pp. 291-292, 299, 324. Pierre Gassendi, *Three Discourses of Happiness, Virtue, and Liberty*, collected by François Bernier (London, 1699), p. 13.

36. *Works of Sir William Temple* (New Edition, London, 1814), III, 202.

37. Stouppe in his *Religion des Hollandais* (1673) wrote: "As for the Libertins, it seems that as many as there are of them, they each have their private opinion. Most of them believe that there is one spirit of God, which is in all living things, which is diffused throughout everything, which is and which lives in all creatures; that the substance and immortality of our soul is nothing else than this spirit of God; that God Himself is nothing other than this spirit; that souls die with their bodies; that sin is nothing, that it's only a simple opinion which vanishes at once when we don't take it seriously; that Paradise is merely an illusion, an agreeable chimera, which the theologians have invented in order to persuade men to embrace what is called virtue. . . ." J. B. Stouppe, *op. cit.*, pp. 62-63 (translated by the writer). Also cf. *Correspondence*, p. 239.

38. "The vogue of Epicurus would seem, therefore, both by its dates, and by its personnel to constitute an aspect of the temporary aristocratic triumph over the bourgeois movement which had culminated politically in the Commonwealth." Cf. Thomas Franklin Mayo, *Epicurus in England (1650-1725)* (Dallas, Texas), 1934, p. 54.

39. Marburg, *op. cit.*, pp. 16-18.

40. Cf. Gustave Cohen, "Le Séjour de Saint-Evrémond en Hollande," *Revue de Littérature Comparée*, V (1925), 444-445.

41. *Ethics*, Part Four, Appendix, Par. XX.

42. Marburg, *op. cit.*, p. 22.

43. Cf. Harcourt Brown, "The Utilitarian Motive in the Age of Descartes," *Annals of Science*, I (1936), 192.

44. Saint-Evremond, *Oeuvres Mêlées*, ed. C. Giraud (Paris, 1865), I, 17-18.

45. *Ethics*, Part IV, Prop. XLII, Prop. XLIII, Prop. XLIV, Appendix, Par. IX.

46. Bishop Burnet complained that Sir William Temple "seemed to think, that things were as they are from all eternity; at least, he thought religion was fit only for the mob. He was a great admirer of the sect of Confucius in China, who were atheists themselves, but left religion to the rabble. He was a corrupter of all that came near him: and he delivered himself up wholly to study, ease, and pleasure." *Works of Sir William Temple* (London, 1814), I, xxii.

47. *Short Treatise*, p. 133.

48. *Ethics*, Part Four, Prop. LXVI, Appendix, Par. II.

49. The close similarity between Spinoza's therapy for "human bondage" and Freud's psychoanalysis has been noticed by several psychoanalysts and psychiatrists. Cf. Walter Bernard, "Freud and Spinoza," *Psychiatry*, IX (1946), 99-109. M. Hamblin Smith, "Spinoza's Anticipation of Recent Psychological Developments," *The British Journal of Medical Psychology*, 1925, Vol. V. The leading expositor of Freud in America, Dr. A. A. Brill, wrote: "I was so readily attracted to Freud because his thoughts, or, if I may say so, his system reminded me of Spinoza to whom I became attached by a very strong bond long before I heard of Freud. After reading *Moses and Monotheism*, I was again reminded of Spinoza and impressed by the fact that throughout all his works Freud consistently and clearly follows almost the same mode of thought as Spinoza." Cf. A. A. Brill, "Reminiscences of Freud," *Psychoanalytic Quarterly*, IX (1940), 182.

50. *Ethics*, Part Five, Prop. III, Part Four, Prop. XXXVII, LVI, XXII, Corol., XVIII, XX, XXV, XXIII.

51. *Ibid.*, Part Five, Prop. IV, X.

52. *Ibid.*, Part Four, Prop. LVII, Scholium, Book III, the Affects, Definition XXIX, Explanation, Prop. XVIII.

53. Cf. Sigmund Freud, *Collected Papers*, ed. James Strachey (London, 1950), V, 329-336.

54. *Ethics*, Part Four, Prop. XX, Part Three, Prop. LIX.

55. The conception of the unconscious was worked out by Spinoza in order to distinguish between the free man and the slave. The occasion of its discovery was in the needs of ethical therapy. Leibniz took over the hypothesis of unconscious mental states; it enabled him especially to reply to Locke's empiricism. Locke had argued on psychological grounds that there were no innate ideas common to all men. If this were true, then we could have no innate idea of God, and the classical demonstration of God's existence from our innate idea of Him would be undermined. With God's existence threatened, the innate principles of ethics were likewise endangered. Leibniz thereupon invoked the notion of the unconscious, and held that though the innate truths were not consciously attended to or expressed in language, they were indeed present in the unconscious of all men: "it is not necessary that we have ever actually thought of them; they are only natural habitudes."

He was then led to investigate the role of the unconscious in dreams and abnormal phenomena. "It may be that such a man has remaining effects of former impressions without remembering them. I believe that dreams often thus revive in us former thoughts." Cf. Gottfried Wilhelm Leibnitz, *New Essays on the Understanding*, trans. Alfred Gideon Langley (New York, 1896), pp. 105-106. Leibniz made a remarkable catalogue of instances of the influence of unconscious mental compulsions where, "the reasons are unknown to us." *New Essays*, pp. 282-283. The conception of the unconscious thus entered modern thought in these diverse ways during the seventeenth century.

56. *Ethics*, Part Four, Prop. IX, XXXIX.

57. *Short Treatise*, p. 33.

58. *Tractatus Theologico-Politicus*, p. 7.

59. *Ethics*, Part Four, Appendix, Par. XIII. Also, Prop. LXIII.

60. *Ibid.*, Part Three, Prop. XXXIX, XVII, XXIII, XLI, Corol.

61. *Ibid.*, Part Four, Prop. XLVI, XXVIII.

62. *Ibid.*, Part One, Prop. XV, Part Five, Prop. XX, XVII, XIX, XVIII.

63. *Ibid.*, Part Four, Axiom, Prop. LVII, LXXIII, Appendix, Par. XXXII, Prop. XVIII.

64. René Descartes, *The Passions of the Soul*, Article LXXIX, in *The Philosophical Works of Descartes*, trans. Elizabeth S. Haldane and G. R. T. Ross (Cambridge, 1911), I, 366.

65. *Ethics*, Part Four, Prop. LXXI, Appendix, Par. XIX, Prop. XLIV.

66. *Ibid.*, Part Three, the Affects, Definition XLVIII, Explanation, Part Five, Prop. X, Part Three, Prop. XXXV.

67. *Ibid.*, Part Four, Prop. XXXIV, Part Three, Prop. XXXV, Prop. LVI, Part Four, Appendix, Par. XX.

68. M. Hamblin Smith remarks: "But we must not suppose that Spinoza had overcome his own sex repressions. There are many indications that he had not done so, in spite of his insistence on the principle that we are to regard nothing in nature with repugnance." Cf. *The British Journal of Medical Psychology, op. cit.*, V (1925), 266.

69. *Ethics*, Part Four, Appendix, Par. XIX, Part Three, the Affects, Definition VI, Explanation.

70. Sigmund Freud, *New Introductory Lectures on Psychoanalysis* (New York, 1933), p. 141.

71. Colerus, *op. cit.*, pp. 396, 417. "The Relations" of Spinoza were also interested in the fate of his desk "because they fancied that it was full of Money." Cf. pp. 388, 404.

72. Johannes Arend Dijkshoorn, *L'Influence Française dans les Moeurs et les Salons des Provinces-Unies* (Paris, 1925), p. 186. Cf. Una Birch, *Anna van Schurman* (New York, 1909), pp. 9, 63. Descartes regretted Anna's theological bent. One day he found her reading the Hebrew Bible, and asked her why she wasted her time. Later Anna joined the sect of Labadie, inspired it anew, and expounded its tenets of mysticism and communism in her

spiritual autobiography *Eukleria,* the first part of which was published in 1673.

73. *Correspondence,* p. 350 ff.

74. Colerus, *op. cit.,* p. 388.

75. "Love that is transitory passeth away with that whereon it depends but that which is not dependent upon aught that is transitory never ceases. An illustration of the former is the love of Amnon and Tamar." *Pirke Aboth* (The Ethics of the Fathers), trans. the Reverend Abrahamsons (Vienna), Chap. V, 19, p. 241. ". . . And be not prone to much discourse with womankind: not even with thy wife, much less with thy neighbor's wife; hence, the wise men say, whoever converses much with women, bringeth evil on himself, and thus neglects the study of the law, and at last will inherit hell." *Ibid.,* Chap. I, 5, p. 217. Spinoza, in language such as that of the *Ethics of the Fathers,* rejects "the love of what is perishable." *On the Improvement of the Understanding,* p. 5.

76. *Ethics,* Part Five, Prop. XL, Corol., XXXVIII, XXXVI.

77. *Ibid.,* Part Two, Prop. XL, Scholium 2, Prop. XXXVIII, Corol.

78. René Descartes, *Meditations on the First Philosophy,* Meditation Two, in *The Philosophical Works of Descartes,* I, 157.

79. *Ethics,* Part Five, Prop. XXXVI, XXXVIII, XXXII, XXI, XXIII.

80. "We may easily conceive the whole of nature to be one individual, whose parts, that is to say, all bodies, differ in infinite ways without any change of the whole individual." *Ethics,* Part Two, Lemma VII.

81. This analogy is explicitly made by Spinoza. "Let us now, if you please, imagine that a small worm lives in the blood, whose sight is keen enough to distinguish the particles of blood, lymph, etc., and his reason to observe how each part on collision with another rebounds, or communicates a part of its own motion, etc. That worm would live in this blood as we live in this part of the universe, and he would consider each particle of blood to be a whole, and not a part. And he could not know how all the parts are controlled by the universal nature of blood, and are forced, as the universal nature of blood demands, to adapt themselves to one another, so as to harmonize with one another in a certain way. . . . Now all the bodies of nature can be and should be conceived in the same way as we have here conceived the blood; for all bodies are surrounded by others, and are mutually determined to exist and to act in a definite and determined manner, while there is preserved in all together, that is, in the whole universe, the same proportion of motion and rest." *Correspondence,* pp. 210-211.

82. *Short Treatise,* pp. 134-135. Spinoza's theory of the mind's eternity was much the same as that which Menasseh ben Israel, using classical and Jewish sources, had expounded in his *Nishmath Chayyim* (The Breath of Life). Cf. Nahum Sokolow, *History of Zionism* (London, 1918), I, 28.

83. *Tractatus Theologico-Politicus,* p. 16.

84. *Ethics,* Part Two, Prop. XL, Scholium 2.

85. André Maurois, *Proust: Portrait of a Genius,* trans. Gerard Hopkins (New York, 1950), pp. 171, 190.

86. *Ethics,* Part One, Definition VIII. Part Two, Definition V.

87. *Ibid.,* Part Five, Prop. XLI. For Spinoza's earlier discussion of "immortality of the soul," cf. *Short Treatise,* p. 162.

88. "Of his friends the most part were Cartesians; they propounded to him difficulties which, they maintained, could only be solved by the principles of their Master. Mr. de Spinosa freed them from a certain error to which the learned men were then committed by satisfying them by means of entirely different arguments . . . ; these friends on returning home were really overwhelmed when they made it public that Mr. des Cartes was not the only philosopher who deserved to be followed." A. Wolf, ed., *The Oldest Biography of Spinoza* (London, 1927), p. 57.

89. Balling adds: "The light, notwithstanding, abides always the same; and therefore, although man by sin, through his love and union to corruptible things, comes to perish, be damned and miss of his everlasting happiness, the light nevertheless, which is in every man that comes into the world, abides forever unchangeable." *The Light Upon the Candlestick,* in William Sewel, *The History of the Rise, Increase, and Progress of the Christian People called Quakers* (London, 1722), p. 637.

90. Florian Cajori, *A History of Mathematics* (2nd ed.; New York, 1919), p. 180. Emile Boutroux, "Descartes and Cartesianism," *The Cambridge Modern History* (New York, 1906), IV, 777.

91. Cf. the pertinent remarks by Clarence Irving Lewis, "Logic and Pragmatism," in *Contemporary American Philosophy,* ed. George P. Adams and William Pepperell Montague (New York, 1930), II, 42.

92. René Descartes, *Meditations on First Philosophy,* Meditation VI, *The Principles of Philosophy,* First Part, Principle LIV, LI, in *The Philosophical Works of Descartes,* I, 192, 239, 241. Also cf. J. P. Mahaffy, *Descartes* (Edinburgh, 1891), p. 140. A deist in the seventeenth century like Lord Herbert of Cherbury had in the year 1624 in his *De Veritate* already written of "Deum Sive Naturam." Cf. W. R. Sorley, "The Philosophy of Herbert of Cherbury," *Mind,* N. S., III (1894), 501. Other English deists later continued this usage. Cf. S. G. Hefelbower, *The Relation of John Locke to English Deism* (Chicago, 1918), p. 58.

93. Cf. Charles Adam, *Vie de Descartes,* p. 351. Mahaffy, *op. cit.,* p. 101. Kuno Fischer, *Descartes and His School,* trans. J. P. Gordy (New York, 1887), pp. 254-255.

94. "The essence of man consists of certain modifications of the attributes of God." Book II, Prop. X, Corol.

95. To Descartes, Regius wrote: "I must say there are many here who believe that you have discredited your philosophy by the publication of your metaphysics. You promised things which are clear, certain, and evident; but, so they contend, it is only obscure and uncertain." Arnold Dresden, "Review of *Henricus Regius,* by M. J. A. DeVrijer," *The Journal of Philosophy,* XV (1918), 500.

96. *Ethics,* Part One, Definition VI.

97. "The human mind cannot attain to knowledge of any attribute of God except these two." *Correspondence,* p. 307.

98. Cf. John Locke, *An Essay Concerning Human Understanding,* Bk. I, Chap. III, Par. 9, Chap. IV, Par. 8. Leibnitz, *New Essays Concerning Human Understanding, op. cit.,* pp. 89, 102-103, 297. Hobbes, *Leviathan* (London, 1914), p. 65.

99. Grant McColley, "The Seventeenth-Century Doctrine of a Plurality of Worlds," *Annals of Science,* I (1936), 385.

100. *Ethics,* Part One, Prop. XVII.

101. *Correspondence,* p. 307.

102. *Ethics,* Part One, Prop. IX.

103. "When we think of nature under the attribute of extension, or under the attribute of thought, or under any other attribute whatever, we shall discover one and the same order, or one and the same connection of causes. . . ." *Ibid.,* Part Two, Prop. VII.

104. Christianus Huygens, *The Celestial Worlds Discover'd: or, Conjectures concerning the Inhabitants, Plants and Productions of the Worlds in the Planets* (2nd ed.; London, 1722), pp. 100, 133, 149, 151, 155-157. Also A. E. Bell, *Christian Huygens* (London, 1947), pp. 200-201.

105. *Ethics,* Part Two, Prop. VII.

106. *Ibid.,* Prop. XIII. Also, for Spinoza's discussion of the meaning of "life" and its application to corporeal objects, cf. *Cogitata Metaphysica,* p. 151.

107. Leibniz, *Monadology, Discourse on Metaphysics, Correspondence with Arnauld,* trans. George R. Montgomery (Chicago, 1908), p. 266. "Those who perceive that there is an infinity of small animals in the least drop of water, as the experiments of M. Leewenhoek have shown, . . . will not find it strange. . . ," says Leibniz, *ibid.,* p. 227.

108. *The Select Works of Antony van Leeuwenhoek,* trans. Samuel Hoole (London, 1798), II, 45. For Spinoza's usage cf. *Ethics,* Part One, Definitions II, VI, Prop. XXXIII, which emphasizes "that things have been produced by God in the highest degree of perfection."

109. "If two things have nothing in common with one another, one cannot be the cause of the other." *Ethics,* Part One, Prop. III. Also, *Select Works of Leeuwenhoek,* II, 344.

110. *Correspondence,* pp. 209-212. For Leeuwenhoek's similar observations on the "exceeding small particles" of the blood, cf. Leeuwenhoek, *op. cit.,* p. 89 ff.

111. Clifford Dobell, *Antony van Leeuwenhoek and his 'Little Animals'* (London, 1932), pp. 176-177.

112. "He had a great esteem for Dr. Cordes, my Predecessor; who was a learned and good natured Man, and of an exemplary Life, which gave occasion to Spinosa to praise him very often. Nay, he went sometimes to hear him preach, and he esteem'd particularly his learned way of explaining the Scripture, and the solid applications he made of it. He advised at the same

time his Landlord and the People of the House, not to miss any Sermon of so excellent a Preacher." Colerus, *op. cit.*, p. 395. Constantine Huygens, says Leeuwenhoek, was a "valuable friend of mine," and Spinoza was acquainted with the Huygens family. Cf. Leeuwenhoek, *Select Works*, II, 143.

113. *Ibid.*, II, 88; I, 17, 76.

114. *Correspondence*, p. 139.

115. Leeuwenhoek, *Select Works*, II, 126-128; I, 287-291.

116. This criticism of Spinoza in a work on tea-drinking enables us to reconstruct Spinoza's relation to the philosophy of medicine in his time. Cornelis Bontekoe (1647-1687), Spinoza's opponent, was the chief representative in Holland of the so-called iatrochemical school. The iatrochemists held that all physiological processes were to be explained on a chemical basis; they opposed the iatrophysical school which affirmed that the laws of mechanics were necessary and sufficient for explaining the processes of life. Descartes was the forebear of the iatrophysical approach, whereas Van Helmont (1577-1644) was the founder of iatrochemical theory. As formulated by the latter, the iatrochemical standpoint invoked a hierarchy of metaphysical agencies in its explanations, *archaei*, which resembled Aristotle's entelechies. Bontekoe's book was iatrochemical in so far as it held that the chemical thickening of the blood was the cause of all disease; tea, he believed, was effective because it was an agent for thinning the blood.

The founder of the Dutch iatrochemical group was the professor of Medicine at Leyden, Franciscus Sylvius (1614-1672). Sylvius' system stressed the role of saliva, pancreatic juice, and bile, but, and this is noteworthy, he condemned the letting of blood as a therapeutic method. We do know that Spinoza resorted to blood-letting in 1665 in dealing with his own illness. On questions, then, of metaphysics and medical practice, Spinoza was at odds with the leaders of the iatrochemical school. On these points, evidently, Spinoza remained a firm adherent of the doctrine of mechanism—the belief that all physical phenomena are, in the last analysis, mechanical ones.

On Bontekoe and Sylvius, cf. C. J. Dijksterhuis, C. Louise Thijssen-Schoute, and collaborators, *Descartes et le cartésianisme hollandais* (Amsterdam, 1950), pp. 214-215. Arturo Castiglione, *A History of Medicine*, trans. E. B. Krumbhaar (New York, 1941), pp. 540-542. Also cf. Charles Singer, *A History of Biology* (rev. ed.; New York, 1950), pp. 357-359. Pollock, *op. cit.*, p. 350. *Correspondence*, p. 202. Bontekoe, despite his aversion to Spinoza's godlessness, "tried very hard" to acquire Spinoza's books after the "atheist's" death. Cf. *The Oldest Biography of Spinoza*, ed. A. Wolf, p. 168. He admired Spinoza's taste in books even if he felt presumably that his taste for tea was not that of a good believer in Dutch foreign mercantile interests. For Bontekoe's philosophy, cf. Victor Vander Haeghen, *Geulincx* (Gand, 1886), pp. 173, 193-196.

117. A. Wolf, *A History of Science, Technology, and Philosophy in the 16th and 17th Centuries* (New York, 1935), pp. 71-72, 76.

118. Clifford Dobell, *op. cit.*, p. 325.

119. As far as animals were concerned, Spinoza remarks: "I by no means

deny that brutes feel. . . ." *Ethics,* Part Four, Prop. XXXVII.

120. The great biological classification of Linnaeus may well have had a Spinozist inspiration. Linnaeus had a mystic's reverence for the "illimitable diversity of nature's products," and many of his turns of phrase were Spinoza's. It is conjectured that Linnaeus derived this outlook from his teacher, the Dutch scientist and disciple of Spinoza, Hermann Boerhave. Cf. Knut Hagberg, *Carl Linnaeus,* trans. Alan Blair (New York, 1953), pp. 185-189. Perhaps one source of the sexual classification was Spinoza's emphasis on desire as the essence of living things.

121. *The Philosophical Works of Leibnitz,* trans. George Martin Duncan (2nd ed.; New Haven, 1908), p. 269.

122. *Ethics,* Part One, Prop. XXVIII.

123. *Short Treatise,* p. 48.

124. *Leviathan,* p. 111.

125. *Ethics,* Part One, Appendix, Part Two, Prop. XXXV, Part Three, Prop. II.

126. "In the mind there is no absolute or free will, but the mind is determined to this or that volition by a cause, which is also determined by another cause, and this again by another, and so on *ad infinitum.*" Entities such as the "free will" are characterized by Spinoza as "fictitious" or "metaphysical or universal entities." Also, *Ethics,* Part One, Prop. XXXII, Part Two, Prop. XLVIII, and Scholium.

127. *Short Treatise,* pp. 115-117.

128. *Ethics,* Part One, Appendix, Part Four, Prop. XIII.

129. Cf. *The English Works of Thomas Hobbes,* ed. Sir William Molesworth (London, 1840), III, 33; IV, Dedicatory Epistle. *The Works of Francis Bacon,* ed. J. Spedding, R. L. Ellis, D. D. Heath (London, 1858), IV, 61. See especially the essays of Richard Foster Jones, "Science and English Prose Style in the Third Quarter of the Seventeenth Century," "The Attack on Pulpit Eloquence in the Restoration," "Science and Language in England of the Mid-Seventeenth Century," reprinted in *The Seventeenth Century* (Stanford, California, 1951), pp. 41-160. Also, Joan Bennett, "An Aspect of the Evolution of Seventeenth-Century Prose," *The Review of English Studies,* XVII (1941), 282.

130. Thomas Sprat, *The History of the Royal Society in London* (London, 1667), pp. 116-118, 347-348, 366, 397. To carry the argument into the enemy's camp, Sprat even affirms that "Christ too performed Philosophical Works when he fed the Hungry," p. 352.

131. *Ibid.,* p. 371.

132. *Ethics,* Part Three, Preface, Part Five, Prop. XXIX.

133. "Owing to the great mercantile activity of Holland between 1575 and 1650, a large number of arithmetics appeared in that country early in the seventeenth century. . . . To this creative period of arithmetic is due a large amount of matter once of importance but now quite obsolete. . . : Proportion (usually in the form of the Rule of Three) was much more often used in practice than at present." David Eugene Smith, "History of

Arithmetic," *The Encyclopedia Americana* (New York, 1943), II, 249. Also, David Eugene Smith, *History of Mathematics* (New York, 1925), II, 486-488.

134. *Philosophical Transactions of the Royal Society* (London, 1668), p. 627.

135. *Philosophical Transactions* (London, 1666), pp. 324-325, 575, 715-716.

136. For an account of Steno's life, cf. Erik Nordenskiöld, *The History of Biology*, trans. Leonard Bucknall Eyre (New York, 1932), pp. 155-158.

137. *Correspondence*, pp. 102-104, 106-107, 325.

138. Richard Foster Jones, *Ancients and Moderns* (St. Louis, 1936), pp. 105-107, 252, 271.

139. Mahaffy, *op. cit.*, p. 107.

140. *Leviathan*, p. 193.

141. *Ethics*, Part One, Prop. XIV, Corol. 1.

142. *Correspondence*, pp. 118-119, 270.

143. "We imagine time because we imagine some bodies to move with a velocity less, or greater than, or equal to that of others." *Ethics*, Part Two, Prop. XLIV.

144. *Ibid.*, Definition 5. Spinoza's distinction between duration and time was accepted doctrine in the seventeenth century. It is exactly the distinction which Newton made between "absolute, true, and mathematical time" and "relative, apparent, and common time." Sir Isaac Newton, *The Mathematical Principles of Natural Philosophy*, trans. Andrew Motte, ed. Florian Cajori (Berkeley, 1934), Definition VIII, Scholium, p. 6.

145. *Correspondence*, p. 117.

146. *Ethics*, Part One, Prop. XVI. Cf. Charles S. Peirce, *Chance, Love, and Logic*, ed. Morris R. Cohen (New York, 1923), p. 98.

147. *Ethics*, Part One, Prop. XVII, Part Two, Prop. IV, Part Five, Prop. XXIX.

148. *Ibid.*, Part Four, Preface. *Correspondence*, pp. 209-212.

149. *Ethics*, Part One, Prop. XVIII, XXIX.

150. *Correspondence*, pp. 161, 162.

151. "Now if you can show that Evil, Error or Villainy, etc. is something which expresses essence, then I will fully admit to you that God is the cause of villainy, evil, error, etc. I think that I have sufficiently shown that that which gives its form to evil, error, or crimes, does not consist in anything which expresses essence, and that therefore it cannot be said that God is the cause thereof." *Ibid.*, p. 190.

152. *Ethics*, Part Four, Prop. XXXII, Scholium.

153. *Correspondence*, pp. 175, 190.

154. Colerus, *op. cit.*, p. 395.

155. *Correspondence*, p. 139. Cf. Lewis S. Feuer, "The Dream of Benedict de Spinoza," *The American Imago*, Vol. 14 (1957) 225-242.

156. "Those who think that the *Tractatus Theologico-Politicus* rests on this, namely, that God and Nature (by which they mean a certain mass,

or corporeal matter) are one and the same, are entirely mistaken." *Correspondence*, p. 343.

157. *Ibid.*, pp. 116-120. *Ethics*, Part One, Prop. XV, Part Three, Prop. XLIV.

158. Balling, Spinoza's Collegiant friend, founded his mysticism on the inadequacy of language: "the light in every man is the means to come to the knowledge of God. And seeing all external signs must needs presuppose this knowledge, therefore must need be immediate, without any external sign . . . for words are created and finite, and God who should make known himself by them, uncreated and infinite. . . ." *The Light Upon the Candlestick*, in William Sewel, *op. cit.*, p. 637.

Epilogue

1. Sir Isaac Newton, *Theological Manuscripts*, ed. H. McLachlan (Liverpool, 1950), p. 1.

2. *Dictionnaire Historique et Critique de Pierre Bayle* (Edition of Paris, 1820), XIII, 417 (translated by the writer).

3. *Tractatus Theologico-Politicus*, p. 44.

4. Colerus, *op. cit.*, pp. 407-408. *The Oldest Biography of Spinoza*, ed. A. Wolf (London, 1927), p. 169.

5. Gottfried Wilhelm Leibnitz, *New Essays Concerning Human Understanding*, trans. by Alfred Gideon Langley (New York, 1896), pp. 535-536.

6. *Short Treatise*, p. 149.

7. ". . . I should have done much better, if in my first letter, I had replied in the words of Descartes. . . ." *Correspondence*, p. 176.

8. *Ibid.*, p. 172.

9. A. Wolf, *The Oldest Biography of Spinoza*, p. 74.

10. *Dictionnaire Historique et Critique de Pierre Bayle*, XIII, 429.

11. *Ethics*, Part Four, Appendix, Par. XXV.

12. J. Freudenthal, "On the History of Spinozism," *The Jewish Quarterly Review*, VIII (1895), 44-46.

13. Mr. Basnage, *The History of the Jews from Jesus Christ to the Present Time*, trans. Tho. Taylor (London, 1708), p. 742.

14. Limborch, in his correspondence with Locke, takes for granted that Locke knows the letters of Spinoza, and their discussions concerning the unity of God. Cf. *Letters inédites de John Locke à ses amis Nicolas Thoynard, Philippe Van Limborch et Edward Clarke*, ed. Henry Ollion and T. J. De Boer (La Haye, 1912), p. 217. Also cf. Leo Pierre Courtines, *Bayle's relations with England and the English* (New York, 1938), pp. 110, 122.

15. William I. Hull, *Benjamin Furly and Quakerism in Rotterdam* (Swarthmore, 1941), p. 87. H. R. Fox Bourne, *The Life of John Locke* (London, 1876), II, 74.

16. Fox Bourne, *op. cit.*, pp. 31-32. Le Clerc, however, rejected Spinoza's determinism, and adhered to a belief in free will. Cf. Paul Vernière,

Spinoza et La Pensée Française avant la Révolution, Première Partie (Paris, 1954), p. 7. Le Clerc's faith in free thought is most eloquently expressed in his *A Funeral Oration upon the Death of Mr. Limborch,* translated from Latin (London, 1713), pp. 12-13, 19. But Le Clerc himself denounced Spinoza as an atheist in 1713 and joined in the outcry against him.

17. Bourne, *op. cit.,* p. 151. Inheritor of Spinoza's liberalism, Locke wrote: "But those whose doctrine is peaceable, and whose manners are pure and blameless, ought to be upon equal terms with their fellow-subjects. . . ; all these things ought to be permitted to presbyterians, independents, anabaptists, nay, if we may openly speak the truth, and as becomes one man to another, neither pagan, nor Mahometan, nor Jew ought to be excluded from the civil rights of the commonwealth, because of his religion. . . . And the commonwealth, which embraces indifferently all men that are honest, peaceable, and industrious requires it not. Shall we suffer a pagan to deal and trade with us, and shall we not suffer him to pray unto and worship God?" John Locke, *Letter Concerning Toleration,* Locke's *Works,* (10th ed., London, 1801), VI, 52.

18. *Ibid.,* pp. 185-186.

19. The first English translation of Spinoza's *Tractatus Theologico-Politicus* was published in London one year after the Revolution of 1688. The translator in his Preface defied, "the Crape Gown and the Long Robe" to prove that "there are any tenets in the whole Treatise, half so dangerous or destructive to the Peace and Welfare of human Society, as those doctrines and Maxims are, which have of late Years been broached by time serving Churchmen and Mercenary Lawyers; for which they justly deserve the hatred and contempt of all Mankind." Spinoza's work was thus being used as a liberal defense of the Revolution prior to the publication of Locke's *Two Treatises on Civil Government* in 1690.

20. As Voltaire further remarked: "Si d'illustres adversaires peuvent servir en quelque sorte à la gloire d'un auteur, on voit que jamais homme n'a été honoré d'ennemis plus respectables. Il a été attaqué par deux cardinaux des plus savants et des plus ingénieux qu'ait eus la France, tous deux chéris à la cour, tous deux ministres et ambassadeurs à Rome. [If illustrious adversaries may contribute in some way to the glory of an author, one sees that no man has ever been honored with more respectable enemies. He has been attacked by two of the most learned and ingenious cardinals whom France has had, both of them cherished at court, both of them ministers and ambassadors at Rome.]" "Les Systèmes," *Satires,* in *Oeuvres Complètes de Voltaire* (Paris, 1877), X, 171.

INDEX

A., W., Fellow of the Royal Society, 268, 276
Aboab, Rabbi Isaac de Fonseca, 1, 3, 8, 23, 25, 28-32, 265
Abrabanel, Jonas Selomo, 12, 25-27, 265
Abraham, 266
Abrahams, Galenus, 280
Abrahams, Israel, 260, 262, 266
Abravanel, Don Isaac, 291
Academic freedom, its decline in Dutch universities, 179-182
Acosta, Uriel, 9, 34; excommunication of, 13 ff.
Adam, 285
Adam, Charles, 302
Adler, E. N., 259, 264
Aguilar, Moses Raphael de, 15
Albigensian heresy, 11
Allen, Phyllis, 278
Alva, Duke of, 71
American Indians, 233, 277
American Revolution, 107, 268
Ames, William, 48-50, 197, 222, 271
Amnon, 301
Amos, 127
Amsterdam, 268, 277-278; Athenaeum, 2; Burgomaster of, 3; radical intellectual circle of, 22, 24, 39; condition during the Anglo-Dutch War in 1653, 41; political intrigue in, 47; freedom, prosperity, and equality in, 66; epidemic of 1656, 89; as oligarchy, 36, 42, 97; given disproportionate representation in the Provincial Estates, 168; theater in, 296; Leibniz on, 286
Amsterdam Jewry, its culture, intermarriage with the Dutch, decline of orthodoxy within, 2-3; its dominance by commercial oligarchy, its trading relations, shares in Dutch East and West India Companies, 5 ff.; loyalty to house of Orange,

concentration of wealth in, 7-9; class differences between Ashkenazic and Portuguese Jews, 8; constitution of, 8-9; its use of excommunication for social purposes, 9 ff.; its *Mahamad* (governing council), 24; assistance to Jews of New Amsterdam and Brazil, 27-28; their attachment to the pseudo-Messiah Sabbatai Zvi, 26, 29; synagogue, 260
Amzalak, Moses Bensabat, 261
Anabaptists, 5, 41, 71, 84, 143, 146; Dutch, 268-269
Angell, Norman, 287
Anglo-Dutch Wars, 40-41, 51
Annals and History of the Netherlands (Grotius), 280
Anxiety, 215
Apion, 284
Apologie for Epicurus (Charleton), 207
Apostles, 97
Aquinas, St. Thomas, 261
Aragon, liberal constitution of its monarchy, 195
Arianism, 268
Aristophanes, 3
Aristotelians, 54
Aristotle, 6, 37, 54, 180, 246, 273, 304
Arminians, 74, 278
Arminius, 74
Army, citizen soldiers as against professional, 43
Aron, Maurice, 262
Asceticism, 203
Asians, 21, 24
Atheism, 19, 247, 268
Athias, Joseph, 260
Atkinson, Geoffrey, 277
Aubrey, John, 276, 288
Augustine, St., 261
Aulard, A., 293

309